The Plotinus Reader

The Plotinus Reader

Edited
With an Introduction and Notes
By

Lloyd P. Gerson

Hackett Publishing Company, Inc.
Indianapolis/Cambridge

23 22 21 20   1 2 3 4 5 6 7

For further information, please address
    Hackett Publishing Company, Inc.
    P.O. Box 44937
    Indianapolis, Indiana 46244-0937

    www.hackettpublishing.com

Cover design by E. L. Wilson and Elana Rosenthal
Interior design by E. L. Wilson and Elana Rosenthal
Composition by Aptara, Inc.

Library of Congress Control Number: 2020930918

ISBN-13: 978-1-62466-895-1 (cloth)
ISBN-13: 978-1-62466-894-4 (pbk.)

The paper used in this publication meets the minimum requirements of American National Standard for Information Sciences—Permanence of Paper for Printed Library Materials, ANSI Z39.48–1984.

∞

Contents

Introduction   *vii*

List of Enneads *as Arranged by Porphyry and the*
Corresponding Chronological Order   *x*

Enneads *in Chronological Order and the*
Corresponding Order of Porphyry   *xi*

Translations

1.1 (53)	*What Is the Living Being and What Is the Human Being?* (complete)	1
1.2 (19)	*On Virtues* (complete)	14
1.4 (46)	*On Happiness* §§1–4	23
1.6 (1)	*On Beauty* (complete)	30
1.8 (51)	*On What Evils Are and Where They Come From* §§1–5	43
3.8 (30)	*On Nature, Contemplation, and the One* (complete)	50
4.1 (21)	*On the Substantiality of the Soul 1* (complete)	65
4.2 (4)	*On the Substantiality of the Soul 2* (complete)	70
4.7 (2)	*On the Immortality of the Soul* §§1–2; 9–15	72
4.8 (6)	*On the Descent of Souls into Bodies* (complete)	82
5.1 (10)	*On the Three Primary Hypostases* (complete)	94
5.2 (11)	*On the Generation and Order of the Things Which Come after the First* (complete)	111
5.3 (49)	*On the Knowing Hypostasis and on That Which Is Transcendent* §§1–9; 13–17	114
5.5 (32)	*That the Intelligibles Are Not outside the Intellect, and on the Good* §§1–2	134
6.4 (22)	*That Being, One and Identical, Is Simultaneously Everywhere Whole 1* §§1–11	139
6.7 (38)	*How the Multiplicity of the Ideas Came to Exist and on the Good* §§1–23; 37–42	154
6.8 (39)	*On the Voluntary and the One's Wishing* §§1–8; 12–16	195
6.9 (9)	*On the Good or the One* §§1–3; 11	216
	Appendix of Classical Sources	*227*
	English Glossary of Important Terms	*275*

Introduction

The genesis of this book is somewhat unusual and contains a story of remarkable cooperation between academic publishers. Around 2001, Hackett Publishing asked John M. Dillon and me to translate and edit a collection of readings from the works of the major Neoplatonists. The result, published in 2004, is *Neoplatonic Philosophy: Introductory Readings*. That work contained roughly 170 pages of material from Plotinus's *Enneads* and amounts to a bit less than 20 percent of the entire corpus. Sometime around 2010, Cambridge University Press asked me to assemble a team of translators who would produce a complete translation of the *Enneads*. That team included besides myself, George Boys-Stones, John M. Dillon, R. A. H. King, Andrew Smith, and James Wilberding. That work, *Plotinus: The Enneads*, appeared in 2018. When we began the project, I asked Hackett if we could use the material from *Neoplatonic Philosophy* as a basis for the translations in the Cambridge volume. Hackett graciously gave permission to use these translations and, though they were altered somewhat, they greatly facilitated the work of the translation team. Last year, Hackett approached me again, this time to produce a stand-alone volume of the Plotinus translations from *Neoplatonic Philosophy*, including naturally all the corrections and changes that were made for the other work. This time, Cambridge returned the favor by allowing me to use the new-old material for *The Plotinus Reader*, which the reader now has in his or her hands. *The Plotinus Reader* contains the revised translations that originally appeared in *Neoplatonic Philosophy* along with the new Cambridge introductions to each treatise and summaries of each section.

The default text used in this translation is that of the editio minor of Paul Henry and Hans-Rudolph Schwyzer, conventionally designated as HS².[1] Unless otherwise noted, this is the text that has been translated for this work. All deviations from that text are noted, citing, for example, the reading of HS⁴ over that of HS². Those who can benefit from the side-by-side Greek text of A.H. Armstrong's Loeb edition can do the same with the editio minor (OCT) and our translation.

---

1. The editio maior is usually labeled HS¹; the editio minor HS²; addenda to HS¹ labeled HS³; textual addenda to HS³ labeled HS⁴; and the article by H.-R. Schwyzer, "Corrigienda ad Plotini textum," Museum Helveticum 44, 1 (1987), 191–210, is labeled HS⁵. Even though Henry's name does not appear on the article (he died in 1984), he no doubt participated in the work that led up to this article and by common agreement he is listed as one of the authors.

In addition to the translations, the original work contains a glossary of terms from Plotinus and from his successors. This, too, was used as the basis for a similar glossary in the Cambridge volume. That glossary now appears in the present work, much enlarged, along with extensive references to the *Enneads* which are illustrative of the definitions given in the Glossary. The reader is invited to make frequent use of this glossary to help with Plotinus's difficult and somewhat technical vocabulary. It should be noted that the references to passages illustrative of Plotinus's terminological usage list works that are not included in this volume. Readers who want to study Plotinus further or read works of his not found here are invited to go to the Cambridge translations where all of Plotinus's writings are to be found.

Those who have had even a brief acquaintance with the *Enneads* know that one of the problems facing the reader or student is that seldom does Plotinus say everything he has to say about a subject in one place. Indeed, for some large subjects, like the nature of the first principle of all, the nature of intellect, soul, and so on, virtually every treatise has something to add to the overall picture. To help the reader, extensive cross-references have been provided in the notes, again including references to works not included here. These were in the original work, but were added to in the successor, although they are not intended to be complete. I caution the reader that a cross-reference does not necessarily mean that Plotinus is saying exactly the same thing in both passages; sometimes one might well wonder if he is even saying consistent things. But at any rate, it is hoped that reading these passages together will enrich the study of this most challenging but fertile philosophical mind. In addition, there are numerous references in the notes to the so-called fontes or sources for Plotinus's writings, first and foremost Plato, but also Aristotle and other Peripatetics, Stoics, and occasionally Skeptics and Epicureans, and even Gnostics. The Appendix includes an array of passages from Plato and cross-references to the text. These should be read alongside the Plotinian texts since they were no doubt very much in his mind as he wrote down his philosophical thoughts.

Translating Plotinus presents many challenges, particularly when space precludes any sort of commentary or explanatory notes. Apart from the obvious challenge presented by the complexity of Plotinus's thought, there is the problem of his rather idiosyncratic Greek and, as his biographer Porphyry tells us, the fact that, owing to his poor eyesight, he never went over anything he had written. In addition, Plotinus is generally conservative in his philosophical vocabulary, introducing relatively few new words. But since he is responding to a complex and contentious tradition (or traditions), his conservatism means that one word is meant to stand for what in other philosophers' works may well mean several different things. Choosing one English word to translate one Greek word that means different things in different authors is quite difficult and sometimes almost impossible. In order to meet these challenges, or at least to ease the path somewhat for readers, a number of techniques have been adopted. Paragraphs have been introduced which are not, of course, in the Greek. Sentences have been shortened to manageable length. The core of Plotinus's philosophy is his hierarchical metaphysics with the intelligible world at the top and the sensible world below. Plotinus often uses the identical Greek word to refer to one element or feature of both. This can sometimes get very confusing. In order to address this, the convention has been adopted of using capital letters for the terms for the principles in the intelligible world and lowercase letters for their images. For example, "Substance" translates the Greek word *ousia* when referring to the intelligible being and "substance" translates the word when referring to sensible being. When the use of the term is unsure or ambiguous or inclusive, lower case is used as the default. The Glossary contains further information for this term and for many others. In the Glossary will be found some indications of the semantic range of the Greek terms in order to try to minimize misunderstandings based on the translations. The Glossary should serve as a de facto index of key terms.

Another feature of the translation is intended to reflect Plotinus's characteristic use of the ordinary Greek letter *eta* (ἤ). This is the word for "or" as in "x ἤ y." But Plotinus uses it consistently after a dialectical clause in which he expresses one possible view or interpretation with which he does not agree. A rather clumsy but accurate translation in these cases would be, "or is it not the case that . . . ?" Apart from the awkwardness of translating one letter by seven words, it is misleading to suggest that Plotinus here means to express a rhetorical question. What he means to do is express his view (the Platonic view) on the matter. So, we translate ἤ . . . as "in fact." To emphasize that what follows is Plotinus's considered view on the matter he has been discussing—sometimes for many lines—we begin a new paragraph. This is meant to be a signpost for the reader to focus on what follows as an important step in figuring out exactly what Plotinus's position is. Other lexical devices, including the use of square brackets to indicate what is only implicit in the Greek, will be evident to the reader.

As for an introduction to Plotinus's philosophy, in lieu of a repetition of the introduction to *Neoplatonic Philosophy*, I refer the reader to the excellent introductions by Dominic J. O'Meara, *Plotinus: An Introduction to the Enneads* (Oxford, 1993, reprinted 2005) and by Eyjólfur K. Emilsson, *Plotinus* (Routledge, 2017). Richard Dufour has done the profession a great service by assembling and keeping up to date a complete online bibliography of works on Plotinus (http://rdufour.free.fr/BibPlotin/anglais/Biblio.html). That bibliography includes all translations of Plotinus into English as well as other major languages.

List of *Enneads* as Arranged by Porphyry and the Corresponding Chronological Order

Enn.	Chron.	Enn.	Chron.	Enn.	Chron.
1.1	53	2.1	40	3.1	3
1.2	19	2.2	14	3.2	47
1.3	20	2.3	52	3.3	48
1.4	46	2.4	12	3.4	15
1.5	36	2.5	25	3.5	50
1.6	1	2.6	17	3.6	26
1.7	54	2.7	37	3.7	45
1.8	51	2.8	35	3.8	30
1.9	16	2.9	33	3.9	13
4.1	21	5.1	10	6.1	42
4.2	4	5.2	11	6.2	43
4.3	27	5.3	49	6.3	44
4.4	28	5.4	7	6.4	22
4.5	29	5.5	32	6.5	23
4.6	41	5.6	24	6.6	34
4.7	2	5.7	18	6.7	38
4.8	6	5.8	31	6.8	39
4.9	8	5.9	5	6.9	9

Enneads in Chronological Order and the Corresponding Order of Porphyry

Chron.	*Enn.*	Chron.	*Enn.*	Chron.	*Enn.*
1	1.6	19	1.2	37	2.7
2	4.7	20	1.3	38	6.7
3	3.1	21	4.1	39	6.8
4	4.2	22	6.4	40	2.1
5	5.9	23	6.5	41	4.6
6	4.8	24	5.6	42	6.1
7	5.4	25	2.5	43	6.2
8	4.9	26	3.6	44	6.3
9	6.9	27	4.3	45	3.7
10	5.1	28	4.4	46	1.4
11	5.2	29	4.5	47	3.2
12	2.4	30	3.8	48	3.3
13	3.9	31	5.8	49	5.3
14	2.2	32	5.5	50	3.5
15	3.4	33	2.9	51	1.8
16	1.9	34	6.6	52	2.3
17	2.6	35	2.8	53	1.1
18	5.7	36	1.5	54	1.7

1.1 (53)

What Is the Living Being and What Is the Human Being?

Introduction

In this very late treatise, Plotinus considers the relation between the person or self and the human being, composed of body and soul. He is, as always, trying to follow Plato as he understands him but also, especially here, to draw on Peripatetic insights. Plotinus will identify the true self with the immortal, undescended intellect and the embodied subject of psychical activities as its image. This distinction between immortal and moral kinds of soul, drawn from *Timaeus*, will provide the basis for his explanation of punishment and moral responsibility: it is only the embodied self that can be held responsible.

This treatise is placed first by Porphyry since in a way the entire structure of Plotinus's philosophy begins with our personal reflections on self-identity.

Summary

§1. What is the subject of embodied states and activities?

§2. What is the soul? Is it itself a composite or is it form?

§3. The various ways in which the soul has been conceived of as related to the body.

§4. The soul imparts life to the body without being mixed with it.

§5. How can the states of the body be transmitted to the soul?

§6. In what sense is the soul actively involved with the body and in what sense is it impassive?

§7. It is not the soul itself that endows the body with life, but its activity.

§8. Relation of the embodied soul to Intellect.

§9. Vice is attributed to the living being, not to the soul itself.

§10. The ambiguity of 'we' between embodied and disembodied self.

§11. The psychical status of children and animals.

§12. Moral responsibility belongs only to the embodied self, the image of the true self.

§13. Again, the ambiguity in the reference to the subject of intellectual activity.

§1.1.1.[1] Pleasures and pains, fears and feelings of boldness, appetites and aversions and feelings of distress—to what do these belong?[2]

5

In fact, they belong either to the soul or to a soul using a body[3] or to some third thing that arises from a combination of these. And this can be understood in two ways: either as a mixture or as something different that arises from the mixture. It is the same for what arises from these states, namely, actions and beliefs. So, then, we must investigate discursive thinking and belief to determine whether they belong to that to which the states belong or whether some of them are like this and some are not. And we should also reflect on how acts of intellection occur and to what they belong, and indeed what is the thing which is itself considering the investigation of these questions and making the judgment. But before that, we should ask: what is the subject of sense-perception? It is appropriate to begin from there, since the [above] states are either acts of sense-perception or else they do not occur without sense-perception.[4]

10

§1.1.2. First, we need to understand if it is the case that soul is one thing and the essence of soul another.[5] For if this is so, soul will be something composite, and there will at once be nothing absurd in its being the subject, I mean, of these kinds of states and, in general, of better and worse habits and dispositions, that is, assuming the argument will turn out this way.

5

In fact, however, if soul and the essence of soul are identical, soul would be a certain form incapable of being subject of all these activities that it imparts to something else, but would have the activity that is natural to itself in itself, whatever the argument reveals this to be. In this case, it will be true to say that the soul is immortal, if indeed that which is immortal and indestructible must be incapable of being affected.[6] It would somehow give what belongs to itself to another while receiving nothing from anything else—or only so much as is present in the things prior to itself, things from which it is not cut off, since they are superior to it.[7]

10

---

1. See Appendix II A.
2. See Pl., *Rep.* 4.429C–D, 430A–B; *Phd.* 83B; *Tim.* 69D; *Lg.* 897A; Ar., *DA* 1.4.408b1–29.
3. See Pl. [?], *Alc.* 1.129E.
4. See Pl., *Tim.* 61C8–D2.
5. See Ar., *Meta.* 7.6.1037a17–b3; 8.3.1042b2–3.
6. See Ar., *DA* 3.4.429a15 on the impassivity of soul; 430a23 on its immortality; and 2.2.413b26 on the indestructibility of intellect which Aristotle variously treats as a 'part of soul' and a 'genus different from soul'.
7. Referring to Intellect and to the One.

Now what would something of this sort fear, since it is not subject to anything outside it? So, that which is afraid is that which is capable 15 of being affected. So, it does not feel courageous either, for how can courage belong to those things to which what is fearful cannot be present? And how can it have appetites, which are satisfied by means of the emptied body being filled up, since that which is emptied and filled up is different from it?

And how could soul be the product of a mixture?

In fact, its essential nature is unmixed.[8] How could other things be introduced into it? If this were to occur, it would be on the way 20 to not being what it is. Being distressed is even more remote from it. For how can something be pained except in regard to something? But that which is simple in substantiality is self-sufficient inasmuch as it is stable in its own substantiality. And will it be pleased if something is added to it when there is nothing, not even any good, that can augment it? For what it is, it is always. 25

Further, it will perceive nothing nor will there be discursive thinking or belief in it. For sense-perception is taking on a form or also a corporeal state,[9] and discursive thinking and belief supervene on sense-perception.

Regarding intellection, if we are going to understand this as being in soul, we should examine how this happens; and regarding pleasure, I mean pure pleasure,[10] whether it has this when it is by itself.

§1.1.3.[11] But as for the soul that is in the body, we should also examine whether it exists prior to this or [only] in this, since it is from the combination of body and soul that 'the entire living being is named'.[12] If, then, on the one hand, it uses the body as an instrument,[13] it does not have to be the subject of states that come through the body, 5 just as craftsmen are not the subjects of the states of their instruments.[14] On the other hand, perhaps it would necessarily be a subject of sense-perception, if indeed it must use this instrument for cognizing the states arising from sense-perception of what is external. Seeing is, after all, the use of the eyes. But there are injuries associated with seeing,

---

8. See Pl., *Phil.* 59C4. The soul is unmixed like the Forms.
9. See Ar., *DA* 2.12.424a18.
10. See Pl., *Phil.* 52C, 63E3.
11. See Appendix III A 1.
12. See Pl., *Phdr.* 246C5.
13. Cf. 1.4.16.22–28; 4.3.23.8–9; 4.7.1.20–24. See Pl. [?], *Alc.* 1.129C5–130A1; *Phd.* 79C3; *Tht.* 184D4.
14. See Ar., *EE* 7.9.1241b18–23.

10 so that there are also pains and distress, as is generally the case for everything that happens to the body. So, too, there are appetites in the soul seeking care for this instrument.

But how will the states go from the body into the soul? For though body will transfer its own states to another body, how will body transfer anything to the soul? For this would be equivalent in a way to say-

15 ing that when one thing experiences something, another thing experiences it. For so long as what uses the instrument is one thing and the instrument it uses is something else, each is separate.[15] At least, anyone who posits the soul as using the body separates them.

But prior to their separation by the practice of philosophy,[16] how were they disposed?

In fact, they were mixed. But if they were mixed, it was either like a

20 blend or like an 'interweaving',[17] or like a form not separated from the body; or the form controlled the body like the pilot of a ship;[18] or one part of it was one way and another part the other. I mean that one part was separated—the part that uses the body—and the other was somehow mixed with it, that is, it belongs among the ordered parts of that which is used. Thus, what philosophy would do is to turn this part

25 toward the part that uses the body, and to divert the part that uses the body—to the extent that its presence is not entirely necessary—away from what it uses, so that it does not always use it.

§1.1.4.[19] So, let us suppose that they have been mixed. But if they have been mixed, the inferior element, the body, will be made better, and the superior element, the soul, will be made worse. The body will be made better by participating in life, and the soul will be made worse by participating in death and non-rationality.

5 Indeed, how could that which has to any extent been deprived of life acquire the added power of sense-perception? On the contrary, the body, by receiving life, would be what is participating in sense-perception and the states that arise from sense-perception. So, it is the body that will desire—for this is what will enjoy the objects of

10 its desires—and fear for itself. For it is this that will fail to acquire pleasures and will be destroyed.

---

15. See Pl. [?], *Alc.* 1.129D11–E7.
16. See Pl., *Phd.* 67C–D.
17. See Pl., *Tim.* 36E2.
18. Cf. 4.3.21.9–17. See Pl., *Phdr.* 247C7; Ar., *DA* 2.1.413a9.
19. See Appendix III A 1.

We should also investigate the way the mixture occurs to see if it is perhaps impossible, as it would be if someone said that a line was mixed with white, that is, one nature mixed with another of a different sort.[20] The concept of 'interweaving'[21] does not imply that the things interwoven are affected in the same way. It is possible for that which is interwoven to be unaffected, that is, for the soul to pass through and not have the states of the body, just like light, especially if it is in this way woven through the whole. It will not, then, have the states of the body just because it is interwoven.[22]

But will it be in the body in the way that a form is in matter?[23] If so, then first, it will be like a form that is separable, if it is indeed a substance, and even more so if it is that which uses the body. But if we assume it to be like the shape of an axe that is imposed on the iron, and the complex that the axe is will do what iron so shaped will do, because of its shape, we would in that case be even more inclined to attribute to the body such states as are common—common, that is, to this sort of body—to the 'natural instrumental body having life potentially'.[24] For Aristotle says that it is absurd to claim that 'the soul is doing the weaving'[25] so that it is also absurd to claim that it has appetites and is in pain; these belong rather to the living being.

§1.1.5.[26] What we should say is that the living being is either a certain kind of body or the conjunction of body and soul, or some other third thing that arises from both of these.[27] But whatever is the case, either one must preserve the soul's unaffected state while it is the cause of the other part of the conjunction being affected, or else it must be affected along with the body. And in the latter case, its affection is identical to the body's or it is affected in a manner that is somehow the same—for example, if the living being's appetites are other than the acting or being affected of the faculty of appetite of the soul. The body that is of this kind should be examined later.[28]

---

20. See Ar., *GC* 1.7.323b25–27.
21. Cf. *supra* 3.19.
22. Cf. 4.3.22.1–7. See Pl., *Tim.* 36E.
23. See Ar., *DA* 2.1.412b10–3.
24. See Ar., *DA* 2.1.412a27–28.
25. See Ar., *DA* 1.4.408b12–13.
26. See Appendix II A.
27. The term τὸ κοινόν (literally 'that which is common'; here 'conjunction') is probably synonymous with the term τὸ συναμφότερον ('the complex') used in the following lines. Cf. *infra* 11.1 where the term τὸ σύνθετον ('the composite') is used.
28. See *infra* 7.

But how, for example, is the complex able to feel pain?[29] Is it
10   because the body is disposed in this way and the state penetrates up to
sense-perception, which has its culmination in the soul? But it is not
yet clear how sense-perception works. And whenever the pain takes
its origin in a belief or judgment of some evil being present either to
oneself or to something one cares about, is there then a painful change
15   in the body and, generally, in the entire living being?[30] But it is also not
yet clear what is the subject of belief, the soul or the complex.

Next, the belief about some evil does not include the state of pain.
For it is possible that when the belief is present, the feeling of pain is
completely absent; or, again, it is possible for the feeling of anger not
20   to be present when the belief that we have been slighted is present; or,
again, for a belief about what is good not to move one's desire. How,
then, are states common to body and soul?

In fact, it is the case that appetite belongs to the soul's faculty of
appetite, and spiritedness belongs to the soul's faculty of spiritedness,
and, generally, the inclination toward something belongs to the soul's
faculty of desire.[31] In this way, though, they will no longer be common,
25   but belong to the soul alone. But, in fact, they belong to the body as
well, because blood and bile must boil, and somehow the body must be
disposed to move desire in the direction of, for example, sexual objects.

Let us agree that the desire for the Good is not a common state but
belongs to the soul [alone], as is the case with some other states—no
account will attribute all of these to both in common. But the human
30   being who has the appetite will be the one having the desire for sexual
objects, though in another way it will be soul's faculty of appetite that
has the appetite. How? Will the human being initiate the appetite and
will the faculty of appetite follow after? But, in general, how could a
human being have an appetite when the appetitive faculty has not been
moved? In that case, it will be the faculty of appetite that initiates it. But
where will it start from if the body is not first disposed in this way?[32]

§1.1.6. Perhaps it is better to say generally that it is due to the
presence of powers[33] that things that have these act according to them,
while these powers are themselves immobile, providing to the things

---

29. See Pl. [?], *Alc.* 1.130A9; *Phil.* 33D–34A; *Tim.* 43C, 45D.
30. See *SVF* 3.459 (= Plutarch, *De virt. mor.* 3).
31. See Ar., *DA* 2.3.414b2.
32. Cf. 4.4.20.
33. Among the 'powers' or 'faculties' meant are: τὸ θρεπτικόν ('growth'), τὸ αἰσθητικόν ('perceptual'), τὸ ὀρεκτικόν ('desiderative'), τὸ κινητικόν κατὰ τόπον ('locomotive'), and τὸ διανοητικόν ('discursive reasoning'). See Ar., *DA* 2.3.414a31–32.

that have them the ability to act. But if this is so, when the living being is affected, the cause that endows the complex with life is itself unaffected by the states and activities that belong to that which has them. But if this is so, living will in every way belong not to the soul, but to the complex.

In fact, the life of the complex will not be that of the soul. And the power of sense-perception will not perceive, but rather that which has the power.[34] But if sense-perception is a motion through the body having its culmination in the soul,[35] how will the soul not perceive?

In fact, when the power of sense-perception is present, it is by its presence that the complex perceives what it perceives. If, though, the power will not be moved, how will the complex still perceive when neither the soul nor the psychical power are counted together with it?

§1.1.7. In fact, assume that it is the complex that perceives, due to the presence of the soul, which is not the sort of thing that can make itself a part of the complex or of the other part,[36] but which can make something else from a body of this type and a kind of light emitted from itself, namely, a different nature, that of the living being, to which sense-perception and other states proper to a living being are said to belong.[37]

But then how is it that we perceive?

In fact, it is because we are not released from such a living being, even if other things more honorable than us are present in the complete substantiality of the human being, which is made of many parts. But the soul's power of sense-perception should not be understood as being of sensibles, but rather of the impressions that arise from sensation and which are graspable by the living being. For these are already intelligible. So, sensation of externals is a reflection of this [grasp of impressions], whereas this [grasp of impressions] is truer in substantiality, since it contemplates only forms, without being affected. Actually, from these Forms,[38] from which soul alone has already received its leadership over the living being, come acts of discursive thinking,

---

34. See Alex. Aphr., *De an.* 23.18–24.
35. See Pl., *Phil.* 34A4–5; *Tim.* 43C4–7, 45D1–2.
36. I.e., the body.
37. This is Plotinus's position, explained at length in 4.4.18. The 'light' refers to the psychical powers of the living being.
38. Here Plotinus is taking the Aristotelian doctrine of cognition of forms without matter and combining it with the Platonic doctrine of Forms, the true paradigms of the forms in and apart from matter.

beliefs, and acts of intellection. And here indeed is where we are.[39]
The things that are prior to these acts are ours,[40] while we ourselves,
controlling the living being, are, actually, located here and higher up.
But there is nothing against calling the whole a 'living being', with the
lower parts being mixed in, although the true human being begins
about there [with thought]. Those lower parts are the 'lion-like' and,
generally, the 'multifaceted beast'.[41] Given that the human being coincides
with the rational soul, whenever human beings engage in calculative
reasoning, it is we who are reasoning because the results of these acts
of reasoning belong to the soul.

§1.1.8. But how are we related to the Intellect? By 'Intellect' I do
not mean that condition that the soul derives from the entities[42] that
accompany the Intellect, but the Intellect itself.

In fact, we have this even though it transcends us. But we have it
either collectively or individually, or both collectively and individually.[43] We have it collectively, because it is indivisible and one, that is,
everywhere identical; we have it individually, because each one of us
has the whole of it in the primary part of the soul.[44] We have the Forms,
then, in two ways: in the soul, in a way, unfolded and separated, but in
Intellect 'all together'.[45]

But how are we related to god?[46]

In fact, it is 'astride the intelligible nature',[47] that is, over real Substantiality,[48] whereas we are in third place, being made, Plato says,
from the 'indivisible Substantiality', which is above us, and from the
'divisible substantiality found in bodies'.[49] We should actually think of
[souls] as divided within bodies because soul gives itself to corporeal
magnitudes, however large each living being may be, even as, being
one, it gives itself to the whole universe; or else because it is imagined
to be present to bodies as shining on them, and makes living beings

39. Cf. 4.4.18.11–15.
40. Prior in time. Sense-perception precedes higher thought.
41. See Pl., *Rep.* 9.588C7, D3, 590A9–B1.
42. Perhaps a reference to our undescended intellects. Cf. 3.4.3.24; 4.3.5.6; 4.3.12.3–4;
4.8.8; 6.7.5.26–29; 6.7.17.26–27; 6.8.6.41–43.
43. Cf. 5.3.3.26–29.
44. I.e., our embodied intellects.
45. See Anaxagoras, fr. B 1 DK.
46. Here 'god' refers to the One or Good; elsewhere, 'god' refers to Intellect. The One
is 'above οὐσία'. See Pl., *Rep.* 6.509B8.
47. See Numenius, fr. 2 Des Places.
48. See Pl., *Soph.* 248A11.
49. See Pl., *Tim.* 35A1–3.

not out of itself and body, but, while remaining in itself, by giving off reflections of itself, like a face in a multiplicity of mirrors.

The first reflection is sense-perception, which is in the composite. Next after this is what is said to be 'another type of soul',[50] each always coming from the previous one. It ends in the generative and growth faculties or, generally, in what produces and is perfective of something other than what productive soul makes, given that productive soul is directed to its own product.[51]

§1.1.9. So, the nature of that soul of ours will be released from being responsible for the evils that a human being does and suffers. These belong to the living being, the composite, that is, composite in the manner stated.[52] But if belief and discursive thinking belong to the soul, how is it inerrant? For belief can be false, and many evils are   5
committed on the basis of false belief.

In fact, evils are done when we are overcome by what is inferior in us—for we are many[53]—either appetite or spiritedness or an evil mental image.

That which is called 'thinking of falsities' is imagination that has not waited for the judgment of the discursive thinking faculty. But in that case, we acted under the persuasive influence of something infe-   10
rior. It is just as in the case of sense-perception, when we see falsely by our common faculty of sense-perception before the discursive faculty makes a judgment.[54] But the intellect has either been in contact with its object or not, so that it is inerrant.[55]

In fact, we should say that we are, in this way, either in contact with the intelligible which is in Intellect or we are not. Actually, we are in contact with the intelligible in us. For it is possible to have it, but not   15
to have it at hand.[56]

We have indeed distinguished what belongs to the composite and what are properties of soul;[57] what belongs to the composite are the things that are corporeal or do not exist without a body, whereas what

---

50. These are the mortal parts of the soul, the spirited and appetitive faculties, housed in the chest and belly. See Pl., *Tim.* 69C7.

51. The ultimate product that does not produce is matter.

52. Cf. *supra* 1.5–7.

53. See Pl., *Lg.* 626E2–627A2.

54. See Ar., *DA* 2.6.418a7–20 with 3.3.428b19–20 where the common faculty of sense-perception is more open to error than is sense-perception of proper sensibles.

55. See Pl., *Rep.* 5.477E6; Ar., *DA* 3.6.430a26–8; *Meta.* 9.10.1051b17–33.

56. See Pl., *Tht.* 198D5–8.

57. See Ar., *DA* 1.1.403a4.

does not need a body for its activity is a property of soul. Discursive thinking, when it makes a judgment on the impressions that come from sense-perception, is at that moment contemplating forms, that is, contemplating them with a sort of self-awareness; this is, at any rate, principally the case for the discursive thinking of the true soul. For true discursive thinking is an actualization of acts of intellection, and there is often a sameness or commonality between things external and internal. The soul, then, will be no less quiet and turned inward, that is, to itself. The changes and the tumult in us coming from the things that are entangled with us—from the states of the composite, whatever exactly that is—are as we have said.[58]

§1.1.10. But if we are the soul, and we have these experiences, the soul would have them and, again, it will do what we do.

In fact, we said that the composite belongs to us, especially when we are not yet separated from it, since we say that we experience the states of our bodies. The term 'we', then, is used in two ways, referring either to that which includes the beast or to that which is at the same time above this. The beast is the body that has been vivified. But the true human being is other, purified of these corporeal states and possessing the virtues that are found in the activity of thinking that is actually situated in the separated soul,[59] separate and separable even when it is in the sensible world.[60] For whenever it removes itself completely, the inferior part of the soul that receives its illumination goes away, too, following after it. But the virtues that do not belong to thought apply to the custom and training of the composite.[61] For the vices belong to this, since occasions of envy and jealousy and compassion do so, too. What do occasions of love belong to?

In fact, some belong to the composite, and some belong to the 'interior human being'.[62]

§1.1.11. When we are children, the faculties of the composite are active; there is little illumination of it from the things above. Whenever they are inactive in us, they are acting in relation to that which is above. But they act in us whenever they reach what is in the middle.[63]

---

58. Cf. *supra* 1.7; Pl., *Phd.* 66D6; *Tim.* 43B6 where the 'tumult' is due to embodiment.
59. These are the purificatory virtues. Cf. 1.2.3–6.
60. Cf. *infra* 11.2–8; 2.9.7.4–10; 4.3.12.3–8.
61. Cf. 1.2.1.15–16. See Pl., *Rep.* 7.518D9–12.
62. Cf. 5.1.10.10. See Pl., *Rep.* 9.589A7–B1.
63. Referring to the faculties of embodied cognition. Cf. 5.3.3.32–46.

What, then? Is not the 'we' prior to this middle ground, too?[64] Yes, 5
but there has to occur an apprehension of what is prior. For we do not
always use that which we have, but we only do so when we arrange the
middle, either in relation to that which is above or in relation to the
opposite of this, or in relation to such potencies or dispositions we take
steps to actualize.

But how do beasts have animality?[65]

In fact, if the souls in them are, as it is said,[66] human souls which 10
have erred, the separable[67] part of the soul does not belong to the
beasts. It is there, but it is not there for them. Rather, what they have
self-awareness of is the reflection of the soul that goes with the body.
Actually, such a body has been in a way made by a reflection of soul.
On the other hand, if the soul of a human being has not entered it, it
becomes the kind of living being it is due to the illumination coming 15
from the soul of the cosmos.[68]

§1.1.12. But if the soul is inerrant, how can there be punishments
for it? Yet this line of reasoning is inconsistent with every argument
that says that the soul errs or acts morally correctly and undergoes
punishments, both in Hades and via reincarnation. One ought to
associate oneself with whichever line of reasoning one wishes—but 5
perhaps we can discover a way in which they do not conflict.

The line of reasoning that makes the soul inerrant assumes that it is
one and totally simple, claiming that soul and the essence of soul are
identical.[69] The one that allows that the soul can err interweaves and
adds to it another form of soul which is in these terrible states.[70] The 10
soul, then, is a composite of all these things and is actually affected as
a whole, and it is the composite that errs; and it is this which undergoes punishment, not the other.[71] Hence, Plato says, 'we have gazed
upon soul like those who have seen the sea-god Glaucus'.[72] But if 15

---

64. Cf. *supra* 7.9–18; 4.8.8.9–11; 5.3.3.32–46.
65. The term is τὸ ζῷον which is usually translated 'animal' or 'living being'. Here, the sense seems to be the generic property of 'animality'. The Living Being of *Tim.* 30C2–31A1 contains generically all animals and plants.
66. See Pl., *Phd.* 81E2–82b7; *Phdr.* 249B3–5; *Rep.* 10.618A3, 620A2–D5; *Tim.* 42C1–D8.
67. The word is χωριστόν which may also mean 'separate'. In that case, Plotinus is referring to the undescended intellect.
68. Cf. 4.7.14.1–5.
69. Cf. *supra* 2.1–2.
70. See Pl., *Tim.* 69C7–D1.
71. See Pl., *Rep.* 10.611B5.
72. See Pl., *Rep.* 10.611C7–D1. Also, *Gorg.* 523A1–6; *Phd.* 107D2–4.

someone really wants to see its nature, he says, he must 'knock off the accretions'[73] and look at 'its philosophy' to see 'what it adheres to' and 'what it owes its kinship to' such that it is the sort of thing it is. The life and other activities of the soul, then, are one thing; what is punished another.

20   The withdrawal and separation of the soul is not only from this body, but also from its accretions. For the accretion occurs during generation.

In fact, generation belongs to another form of soul entirely. How the generation takes place has already been explained.[74] It is because of the soul's descent, when something else arises from it due to its declination. Does it, then, abandon its [embodied] reflection? And how is

25   the declination itself not a moral error? For if the declination is an illumination of what is below, it is not a moral error, any more than what remains in shadow is. What is illuminated is responsible; for if that did not exist, the soul would not have anything to illuminate.[75]

To descend or to decline, then, means that what is illuminated by it is so because it shares its life with it.[76] The soul, then, abandons its

30   reflection if there is nothing nearby to receive it. But it abandons it not by being cut off, but because the reflection no longer exists. And it no longer exists if the whole soul is looking to the intelligible world. The poet seems to be separating the reflection in the case of Heracles when he puts it in Hades, but places Heracles himself among the gods.[77] Maintaining both stories, namely, that Heracles was among the gods

35   and that he was in Hades, he then divided him. Perhaps the account would be plausible if the idea is actually that Heracles had practical virtue and was thought worthy of being a god due to that excellence, but because his virtue was practical and not theoretical—in which case he would have been entirely in the intelligible world—he is above, though a part of him is also still below.

§1.1.13. That which has investigated these matters: Is it we or the soul?

In fact, it is 'we', but by means of the soul. How have we done this by means of the soul? Is it by having that which was being investigated, namely, soul?

---

73. See Pl., *Rep.* 10.611E1–612A4.
74. Possibly a reference to 4.8 or to 6.4.16.
75. A reference to matter.
76. This is the 'vivified body' at 1.1.10.6–7.
77. See Homer, *Od.* 11.601–602.

In fact, it is insofar as we are soul. Is it, then, in motion?

In fact, we should attribute to it the sort of motion that is not corpo-real but belongs to its life.[78] And intellection is like this for us, because   5
the soul is intellectual, and intellection is its better life—when the soul
thinks, or when intellect is active in us. For this is also a part of us, and
it is to this that we ascend.

---

78. See Pl., *Lg.* 897D3 on 'intellectual motion'.

1.2 (19)

On Virtues

Introduction

This treatise springs from a commentary on Plato's *Theaetetus* 176A, in which Socrates urges his interlocutors to escape from this realm and, by cultivating virtue, to assimilate themselves to the divine. Reflecting on this passage leads Plato to an account of grades of virtue, especially a distinction between the practical and the theoretical, and an argument that the latter is in an important sense higher than the former. Although this fact could be taken to suggest the unimportance of practical ethics for Platonists, Plotinus takes pains to show that the possession of the higher virtues entails the possession of the lower, even if the practice of the lower is not an end in itself.

Summary

§1. How can the practice of virtue bring about assimilation to the divine when the gods themselves do not practice virtue?

§2. Discussion of different senses of 'being likenesses of'.

§3. Virtues as purifications.

§4. The results of purification.

§5. The effects of purification on the soul.

§6. Purification and assimilation.

§7. Whether the higher and lower virtues imply each other.

---

§1.2.1.[1] Since evils exist in the sensible world and 'of necessity circulate in this place,'[2] and the soul wants to flee evils, it should flee from the sensible world. What, then, is this flight? Plato says that it is assimilating oneself to god. And this would occur if we were to
5 become 'just and pious with wisdom,'[3] that is, generally, if we were in a virtuous state. If, then, it is by virtue that we are assimilated to god, are we assimilated to one who has virtue? Moreover, to which god will it be? Would it be, then, to one who seemed to have these virtues more, that is, to the soul of the cosmos, and to that part of it which governs,

---

1. See Appendix II G; III C 4.
2. See Pl., *Tht.* 176A5–B3; Ar., *EN* 10.7.1177b33, 8.1179b27.
3. See Pl., *Tht.* 176B2–3.

in which there exists a marvelous wisdom?[4] For it is reasonable that, because we live in the sensible world, we should assimilate ourselves to this god.

First, however, it is questionable if all the virtues exist in this god, for example, whether it has self-control or[5] courage as one to whom there is nothing fearful.[6] For there is nothing outside it. Nor could something pleasurable which it does not already have present itself as an object of appetite for it to have or want to have. But if it is in a state of desiring the intelligibles which our souls desire, too, it is also clear that the cosmos and the virtues in us come from the intelligible world.

Is it the case, then, that the divine has these virtues?

In fact, it is not reasonable that it should have the civic virtues,[7] I mean, wisdom in the faculty of calculative reasoning, courage in the spirited faculty, self-control in the agreement or concord of the spirited faculty with the faculty of calculative reasoning, and justice consisting in each faculty of the soul doing its own job of ruling and being ruled.[8] If this is so, then it is not according to the civic virtues that we are assimilated, is it, but rather according to those which are greater though they bear the identical name?

But if it is according to other virtues, is the assimilation not according to the civic virtues at all?

In fact, it would be irrational to maintain that we are not in any way assimilated according to these—legend at least has it that those who practiced these are divine, too, and should be said somehow or other to be assimilated according to them—but that the actual assimilation is according to the greater virtues. At least, it follows either way that god possesses virtues even if not these. If, then, someone concedes that, even if god does not have these, it is possible to assimilate oneself to god, and we are in different states with regard to different virtues, nothing prevents us, even if we are not assimilated with regard to virtues, from assimilating by our virtues to that which does not possess virtue. How? In this way.

If something becomes hot by the presence of heat, is it also necessary that that from which the heat comes be heated? And if something is hot by the presence of fire, is it necessary that the fire itself should be

---

4. Τὸ ἡγεμονικόν ('the governing or leading part of the soul') is the Stoic term. See *SVF* 1.529 (= Sext. Emp., *M.* 9.8), 564 (= Themistius, *Or.* II 27 C).
5. Inserting ἢ between σώφρονι and ἀνδρείῳ with Kirchhoff.
6. See Ar., *EN* 10.8.1178b10–23.
7. See Pl., *Phd.* 82A11–B2; *Rep.* 4.430B9–D2, 433B8–C2, 434C8.
8. See Pl., *Rep.* 4.427E–434D, 443B2.

35   heated by the presence of fire? In regard to the first point, one might say
      that in the fire there is heat, though it is intrinsic. The consequence of
      this, if the analogy holds, is that virtue has to be added to the soul but
      is intrinsic to that which the soul imitates. In regard to the point about
40   fire, one might reply that then the divine just is virtue. We, though,
      judge it to be greater than virtue.[9] But if that in which the soul par-
      ticipates were identical with that from which it comes, it should have
      been expressed in that way. Now, though, we are saying that the divine
      is one thing and virtue another. For the sensible house is not identical
      with the intelligible house, even though it is made to be like it.[10] And the
      sensible house participates in order and arrangement, whereas in the
45   intelligible world, in the house's expressed principle, there is not order
      or arrangement or symmetry. In the same way, then, we participate in
      order and arrangement and consonance coming from the intelligible
      world, and these, when in the sensible world, are virtue; but Beings in
      the intelligible world do not themselves need consonance or order or
      arrangement, so that they also have no need for virtue. Nonetheless,
50   we are assimilated to the things in the intelligible world because of the
      presence in us of virtue.
          So much for the fact that there is no need for virtue in the intelli-
      gible world even if we are made to be assimilated by virtue. But one
      should add persuasion to the argument and not rely on its force alone.

      §1.2.2. So, first, we need to grasp the virtues according to which we
      claim to be assimilated in order that, again, we may discover the very
      thing whose imitation in us is virtue, but which in the intelligible world
      is a sort of archetype and not virtue. This will show how there are two
5   types of assimilation: the first requires that there be something identical
      in the things that are the same, such that their sameness derived
      equally from that which is identical. But in cases where one thing is
      assimilated to another, but that other is primary, the relationship is not
      reciprocated, and the primary thing is not said to be the same as the
      other. In this case, the assimilation should be taken in another sense,
10   not requiring the identical form, but rather a different one in each case,
      if indeed it is assimilated in this other sense.
          What, then, is virtue exactly—universally and in particular? The
      argument will be clearer if we consider each particular virtue, for in
      this way what is common to them, that according to which they are
      virtues, will easily be made evident.

      _____

      9. See Alcinous, *Didask.* 28.181.44–45.
      10. The ὁμοίωσις ('assimilation') comes from the verb ὁμοιοῦσθαι ('to be made like').

So, the civic virtues, which we have spoken of above, do really give
order to us and make us better; they limit and give measure to our appe-   15
tites and, generally, give measure to our affective states and remove our
false beliefs by means of that which is generally better and by imposing
limits on us and by the fact that that which is measured is placed outside the things that are unmeasured and unlimited. And these virtues,
which are themselves limited insofar as they are measures in 'matter',
that is, soul, are assimilated to the measure that is in the intelligible
world and they have a trace of the best that is there.[11] For matter, being   20
in every way unmeasured, is unassimilated to everything. But insofar
as it participates in form, to that extent is it assimilated to that formless
reality [the Good].[12] Things that are closer participate more. Soul is
nearer than body, and more closely related. Due to this, it participates   25
more, so that, having appeared to us as a god, it deceives us into thinking that it is the entirety of god. Those, then, who are virtuous in this
way are assimilated to god.

§1.2.3.[13] But since Plato reveals the other type of assimilation as
belonging to a greater virtue,[14] we should speak about that. In this
account, the substantiality of civic virtue will also be made even clearer,
as well as the substantiality of the greater virtue, and, generally, the fact
that there is a type of virtue different from the civic. Given that Plato   5
is indeed saying that assimilation to god is a flight from the sensible
world,[15] and does not name the virtues of civic life unqualifiedly
'virtue' but adds the qualification 'civic', and given that elsewhere he
says that all the virtues are purifications,[16] it is clear that he maintains
that there are two sorts of virtue, and does not think that assimilation
is according to civic virtue. In what sense, then, should we say that   10
virtues are purifications, and, once we are purified, in what sense are
we assimilated to the highest degree?
    In fact, since the soul is evil when it is enmeshed in the body, and
has come to experience the same things as it, and has come to believe
the same things, it would be good, that is, it would have virtue if it
were not to believe these things, but were to act alone—which is what   15

---

11. On virtues as measures see Pl., *Protag.* 356D1–357B3; *Sts.* 284A8–E8; *Soph.*
228C1–D4; *Phil.* 64D9–E7.
12. Cf. 5.5.6.4–5; 6.7.32.9; 6.9.3.43–44 on the Good as ἀνείδεος ('formless'). On matter
as unmeasured, cf. 1.8.3.13–34.
13. See Appendix II B; II G.
14. See Pl., *Tht.* 176C4–D1; *Lg.* 716D1–E3.
15. See Pl., *Tht.* 176B1–8.
16. Cf. 3.6.5.13–29. See Pl., *Phd.* 69C1, 82A11.

thinking and being wise is—and not feel the same things as the body—
which is what self-control is—and not fear being separated from the
body—which is what it is to be courageous—and if reason or intellect were to lead it, with the appetites not opposing it—which is what
justice would be. Indeed, as for such a disposition of the soul, one in
20   which one thinks and is unaffected in this way, if someone were to say
that it is a kind of assimilation to god, he would not be mistaken. For
the divine is pure and this is its sort of activity, so that someone who
imitates it has wisdom.

Why, then, is the divine not disposed in this way?

In fact, it does not have a disposition; disposition belongs to soul.
And the soul thinks in one way, but, among the things in the intelligi-
25   ble world, one sort [Intellect] thinks in a different way, and the other
[the One] does not think at all. But, again, we may ask if the word
'thinking' is equivocal? Not at all. But there is a primary type of thinking and one derived from it, which is different. For as a spoken word is
an imitation of a word in the soul, so a word in the soul is an imitation
of something in something different.[17] As, then, that which is in an
30   utterance is divided from that which is in the soul, so, too, is that which
is in soul divided, being an interpretation of that which is prior to it.
Virtue belongs to soul, not to Intellect nor to that which transcends it.

§1.2.4.[18] We should, then, examine if the purification is identical
with this sort of virtue, or if the purification comes first and then the
virtue follows, that is, whether the virtue lies in the process of being
purified or in the state one is in once one has been purified.

Virtue in the process of being purified would be less complete than
5   in the state one is in once having been purified, for having been purified is in a way already a completion. But to have been purified is the
elimination of something alien, whereas that which is good is different
from this.

In fact, if the good were there prior to the impure state, then the
purification would do the job; but if the purification will do the job,
what remains will be that which is good, not the purification.

10   And what it is that remains should be examined. For perhaps the
nature that remained would not be that which is good after all; for it
would not have been there in the [unpurified] evil. Should we, then,
say that this nature is Good-like?[19]

---

17. What is in the soul is an imitation of what is in Intellect. Cf. 3.8.6.27–29; 5.1.3.7.
18. See Appendix II E.
19. See Pl., *Rep.* 6.509A3.

In fact, we should say that it was not up to staying in a truly good state, for it was naturally inclined to both good and evil. Its good, then, will be associating with what is akin to it, and its evil associating with the opposite. It will be associating, then, once it has been purified, but it will be doing so having turned itself around. Does it turn around after the purification, then?

In fact, after the purification it has already turned around. Is this, then, its virtue?

In fact, its virtue is what comes to it from turning around. What, then, is this? A seeing and an impression of that which has been seen embedded in it and now active—like seeing in relation to the object seen.[20]

Did it, therefore, neither have them nor recollect them?

In fact, it had things that were not active, but dispersed and unilluminated. If they are to be illuminated and it is to know them as being present, it must impel itself toward that which does the illuminating. And it did not have the things themselves, but impressions. It must, then, harmonize the impressions with the true Beings of which they are impressions. And perhaps it is in this sense that this nature 'has' them, because the Intellect is not alien to it, especially not when it looks toward the Intellect. If this were not so, the Intellect would be alien even when it is present. For even areas of scientific understanding in which we are not wholly engaged are alien.

§1.2.5.[21] But the extent of purification should be addressed. For in this way, it will be clear what the assimilation is to and with what god we are identified. And we should especially examine purification in regard to anger and appetite and the rest, pain and related feelings, and to what extent separation from the body is possible. Perhaps the soul actually collects itself in some sort of place apart from the body, where it is incapable of being affected, producing only those perceptions of pleasures that are inevitable, using them as treatments and relief from pain so that it should not be disturbed—eliminating pains, and, if that is not possible, bearing them easily and lessening them by not suffering alongside the body. It would also eliminate anger as much as possible and, if possible, entirely, but if not, at least not flaring up along with the body, but treating it as the involuntary act of something else, and reckoning what is involuntary to be small and weak. It eliminates fear

---

20. These are the intelligible objects of which the one purified is now aware.
21. See Appendix II B.

altogether. For it will be fearful of nothing—though the involuntary is here, too—except when fear serves as a warning.

And what about appetite? Clearly, it will not be for anything base, and the soul itself will not have the appetite for food and drink needed for replenishment. Nor will it have appetite for sexual pleasures.[22] If it does have appetite, it will be for natural things, I think, and will not be involuntary. But if it does have this, it will only have it to the extent of a spontaneous impression in the imagination, and no more.

In general, the soul will be pure of all these, and it will want to make the non-rational [part of the soul] pure, too, so that it is not disturbed. But if it is, it will not be disturbed excessively; rather, its disturbances will be few, and immediately dislodged by the proximity of the [faculty of calculative reasoning]. It is just as if someone with a wise person living nearby should benefit from the proximity of wisdom, either becoming like him or being ashamed of daring to do something that the wise person would not want him to do. There will, then, be no conflict. For it is sufficient that reason is present, which the inferior element will so stand in awe of that the inferior element itself will be disgusted if the soul were to be moved at all because it did not remain still when the master was present, and will reproach itself for its own weakness.

§1.2.6.[23] There is, then, no moral error in anything of this sort for a human being, but only [the occasion for] morally perfect acting.[24] The focus is not on being exempt from moral error, but on being god. If, then, there were to remain anything involuntary in their actions, a human being in this state would be a god or a daemon by being double, or rather by having with himself someone else with another virtue.[25] If he had nothing of this sort, he would be only a god, a god among those following the first god.[26] For he himself is a god who came from the intelligible world, and what he is in himself, if he remains as he was when he came, is in the intelligible world. But as for the one with whom he dwells when he came here, he will assimilate this one to himself as much as he is able so that, if possible, he is impervious or at least incapable of doing those things that do not seem right to the master.

---

22. See Pl., *Phd.* 64D2–7.
23. See Appendix II D.
24. Cf. 3.2.10.7–11; 4.8.5.16–24. See *SVF* 3.500 (= Stob., *Ecl.* 93.14), 501 (= Stob., *Ecl.* 96.18), 502 (= Stob., *Ecl.* 97.5) on ἁμαρτία ('moral error') and κατόρθωσις ('morally perfect acting').
25. This is the civic virtue of *supra* 1.16ff.; 2.13–18; 3.9. Cf. 1.1.10.7–14.
26. See Pl., *Phdr.* 246E5–6. The first god is Zeus.

What, then, are the particular virtues for such a person?

In fact, theoretical and practical wisdom consist in the contemplation of that which Intellect possesses, though Intellect has them by
touching.[27] Each of these is twofold: one is in Intellect, one in Soul.
And in the intelligible world, there is no virtue; virtue is in the soul.   15
What, then, is in the intelligible world? Its own activity, that is, what it
really is. But in the sensible world, when what comes from the intelligible world is found in another, that is virtue. For neither Justice itself,
nor any of the others, is a virtue, but rather a paradigm. That which
comes from it in the soul is a virtue. For virtue is someone's virtue. But
that which is in itself belongs to itself, and not to something else.

But if justice is indeed taking care of one's own affairs,[28] is it always   20
found in a multiplicity of parts?

In fact, the virtue is in a multiplicity when the parts are many, but
taking care of one's own business is wholly present even if there were
to be a unity. Indeed, true Justice itself belongs to a self-related unity
in which there are no parts. So, the justice in the soul that is greater is
activity in relation to intellect, and the greater self-control is a turning   25
inward toward intellect, and the greater courage is a lack of affection
inasmuch as there is an assimilation of itself to the unaffected nature
toward which it is looking. This assimilation comes from virtue, and
ensures that the soul does not share affections with the inferior element
with which it lives.

§1.2.7. The virtues themselves in the soul are, then, mutually
implicating just as are their paradigms prior to virtue in Intellect.[29]
For intellection in the intelligible world is scientific understanding or
theoretical wisdom, and being self-related is self-control, and taking
care of one's own affairs is one's proper function, and courage is in a   5
way the immaterial state[30] of remaining pure in oneself. In soul, then,
theoretical wisdom and practical wisdom in relation to Intellect are
the act of seeing. These are virtues belonging to it, for it itself is not
these virtues, as is the case in the intelligible world. And the others
follow similarly. And as for purification, if indeed all the virtues are

---

27. Cf. 6.2.21.28. See Pl., *Phd.* 79D6; *Symp.* 212A4; *Tim.* 37A6; Ar., *Meta.* 12.7.1072b21.
28. See Pl., *Rep.* 4.434C8.
29. On the Stoic doctrine of the mutual implication of the virtues, see *SVF* 3.295 (= D.L.,
7.125), 299 (=Plutarch, *De St. repug.* 27). Also, see Ar., *EN* 6.13.1144b32–1145a2.
30. The word ἀϋλότης ('immaterial [state]') is a *hapax* in Plotinus and is perhaps
odd in this context, although it is the reading of all the mss. Porphyry, *Sent.* 32.29.6,
reads ταὐτότης ('identical [state]'), presumably indicating the identity discussed in the
previous section.

10   purifications, in the sense that they are states of having been purified,
        purification necessarily produces all of them; otherwise, none would
        be complete.

        Whoever has the greater ones will have the lesser in potency, too,
        necessarily, though one who has the lesser will not necessarily have
        the greater. This is actually in a nutshell the life of the virtuous per-
        son. Whether he who has the greater has the lesser in actuality, too, or
15   has them in another manner, should be investigated in each case. For
        example, consider practical wisdom. If it requires the use of other prin-
        ciples, how will it still be there when it is not active? And if one virtue
        by nature consists in being in a state to a certain extent and another
        to another extent, and one sort of self-control imposes measure on
        feelings, will the other type eliminate them entirely? But the identical
        question arises for the other virtues generally once it has been raised
        for practical wisdom.

20   Should we state, at least, that the virtuous person will know them
        and how much he will have of them? Perhaps he will act according
        to some of them if circumstances demand. But advancing on to the
        greater principles, and the other measures, he will act according to
        those. For example, he will not locate the act of self-control in imposing
        a measure, but in separating himself entirely as far as possible, abso-
25   lutely not living the life of the good human being, which civic virtue
        values, but leaving this, and opting for another, the life of the gods.
        For assimilation is to the gods, not to good human beings. Assimila-
        tion to good human beings is making an image of an image, one from
30   another. But the other assimilation is like making an image according
        to a paradigm.

1.4 (46)

ON HAPPINESS

Introduction

In this treatise, Plotinus draws upon Peripatetic, Stoic, and Epicurean accounts of happiness to compare them with that of Plato. He draws on elements of the former in order to demonstrate that the best life for a human being is ascent to and immersion in the intelligible world. Happiness, as the Platonist understands it, is the result of the assimilation to the divine. At one level, Plotinus has an affinity with the Stoic view that virtue, properly understood, is sufficient for happiness. And yet the Stoics, owing to their materialism and their denial of the immortality of the soul, are in no position to justify their discounting of the travails of embodiment and so they defend the identity of the person with the intellect.

Summary

§1. If Aristotle is right that the best life is the achievement of something's function, then even non-rational animals and plants can be happy.

§2. The unsustainability of the Epicurean position that identifies happiness with the pleasant life. The Stoic position, that happiness is the rational life, is better, but not if rationality is understood as following nature.

§3. The happy life can only be the life of the Intellect in relation to the Good.

§4. The happy life is not only found in Intellect but it requires the recognition of our true identity with our intellects.

§5. Peripatetic objects to the Platonic position based on the role of externals in the happy life.

§6. Responses to the Peripatetics. Externals make no contribution to our happiness.

§7. Not even great personal misfortunes, whether our own or those of others close to us, can detract from our happiness.

§8. Bodily pains do not detract from happiness.

§9. Do we need to be conscious to be happy?

§10. Primary intellectual activity is beyond mental representations.

§11. Externals do not increase happiness.

§12. The unique pleasure of the intellectual life.

§13. The happy person is impervious to fortune.

§14. The happiness we are talking about refers only to the real person, the intellect.

§15. The truly happy person is indifferent to the state of the embodied individual, although this does not require disregard for the body.

§16. The focus of the happy life is only the Good.

---

§1.4.1.[1] If we suppose that living well and being happy are identical, will we in that case be endowing other living beings with these, too?[2] For if it is natural for them to live their lives without impediment, what prevents us from saying that they also live well?[3] Also, whether one supposes that living well is being in a good state or performing the function appropriate to oneself, both alternatives will apply to other living beings as well.[4] For it would be possible to be in a good state or to perform one's function by nature; for example, musically disposed animals, who are otherwise in a good state, certainly sing naturally, and have a life that is in this respect choice worthy for them.

So, if we suppose that being happy is a certain goal,[5] that is, the ultimate goal of natural desire,[6] we would in that case be endowing with happiness those who achieve this ultimate goal, where, for those who arrive there, the nature within them rests having been present their entire life and having been fulfilled from beginning to end. Someone might disapprove of extending happiness to other living beings—for to do this is to endow with happiness even the basest living beings[7]—and plants, too, since they are themselves alive, that is, they have a life that also unfolds in the direction of a goal.

But, first, will it not seem absurd for him to be saying that other living beings do not live well because they do not seem to be worth much to him? And one would not be forced to attribute to plants that which one attributes to living beings in general, because they have no

---

1. See Appendix III C 2; III C 3.

2. See Ar., *EN* 1.8.1098b21, 9.1099b33–35; 10.8.1178b24–28; *EE* 2.10.1219b1; *SVF* 3.17 (= Michael of Ephesus, *In EN* 598.30–32).

3. See Ar., *EN* 7.14.1153b11.

4. See Ar., *EN* 1.7.1097b7–8; 11.1101a18–19; 2.5.1106a23–24; 10.7.1177a16–17; *SVF* 3.16 (= Stob., *Ecl.* 2.77.16–27); 3.431 (= D.L., 7.115).

5. See Ar., *EN* 10.6.1176a31–32; Alex. Aphr., *De an. mant.* 152.17–22.

6. See *SVF* 3.65 (=Alex. Aphr., *De an. mant.* 162).

7. See Sext. Emp., *M.* 11.97, where the objection is directed against Epicureans.

sense-perception.[8] And then, one might include plants if indeed they are alive, too; there is life that is good and life that is the opposite, which in the case of plants is being in a good state or not, for example, bearing fruit or not bearing fruit.[9] If, then, pleasure is the goal and living well consists in this,[10] it is absurd for someone to deny that other living beings live well. If freedom from disturbance is the goal, the same applies.[11] And it applies to 'living according to nature' if one were to say that this is living well.[12]

§1.4.2.[13] So, those who do not include plants because they do not have sense-perception will by that token risk not including all living beings,[14] for if they say that sense-perception is this—being not unaware of one's state—then the state should be good prior to being aware.[15] For example, being in a natural state is good even if one is not aware of being in that state, and similarly being in one's proper state, even if one is not yet cognizant that it is proper and that it is pleasurable—for it should be pleasurable. So, if the state is good and it is present, that which has it is thereby living well. So, why should we add sense-perception? We should not, unless in response they attribute good not to a state or condition that has come to be, but to the cognizance, or sense-perception, of this.

But if they say this, they will be saying that it is the sense-perception itself that is good, that is, the actuality of the perceptual life regardless of what things are apprehended. But if they attribute good to the combination of both, so that it is the sense-perception of a certain type of object, how can they say that the combination is good when each member of the combination is neutral? But if it is the state that is good, and living well is the condition wherein someone is cognizant that the Good is present to him, we should ask them if such a one lives well just by being cognizant that this is actually present to him, or if he should also be cognizant not only that its presence is pleasurable but that it is good, too.

But if he must be cognizant that it is good, living well is at once no longer the function of sense-perception but of an ability different from

---

8. See Ar., *EN* 1.6.1097b33–1098a2.
9. See *SVF* 3.178 (= D.L., 7.85).
10. Probably, given the above, a reference to the Epicurean view.
11. See D.L., 10.128, quoted from Epicurus's *Ep. to Menoeceus*.
12. See *SVF* 1.183 (= Plutarch, *De comm. not.* 23.1); 3.16 (= Stob., *Ecl.* 77.16).
13. See Appendix III C 4; IV B; IV C.
14. See Ar., *EN* 10.9.1178b28; *EE* 1.5.1216a2–10.
15. Cf. 4.4.8.8–13. See Pl., *Phil.* 33D8–9.

and greater than sense-perception. So, living well will not belong to those who are experiencing pleasure, but to one who has the ability to recognize that the good is pleasure. But then the cause of living well will actually not be pleasure, but being able to discern that pleasure is
25 good. And that which does the discerning is better than that which is in the state, for that is reason or intellect whereas pleasure is a state, and nowhere is the non-rational superior to reason.

How, then, will reason, excluding itself, suppose something else located in a contrary genus to be superior to it? For it seems that those who deny that plants live well and those who claim that living well
30 consists in a certain type of sense-perception lack awareness that they are seeking living well in something greater and that they are supposing the better life to consist in a life of greater clarity.

Those who say that living well is found in the rational life, not simply in life, nor even perceptual life, would perhaps be correct.[16] But it
35 is appropriate to ask them why they thus place happiness only in the rational living being: 'Do you add[17] the qualification "rational" because reason is more efficient and more easily able to discover and procure the basic natural needs, or would you still do this even if it were not able to discover or procure these? But if you say this because reason is better able than anything else to discover these, happiness will belong
40 even to living beings without reason provided they are able to acquire the basic natural needs. And then reason would become subservient and would not be choice worthy in itself, nor in turn would its perfection, which we say is what virtue is.[18] But if you say that reason is more honorable not because it is better at meeting the basic natural needs,
45 but because it is desirable in itself, you should say what other function it has and what its nature is and what makes it perfect.'[19]

For it should not be contemplation of these basic natural needs that makes it perfect, but something else of another nature that makes it perfect, and it is itself not one of these basic natural needs, nor does it
50 come from the source from which these basic natural needs arise, nor, generally, is it of this kind, but it is better than all these.

In fact, I do not see how they will account for its being honorable. But until they find a nature better than those things at which they are now stopping, let them remain at this level, where they want to remain,

---

16. See Ar., *EN* 1.6.1098a3–7; *SVF* 3.687 (= D.L., 7.130).
17. Reading προσλαμβάνετε with Armstrong.
18. See Ar., *Phys.* 7.2.247a2.
19. See Alex. Aphr., *De an.* 2.164.3–9; Plutarch, *De comm. not.* 1070f–1071e, 1072e–f.

being at a loss to say how living well belongs to those capable of attain-   55
ing this by meeting these basic natural needs.[20]

§1.4.3. But as for us, let us state from the beginning what we take
happiness to be. Having indeed supposed that happiness is something
that is found in life,[21] if we made 'living' univocal in all cases, we would
be claiming that all living beings are capable of acquiring happiness,
and that those that are actually living well are those in which is present   5
some identical thing, something which all living beings are capable
of acquiring by nature. In doing this, we would not be endowing
rational beings with the ability to live well while denying it to non-
rational beings, for life was assumed to be something common to both
and something which, by being receptive of the identical thing, was
intended to be capable of achieving happiness—if indeed happiness
was to be found in any sort of life.[22]

Hence, I think that those who say that happiness occurs in a rational   10
life, by supposing that it is not found in life in general, do not realize
that they are presuming that being happy is not just living. They would
be forced to say that the rational capacity in which happiness consists
is a quality of life. But for them, the substrate of this quality was a life
that is rational, for happiness consists in the whole [rationality plus   15
life], so that it consists in some other 'form' of life [and not just life]. I
mean this not in the sense of a logical distinction within a genus, but
in the sense in which we speak of one thing being prior and another
being posterior.[23]

So, the term 'life' is spoken of in many ways, differentiated according to the primary way, the secondary way, and so on in order.[24] The   20
term 'living' is said equivocally, that is, it is said in one way of a plant
and in another of a non-rational animal, according to the clarity and
dimness of the lives they have.[25] Analogously, it is clear that 'living well'
is said homonymously, too. And if one sense of the term 'living' is a
reflection of another, it is also clear that one sense of 'living well' is a
reflection of another.

---

20. Cf. 5.9.1.10–16.
21. See Ar., *Meta.* 9.8.1050b1–2.
22. Cf. 3.2.3.31–33. Whatever has life of any sort can live a good life, but only rational
creatures can be happy.
23. Cf. 5.1.1.28; 5.2.1.7–9; 5.5.9.5–7; 6.2.1.17–19; 6.9.2.31–32. See Ar., *Cat.* 13, 14b33–
15a1; *Meta.* 2.3.999a6–7.
24. Cf. 6.7.18.15–33.
25. See Ar., *DA* 1.5.410a13 where the question of homonymy regards 'soul', not 'life'.

25   If, then, living well[26] belongs to something living fully—meaning to
something that is in no way deficient in life—being happy will belong
only to one living fully, for the best will belong to this, if indeed that
which is really best in life, that is, the perfect life, is something that
exists. For in this way, the goodness that exists in happiness would not
be something superadded nor will something else from somewhere
30   else provide the substrate for its being good. For what, added to a perfect life, would turn it into the best life? But if someone will say that
what does this is the nature of the Good,[27] that is a congenial argument
to us, but now we are not seeking the cause of goodness, but that in
which it exists.

It has been said many times that the perfect life and the true and
35   real life is in that intellectual nature and that the other sorts of life are
imperfect and reflections of life and do not exist perfectly or purely,
and are no more lives than the opposite of this.[28] And now let it be said
summarily that so long as all living beings are from one source and
they do not have life in the same way that it does, it is necessary that
40   the source is the primary life, that is, the most perfect life.

§1.4.4.[29] If, then, it is possible for a human being to have the perfect
life, a human being who has this life is happy. If not, one would suppose
happiness to be found among the gods, if such a life is found among
5   them alone. So, since we are now saying that this happiness is found
among human beings, we should examine how this is so.

What I mean is this: it is clear also from other considerations that
the fact that a human being has a perfect life does not mean that he
only has a perceptual life, but rather that he has a faculty of calculative
reasoning and a genuine intellect as well. But is it the case that he is one
thing and this life is another?

10   In fact, he is not a human being at all if he has this neither in potency
nor in actuality, where we actually locate happiness.[30] But will we say
that he has this perfect form of life in himself as a part of himself?

In fact, the other human being has it in potency as a part, whereas
15   the one who has already achieved happiness is this in actuality and
has transformed himself in the direction of being identical with this.[31]
Everything else is just something he happens to be wearing, which no

---

26. Reading εὖ with HS⁴ to pick up the question initiating the treatise.
27. See Pl., *Phil.* 60B10.
28. Cf. 5.5.2.18; 6.6.18.12–13; 6.7.15.1–10; 6.9.9.15. See Pl., *Soph.* 248E6–249A1.
29. See Appendix II A.
30. Cf. 5.1.1.1–3; 6.7.5.26–29.
31. Cf. 1.1.8.1–6; 5.3.4.29–31.

one would actually suppose to be a part of him, since he does not want to wear these things.[32] They would be parts of him if they were connected to him according to his will.

So, what is the good for this human being?

In fact, it is, for him, what he possesses.[33] And the transcendent cause of goodness in him,[34] which is good in one way, is present to him in another. Evidence for the fact that this is so is that one who is like this does not seek anything else. What else would he seek? It would, of course, not be something worse; the best is already in him. The way of life of one living in this way, then, is self-sufficient.[35] And if he is virtuous, he has what he needs in order to be happy and to possess the good, for there is no good that he does not have.

What he seeks he seeks as something necessary, and not for himself but for one of the things that belong to him, for he is seeking something for the body that is attached to him. And even if that body is alive so that what belongs to it belongs to a living being, namely, this body, it does not belong to such a human being. He knows these things [what the body needs] and gives what he gives to it without taking anything away from his own life. So, his happiness will not be diminished by adverse fortune, for this sort of life remains as it is. And when relatives and friends are dying, he knows what death is; the dying themselves do, too, if they are virtuous. Even if the dying of relatives and close ones causes pain, it does not pain him, but only that in him which is apart from intellect, that whose pains he will not accept.

---

32. Cf. 1.1.3.21–26; 5.1.3.12–13.
33. Cf. 3.8.6.40; 6.9.3.18–22.
34. I.e., the Good. Cf. 6.9.6.56–57.
35. See Pl., *Rep.* 3.387D5–E1; Ar., *EN* 10.6.1176b5–6.

1.6 (1)

On Beauty

Introduction

This treatise is listed as first in Porphyry's chronological ordering of the *Enneads*. Although the work has frequently served as a relatively accessible introduction to Plotinus's difficult systematic thought, there is no reason to believe that Plotinus intended it as such. The work focuses on the nature of physical beauty and its relation to moral and intellectual beauty. It relies heavily on Plotinus's understanding of Plato's *Symposium* and *Phaedrus*. Treatise 5.8 (31), 'On the Intelligible Beauty', provides a companion argument. One central theme of this work is the inseparability of aesthetic and ethical considerations. Beauty is here presented as hierarchically ordered manifestations of a property of intelligible reality, namely, its attractiveness to us.

Summary

§1. What is the nature of beauty and what causes things to be beautiful? Criticism of the Stoic view.
§2. Something is beautiful owing to the presence of intelligible form.
§3. The beauty of shapes, colors, and sounds and the means to their recognition.
§4. The beauty of virtue.
§5. The relation between the beauty of virtue and the intelligibles.
§6. The process of purification leading to the recognition of intelligible beauty.
§7. The ascent to the Good.
§8. The method of ascent.
§9. The development of interior sight through the practice of virtue.

§1.6.1.[1] Beauty is found for the most part in what is seen, although it is also found in sounds, when these are composed into words, and in all the arts generally.[2] For songs and rhythms are beautiful, too. And

---

1. See Appendix II C.

2. The word μουσική ('art') is, literally, all that is governed by the Muses, including poetry, literature, music, and dance. Later these came to include philosophy, astronomy, and intellectual practices generally.

beauty is also found by those who turn away from sense-perception toward the higher region; that is, practices,[3] actions, habits, and types of scientific understanding are beautiful, to say nothing of the beauty of the virtues.[4] If there is some beauty prior to these, this discussion will show it.

What, then indeed, is it that has actually made us imagine bodies to be beautiful and our sense of hearing incline to sounds, finding them beautiful? And as for the things that depend directly on the soul, how are all of these beautiful? Is it because all of them are beautiful by one identical beauty, or is it that there is one sort of beauty in the body and another in other things? And what, then, are these sorts of beauty, or what is this beauty?

For some things, such as bodies, are not beautiful due to their substrates, but rather by participation, whereas some things are beautiful in themselves, such as the nature of virtue.[5] This is so because bodies themselves sometimes appear beautiful and sometimes do not[6] since what it is to be a body is distinct from what it is to be beautiful. What is it, then, that is present in bodies that makes them beautiful? It is this that we must examine first. What is it, then, that moves the eyes of spectators and turns them toward it[7] and draws them on and makes them rejoice at the sight? By finding this and using it as a stepping-stone,[8] we might also see the rest.

It is actually said by everyone that the symmetry of parts in relation to each other and to the whole added to fine coloration makes something beautiful to see.[9] And, generally, in regard to the objects of sight and all other things, their beauty consists in their symmetry or measure. For those who hold this view, no simple thing will be beautiful; necessarily, beauty will exist only in the composite. The whole will be beautiful for them, while each of the parts will not have its own beauty

3. The word ἐπιτηδεύματα ('practices') here refers to habitual activities that lead to the acquisition of moral virtue. See Pl., *Rep.* 4.444E; *Lg.* 793D.

4. See Pl., *Hip. Ma.* 297E6–298B4; *Symp.* 210B6–C7.

5. See Pl., *Hip. Ma.* 288A8–289D5; *Gorg.* 474D3–475A2; *Phd.* 100C10–103C1; *Symp.* 211B21–25.

6. See Pl., *Symp.* 211A3.

7. The word ἐπιστρέφειν ('reverting to', here 'turns') is a central semi-technical term in Plotinus for the (re-) orientation of the soul in the direction of the One. Cf. 1.2.4.16; 2.4.5.34; 5.2.1.10.

8. See Pl., *Symp.* 211C3.

9. Cf. 6.7.22.24–26. This is in particular the Stoic view, although it was widely held by others as well. See *SVF* 3.278 (= Stob., *Ecl.* 62, 15); 279 (= Cicero, *Tusc.* 4.13. 30); 472 (= Galen, *De plac. Hip. Etrr Plato.* 5.3). Also, Pl., *Tim.* 87C4–D8; Ar., *Meta.* 13.3.1078a36–b1.

but will be a contributing factor in making the whole beautiful. But it should be the case that if the whole is indeed beautiful, the parts are also beautiful. For beauty is surely not made up out of ugly things; all of its parts are beautiful.

30   For these people, the beauty of colors, for example, and the light of the sun, since they are simple, do not have proportion and so will be excluded from being beautiful. Indeed, how [on this view] is gold beautiful? And how about lightning in the night and the stars, which

35 are beautiful to see? And as for the beauty of sounds, the simple ones will be eliminated for the same reason, although it is frequently the case that in the beauty of a whole composition, each sound is itself beautiful.

Further, when the identical face sometimes actually appears beautiful and sometimes not, though the symmetry remains identical, would

40 we not have to say that beauty is other than the symmetry and that the symmetry is beautiful because of something other than itself?[10]

But if they actually pass on to beautiful practices and discourses and attribute their beauty to symmetry, what does it mean to say that there is proportion in beautiful practices or customs or studies or types of

45 scientific understanding?[11] For how could theorems be proportional to each other? If it is because they are in concord, it is also the case that there is agreement or concord among bad theorems. For example, to say 'self-control is stupidity' and 'justice is laughable nobility' is to say two things that are in concord, or in tune, or agree with each other.[12]

50   Further, then, the beauty of soul just is its virtues and a beauty that is truer than the previous ones. But how are these proportioned? It is not as magnitudes or numbers that they are proportioned. And since there are several parts of the soul, what is the formula for the combination or the blending of the parts or of the theorems? And what would be the beauty of Intellect taking it in isolation?

§1.6.2. Taking up the matter again, let us say what, then, is the primary beauty in bodies. There is, of course, something that is perceived at first glance, and the soul speaks about it as it does about that with which it is familiar, and takes it in as something that it

5 recognizes and, in a way, is in concord with it. But when it encounters the ugly, it holds back and rejects it and recoils from it as something

---

10. Cf. 6.7.22.24–26.
11. See Pl., *Symp.* 210C3–7, 211C6.
12. See Pl., *Rep.* 3.348C11–12, 8.560D2–3; *Gorg.* 491E2.

with which it is not in harmony and as something that is alien to it.[13] We indeed say that the soul, having the nature it does, and finding itself among Beings in the presence of the greater Substantiality,[14] when it sees something to which it has a kinship[15] or something that is a trace of that to which it has a kinship, is both delighted and thrilled and returns to itself and recollects itself and what belongs to itself. 10

What sameness is there, then, between the things here and the things that are beautiful in the intelligible world? For if there is a sameness, then we assume that the things are the same. How, then, are things here and there both beautiful? We say that these are beautiful by participation in Form. For everything that is shapeless but is by nature capable of receiving shape or form, having no share in an expressed 15 principle or form, is ugly, and stands outside divine reason.[16] This is complete ugliness.[17]

But something is also ugly if it has not been mastered by shape and an expressed principle due to the fact that its matter has not allowed itself to be shaped completely according to form.[18] The form, then, approaches the matter and organizes what is going to be a single composite made from many parts, and guides it into being a completed 20 unity, and makes it one by the parts' acceptance of this; and since the form is one, that which is shaped had to be one, to the extent possible for that which is composed of many parts.

Beauty is, then, situated over that which is shaped at the moment when, the parts having been arranged into one whole, it gives itself to the parts and to the wholes. Whenever beauty takes hold of something that is one and uniform in its parts, it gives the identical thing to the 25 whole. It is, in a way, like craftsmanship, that sometimes gives beauty to a whole house along with its parts, but sometimes it is like the particular nature that gives beauty to a single stone.[19] Thus, a body actually comes to be beautiful by its association with an expressed principle coming from divine Forms.

13. See Pl., *Symp.* 206D6.

14. Substance in the intelligible world is greater than substance in the sensible world. When the soul finds itself among Forms and undescended intellects, it finds itself in the presence of Substantiality.

15. See Pl., *Phd.* 79D3; *Rep.* 10.611E2; *Tim.* 90A5–7.

16. See Pl., *Tim.* 50D7.

17. Cf. 1.8.9.14–18; 3.6.11.15–27.

18. See Ar., *GC* 4.3.769b12, 4.770b16–7.

19. Presumably, the nature that is the ensouled earth. Cf. 6.7.11.17–36.

§1.6.3. The power in the soul that has been made to correspond to beauty recognizes it, and there is nothing more authoritative in judging its own concerns, especially when the rest of the soul judges along with it. Perhaps the rest of the soul also expresses itself by bringing into concord the beautiful object with the form inside itself, using that for judgment like a ruler used to judge the straightness of something.[20]

But how does the beauty in the body harmonize with that which is prior to body? How can the architect, bringing into concord the external house with the form of the house internal to him, claim that the former is beautiful?

In fact, it is because the external house is—if you consider it apart from its stones—the inner form divided by the external mass of matter. Being in fact undivided, it appears divided into many parts. Whenever, then, sense-perception sees the form in the bodies binding together and mastering the contrary nature, which is shapeless—that is, whenever it sees an overarching shape on top of other shapes—it gathers together that which was in many places and brings it back and collects it into the soul's interior as something without parts, and at that moment gives it to that which is inside as something which has the harmony and concord that is dear to it. This is just as when a good man sees in the fresh face of a youth a trace of the virtue that is in harmony with the truth that is inside himself.

The simple beauty of a color resides in shape and in the mastery of the darkness in matter by the presence of incorporeal light and of an expressed principle or form. This is the reason why fire, above all the other bodies, is beautiful; it has the role of form in relation to the other elements, highest in position, finest of the other bodies, being as close as possible to the incorporeal, and is alone not receptive of the other elements, though the others receive it.[21] For it heats them, but is itself not cooled, and is primarily colored, whereas the others get the form of color from it. So, it shines and glows as if it were form. That which fades in a fire's light, unable to dominate the matter, is no longer beautiful, since the whole of it[22] does not partake of the form of the color.

As for the non-sensible harmonies in sounds that make the sensible ones,[23] they make the soul grasp them so as to have comprehension of beauty in the same way, showing the identical thing in another way.

---

20. Cf. 5.3.4.15–17.
21. See Ar., *GC* 2.8.335a18–21.
22. Reading ὅλον with Kalligas.
23. See Heraclitus, fr. 22 B 54 DK.

It is logical that sensible harmonies be measured by numbers, though not by every formula but only by one that serves in the production of form for the purpose of dominating the matter. And so regarding sensible beauties, which are actually reflections and shadows that come to matter as if they were making a dash there to beautify it and thrill us when they appear, enough said.

§1.6.4.[24] Regarding the more elevated beauties not given to sense-perception to see, soul sees them and speaks about them without the instruments of sense-perception, but it has to ascend to contemplate them, leaving sense-perception down below.[25] But just as in the case of the beauties perceived by the senses it is not possible to speak about them to those who have not seen them or to those who have never grasped them for what they are, for example, those who have been blind since birth; in the same way, it is not possible to speak about the beauty of practices to those who have not accepted their beauty nor about types of sciences and other such things. Nor can one speak about the 'splendor'[26] of virtue to those who have not even imagined for themselves the beauty of the visage of Justice and Self-Control, 'not even the evening nor the morning star are so beautiful'.[27]

But such a sight must be reserved for those who see it with that in the soul by which it sees such things, and seeing it are delighted and shocked and overwhelmed much more than in the previous cases, inasmuch as we are now speaking of those who have already got hold of true beauties.[28] For these are the states one should be in regarding something which is beautiful; astonishment, and a sweet shock, and longing, and erotic thrill, and a feeling of being overwhelmed with pleasure. It is possible to have these emotions, and practically all souls do have them in regard to all the unseen beauties, so to say, but in particular those souls who are more enamored of these. It is the same with regard to the bodies that all can see, though not everyone is 'stung'[29] equally by their beauty. Those who are stung especially are those who are called 'lovers'.

---

24. See Appendix II D.
25. See Pl., *Symp.* 210B6–D1; Alcinous, *Didask.* 5.157.16–20, 10.165.27–30.
26. See Pl., *Phdr.* 250B3.
27. Cf 6.6.6.39. See Ar., *EN* 5.3.1129b28–9 quoting Euripides, *Melanippe* fr. 486 Nauck².
28. Cf. 6.7.36.4; 39.19; 6.9.4.27. See Pl., *Symp.* 206D8, 212A4–5; *Phdr.* 259B8; *Rep.* 9.572A8, 10.600C6, 608A7.
29. See Pl., *Phdr.* 251D5.

§1.6.5.[30] We should next ask those who are indeed enamored of the beauties not available to the senses: 'What state are you in regarding the practices said to be beautiful and in regard to beautiful ways of being in the world and to self-controlled characters and, generally, to products of virtue or dispositions, I mean the beauty of souls?'[31] And 'When you see your own "interior beauty",[32] what do you feel?' And 'Can you describe the frenzied[33] and excited state you are in and your longing to be united with yourselves,[34] when extricating yourselves from your bodies?' For this is how those who are truly enamored feel.

But what is it that makes them feel this way? It is not shapes or colors or some magnitude, but rather they feel this way about soul, it being itself 'without color'[35] and having self-control that is also without color and the rest of the 'splendors'[36] of virtues. You feel this way whenever you see in yourselves or someone else greatness of soul or a just character or sheer self-control or the awe-inspiring visage of courage[37] or dignity and reserve circling around a calm and unaffected disposition with divine intellect shining on them all.

We then love and are attracted to these qualities, but what do we mean when we say that they are beautiful? For they are real and appear to us so, and no one who has ever seen them says anything other than that they are real Beings. What does 'real Beings' mean?

In fact, it means that they are beautiful Beings. But the argument still needs to show why Beings have made the soul an object of love. What is it that shines on all the virtues like a light?

Would you like to consider the opposites, the ugly things that come to be in the soul, and contrast them with these beauties? For perhaps a consideration of what ugliness is and why it appears as such would contribute to our achieving what we are seeking. Let there be a soul that is actually ugly,[38] one that is licentious and unjust, filled with all manner of appetites and every type of dread, mired in fear due to its cowardice and in envy due to its pettiness, thinking that everything it can actually think of is mortal and base, deformed in every way, a lover

---

30. See Appendix II D; II G.
31. See Pl., *Symp.* 210B6–C4.
32. See Pl., *Phdr.* 279B9; *Phd.* 83A7.
33. Cf. 6.7.22.9. See Pl., *Phd.* 69D1. The allusion to 'Bacchic' frenzy adds an emotional dimension to the fundamentally rationalist account of beauty here.
34. Cf. 6.7.30.36–38. Presumably, a reference to our undescended intellects.
35. See Pl., *Phdr.* 247C6.
36. See Pl., *Phdr.* 250B3.
37. See Homer, *Il.* 7.212.
38. See Pl., *Gorg.* 524E7–525A6.

of impure pleasures, that is, one who lives a life in which corporeal   30
pleasures are measured by their vileness. Shall we not say that, just as
in the case of something beautiful added to the soul, this very vileness
supervenes on the soul, and both harms it and makes it impure and
'mixed with much evil',[39] no longer having a life or sense-perceptions
that are pure, but rather living a murky life by an evil adulteration that   35
includes much death in it, no longer seeing what a soul should see, no
longer even being allowed to remain in itself due to its always being
dragged to the exterior and downward into darkness?[40]

This is indeed what I regard as an impure soul, dragged in every   40
direction by its chains toward whatever it happens to perceive with its
senses, with much of what belongs to the body adulterating it, deeply
implicating itself with the material element and, taking that element
into itself due to that adulteration that only makes it worse, it exchanges
the form it has for another. It is as if someone fell into mud or slime
and the beauty he had is no longer evident, whereas what is seen is   45
what he smeared on himself from the mud or slime. The ugliness that
has actually been added to him has come from an alien source, and his
job, if indeed he is again to be beautiful, is to wash it off and to be clean
as he was before.

We would be speaking correctly in saying that the soul indeed
becomes ugly by a mixture or adulteration and by an inclination in the
direction of the body and matter. And this is ugliness for a soul; not   50
being pure or uncorrupted like gold, but filled up with the earthly. If
someone removes that, only the gold is left, and it is beautiful, isolated
from other things and being just what it is itself. Indeed, in the identical manner, the soul—being isolated from appetites which it acquires   55
because of that body with which it associates too much—when it
is separated from other affections and is purified of what it has that is
corporeal, remains just what it is when it has put aside all the ugliness
that comes from that other nature.

§1.6.6.[41] For it is indeed the case, as the ancient doctrine[42] has it,
that self-control and courage and every virtue is a purification and
is wisdom itself. For this reason, the mysteries correctly offer the
enigmatic saying that one who has not been purified will lie in Hades
in slime, because one who is not pure likes slime due to his wickedness.   5

---

39. See Pl., *Phd.* 66B5.
40. See Pl., *Phd.* 79C2–8.
41. See Appendix II B; II C; II G.
42. Cf. 1.8.13.17–25. See Pl., *Phd.* 69C1–6.

They are actually like pigs that, with unclean bodies, delight in such a thing.[43]

What would true self-control be, besides not having anything to do with the pleasures of the body and fleeing them as impure and as not belonging to one who is pure? And what is courage but the absence of fear of death? But death is the separation of the soul from the body.[44] And this is not feared by one who longs to be alone. And greatness of soul[45] is actually contempt for the things here below. And wisdom is the intellection that consists in a turning away from the things below, leading the soul to the things above.

The soul, then, when it is purified, becomes form,[46] and an expressed principle, and entirely incorporeal and intellectual and wholly divine, which is the source of beauty and of all things that have a kinship with it. Soul, then, being borne up to Intellect, becomes even more beautiful. And Intellect and the things that come from Intellect are soul's beauty, since they belong to it, that is, they are not alien to it, because it is then really soul alone. For this reason, it is correctly said that goodness and being beautiful for the soul consist in 'being assimilated to god',[47] because it is in the intelligible world that Beauty is found as well as the fate of the rest of Beings. Or rather, Beings are what Beauty is and ugliness is the other nature, primary evil itself, so that for god 'good' and 'beautiful' are identical, or rather the Good and Beauty are identical.[48]

In a similar way, then, we should seek to discover that which is beautiful and good and the ugly and evil. And first we should posit Beauty,[49] which is the Good from which Intellect comes, which is itself identical with Beauty. And Soul is beautiful by Intellect. Other things are beautiful as soon as they are shaped by Soul, including examples of beauty in actions and in practices. Moreover, bodies that are said to be beautiful are so as soon as Soul makes them so. For inasmuch as it is divine and, in a way, a part of Beauty, it makes all that it grasps and masters beautiful insofar as it is possible for them to partake of Beauty.

---

43. See Heraclitus, fr. 22 B 13 DK; Sext. Emp., *PH* I 56.

44. See Pl., *Phd.* 64C2–65A3.

45. See Ar., *EN* 2.7.1107b22; 4.7.1123a34–b4.

46. Or 'Form'. Cf. 5.7 on Forms of individuals. Also, 1.1.2.6–7.

47. See Pl., *Rep.* 10.613B1; *Tht.* 176B1; *Lg.* 716C6–D4.

48. The Good is both beyond Beauty because it is beyond Substantial Being (cf. 6.2.18.1–3; 67.32.22) and identical with Beauty because it is the cause of all that is beautiful, that is, the Forms.

49. The unusual term here is ἡ καλλονή who appears as a goddess in Plato's *Symp.* 206D. Cf. 6.2.18.1–3, 6.7.33.22.

§1.6.7.[50] We must, then, ascend to the Good, which every soul desires.[51] If someone, then, has seen it, he knows what I mean when I say how beautiful it is. For it is desired as good, and the desire is directed to it as this, though the attainment of it is for those who ascend upward and revert to it and who divest themselves of the garments they put on when they descended. It is just like those who ascend to partake of the sacred religious rites where there are acts of purification and the stripping off of the cloaks they had worn before they go inside naked.[52] One proceeds in the ascent, passing by all that is alien to the god until one sees by oneself alone that which is itself alone uncorrupted, simple, and pure,[53] that upon which everything depends,[54] and in relation to which one looks and exists and lives and thinks. For it is the cause of life and intellect. And, then, if someone sees this, what pangs of love will he feel, what longings and, wanting to be united with it, how would he not be overcome with pleasure?[55]

For though it is possible for one who has not yet seen it to desire it as good, for one who has seen it, there is amazement and delight in beauty, and he is filled with pleasure and he undergoes a painless shock, loving with true love and piercing longing. And he laughs at other loves and is disdainful of the things he previously regarded as beautiful. It is like the states of those who have happened upon apparitions of gods or daemons after which they can no longer look at the beauty of other bodies in the same way.

What, then, should we think if someone sees pure Beauty itself by itself, not contaminated by flesh or bodies, not on the earth or in heaven, in order that it may remain pure?[56] For all these things are added on and have been mixed in and are not primary; rather, they come from the Good. If, then, one sees that which orchestrates everything, remaining by itself while it gives everything, though it does not receive anything into itself, if he remains in sight of this and enjoys it by assimilating himself to it, what other beauty would he need? For this, since it is itself supremely beautiful and the primary Beauty, makes its lovers beautiful and lovable.

---

50. See Appendix II B; II C; II D; III B 1.
51. See Pl., *Rep.* 7.517B4–5.
52. See Pl., *Gorg.* 523C–E.
53. Cf. 5.1.6.11–12; 6.7.34.7–8; 6.9.11.51. See Pl., *Symp.* 211E1.
54. Cf. 3.8.10.1–4; 5.3.16.35–38; 6.7.18.16–31. See Ar., *DC* 1.9. 279a28–30; *Meta.* 12.7.1072b14.
55. Reading ἀν <οὐκ> ἐκπλαγείη with HS⁴. Cf. 6.7.27.24–28.
56. See Pl., *Symp.* 211A8, 211D8–E2.

And with the Good as the prize actually the greatest and 'ultimate battle is set before souls',[57] a battle in which our entire effort is directed toward not being deprived of the most worthy vision. And the one who attains this is 'blessed',[58] since he is seeing a blessed sight, whereas the one who does not is luckless.[59] For it is not someone who fails to attain beautiful colors or bodies, or power or ruling positions or kingship who is without luck, but the one who does not attain this and this alone. For the sake of this, he ought to cede the attainment of kingship and ruling positions over the whole earth, sea, and heaven, if by abandoning these things and ignoring them he could revert to the Good and see it.

§1.6.8.[60] How, then, can we do this? What technique should we employ? How can one see the 'inconceivable beauty'[61] which remains in a way within the sacred temple, not venturing outside, lest the uninitiated should see it? Indeed, let him who is able go and follow it inside, leaving outside the sight of his eyes, not allowing himself to turn back to the splendor of the bodies he previously saw. For when he does see beauty in bodies, he should not run after them, but realize that they are images and traces and shadows, and flee toward that of which they are images.[62] For if someone runs toward the image, wanting to grasp it as something true, like someone wanting to grasp a beautiful reflection in water—as a certain story has it, hinting at something else, in an enigmatic way, I think, who then falls into the water and disappears[63]—in the identical manner, someone who holds onto beautiful bodies and does not let them go, plunges down, not with his body but with his soul, into the depths, where there is no joy for an intellect, and where he stays, blind in Hades, accompanied by shadows everywhere he turns.

Someone would be better advised to say: 'Let us flee to our beloved fatherland'.[64] But what is this flight, and how is it accomplished? Let us

---

57. See Pl., *Phdr.* 247B5–6.
58. See Pl., *Phdr.* 250B6.
59. Or: ἀτυχὴς δὲ <ὄντως > 'truly' luckless, according to the emendation of Vitringa, endorsed by Kalligas.
60. See Appendix II E.
61. Cf. 5.1.6.12–15; 6.9.11.17–21. See Pl., *Rep.* 6.509A6; *Symp.* 218E2.
62. See Pl., *Tht.* 176B1.
63. Cf. 5.8.2.34–35.
64. See Homer, *Il.* 2.140.

set sail in the way Homer, in an allegorical[65] way, I think, tells us that Odysseus fled from the sorceress Circe or from Calypso. Odysseus was not satisfied to remain there, even though he had visual pleasures and   20 passed his time with sensual beauty. Our fatherland, from where we have actually come, and our father are both in the intelligible world.[66]

What is our course and what is our means of flight? We should not rely on our feet to get us there, for our feet just take us everywhere on earth, one place after another. Nor should you saddle up a horse or prepare some sea-going vessel. You should put aside all such things   25 and stop looking; just shut your eyes, and change your way of looking, and wake up. Everyone has this ability, but few use it.

§1.6.9.[67] What, then, is that inner way of looking? Having just awakened, the soul is not yet able to look at the bright objects before it.[68] The soul must first be accustomed to look at beautiful practices, next beautiful works—not those works that the crafts produce, but those that men who are called 'good' produce—next, to look at the   5 soul of those who produce these beautiful works.[69]

How, then, can you see the kind of beauty that a good soul has? Go back into yourself and look. If you do not yet see yourself as beautiful, then be like a sculptor who, making a statue that is supposed to be beautiful, removes a part here and polishes a part there so that he makes the latter smooth and the former just right until he has given the   10 statue a beautiful face. In the same way, you should remove superfluities and straighten things that are crooked, work on the things that are dark, making them bright, and not stop 'working on your statue'[70] until the divine splendor of virtue shines in you, until you see 'Self-Control   15 enthroned on the holy seat'.[71]

If you have become this and have seen it and find yourself in a purified state, you have no impediment to becoming one in this way[72] nor do you have something else mixed in with yourself, but you are entirely yourself, true light alone, neither measured by magnitude nor reduced

---

65. The word αἰνίττεσθαι (literally 'to riddle') seems to be rendered best in the above manner.
66. Πατήρ ('father') sometimes refers to the One and sometimes to Intellect. Cf. 5.1.1.1; 5.8.1.3.
67. See Appendix II E; II J.
68. Cf. 5.8.10.4–8. See Pl., *Rep.* 7.515E1–516A8.
69. See Pl., *Symp.* 210B–C.
70. See Pl., *Phdr.* 252D7.
71. See Pl., *Phdr.* 254B7.
72. Cf. 1.3.4.18; 6.9.1.16–17. See Pl., *Rep.* 4.443E1.

20   by a circumscribing shape nor expanded indefinitely in magnitude but
being unmeasured everywhere, as something greater than every measure and better than every quantity. If you see that you have become
this, at that moment you have become sight, and you can be confident
about yourself, and you have at this moment ascended here, no longer
25   in need of someone to show you. Just open your eyes and see, for this
alone is the eye that sees the great beauty.

But if the eye approaches that sight bleary with vices and not having
been purified, or weak and, due to cowardice, is not able to see all the
bright objects, it does not see them even if someone else shows that
they are present and able to be seen. For the one who sees has a kinship
30   with that which is seen, and he must make himself the same as it if he is
to attain the sight. For no eye has ever seen the sun without becoming
sun-like,[73] nor could a soul ever see Beauty without becoming beautiful.
You must first actually become wholly godlike and wholly beautiful if
you intend to see god and Beauty.

35   For first, the soul in its ascent will reach Intellect, and in the intelligible world it will see all the beautiful Forms and will declare that these
Ideas are what Beauty is.[74] For all things are beautiful due to these; they
are the offspring of Intellect and Substantiality. But we say that that
which transcends[75] Intellect is the Idea of the Good, a nature that holds
40   Beauty in front of itself. So, roughly speaking, the Good is the primary
Beauty. But if one distinguishes the intelligibles apart, one will say that
the 'place' of the Forms[76] is intelligible Beauty, whereas the Good transcends that and is the 'source and principle'[77] of Beauty. Otherwise, one
will place the Good and the primary Beauty in the identical thing.[78] In
any case, Beauty is in the intelligible world.

---

73. Cf. 2.4.5.10; 5.3.8.19–25. See Pl., *Rep.* 6.508B3, 509A1.

74. Plotinus uses εἴδη ('Forms') and ἰδέαι ('Ideas') synonymously as, apparently, does
Plato. Cf. 5.8.10.

75. See Pl., *Rep.* 509B9; Simplicius, *In Cat.* 485.22 (= fr. 49 Rose³, p. 57 Ross).

76. See Pl., *Rep.* 7.517B5; Ar., *DA* 3.4.429a27–28.

77. See Pl., *Phdr.* 245C9.

78. See Pl. [?], *Alc.* 1.116C1–2.

1.8 (51)

ON WHAT EVILS ARE AND
WHERE THEY COME FROM

Introduction

In this treatise, Plotinus addresses the problem of the existence of evil given the omnipotence of the Good. He argues against the interpretation of Plato according to which evil is somehow a principle independent of the Good which would establish what Plotinus takes to be an unjustifiable dualism. He argues here extensively for the identification of evil with matter, crucially rejecting Aristotle's distinction between potency and privation. Matter is both pure potency and unqualified privation, which disqualifies it from being a separate principle although at the same time making it an inevitable result of the outflow of the universe from the Good or the One. Where all trace of intelligibility ceases, there matter must be.

Summary

§1. What is evil and how is it known?

§2. There can be no evil in the intelligible world.

§3. It must, therefore, be absolutely bereft of intelligibility and measure.

§4. Bodies are evil only in the element of unintelligibility which they necessarily possess and souls are evil only insofar as they associate with the evil in bodies.

§5. Matter is unqualified privation and so evil.

§6. Commentary on Plato's *Theaetetus* 176A in relation to the problem of evil.

§7. The use of *Timaeus* 47E–48A to interpret *Theaetetus*.

§8. Evils in the soul are vice and they arise from the association with matter.

§9. How can that which is utterly unintelligible be known?

§10. Matter is evil because it is without any qualities.

§11. Evil does not belong to the soul.

§12. Evil is not partial privation.

§13. The distinction between evil and vice.

§14. Vice is psychical illness.

§15. Evil and the Good.

§1.8.1.[1] Those who are seeking to discover where evils come from—whether they belong among beings in general or to a particular genus of beings—would be making an appropriate start to their search if they first offered a hypothesis as to what evil is, that is, what its nature is. For in this way it would also be known where evil comes from and where it is located and in what sort of thing it occurs, and, in general, some agreement could be arrived at as to whether it is something that exists.

But if it is the case that we understand each thing by being the same as it, we would be at a loss to know by what capacity we know the nature of evil, for intellect and soul, being forms, would produce the knowledge of Forms, and would have a desire for these.[2] Yet how could one imagine that evil is a Form, when it is situated in the absence of every good? If, however, the scientific understanding of one contrary is identical to the scientific understanding of what is contrary to it, and evil is contrary to good, the scientific understanding of good will be of evil,[3] too; so, it is necessary for those who intend to know evils to comprehend good, since the better precedes the worse, that is, among Forms, and some of the worse are not Forms but rather a privation of Form. It is, all the same, a matter for investigation how good is contrary to evil, with perhaps one a beginning and the other an end, or the one as Form and the other privation. But these questions will be addressed later.[4]

§1.8.2.[5] Now we should say what the nature of the Good is to the extent that is appropriate for the present discussion. The Good is that upon which all beings depend and that 'which all beings desire';[6] they have it as their principle and are also in need of it. It itself lacks nothing, being sufficient unto itself and in need of nothing.[7] It is also the measure and limit of all beings, giving from itself Intellect and Substantiality and Soul and Life and the activity of Intellect. And all of these up to the Good are beautiful, but it itself is above Beauty and is the transcendent ruler of all that is best, all that is in the intelligible world.[8] Intellect there is not like the intellects we are said to have, intellects that are filled with propositions and are capable of understanding

---

1. See Appendix IV B.
2. See Ar., *DA* 1.2.404b17–18, 405.b15–19; 3.8.432a2–3. In knowing Forms, we are cognitively identical with them.
3. See Pl., *Phd.* 97D4–5; Ar., *Pr. An.* 1.24a21–22.
4. Cf. *infra* 3 and following.
5. See Appendix III B 1; III C 1.
6. See Pl., *Phil.* 20D8; Ar., *Meta.* 12.7.1072b14; *EN* 1.1.1094a3.
7. Cf. 5.3.13.18, 17.14; 5.5.13.6; 6.7.23.7, 33.18.
8. See Pl., *Rep.* 6.509B5–9.

things that are said and of calculative reasoning and so observing what follows, intellects which consequently observe beings that they did not formerly possess, since they were empty before learning them, despite being intellects.

Intellect there is actually not like that; rather, it has all things and is all things and is present with them when it is present to itself and has all things while not having them, for they are not one thing and it another. Nor is each thing separate in it. For each is the whole, and everything is everywhere. Yet they are not mixed up, but each is in its turn separate. At least, that which shares in it does not share in all of them in the same way, but rather in the way that it is able to share. Intellect is the primary activity that comes from the Good,[9] and the primary Substance that comes from it, while it remains in itself. But Intellect is active with reference to the Good, in a way living around it.[10] Soul dances outside this, looking at it and, in contemplating its interior, looks at god through Intellect.

And 'this is the life of the gods,'[11] carefree and blessed, and evil is nowhere here. And if [the procession] had stopped here, there would be no evil but only the first and the second and the third order of goods. 'All things are around the king of all, and that is the cause of all beauties, and all things come from that, and second things are around the second, and third things around the third.'[12]

§1.8.3.[13] Indeed, if all that exists were these Beings and what transcends them, evil would not exist among Beings, or in what transcends them. For these Beings are good. So, it remains that if indeed evil does exist, it exists among non-beings as a sort of form of non-being and is involved in some way with that which is mixed or associated with non-being. 'Non-being' does not mean 'that which is absolutely non-existent' but only something different from being.[14] Nor does it refer to the non-being that Motion and Stability have in relation to Being but rather to an image of Being or to something that has even more non-being than that.[15] This non-being belongs to every sensible object and every state sensible objects are in, whether as something

---

9. Cf. 5.3.5.36; 6.7.40.18.
10. Cf. 6.9.9.17. See Ar., *Meta.* 12.7.1072b19–23, 9.1074b21–1075a5.
11. See Pl., *Phdr.* 248A1.
12. See Pl. [?], *2nd Ep.* 312E1–4.
13. See Appendix III C 1.
14. Cf. 2.4.16.1–4. See Pl., *Parm.* 162A4–B3; *Soph.* 257B3–4, 258E7–9.
15. See Pl., *Soph.* 240B11.

posterior to or accidental to them or as a principle of these or as some
one of the elements that together comprise being of this sort.

On this basis, someone might immediately arrive at a conception of
evil as a sort of absence of measure as opposed to measure, or absence
of limit as opposed to limit, or absence of form as opposed to what is
15   productive of form, or what is always in need as opposed to what is
self-sufficient; always indefinite, in no way stable, absolutely passive,
insatiable, and completely impoverished. And these properties are not
accidental to it, but in a way its substantiality. Whichever part of it you
look at, it, too, is all these things. All other things that partake of evil
20   and are assimilated to it become evil, though they are not essentially
evil.

What, then, is the sort of existence in which these properties are
present, not as being something different from it, but as being identical
with what it is? For indeed if evil occurs in something else, it must be
something prior to that occurrence, even if it is not a substance. For just
as the Good itself is one thing and the property of being good another,
so evil is one thing and the property of being evil, which immediately
derives from that, another.

25   What, then, is absence of measure if it is not just whatever is in that
which is without measure? But just as there is measure that is not in
that which is measured, so there is absence of measure that is not in
that which is without measure. For if it is in something else, either it is
in that which is without measure—but this thing does not need to partake of the absence of measure, since it is unmeasured—or it is in that
30   which is measured. But it is not possible for that which is measured to
have absence of measure, just to the extent that it is measured.

And, then, there must be something that is absence of limit in itself
and, again, absence of form in itself and all the other properties mentioned above which characterize the nature of evil.[16] And if there is
something like it that comes after it, either it has evil mixed in with
it, or it looks toward evil and so is like it, or it is productive of this
35   sort of thing.[17] So, the substrate of figures and forms and shapes and
measures and limits and whatever is ordered by an ordering alien to
it, not having good from itself, but being like a reflection in relation to
beings—that is actually the substantiality of evil, if indeed something
can be the substantiality of evil. The argument has found this to be
40   primary evil or evil itself.

---

16. Plotinus will identify this with matter. Cf. 3.6.7.23–30.

17. This is 'secondary evil', that is, anything mixed with primary evil (i.e., matter).
Cf. 2.4.12.8–10.

§1.8.4. It is the nature of bodies, insofar as they partake of matter, to be evil, but not to be primary evil. For bodies have some form, though it is not genuine, and they are deprived of life, and they destroy each other, and their motion is disordered and they are an 'impediment'[18] to the soul in regard to its own activity, and they flee substantiality inasmuch as they are continually in flux, and so they are secondary evil.

But soul in itself is not evil nor, again, is all soul evil. What is the evil soul? It is the sort of thing Plato is referring to when he says: 'Those who have been enslaved by the part of the soul that naturally brings evils to it',[19] because the non-rational form of the soul is receptive of evil, that is, of absence of measure, and of excess and defect, from which also come licentiousness and cowardice and the other evils of the soul, and involuntary states which produce false beliefs, and the thinking that evils and goods are what it is actually fleeing and pursuing.

But what is it that produces this evil, and how will you connect it to its principle or cause?

In fact, first, this type of soul does not transcend matter, nor does it exist in itself. It has, then, been mixed with absence of measure and is without a share in the form that orders it and connects it to measure, for it is mixed up with a body that has matter.

Next, the faculty of calculative reasoning, if it is harmed, is prevented by these corporeal states from seeing, and by being darkened by matter and inclined to matter and, generally, by looking not toward substantiality but toward becoming, whose principle is in this way the nature of matter. Being evil, it fills with its own evil even that which is never in it, but is only looking at it. For since it is absolutely without a share of good and is a privation or unmixed lack of it, it assimilates to itself everything that comes into contact with it in any way.

The soul, then, that is perfect and inclines toward Intellect is always pure and turns away from matter and all that is indefinite and without measure and neither sees evil nor approaches it. It, then, remains pure when it is absolutely made definite by Intellect. That which does not remain like this but proceeds from itself by not being perfect or primary is like a reflection of that pure soul, due to its deficiency, just to the extent that it is deficient, and is filled up with indeterminateness and sees darkness and at that moment acquires matter and looks at that which it does not see—in the sense that we talk about seeing darkness, too.

---

18. See Pl., *Phd.* 65A10.
19. See Pl., *Phdr.* 256B2–3.

§1.8.5. But if the lack of that which is good is the explanation of seeing and consorting with darkness, evil would consist in the lack that is in the soul and would be primarily there—let the darkness be evil secondarily—and the nature of evil will no longer be in matter but in
5   that which is prior to matter.

In fact, evil consists not in any particular type of lack but in absolute lack. At least, that which is slightly lacking with respect to that which is good is not evil, for it is still able to be perfect according to its own nature. But when something is absolutely lacking—which is what matter is—this is really evil, having no share of
10   good.[20] For matter does not even have existence, which would have allowed it to partake of good to this extent; rather, we say that 'existence' is said of it equivocally, so that the true way to speak of it is as non-existent.[21]

Lack, then, amounts to not being good, but evil is absolute lack. The greater lack consists in being able to fall into evil and thereby being evil
15   already.[22] Accordingly, it is necessary to think of evil not as a particular evil, such as injustice or some other kind of vice, but as that which yet is none of these, since these are in a way species of evil specified by their own additional [differentiae]. For example, wickedness in the soul and its species are differentiated either by the matter with which they are concerned or by the parts of the soul or by one being a sort of seeing and one an impulse or state.

20   But if someone were to suppose that things outside the soul, like sickness or poverty, can be evils, how will he connect it to the nature of matter?

In fact, sickness is a lack or excess in the materialized bodies that do not maintain order or measure.[23] Ugliness is matter not conquered by form, and poverty is a lack or privation of that which we need due
25   to the matter to which we are joined, a nature that has neediness.

If this is indeed rightly stated, the principle of evils should not be supposed to be in the evils that are within ourselves but to be prior to us. Whatever evils take hold of human beings, they take hold of us

---

20. See Pl., *Phil.* 20D1, 54C10, 60B4.
21. Cf. *supra* 3.6–7; *infra* 15.1–3; 2.4.11.1–12, 28.
22. Following the punctuation of HS[1] with a full stop before τῷ.
23. See Pl., *Tim.* 81E–82B.

unwillingly.[24] Indeed, there is a 'flight from evils in the soul'[25] for those   30
who are able, though not all are able.

Though matter is present to the sensible gods,[26] evil is not present,
I mean the vice which human beings have, because that is not even
present in all human beings. For these gods master matter—though
the gods in whom matter is not present are better—and they master it
by that in them which is not enmattered.

---

24. See Pl., *Gorg.* 488A3; *Protag.* 345D8, 358C7, 358E2–359A1; *Rep.* 9.589C6; *Tim.*
85D2, E1; *Lg.* 731C2, 860D1–9. The evils are the types of wickedness mentioned *supra*
ll. 17–19.
25. See Pl., *Phd.* 107D1.
26. These are the heavenly bodies.

3.8 (30)

ON NATURE, CONTEMPLATION, AND THE ONE

Introduction

This treatise forms the first part of a longer work (which includes 5.8, 5.5, and 2.9), which Porphyry split up in his edition. It is Plotinus's most ambitious discussion of the vital role of contemplation and of all its different forms and intensities at every level of reality. Although he is primarily concerned with the structure of reality itself the activity of individual human contemplation surfaces frequently throughout.

Summary

§1. Let us suppose in a playful way that all things contemplate.

§2. At the lowest level nature, like a craftsman, works on matter by means of its contemplation and the expressed principle.

§3. Nature's contemplation produces without being itself affected.

§4. Nature would say that its product flows from its contemplation, just as it flowed from its producer. Its contemplation is only an image of a higher form of contemplation and its product a by-product.

§5. Contemplation at the level of soul.

§6. Action also leads to contemplation.

§7. Contemplation at the level of Being produces active contemplative expressed principles which give form at every level. Failure is due to the progressive weakening of contemplation.

§8. In Intellect contemplation is identical with the object of contemplation. It is the primary life and all life at every level is contemplative.

§9. Intellect is not the first. The One, the Good, is beyond it. We can have access even to this.

§10. The One is not everything but is the productive power and source of everything.

§11. Intellect needs the Good, but the Good is not in need of anything.

§3.8.1. If, before attempting to be serious, we were actually to begin by playing and say that all things aim at contemplation and look to this goal, not only rational but also non-rational animals[1] and nature in

---

1. Cf. 1.4.1.1–2.33. See Ar., *EN* 10.2.1172b10, on the view of Eudoxus.

plants and the earth which produces them, and that all things achieve   5
it as far as they can in their natural state, but contemplate and achieve
it in different ways, and some in a genuine manner, others by acquiring
an imitation and image of it, would anyone put up with the oddity of
the statement?

In fact, when the issue has been raised among ourselves, there will
be no harm in playing with what is ours.

Are we, too, then contemplating right now when we are playing?   10

In fact, both we and all who play are contemplating or at least desire
this when we are playing. And, as it happens, whether it is a child
or a man that plays or is serious, he is going to be playing or he is
being serious for the sake of contemplation; and every action is going   15
to involve a serious tendency to contemplation; compulsory action[2]
in a stronger manner,[3] drawing contemplation toward externals, but
so-called voluntary action less so while still originating in a desire for
contemplation. But we will deal with this later.[4]

For now, let us ask about earth itself and trees and plants in general   20
what contemplation is in their case, how we will trace back what is
produced or generated from the earth to the activity of contemplation,
and how nature, which they[5] say is without a mental image and reason,
both possesses contemplation within itself and produces what it produces through contemplation which it does not have and yet somehow
does have.[6]

§3.8.2. It is, I think, clear to everyone that there is no question here
of hands or feet or of any instrument, whether acquired from outside or
built in, but of matter for it [nature] to work on and to which it applies
form. And one must also exclude levering from natural production; for   5
what kind of pushing or leverage produces different colors of all shades
and shapes? Not even the fashioners of wax models[7] can produce
colors without bringing them in from elsewhere to what they are
fashioning; and people looked at them and really thought that nature's
creation is similar.

Those, however, who are making this comparison ought to have   10
considered that just as in the case of those who practice such crafts
something must remain in them in accordance with which, while still

---

2. Deleting καὶ with Theiler.
3. Comma inserted here with Theiler.
4. Cf. *infra* 5–6.
5. See *SVF* 2.1016 (= Sext. Emp., *M.* 9.111–115), 2.458 (= Philo, *Leg. Alleg.* 2.22).
6. Reading καὶ πως ('somehow') with Kirchhoff.
7. See Pl., *Tim.* 74C6.

remaining in them, they produce their artifacts by means of their hands,
they must also go back to a similar thing in nature and understand that
15   here, too, all the power that produces not by means of hands must
remain and remain entire. For there is indeed no need for it [power] to
have some parts that remain and others that are in motion, for matter
is what is in motion, but nothing in power is in motion; otherwise, it
[power] will not be the prime mover, nor will nature be this [the prime
mover], but that which is unmoved in the whole [of nature].

Someone might indeed say that the expressed principle is unmoved,
20   whereas nature itself is different from the expressed principle and is in
motion. But if they go on to say that nature is entirely in motion, the
expressed principle, too, will be in motion. But if any part of nature is
unmoved, this would, in fact, be the expressed principle.[8] For nature
must be a form and not composed of matter and form;[9] for what need
does it have of warm or cold matter?

In fact, the matter which underlies and is worked on comes bring-
25   ing this, or rather the matter, though not possessing quality, becomes
such, when subject to an expressed principle. For it is not fire that has
to approach for matter to become fire, but an expressed principle.

This is no minor sign that in animals and in plants expressed principles are what produce and that nature is an expressed principle, which
30   makes another expressed principle, its production, which in turn gives
something to the substrate while it itself remains. And so the final
expressed principle, which is in the visible shape,[10] is at this stage a
corpse and is unable to make another expressed principle, but the one
which possesses life, as the brother of the one which made the shape
and itself having the identical power, produces something in what has
come to be.[11]

§3.8.3. How, then, while the expressed principle produces, that is,
produces in this way, could it attain to any kind of contemplation?

In fact, if it produces while remaining, that is, both remaining in
itself and an expressed principle, it would itself be contemplation.
For action would occur in accordance with an expressed principle
5   being clearly different from it; but the expressed principle, which

---

8. Cf. 3.2.4.12–16.
9. See Ar., *Phys.* 2.1.193b12, 18.
10. Cf. 5.8.7.12–16; 5.9.6.20–24.
11. Here nature is distinguished from its image, which gives 'shape' to bodies. The
'brother' here probably refers to souls of individual bodies. Cf. 4.3.6; 2.9.18.14–17. On
sensible bodies as corpses, cf. 2.4.5.16–18; 3.4.1.7.

accompanies action and looks after it, would not be action.[12] Then, if it is not action but an expressed principle, it is contemplation. And in the case of every expressed principle, the one that is last is derived from contemplation and is contemplation in the sense that it is what has been contemplated, but the one prior to this is all contemplation, though, part of it is contemplation in a different way, that is, not as nature but as soul, and the other part is in nature, that is, is identical   10
to nature.

Does nature itself also really derive from contemplation? Yes, entirely from contemplation. But is it itself [produced] by contemplating itself?

In fact, how else? For it is the result of contemplation and of something that has contemplated.[13] But how does nature have contemplation? It doesn't have it, certainly, from reasoning; by 'from reasoning' I mean looking over its own contents. Why, then, is this so given that it   15
is a life, an expressed principle, and productive power? Is it because to 'look over' is not yet to possess? But it does possess and it is precisely because it possesses that it also produces.

So its being what it is for it is the act of producing and being something that produces is precisely what it is. But it is contemplation and object of contemplation, since it is an expressed principle. And so by being contemplation, object of contemplation, and an expressed prin-   20
ciple, it also produces insofar as it is these things. Its producing has, therefore, been shown by us to be contemplation. For it is the result of a contemplation that remains, a contemplation which has not done anything else but has produced by being contemplation.[14]

§3.8.4. And if someone were to ask nature why it produces, if it were willing to listen and answer the questioner it would say: 'You should not ask but understand and fall silent yourself, as I am silent and not accustomed to speak. Understand what, then? That what   5
comes to be is my vision, in my silence,[15] an object of contemplation that comes to be by nature, and that since I come to be from this sort of contemplation, it is necessary for me to have a contemplation-loving nature. And my contemplating produces an object of contemplation, just as geometricians draw lines as they contemplate. But without my drawing, while I contemplate, the lines of bodies come to exist as though   10

---

12. See Ar., *DA* 3.11.434a16–21.
13. Cf. 4.8.8.13–16. Nature is the lowest part of the soul of the universe.
14. Cf. 3.2.1.34–45.
15. Reading ἐμὸν σιωπώσης with HS⁴.

falling out of me. And my experience is the same as that of my mother and those who begat me.[16] For they, too, are a result of contemplation and my birth has come about without them doing anything, but since they are greater expressed principles and contemplate themselves, I have come to be'.[17]

15   What, then, does this mean? It means that what we call 'nature' is a soul, offspring of a prior soul having a more powerful life, holding contemplation still within itself not directed to what is above, nor even

20   to what is below, but stationary in what it is, in its own stable position, it saw what comes after it by a comprehension of this kind and a sort of self-awareness[18] as far as it can and it no longer searched but has perfected a beautiful and graceful vision.

And if anyone wants to grant it some kind of comprehension or perception, it is not what we call perception and comprehension in

25   other cases, but as if someone were to compare awareness in sleep to the self-awareness of someone awake. For it is at rest in contemplating itself as object of contemplation which has come to it from its abiding in and with itself, and from its being an object of contemplation. And its contemplation is soundless, but more clouded.

For there is another type of contemplation clearer than it in its vision, and nature is an image of this other type. Indeed, for this reason, what

30   is generated by it is also completely weak because a contemplation that is weak makes a weak object of contemplation. Human beings, too, when they are weak in contemplation, produce action as a shadow of contemplation and reason. For their faculty of contemplation is not adequate for them due to weakness of soul, and being unable to grasp

35   adequately the object of their vision and because of this not being filled [by it], yet still desirous of seeing it, they are carried toward action so that they can see [with their eyes] what they cannot see with their intellect. Whenever they do succeed in producing something, they also want to see it for themselves and others to contemplate and perceive it, whenever their project is realized as far as it can be in action.

40   Indeed, everywhere we will find that production and action are a weakened form of contemplation or a consequence of contemplation; a weakness where a person has nothing in mind beyond what has been made, a consequence where he has something prior to this

---

16. 'Mother' refers to the soul of the cosmos and the 'begetters' refers to the expressed principles in soul derived from Forms in Intellect.

17. On the self-contemplation of Forms, cf. 5.1.4; 3.9.6.

18. Reading in ll. 19–20 καὶ [οἷον συναισθήσει] τῇ συννέσει ταύτῃ καὶ <οἷον> συναισθήσει with HS⁴.

to contemplate which is superior to what has been produced. For why would anyone go after the image of what is genuine as their first choice, if he can contemplate what is genuine? And less intelligent children are   45
also evidence of this; not being capable of study and theory, they turn to crafts and manual work.

§3.8.5.[19] But now that, in our discussion of nature, we have said in what way generation is contemplation, let us go to the soul before this[20] and say how its contemplation, its love of learning, its inquisitive nature,[21] the birth pangs from the things it recognized and its completeness have produced it, so that when it has become entirely an   5
object of contemplation, it produces another object of contemplation [i.e., nature]. It is like the way in which craft produces; when each craft is complete it produces a kind of little craft in a toy which possesses a reflection of everything. But in other respects these visions and objects of contemplation are like things dim and unable to help themselves.

So the first part of soul[22] which is above and is always being filled   10
and illuminated by what is above remains in the intelligible world, while the other part, by means of the first participation in it as participant, goes forth[23] in participation.[24] For life always goes forth from life, since activity reaches everywhere and is not absent from anywhere. Yet as it goes forth, it allows the prior part to remain where it left it; for   15
if it were to abandon its prior part, it would no longer be everywhere but only at the last point which it reached. But what goes forth is not equivalent to what has remained.

If, then, it must be everywhere and there must be nowhere where its activity is not present and the prior must be different from the posterior, and if activity derives from contemplation or action—and action   20
did not yet exist for it cannot precede contemplation—it is necessary that one activity is weaker than another, but all of it is contemplation. And so the action which appears to be in accordance with contemplation is the weakest contemplation; for what is produced must always be of the same kind [as what produces it], but weaker because it becomes   25

19. See Appendix II D.
20. This is the soul of the universe, which is itself produced by the contemplation of what is prior to it. Cf. 5.1.7.36–38; 5.2.1.16–21.
21. See Pl., *Phdr.* 251B5f.
22. Deleting τὸ λογιστικὸν with HS⁴, following Kirchhoff, which may be a gloss.
23. Reading μεταλαμβάνον <πρόεισι> with HS⁴.
24. The distinction between the soul of the cosmos and nature is analogous to the distinction between the undescended and descended parts of the intellect. Cf. 3.2.2.18–33.

attenuated[25] as it descends. Indeed, everything goes forth without sound because there is no need of any visible and externally originating contemplation or action, while both the soul which contemplates and that which contemplates in the way described [i.e., nature], inasmuch as it does so externally and not in the same way as what went before it, produces what comes after it and contemplation produces
30   contemplation. For contemplation does not have a limit nor does the object of contemplation.

This is why [soul contemplates]; in fact, this is why it is everywhere. For where is it not present since it is also identical in every soul? For it is not circumscribed by magnitude. Yet it is not present in the same way in everything with the result that it is not even present in every part of
35   soul in the same way. For this reason, the charioteer[26] gives the horses something of what he saw, while it is obvious that the horses which have taken it would have a desire for what they saw. For they did not receive all of it. But if they are to act on this desire, they are acting for the sake of what they desire. And that was an object of contemplation and contemplation.

§3.8.6. Action, therefore, is for the sake of contemplation and for an object of contemplation. And so contemplation is the goal even for those who are acting, and what they are unable to obtain in a straight line, in a way, they seek to grasp by a circuitous route. For whenever
5   they succeed in achieving the object of their desire, which they want to come to be, not because they want to be ignorant of it, but rather to know and see it present in their soul; in this case, it is clear that it lies there as something to be contemplated. And that is also because they act for the sake of a good. And they do this not so that it should be outside them nor that they should not possess it, but so that they should possess the good that comes from action.
10   Where is this? In the soul. Action, then, turns back again to contemplation. For what else could that be which someone receives in his soul, which is itself an expressed principle, than a silent expressed principle? And all the more silent the more [the soul possesses it within]. For then it holds its peace and seeks nothing since it has been filled. And contemplation in such a person lies within because he is confident in its
15   possession. And as the confidence becomes clearer, the contemplation, too, becomes stiller, which enables the soul to bring the contemplation

---

25. See Pl., *Rep.* 6.497B4, of a seed.
26. See Pl., *Phdr.* 247D1–E6.

into unity. And that which knows insofar as it knows—for now we must be serious[27]—comes into unity with what is known.[28]

For if they are two, the knower will be one thing and the known another, so that they lie side by side, in a way, and this pair is not yet reconciled by the soul, just like expressed principles which although present in the soul produce nothing. For this reason, the expressed   20
principle must not remain external but be unified with the soul of the learner until he discovers what is his own.

The soul, then, when it has become reconciled to [the known] and disposed [in accordance with an expressed principle], still proceeds to bring it forth and set it to the fore—for it did not possess it in a primary way—and to learn it. And by bringing it forth it becomes, in a way, different from it and, when it reasons, looks upon it as being   25
other than itself. And yet soul was itself an expressed principle and a sort of intellect, but one that is looking at another; for it is not full, but lacking compared with its prior. It, too, however, sees in stillness what it brings forth. For it no longer brings forth what it has brought forth well, but by its very deficiency brings forth for investigation and learns what it has.

But in active persons, the soul fits what it has to the external. And   30
by its greater possession, it is stiller than nature, and by its being fuller it is more contemplative, but because it does not possess perfectly, it desires to have to a greater degree the knowledge of what it has con-templated and the contemplation which is the result of the investiga-tion of it. And when the soul abandons itself and comes into the com-pany of other things, and next is returning once again, it sees with the   35
part which it left behind; but the soul which remains stationary in itself does this less. For this reason, the virtuous person has already com-pleted reasoning when he reveals what is within him to another, but in relation to himself he is vision.[29] For this person is already directed toward the One and to stillness not only among externals, but also with   40
respect to himself and everything internal.

§3.8.7. That everything, then, comes from contemplation and is contemplation, both the Beings that truly are and those things that come from them when they contemplate and which are themselves objects of contemplation, some for sense-perception, others for knowing or belief; that actions, too, have their goal in knowing and their desire   5

---

27. Cf. *supra* 1.1ff.
28. Cf. 1.3.4.18.
29. Cf. 4.4.12.5–18.

is for knowing and that what is produced from contemplation has its goal in a further form and object of contemplation; that, in general, each thing is an imitation of what produced it and produces [further] objects of contemplation and forms, and the beings that come to exist, being imitations of Beings, reveal that their producers have as their
10 goal not acts of production and actions, but the finished product in order to contemplate it; that both acts of discursive reason and even before them acts of sense-perception, whose aim is to know, want to look upon this; and that before these, nature produces the object of
15 contemplation and an expressed principle in itself, perfecting another expressed principle, all this is, I think, clear, some of it is self-evident, and some again our account has brought back to mind.

This, then, too, is clear, namely, that when the primary Beings are engaged in contemplation everything else, too, of necessity desires this, if indeed for all things their starting point is their goal.[30] Another reason is as follows: whenever living beings generate, the expressed principles that are within them cause the motion, and this is an activ-
20 ity of contemplation and the birth pain of producing many forms and objects of contemplation, and filling everything with expressed principles and a sort of continuous contemplation. For to produce is to make a form exist and this means to fill everything with contemplation. And the failures, both in what comes to be and in actions, are due to the divergence of those that contemplate from the object of contempla-
25 tion. And the bad craftsman is like someone who produces ugly forms. Lovers, too, are among those who see and hasten on toward a form.

§3.8.8.[31] This is our account of the matter. But when contemplation ascends from nature to Soul and from Soul to Intellect, the acts of contemplation are even more fully appropriated by, that is, more unified with, the contemplators.[32] In the case of the virtuous person's
5 soul, that which is known approaches becoming identical with the substrate which contemplates, inasmuch as it hastens to Intellect. In Intellect, it is clear that the two are already one not by appropriation, as in the case of the best soul, but in Substantiality because 'thinking and Being are identical'.[33] For there is no longer one thing and another;
10 if there were, there would then be yet another again, which would

30. See Pl., *Lg.* 715E8, which Plotinus here understands as a reference to the One.
31. See Appendix I B.
32. Cf. 5.3.5.26–28, 41–48; 5.9.5.1–7.
33. Cf. 1.4.10.6; 5.1.8.17–18; 5.6.6.22–23; 5.9.5.29–30; 6.7.4.18. See Parmenides, fr. 28 B 3 DK.

no longer be one thing and another. It must be, then, that Intellect comprises both as really one.

But this is a contemplation that is alive, not an object of contemplation like that in another.[34] What is in another is living on account of that, but not living for itself. If, then, an object of contemplation or thought is to be alive, it must be a life itself, not the life of the faculties of growth and of sense-perception or of the rest of soul. For other lives are also somehow acts of intellection; but one kind of intellection is that of the faculty of growth, another belongs to the faculty of sense-perception, and another to the [higher] soul. How are they instances of intellection? Because they are expressed principles. And every life is intellection of a sort, but one kind more obscure than another, just as life is, too.

This life, however, is more clear and is the primary Life[35] and primary Intellect, and these are one. And so the first life is intellection and the second life is a second kind of intellection, and the last life is a final form of intellection. And so all life is of this kind and is intellection. People might perhaps say that there are different kinds of life, though they do not say these are different kinds of intellection, but rather that some are instances of intellection, others not intellection at all, doing this because they do not investigate what life in general is. But we really must point out the following, that our argument demonstrates once again that all beings are a by-product of contemplation. So, if the truest life is life with intellection, and this is identical with the truest intellection, then the truest intellection is alive, and contemplation and the object of the highest kind of contemplation are alive and are life, and the two are together one.

If, then, these two are one, how can this one also be many?[36]

In fact, it is because it does not contemplate what is one. Since even when it contemplates the One, it does so not as one. If this were not so, it would not become Intellect. But beginning as one, it did not remain as it began, but, becoming many without noticing it, in a way 'weighed down'[37] it unfolded itself in its wish to have everything—how much better it would have been for it not to want this, for it became second— as a circle comes to be by deploying itself; shape, plane, circumference, center, radii, some parts above, others below.[38] Hence, the starting

---

34. Cf. 1.4.3.33–40; 3.7.3.11–23.
35. See Ar., *Meta.* 12.7.1072b26–30.
36. Cf. 4.8.3.10; 5.1.8.26; 5.3.15.10–22; 5.4.1.20–21; 6.7.14.1–18, etc.
37. See Pl., *Symp.* 203B7.
38. Cf. 6.8.18.7–18.

40 points are better, the end points inferior. For the goal is not of the same kind as the origin-and-goal nor again the origin-and-goal the same as the origin alone.

And, to express it differently, Intellect is not the intellect of one particular thing, but Intellect as a whole. And being Intellect as a whole, it is the Intellect of everything. And so since it is all Beings and belongs to all Beings even its part must possess all Beings. If this is not so, it will have some part that is not Intellect and it will be composed from
45 non-intellects; and it will be a heap gathered up waiting to become an intellect out of all things. For this reason, it is unlimited in this way and, if anything comes from it, there is no diminution, neither of that which comes from it, because it, too, is everything, nor of that from which it comes, because it was not a compound formed from parts.

§3.8.9.[39] This, then, is what Intellect is like; for this reason, it is not the first, but there must be what is 'beyond'[40] it—the previous arguments also lead up to this—first, because a multiplicity comes after unity. And while Intellect is Number,[41] the real One is the principle of Number
5 and Number of this kind. And this Intellect is also at the same time intelligible,[42] so that at the same time there are two. But if there are two, we must grasp what is before the two. What, then, is it? Is it just Intellect on its own? But the intelligible is yoked to every intellect; so if the intelligible is not to be yoked with it, Intellect will not exist either. If, then, it is not Intellect, but shuns duality, what is before these two
10 transcends Intellect.

Why, then, couldn't it be the intelligible?

In fact, it is because that which is intelligible, too, is yoked to Intellect. Then, if it is to be neither Intellect nor intelligible, what could it be? We will say that it is that from which comes Intellect and the intelligible that is with it. What, then, is this and what sort of thing are we to imagine it to be? For it is certainly going to be either something that
15 thinks or something that is without thought. If, then, it is thinking, it will be Intellect, but if it is without thought it will be ignorant even of itself. Where is the dignity in that?[43] For if we were to say that it is the Good and is the most simple thing, we will still not be saying anything clear and distinct, even if we are saying what is true, so long as we

---

39. See Appendix II E; II H.
40. Cf. 1.7.1.19–24; 5.5.4.9–15. See Pl., *Rep.* 6.509B9.
41. Cf. 5.1.5.6–17; 5.5.5.2–14.
42. See Ar., *DA* 3.4.430a2–3.
43. See Pl., *Soph.* 249A1; Ar., *Meta.* 12.9.1074b17–18.

do not possess a firm foundation for our discursive thinking when we speak.

For, again, if knowledge of other things comes about by means of   20
intellect and it is by intellect that we are able to know Intellect, with what sort of direct grasp will that be seized which transcends the nature of Intellect? We shall say to the person to whom we must make clear how this is possible that it is by means of that in us which is the same as it.[44] For there is something of it even within us.[45]

In fact, there is nowhere where it is not, for those able to partake of it.[46] For wherever you place that which is able to possess what is omni-   25
present, it is from there that you possess it. Just as when a voice fills an empty space or human beings, too, as well as the space, in whatever part of the empty space you place your ear you will receive the voice as a whole and yet not all of it.

What, then, is it that we receive when we apply our intellect?   30

In fact, the intellect must, in a way, retreat to what is behind it and somehow let go of itself to what is behind it, since it looks both ways, and in the intelligible world,[47] if it wants to see the One, it must be not entirely intellect. For Intellect is itself the primary Life since it is activity engaged in its progression through everything, not a progression which is progressing but one which has progressed.[48] If, then, it is   35
indeed both Life and is progression and possesses everything precisely and not in a general way—for it would then possess them imperfectly and in an inarticulate way—it must itself come from something else which is no longer in progression, but is the principle of progression, the principle of Life, the principle of Intellect and of all things. For all things are not a principle, but all things are from a principle. And this   40
is no more all things, nor any of them, to enable it to generate all things and not be a multiplicity, but the principle of multiplicity. For that which generates is everywhere simpler than that which is generated.

If, then, this generated Intellect, it must be simpler than Intellect. And if someone were to suppose that the One itself is everything,   45
either it will be each one of everything one by one or all together. Now, if it is all gathered together, it will be subsequent to everything. But if it is prior to everything, everything will be other than it and it will be

---

44. Cf. 6.9.4.26–28, 11.30–32.
45. Cf. 5.1.11.6–7.
46. Reading αὐτοῦ. τὸ with HS⁴.
47. Reading κἀκεῖ[να] with Armstrong.
48. Intellect's 'progression' implies no discursivity. It is an 'activity' (ἐνέργεια) which is complete at every moment.

other than everything. And if it is itself and everything at the same
50   time, it will not be a principle. It must, however, be a principle and
be prior to everything so that everything can exist after it. And if it is
each one of all things separately, first any one will be identical with any
other and next, all will be together and nothing will be distinct. And
for this reason, it is none of all things, but prior to all things.[49]

§3.8.10. What indeed is it? It is the productive power of all things.[50]
If it did not exist, neither would all things, nor would Intellect be the
primary total Life. And that which is beyond Life is cause of Life.[51] For
the activity of life which is all things is not primary, but is poured forth
5   as though from a spring. Think of a spring which has no other source,
but gives all of itself to rivers while not exhausting itself in the rivers
but quietly remaining itself, while the streams which go forth from
it are still all together before they flow their separate ways, yet at this
point they already each know as individual rivers in what direction
10   they will release their waters; or of life in a huge plant passing through
its entirety while the source remains as though seated in the root and
is not scattered around it all. So, this source presents life in its total
multiplicity to the plant, but itself remains non-many. And this is no
great wonder.
15   The wonder is, rather, how the multiplicity of life has come from
what is not a multiplicity and how the multiplicity would not exist
unless what preceded the multiplicity was a thing that was not a multiplicity. For the source is not divided into the whole, since if it had
been so divided it would have destroyed the whole as well; nor would
the whole continue to exist if the source did not continue to remain in
20   itself and different.[52] For this reason, in all cases [of multiplicity], the
ascent is to a one. And there is some one in each case to which you will
trace it back; and this whole you will trace back to a one before it, not
an absolute one, until you come to the absolute One; and this no longer
[goes back] to another one.
        But if you take the one of the plant, and this is also its source which
25   remains, the one of a living being, the one of the soul, and the one of
the universe, you take in each case the most powerful and valued thing.

---

49. Cf. 3.9.4.3–9; 5.2.1.1–2; 5.3.11.14–21, 13.2–3; 5.4.2.39–42; 5.5.13.33–36.
50. Cf. 5.1.7.9–10; 5.3.15.32–35; 5.4.1.36, 2.38; 6.9.5.36. See Pl., *Rep.* 6.509B9–10.
51. 1.6.7.11–12; 5.3.16.35–38; 6.7.18.16–31.
52. Cf. 5.2.2.13–17.

But if you take the One belonging to true Beings, their 'principle and source'[53] and power, are we to lose faith and suppose it to be nothing?

In fact, it is none[54] of the things whose source it is, yet is the sort of thing which, because nothing can be predicated of it, not Existence, not Substantiality, not Life, is a thing beyond them. And if you grasp   30
it after removing Existence from it, you will be amazed. Cast yourself toward it and encounter it taking rest within it; unite your thought with it more and more by knowing it through immediate contact with it and by beholding its greatness through what comes after it and is caused by it.

§3.8.11.[55] And you can consider it further in the following way. Since Intellect is a kind of sight and a sight that is seeing, it will be [like] a potency which is actualized. So, there will be its matter and its form, though matter here is intelligible. Besides, actual seeing, too, is two-   5
fold; before seeing it was one; then, the one became two and the two one. The completion and, in a way, perfecting of sight, then, comes from the sensible, but for the sight of Intellect it is the Good which completes it; for if Intellect was the Good, what need would it have to see or be active at all?

For other things have their activity with respect to and for the sake   10
of the Good, whereas the Good has no need of anything. And so it has nothing but itself. For this reason, when you have uttered 'the Good', don't make any mental additions. For if you add anything, you will make that to which you have added something deficient.[56] For this reason, don't, then, even add thinking so as not to make it into something else and make it two, Intellect and Good. For while Intellect needs the   15
Good, the Good does not need Intellect. Hence, even when it acquires the Good it becomes Good-like[57] and is perfected by the Good when the form which comes upon it from the Good makes it Good-like. One   20
should conceive of the archetype as being similar by forming an idea of its true archetype from the trace which comes upon Intellect.

The Good has bestowed its trace upon Intellect to have by seeing it, so that whereas in Intellect there is desire and it both desires and attains forever, the Good neither desires—what would it desire?—nor   25

---

53. See Pl., *Phdr.* 245C9.
54. Omitting the τὸ in l. 28 with Ficino, Theiler, and Kalligas.
55. See Appendix II D; II E.
56. Cf. 5.3.16.5–16; 6.7.41.14–17.
57. See Pl., *Rep.* 6.509A3.

attains, for it did not even desire. So, it isn't even Intellect. For in Intellect there is desire and convergence with its form.

Indeed, since Intellect is beautiful and the most beautiful of all, and lies in pure light and a 'pure ray of light'[58] and embraces the nature of
30 Being, whose shadow and image is also seen in this beautiful universe of ours, and since it lies in total splendor, because there is nothing non-intelligible, dark or unmeasured in it, living a blessed life, awe takes hold of the one who sees it and who, plunging into it in the way he should, becomes one with it. And just as someone who looks up to
35 heaven, as he sees the brilliance of the stars, certainly thinks of their creator and seeks it, so, too, when someone who has contemplated the intelligible world, looked into it, and also marveled at its creator, therefore must also inquire what it was that brought such a thing into existence or how, a creator who has begotten such a child as Intellect, a beautiful boy, who derived his fullness from it.[59]
40 For surely there is no way in which the Good can be either Intellect or fullness, but is prior to Intellect and fullness. For Intellect and fullness are after it, since they have need of it to be filled and to complete their thought. And they are close to what has no needs and does not in any way need to think, but they possess true fullness and intellection, because they have it primarily. But what is before them neither needs
45 nor possesses anything; otherwise, it would not be the Good.

---

58. See Pl., *Phdr.* 250C4.
59. A pun on κόρος ('boy' and 'fullness').

4.1 (21)

ON THE SUBSTANTIALITY OF THE SOUL 1

Introduction

This little essay is a sort of appendix, or follow-up, to the early treatise 4.7 (second in Porphyry's chronological list), *On the Immortality of the Soul*. Plotinus's concern here is to highlight the intermediate nature of soul, between the completely indivisible nature of Intellect and the entirely divisible nature of bodies. In this, he is, as elsewhere, provoked to thought by what he regards as the 'riddling utterance' of Plato at *Timaeus* 35A1–3, that the soul contains an element which is 'divided about bodies'. To a certain extent, this essay looks forward to the fuller discussion in 6.4–5, where the same preoccupation exercises him.

The essay is placed first in the fourth *Ennead* by Porphyry himself, but Marsilio Ficino, the first modern editor of Plotinus, chose to place it second, after the little note which follows it, which explains the residual confusion in its numbering.

Summary

§1. The real nature of soul being a recapitulation of the latter chapters (9–14) of 4.7: soul is a divine and intelligible reality, intermediate between the intelligible realm proper, which is the 'indivisible' of *Tim.* 35A, and the physical realm, which is the 'divisible', it itself being indivisible of its own nature, but 'divisible' insofar as it is incorporated.

§2. A systematic analysis of the claims that the soul is divisible and that it is entirely indivisible, and refutations of both. In fact, the soul is both divisible and indivisible, 'one and many'.

---

§4.1.1. In investigating the substantiality of the soul,[1] once we have demonstrated that it is not a body, and that, among incorporeals, it is not a harmony; and rejecting its description as an entelechy as not correct, in the sense in which it is asserted, and as not being indicative of its essence; and, further, when we declare that it is of an intelligible   5

---

1. Cf. 4.7, esp. 8⁴ and 8⁵ to which this little piece is a kind of appendix. The reference throughout is to soul in general, and implicitly to the hypostasis Soul.

nature and of divine kinship, perhaps then we will have made some
clear statement about its substantiality.

However, it seems better now to probe this question somewhat
further. Then, after all, we made a simple division, distinguishing the
sensible from the intelligible nature, and situating the soul in the intel-
10   ligible world.[2] Now, though, let us accept it as given that it belongs to
the intelligible; what we need to do next is to track down the precise
quality of its nature, by employing a different approach.

Let us specify, then, that there are some things that are primarily
divisible and by their very nature subject to dispersion;[3] and these are
those things that have none of their parts identical either to any other
part or to the whole, and in which the part must be less than the total-
15   ity as a whole. These things are sensible magnitudes or masses, each
of which occupies a unique place, and is such as not to be capable of
being simultaneously in a plurality of places while remaining identical.

There is, on the other hand, a type of substantiality contrasted with
this, which is in no way receptive of division, and is partless and indi-
20   visible, admitting of no extension even conceptually, having no need of
place nor coming to be in any sort of being either part by part or as a
whole; it is, in a way, riding on all beings together, not so as to fix itself
upon them, but because the other things cannot—nor indeed do they
want to—exist without it, a substance always maintaining the identical
state, being common to all those things that follow upon it like the cen-
25   ter in a circle, from which all the lines to the periphery depend; nonetheless, they allow it to remain alone by itself, though drawing upon it
for their generation and [continued] existence; they participate, on the
one hand, in the point, and its partlessness is a principle for them, but
they have proceeded forth from the intelligible world while yet binding
themselves to it.

30   So, there is indeed this primarily indivisible Being among intelligibles, as guiding principle among Beings, and there is that being among
sensibles which is divisible in every way; but prior to the sensible,
though contiguous with it and indeed immanent in it, there is another
nature, not itself primarily divisible, as are bodies, but yet such as to
35   become divided among bodies; so that, when bodies are divided, the
form in them becomes divided as well, yet exists as a whole in each
of the divided parts, becoming many and yet staying identical, while
each of the many separates entirely from any other, inasmuch as it has

---

2. Cf. 4.7.9–12.
3. See Pl., *Tim.* 37A5.

become completely divided.[4] It is even so with colors and all qualities and each shape, which can exist simultaneously as a whole in many separated things, while having no part that is affected in the identical manner any other part is affected; for which reason indeed this, too, is to be reckoned entirely divisible.

But again, in addition to that completely indivisible nature, there is another [type of] substantiality following next upon this, deriving its indivisibility from that source, but which, through striving in its procession from that toward the opposite nature, finds itself situated between the two, that is to say, the indivisible and primary and that which is divided in bodies, which has immersed itself in bodies—not in the way that color and quality is in many places identical in its entirety, in a multiplicity of corporeal masses—but that which is in each is entirely separate from any other, inasmuch as one mass is also distinct from any other; and even if the magnitude is one, yet that which is identical in each part possesses no commonality that would contribute to shared experience, because the identity is in fact different in each case; for it is the affection that is identical, not the substantiality itself.

But the [type of] substantiality which we say rests upon this nature, while still contiguous with the indivisible Substantiality, is both itself a [type of] substantiality and comes to be present in bodies, where it happens to experience division, while not having suffered this experience previously, before it had given itself to bodies. In the bodies, then, in which it comes to be, even when it comes to be in that which is greatest and all-embracing, having given itself to the whole of each, it still does not itself abandon its unity.[5] For it is not one in the way that a body is one; for a body is one by its continuity, while each of its parts is different from another and in a different place. Nor is it one in the way that a quality is. For that nature at once divisible and indivisible which we want to say that soul is, is not one in the manner of a continuous entity, which has one part in one place and another in another; but while it is certainly divisible, in that it is present in all the parts of that in which it is present, it is nonetheless indivisible, because it is present as a whole in all the parts, and in any one of them as a whole also.

And he who beholds this greatness of the soul, and who beholds its power, will acknowledge how divine a thing it is, and how marvelous, and how it is among the natures which transcend the physical world. Though it does not itself possess magnitude, it is present to objects of every magnitude, and it is present, now here, now there, not with a

---

4. See Pl., *Tim.* 35A2–3.
5. Cf. 4.3.8.2–4; 5.1.2.35–38.

different part of itself, but as identical; the result is that it is divided and yet again not divided, or rather not divided in itself, nor has it come to be divided; for it remains with itself as a whole, but yet it is divided
75 among bodies, since bodies are incapable, by reason of their own characteristic dividedness, of receiving it undividedly. So, divisibility would be a state of bodies, not of it itself.[6]

§4.1.2. It is clear from this, then, that the nature of the soul should be of this sort, and that anything different from this cannot be soul, either something solely indivisible or something entirely divisible, but that it must necessarily be both of these, in the way described above.
5 For if it were constituted in the way that bodies are, with one part here and another there, it would not be the case that, when one part was affected, another part would have perception of the part affected, but that the particular soul, let us say of a finger, being distinct and independent, would have the perception; there would then be,
10 generally, a multiplicity of souls administering each of us—and indeed it would not be just one soul that would be directing this universe, but an unlimited multitude, all separate from one another.

The fact of continuity, after all, if it does not result in unity, is of no relevance; for we must certainly not accept, as they claim in a state of self-deception, that acts of sense-perception proceed to the 'ruling principle' by a process of 'transmission.'[7] For first of all, the claim that
15 there is a part of the soul that is a 'controlling principle' is made without due consideration. For how are they going to divide up the soul, and speak of this part and that, and then the 'controlling principle'? By what sort of quantitative criterion, or by what differentiation of quality, will they make the division between each part, when the mass involved is one and continuous?

And [second,] will it be only the controlling principle or the other parts, too, that will have sense-perceptions? And if only the former, if
20 a sense-perception falls upon the controlling principle, in what place will the sense-datum be perceived as being situated? If in some other part of the soul, since it is not this part's nature to perceive, it will not transmit its experience to the controlling principle, and so there will not be a sense-perception at all. And, on the other hand, if it falls upon
25 the controlling principle itself, either it will fall upon a part of it, and when it perceives the item the other parts will not—for there would be

---

6. Cf. 6.4.441–52.
7. The Stoics. See *SVF* 2.441 (= Alex. Aphr., *De mixt.* 223, 25), 854 (= Aëtius, *Plac.* 4.23, 1); Alex. Aphr., *De mixt.* 10, Suppl. Aristot. 2.2.223.28–34.

no point in that—or there will be a multiplicity of sense-perceptions, and indeed an unlimited number of them, and they will not be all the same; but one will say, 'I was the first to experience that!', and another will say, 'I perceived the experience of another part!'; but, except for the first one, each of them will be ignorant of where the experience first arose. Or else each part of the soul will be deceived into imagining that the experience originated where it happens to be.

If, by contrast, not only the controlling principle, but also every other part, is going to be endowed with sense-perception, why would one be the controlling principle and another not? Or why would the sense-perception have to ascend as far as that? And how, in the case of the products of multiple sense-organs, such as, for example, ears and eyes, will one single item be cognized?

But if, on the other hand, the soul were entirely unitary, that is to say totally indivisible and one by itself, and if it entirely escapes all multiplicity and division, the result would be that nothing which was occupied by soul will be ensouled as a whole; but as if basing itself around a central point of each living being, it would have left the whole mass of it soulless.

The soul must, therefore, be in this way both one and many,[8] and divided and indivisible, and we should not be incredulous as to the possibility of a thing's being identical and one in many places. For if we were not prepared to accept this possibility, the nature holding all things together and administering them will not exist. As it is, it is that which encloses all things in one embrace and directs them with wisdom, constituting on the one hand a multiplicity—since there is a multiplicity of beings—but also one, in order that the coordinating force may be one, and while orchestrating life in all its parts due to its multiple unity, exercising a wise leadership due to its indivisible unity. In those things which are devoid of wisdom, the controlling unity imitates this.

This, therefore, is the meaning of the divinely inspired riddling utterance: 'From the indivisible and ever-unchanging Substantiality and from the divisible substantiality which comes to be in bodies, he mixed from both a third type of substantiality'.[9] The soul, then, is one and many in this way; and the forms in bodies are many and one; bodies, in turn, are many only; and that which is highest is one only.[10]

---

8. Cf. *infra* 53; 4.3.3.10; 4.9 *passim*; 6.2.4.30–35, 5.14. See Pl., *Parm.* 155E5.
9. See Pl., *Tim.* 35A1–4.
10. Probably a reference to Intellect, a one-many. The One cannot, strictly speaking, even be said to have 'one' predicated of it.

4.2 (4)

ON THE SUBSTANTIALITY OF THE SOUL 2

Introduction

This little note, ranked by Porphyry as twenty-first in his chronological listing, also concerns the question of the intermediate nature of soul, and, like 4.1, involves a meditation on *Timaeus* 35A1–3: In what sense can the soul be said to be 'divisible about bodies'? It would have fitted well as one of the 'miscellaneous topics of inquiry' gathered by Porphyry as 3.9, and that is where it seems to have been placed in the archetype of our existing manuscripts. Porphyry, however, required it to make up his fourth *Ennead*, so he lists it separately in the *Life*, and seems to have placed it at the head of this *Ennead*. Marsilio Ficino, in his translation, followed by the *editio princeps*, places it second, and modern editors have followed this lead.

---

§4.2.1. It is in the intelligible cosmos that true Substantiality is to be found. Intellect is the best part of it. Souls are also in the intelligible world; for it is from there that they come to be in the sensible world, too.[1] And that cosmos contains souls without bodies, whereas this one contains those which have come to be in bodies and are divided among them. In the intelligible world, Intellect is all together and [its contents are] not separated or divided, and all souls are together in a world of eternity, not one of spatial extension.

Intellect, then, is always without separation and is indivisible, and Soul in the intelligible world is without separation and undivided; it has, though, a natural propensity to be divided. For its propensity to division involves its departure from that world and its coming to be in body. So, then, it is plausibly said to be 'divided among bodies',[2] because it departs in this way and is subject to division.

How, then, is it also undivided? The reason is that it does not totally depart, but there is an element of it that has not gone forth, whose nature it is not to be divided.[3] The phrase, then, 'from the indivisible and ever-unchanging [Substantiality] and from the divisible [substantiality] which comes to be in bodies' is identical to saying that the soul

---

1. Cf. 4.8.8.1–3.
2. See Pl., *Tim.* 35A1–3.
3. See 4.9.3.13–14. This is probably a reference to the undescended intellect.

is composed of that which exists above[4] and that which depends upon the intelligible world, but has flowed forth as far as the sensible world, like a line from a center. But having come to the sensible world with this part, observe how[5] with this very part it preserves the nature of the whole. Not even in the sensible world, after all, is it solely divided, but it is also undivided; for that in it which is divided is divided indivisibly.[6] In giving itself to the whole body, it is divided even while not being divided, by being whole in all the parts of the body.

20

---

4. Deleting καὶ κάτω with Bréhier, and adopting οὔσης, with the majority of mss.
5. Reading ὁρᾷ ὡς with Igal.
6. Cf. 4.3.19.30–34.

4.7 (2)

ON THE IMMORTALITY OF THE SOUL

Introduction

This early treatise (only second in Porphyry's chronological list) is a survey, in a rather scholastic mode, of a sequence of doctrines on the nature of the soul adopted by other schools—Epicureans, Stoics, Pythagoreans who hold that the soul is merely a harmony of the body, and Aristotelians—in ascending order of acceptability (§§1–8⁵), leading up to an exposition of the true Platonic doctrine that the soul is not a body, but an immaterial, eternal substance (§§9–15).

A peculiarity of this treatise is that a number of chapters (now numbered 8¹-8⁵), containing much of the critique of other schools, were omitted from the existing manuscripts of the *Enneads*, and appear only in extracts from the treatise quoted by the church historian Eusebius. Since these were not known to Marsilio Ficino, the first editor of the *Enneads*, who is responsible for the division of the tractates into chapters, they have had to be added to the original numbering.

Summary

§1. An introductory chapter, spelling out the nature of the human being, and the respective roles of body and soul.

§§2–4. Plotinus proceeds to a refutation, first, of the materialist psychology of the Stoics (and incidentally, at the beginning of §3, of the Epicureans), refuting the notion that the soul is any kind of material entity, atomic or otherwise, nor yet a pneumatic entity (in the Stoic sense), nor yet a 'mode' of body (§4).

§5. Body cannot be a principle either of existence or of movement.

§§6–7. If the soul were a body, it would not be possessed of sense-perception, at least in any conscious or coherent way, nor could it properly analyze the source of pains or other sensations; this against the Stoics.

§8. If the soul were a body, it would not be capable of thought.

§8¹. Soul is not a quantity.

§8². If soul were material it would not penetrate bodies entirely, as in fact it does; this serves as a rejection of the Stoic doctrine of total mixture.

§8³. Soul and intellect are naturally prior to nature and to body.

§8[4]. Refutation of (a misunderstanding of) Pythagorean doctrine that the soul is an ἁρμονία or 'attunement' of body, and nothing more than that (the suggestion of Simmias in Plato's *Phaedo*).

§8[5]. Refutation of the Aristotelian doctrine (in *On the Soul* 2.1) of the soul as *entelekheia*, or 'realized actuality' of the body.

§9. The soul as a principle of life, being life of itself.

§10. Soul is of a divine nature; when it discovers its own true nature, that endows it with happiness.

§§11–12. The soul is of its nature immortal and indestructible; having no parts, it is not liable to alteration, or, therefore, dissolution.

§13. The purely intellective part of soul does not descend into body; only that which acquires desire comes into relation to body, without actually being in the body; it produces, embellishes, and directs all things in this world.

§14. Even the souls of non-human living things subsist separately from their bodies, though an element of their souls derives from nature.

§15. Concluding theological postscript. Evidence adduced from divine pronouncements, prophetic shrines, and suchlike.

---

§4.7.1.[1] Whether each one of us is immortal, or, on the contrary, is destroyed entirely, or if some parts of the individual depart into dispersion and destruction, while other parts persist forever—those which constitute the self—this is something that one might discover if one conducted the inquiry with a view to our nature.[2] A human being   5
is certainly not something simple, but there is in him a soul, and he also has a body, whether in the role of an instrument for us, or connected to us in some other way. At any rate, let the division be made along these lines, and let us examine the nature and substantiality of each.

The body, being itself actually composite, too, cannot logically be assumed to be permanent and, in fact, sense-perception observes it   10
dissolving and wasting away and being prone to all sorts of destructive forces, as each of its component parts is borne to its proper place, one destroying another and changing into another and self-destructing, and especially when the soul which makes them all work together is no longer present to the parts of its mass. And even when each part is   15
isolated and to that extent becomes one, it is not one,[3] since it admits of

---

1. See Appendix II A.
2. Cf. 6.4.4.39–46.
3. Reading <ἕν> οὐκ ἔστιν with Igal and HS³.

dissolution into form and matter, which are the necessary constituents of even simple bodies.

Further, bodies, inasmuch as they are bodies, have magnitude, and so are liable to being cut up and broken into little pieces, and in this

20   way meeting with destruction. So, if this is a part of us, we are not entirely immortal, while if it is an instrument which has been assigned to us for a certain period of time, it should be endowed with a nature corresponding to that. The dominant part of us, and that which constitutes the human being himself, if indeed it is this, is related to the body as form to matter, or as user to instrument. In either case, the soul is the self.[4]

§4.7.2. What, then, is its nature?

In fact, if it is a body, it is at all events subject to dissolution; for every body is, after all, composite. If it were not to be a body, but of some other nature, then that nature, too, would have to be examined either by the identical method or by some other. But first we must examine

5   what components into which we must analyze this body which they claim soul to be.[5] For since life is of necessity present to soul,[6] it is necessary that, in the case of this [supposed] body which is the soul, if it is composed out of two or more bodies, either or each of them must possess life innately, or one of them would possess it and the other not,

10 or neither or none of them. After all, if life were actually present to any one of them, then this very one would be soul.

What, then, would the body be that possesses life in itself? For fire and air and water and earth are in themselves soulless; in the case of any one of these to which soul is present, this enjoys a borrowed life, and there are no other bodies apart from these. And those who take the view that there are other elements in addition to these have asserted

15 that those are bodies, not souls, and so not possessing life.[7] But if, when none of them possesses life, the conjunction of them creates life, that is an absurdity; whereas if each of them were to have life, even one would be sufficient. But it is quite impossible for a composition of bodies to generate life, and for things devoid of thinking to generate intellect.

---

4. Cf. 1.1.10.7–11; 4.4.18.10–19. See Pl. [?], *Alc.* 1.129E5, 130C3; Ar., *Meta.* 7.10.1035b14–16; 8.3.1043b3–4; Alex. Aphr., *De an.* 2.1–2; *De an. mant.* 115.14–15.

5. See *SVF* 1.142 (= Iamblichus, *De an. apud* Stob., *Ecl.* 1.49.33), 518 (= Nemesius, *De nat. hom.* 2.32), 2.780 (= Galen, *Def. med.* 29.19.355), 790 (= Nemesius, *De nat. hom.* 2.46).

6. See Pl., *Phd.* 105D3–4.

7. These are Atomists. See Democritus *apud* Ar., *DA* 1.2.403b31–404a3; Epicurus, *Ep. Hdt.* (= D.L., 10.65); Alex. Aphr., *De an.* 12.2–3.

Moreover, they are not also going to claim that these bodies are mixed   20
together in any random way. So, therefore, there should be something
that orders them and constitutes the cause of their mixture so that this
could assume the role of soul. For, quite apart from a composite, there
would not even exist a simple body without soul's presence in the
universe, if it is indeed true that it is the approach of the expressed
principle to matter that generates body, with the expressed principle
proceeding from no other source than from soul.   25

§4.7.9. The other nature [i.e., the incorporeal], however, that which
has its existence from itself, is all that is really Being[8] which neither
comes to be nor is destroyed; indeed, all other things will pass away,
and never return again, if that suffered destruction which preserves
them, and, above all, this universe as a whole which is preserved and   5
endowed with order by means of soul. For this serves as 'principle of
motion,'[9] providing motion to all other things, while it is itself moved
by itself, bestowing life on the ensouled body, while possessing it of
itself, which it never loses, inasmuch as it has it from itself.

For indeed it is not the case that everything enjoys a life sourced   10
from outside—that would lead to an infinite regress—but there must
be some nature that is primarily alive, which must necessarily be
'indestructible and immortal,'[10] inasmuch as it serves as a principle of
life for all other things as well.

It is certainly there that the divine as a whole and the blessed must
have its seat, having life by itself and being by itself, being primarily, 15
that is, primarily alive, having no part in change to its substantiality,
neither coming to be nor perishing.[11] For where would it come from,
or into what would it perish?[12]

And if we are to employ the term 'being' in its truest sense, it will be
necessary that it not be at one time and not at another. Even as in the
case of whiteness, just the color itself, it is not at one time white and at 20
another not white; and if the whiteness were also a being along with
being white, it would have been eternal; but, in fact, it has only the
characteristic of being white. That, on the other hand, which has being
present to it of itself and primarily, will be always. So, this thing which
is primarily and always, is not something dead, like a stone or a log, but

---

8. πᾶν τὸ ὄντως ὄν ('all that is really Being') often refers to Intellect and the Forms;
here the term refers to the incorporeal, including Soul.
9. See Pl., *Phdr.* 245C9.
10. See Pl., *Phd.* 95C1; Alcinous, *Didask.* 177.18–20.
11. See Pl., *Symp.* 211A1.
12. See Parmenides, 28 B 8.19 DK.

25   must be always living, and must enjoy a pure life, at least as much of it as remains on its own; but whatever is mixed with a worse element, possesses an impediment as regards what is best[13]—though it does not, for all that, lose all contact with its own nature—but it can recover 'its ancient state'[14] by ascending to what belongs to itself.[15]

    §4.7.10. That the soul is akin to 'the more divine nature and the eternal' is something that is made plain by our demonstration that it is not a body.[16] Further, it has no shape or color, and is impalpable. All this may also be demonstrated from the following considerations.

5   Since we are indeed agreed that all that which is divine and really Being is endowed with 'a life of goodness and intelligence',[17] we must consider next after this, taking our start from our own soul, what would be its nature. Let us for this purpose focus on a soul that has not, in the body, taken to itself non-rational appetites and passions and made itself the receptacle of other emotions, but one that has cleansed

10   itself of these, and as far as possible has nothing in common with the body. The postulation of such a soul as this will make it clear that vices are accretions to the soul and come in from elsewhere,[18] while when it is purified what inheres in it are the best things, 'wisdom and the rest of virtue',[19] which are its proper inhabitants.

    If, then, the soul is such as this, when it rises up so as to be on its

15   own, how can it not belong to that nature, such as we declare to be that of the whole divine and eternal world? For wisdom and true virtue, divine as they are, would not come into being in any low-grade mortal receptacle; rather, it is necessary that such a thing should be itself divine, inasmuch as it partakes in divinity through kinship or sameness in being.

20   For this reason, any of us who is like this would be very little different from the inhabitants of the world above in respect of his soul itself, being inferior only as regards the embodied soul. For this reason indeed if every human being were like this, or even if a substantial multitude were endowed with such souls, there would be no one so skeptical as not to be convinced that the part of them which is soul is entirely

25   immortal. As it is, however, seeing the soul in the great majority of

---

13. Cf. 1.1.12.10–28; 1.8.13.24–25, 14.44–49; 4.8.4.25–30. See Pl., *Phd.* 65A9–B1.
14. See Pl., *Rep.* 8.547b6–7.
15. Cf. 6.4.1.17–29.
16. Cf. *supra* 2–3. See Pl., *Rep.* 10.611E2–3.
17. See Pl., *Rep.* 7.521A4 (referring to the life of the Guardians).
18. See Pl., *Rep.* 10.611B10–C5.
19. See Pl., *Symp.* 209A3–4.

people to be in various ways corrupted,[20] they do not regard it as being
a thing either divine or immortal. But one must view the nature of each
thing rather by looking to its purified state, since the state that accrues
from without tends always to get in the way of knowledge of that to
which it accrues.[21]   30

Examine it by actually subtracting that element,[22] or rather let one
subtract himself and then look, and he will come to believe that he is
immortal, when he contemplates himself as having come into the intelligible, that is, the pure world. For he will see an intellect viewing no
sensible, nor any of mortal things here, but grasping with the everlasting aspect of itself the everlasting reality, all the contents of the intel-   35
ligible world, a world itself intelligible and suffused with light, being
illuminated by the truth radiating from the Good,[23] which beams its
truth upon all the intelligibles; so that often it should occur to him that
this is indeed well said:

'Hail, I am to you as an immortal god'![24]—as he ascends to the
divine, and focuses his attention on the sameness he has to it.   40

But if this purification results in him realizing the knowledge of the
best things, then the branches of scientific understanding come to be
revealed as being within him, those ones that are actually branches of
scientific understanding. For it is certainly not by running away from
itself that the soul 'beholds Self-Control and Justice',[25] but all by itself,
in the process of its grasping of itself, and of what it formerly was,   45
beholding in a way statues set up within itself, which it has cleaned up
after their infection by the rust of time.[26] It is as if gold were to become
ensouled, and next, knocking off the earthy element that pervades it,
having been previously in a state of ignorance as regards itself, which
caused it not to see itself as gold, but then seeing itself on its own,   50
would at once be astonished at its own nature, and would reflect that it
had no need, after all, of beauty imported from without, since it itself
emerged as supreme, provided that one let it be by itself.

§4.7.11. Regarding a thing of this sort, who endowed with good sense
would dispute that it is immortal? It is, after all, something endowed of
itself with life, which it is not capable of losing. How indeed could soul

---

20. See Pl., *Rep.* 10.611B10–C1.
21. See Pl., *Phd.* 65A10; *Rep.* 10.611E5–612A2.
22. See Pl., *Rep.* 7.534B9.
23. Cf. 5.1.3.12. See Pl., *Rep.* 6.508D5.
24. Cf. 5.3.17.28–38. See Empedocles, fr. 31 B 112.4 DK.
25. See Pl., *Phdr.* 247D6.
26. See Pl., *Symp.* 216E6.

be destroyed, since life is not added to it from outside, nor does it have
5   it in the way that heat is present to fire?[27] I do not mean to imply that
heat is something externally introduced into fire, but rather that, even
if it is not introduced into fire, it is into the matter underlying the fire;
for it is through this that the fire is extinguished.

Soul, however, does not have life in this way, as matter that underlies
10   it, but it is life coming to be in it that renders it a soul. For either life is a
substance, and a substance such that it possesses life of itself—which is
just that thing that we are in search of, the soul—and this they agree to
be immortal; or they will have to analyze this, too, in turn as a composite, until they arrive at something immortal which is moved of itself,
for whom it is not licit to 'receive the portion of death.'[28] Otherwise, if
15   they declare that life is an affection externally introduced into matter,
they will be compelled to admit that that very thing from which this
affection is introduced into matter is itself immortal, being incapable
of receiving into itself the opposite of what it introduces.[29] But, really,
there is a single nature which is alive in actuality.

§4.7.12. Further, if they[30] are going to maintain that every soul is
destructible, it would be necessarily the case that all things should have
perished long ago. If, on the other hand, one class of soul is perishable
and another not, as, for example, the soul of the universe is postulated
to be immortal, but our own are not, then they will have to give us the
explanation for that; for each of them is a first principle of motion,[31]
5   and each of them lives of itself,[32] and each of them acquaints itself with
the identical things by the identical means, thinking both what is in
heaven and what transcends heaven, seeking out everything which has
Substantiality,[33] and ascending as far as the first principle. And this
grasping of the 'what it is of each thing,'[34] which it actually derives
from its own resources from the acts of contemplation of that which
10   is within it arising from the process of recollection, endows it with an

---

27. See Pl., *Phd.*102A10–107B10.
28. See Pl., *Tim.* 41B4.
29. See Pl., *Phd.* 105D10–11.
30. The Stoics. See *SVF* 2.809 (= Eusebius, *Pre. ev.* 15.20.6), 2.774 (= D.L., 7.156).
31. See Pl., *Phdr.* 245C9.
32. I.e., soul alone has life essentially. Cf. *supra* 11.18.
33. Along with the words πᾶν ὅ ἐστι κατ᾽ οὐσίαν the word ὄντως *vel sim.* should be understood.
34. Cf. *supra* 4.7.8.16.

existence that is prior to the body, and, since it makes use of everlasting types of scientific understanding, allows that it is everlasting as well.[35]

Everything, after all, that is dissoluble, having assumed composition for the purpose of existing, is naturally disposed to suffer dissolution according to the method of its composition. But the soul is one and a simple nature, whose actuality consists in its living;[36] so, due to this, it will be indestructible. 15

But [one might say] as it is divided,[37] therefore, by reason of being split up into individual bits, it would be prone to perishing. No, the soul is not any sort of physical mass or quantity, as has been demonstrated.[38]

Well, then, it is through experiencing change that it will meet with destruction.[39] But the process of change, insofar as it is destructive, does away with the form, and leaves the matter as it is; thus, this is something experienced by a composite.[40] If, then, the soul is not susceptible 20 to destruction by any of these means, it necessarily follows that it is indestructible.

§4.7.13. How is it, then, that, whereas the intelligible world is entirely separate, the soul enters into contact with the body? This is because whatever is intellect alone remains eternally incapable of being affected there among the intelligibles, enjoying a life that is solely intellectual—for there is in it no element of impulse or desire— whereas if that which follows immediately upon that intellect takes on 5 desire, by the addition of that desire it in a way proceeds already a stage further, striving to impose order on the model of what it has seen in Intellect, as if pregnant from that source and straining to beget, it is eager to produce something, that is, to create.[41]

And being keyed up with this enthusiasm for the world of sense, it is on the one hand in cooperation with the soul of the universe as a whole that it dominates the external object of its administration and joins 10 in the supervision of the cosmos, but through its wish to administer a part and finding itself isolated and increasingly attached to that in

---

35. See Pl., *Phd.* 72E3–73A3,78C1–2.
36. Countering Ar., *DA* 2.4.415b13–15, who says that living is the actuality of an animal's body, not of its soul.
37. I.e., the individual soul.
38. Cf. *supra* 5.24–51.
39. Cf. 3.6.1–5.
40. Cf. 1.1.2.22–23; 4.2.1.59–76; 6.2.4.21–28.
41. Cf. 5.3.17.15–17.

which it is involved, it yet does not give itself over whole and entire to its body, but retains as well some element outside the body.[42]

15 Not even in the case of such a soul, then, is its intellect subject to affections; but this soul is sometimes in the body, and sometimes out of the body, driven forth by its impulse from the primary Beings, and proceeding as far as the third level of Being,[43] to the world this side of Intellect, by the activity [of Intellect],[44] which remains itself ever in the identical state and, by means of Soul, fills all things with various types of beauty, and adorns them, immortal by means of an immortal, since 20 Intellect itself, in its eternal existence, will be engaged in unceasing activity.

§4.7.14. Concerning the souls of other living beings, such of them as have failed as humans, and have descended into the bodies of beasts, they, too, will necessarily be immortal.[45] But if there is another type of 5 soul, this must derive from no other source than that of living nature, it itself being also a cause of life to living beings, including indeed the soul in plants; for all have sprung forth from the identical principle, possessing their own proper life, and being themselves incorporeal and partless and substances.[46]

Now if it is asserted that the human soul, seeing as it is tripartite,[47] 10 will be subject to dissolution by reason of being composite, we in turn will say that the pure souls, when set free, will rid themselves of what has been tacked on to them at birth, while others will maintain this association for a very long time; and even when the worse element is disposed of, it itself will not perish, so long as that persists from which it takes its origin. For nothing from Being will ever perish.

§4.7.15. We have, then, said what was required for those who are in need of a demonstration. But for those who also have need of conviction fortified by sense-perception, we must make a selection from the considerable store of information relative to such matters, 5 and specifically from what the gods have handed down in ordering us to appease the wrath of souls that have suffered wrongs,[48] and granting honors to the dead as if they were still able to perceive them as indeed

---

42. Cf. 1.1.12.11–18; 4.8.4.30–35.
43. See Pl. [?], *2nd Ep.* 312E1–4.
44. Reading ἐνεργείᾳ τοῦ μένοντος with Harder.
45. Cf. 2.9.9; 3.2.13, 15, 17; 3.3.8; 3.4.2; 4.3.24.27; 6.4.16; 6.7.6. See Pl., *Tim.* 90E–92C.
46. Cf. 1.1.11.8–15.
47. See Pl., *Rep.* 4.439D–E, 441A.
48. See Pl., *Hip. Ma.* 282A7.

all human beings do in respect of those who have departed. Also, it is a fact that many souls which were formerly in human bodies, when they have departed from their bodies, have not ceased to confer benefits on human beings;[49] indeed, by instituting oracles and prophesying by other means, they both grant us benefits and demonstrate also by their own examples, too, that the rest of souls have not in fact perished.

10

---

49. See Pl., *Lg.* 927A1–3.

4.8 (6)

ON THE DESCENT OF SOULS INTO BODIES

Introduction

This is also an early treatise (sixth on Porphyry's chronological list), but it is of peculiar importance in revealing certain salient aspects of Plotinus's thought. First of all, it shows that he is prepared to recognize tensions, if not contradictions, in Plato's thought, and to address them constructively (§§1–4). Then, it illustrates both his essentially 'world-affirming' attitude to the creation of the physical world and the embodiment of the soul (§§5–7), together with his rather distinctive conviction that even our souls do not descend, but an element in each of us remains 'above' (§8).

Summary

§§1–2. Beginning with a vivid 'autobiographical' passage, Plotinus turns to an inquiry into the role of soul in general in the physical world. Following a survey of the opinions of the early 'sages', such as Empedocles, Heraclitus, and Pythagoras, the question is raised as to the true position of Plato, who seems to present conflicting views.

§§3–4. Is the descent of the individual soul a misfortune or is it an integral aspect of the structure of the universe? In the latter case, it must be accepted, if not welcomed.

§5. Plato's apparently contradictory remarks on this topic can in fact be reconciled. Descent for the individual soul is necessary; all depends on the quality of the life lived after the descent.

§6. The power inherent in the first principle must project itself outward and 'downward', though Soul, to create a world of multiplicity.

§7. It is the nature of soul to be intermediate between the intelligible and physical realms, and it need not be harmed by this.

§8. A part of the individual soul always remains 'above', in the intelligible world, even if we are not always conscious of this.

§4.8.1.[1] Often, after waking up to myself from the body,[2] that is, externalizing myself in relation to all other things, while entering into myself, I behold a beauty of wondrous quality, and believe then that I am most to be identified with my better part, that I enjoy the best quality of life, and have become united with the divine and situated   5
within it, actualizing myself at that level, and situating myself above all else in the intelligible world. Following on this repose within the divine, and descending from Intellect into acts of calculative reasoning, I ask myself in bewilderment, how on earth did I ever come down here, and how ever did my soul come to be enclosed in a body, being such as it   10
has revealed itself to be, even while in a body?

Of our predecessors, Heraclitus, who exhorts us to investigate this very thing, postulating the necessity of 'reciprocal changes' from opposite states, and talking of 'the way up and the way down', and 'in change there is rest', and 'it is laborious always to be toiling at and being sub-   15
jected to the identical tasks',[3] has presented us with these hints, having no concern to clarify his utterance for us, indicating perhaps that we must search the answer out for ourselves, even as he discovered it by searching.[4]

Empedocles, in turn, having stated that it is the law for souls that have erred to fall down to the sensible world, and that he has descended after becoming 'a fugitive from the gods, entrusting myself to raving   20
strife',[5] has in my view revealed as much as has Pythagoras, too, and his followers who have spoken enigmatically on this matter, as upon many others. In the case of Empedocles, however, there is the excuse for lack of clarity that he is writing in verse.

There remains for us, then, the divine Plato, who, among many other beautiful pronouncements on the soul, has in many places in his works spoken of its arrival in this world in such a way as to arouse   25
in us some hope of clarification on the subject. What, then, does this philosopher say?

Well, it will be plain that he does not say the identical thing in every instance, so that one might easily discern his intention, but granting in all cases scant respect for the sensible world, and blaming the soul for

---

1. See Appendix I A; I D; II B; II D; II I.
2. Cf. 6.9.7.17. See *Life of Plotinus* 23.15–16, where, however, union with the One, not Intellect, is described.
3. See frs. 22 B 90, B 60, and B 84a–b DK, respectively, the last pair only known from this passage of Plotinus.
4. See fr. 22 B 101 DK, 'I searched into myself'.
5. See Empedocles, fr. 31 B 115, ll. 13–14 DK.

30   its association with the body, he declares that the soul is 'in bondage'[6]
and has buried itself within it, and that 'the pronouncement made in
secret rites is a great one', to the effect that the soul is 'in prison'[7] here.
And his 'Cave',[8] like the cavern of Empedocles,[9] is to be taken, it seems
35   to me, to be referring to this universe, seeing as the 'release from the
shackles' and the 'ascent' from the Cave he declares to be the journey toward that which is intelligible.[10] And in *Phaedrus* he identifies
'molting of feathers' as the cause of its arrival in the sensible world;[11]
and 'periodic cycles'[12] bring the soul which has ascended back down
40   here, and judgments send others down here, and lots, chances, and
necessities.[13]

But then again, while in all these passages he has blamed the soul
for its arrival in the body, in *Timaeus*, in speaking of this universe, he
commends the cosmos and declares it to be a 'blessed god',[14] and that
the soul was bestowed by the Demiurge in his goodness so as to render
this universe intelligent, since it had to be intelligent, and this could
45   not come about without soul.[15]

The soul of the universe, then, was sent down into it by the god for
this purpose, while the soul of each one of us was sent to ensure its perfection; since it was necessary for the identical genera of living being in
50   the intelligible world also to exist in the sensible world.[16]

§4.8.2.[17] So, when we seek to learn from Plato about the situation
of our own soul, we find ourselves necessarily involved also in an
inquiry into soul in general, how it ever acquired a natural impulse
to associate itself with body, and what we should posit as being the
5   nature of the cosmos in which soul involves itself, whether under
compulsion or voluntarily or in some other way;[18] and also about

---

6. See Pl., *Phd.* 67D1.
7. See Pl., *Phd.* 62B2–5, taking ἐν φρουρᾷ in the sense of 'in prison', rather than 'on
guard-duty', as Plato may well have intended.
8. See Pl., *Rep.* 7.514A ff.
9. See Empedocles, fr. 31 B 120 DK.
10. See Pl., *Rep.* 7.532E.
11. See Pl., *Phdr.* 246C2, 248C9.
12. See Pl., *Phdr.* 247D5.
13. The 'judgments, lots, chances, and necessities' represent a blend of *Phdr.* 249B2
with *Rep.* 10.619D7.
14. See Pl., *Tim.* 34B8.
15. See Pl., *Tim.* 30B3.
16. Cf. *infra* 3.27–30; 6.1ff. See Pl., *Tim.* 39E7–9, 41B7–C3, 92C5–9.
17. See Appendix II B; II D; II I.
18. Cf. 4.3.13.17–20.

the creator of the cosmos, whether he has been able to do his work without impairment, or whether perhaps he is affected like our souls, which by reason of having to administer bodies of inferior nature are constrained to descend deep inside them, if indeed they are going to master them, each element of them otherwise being scattered and carried to its proper place[19]—whereas in the universe as a whole all things are already by nature in their proper places—and requiring a great deal of onerous providential care, inasmuch as there are many external influences falling upon them, and they are constantly in need of support, and the difficult situation that they are in requires every sort of assistance.[20]

The body [of the cosmos], on the other hand, being perfect and sufficient to itself[21] and autonomous, and containing nothing in it contrary to nature, needs only a brief prompting; and the soul of the cosmos is always in the state that it wants to be in, and it is subject to no appetites or affections; 'for nothing goes out from it, nor does anything enter into it'.[22] It is just for this reason that Plato says that our soul, too, if it would come to associate with that perfect soul, would come to be perfected itself, and would also 'walk on high and govern the whole world';[23] when it stands apart in such a way as not to be enclosed within any body nor involved with it, then it, too, even as is the case with the soul of the universe, will cooperate readily in the administration of the cosmos, since it is not in any way an evil thing for the soul to provide the body with the power of flourishing and existing, because not every form of providential care for what is inferior deprives the carer of remaining in its best state.

For there are two kinds of care of everything, that of the totality being achieved at the bidding of an agent ordering by a 'royal' supervision that calls for no exertion, while that of particular things involves a sort of 'hands-on' activity, in which the contact with what is being acted upon suffuses the agent with the nature of the object of his action. Now, since the divine soul is said always to administer the whole heaven in the former way, transcending its subject in respect of its higher aspect, but sending forth its power into its deepest recesses,[24] god could not be said to be the cause of placing the soul of the universe in a worse

---

19. See Pl., *Tim.* 32B5–6.
20. See Pl., *Tim.* 43B8–C1.
21. See Pl., *Tim.* 34B2, 34B8–9.
22. See Pl., *Tim.* 33C6–7.
23. Cf. 4.7.13.9. See Pl., *Phdr.* 246E1–2.
24. See Pl., *Phdr.* 247E3–4.

state, while the soul is not deprived of its natural state, as it possesses this from all eternity and will continue to possess it, this state not being something that can be rendered unnatural, since it pertains to it eternally and never had a beginning.

And when Plato declares that the souls of the stars relate in the identical manner to their bodies as does that of the universe—for the Demi-
40 urge 'inserts' their bodies also 'into the circuits' of the soul[25]—he would thereby preserve also for them their proper state of happiness. There being, after all, two aspects of the association of soul with body that are troublesome, first,[26] that it constitutes an obstacle to acts of thinking,
45 and second,[27] that it infects the soul with pleasures and appetites and pains;[28] none of these would befall a soul which has not entered into the innards of a body, nor belongs to a given body, nor has come to be the soul of that body, but rather that body belongs to its soul,[29] and is such as neither to desire anything nor to be deficient in any respect, so
50 that that soul will not be infected with appetites or fears. For it does not ever expect anything alarming to derive from such a body as that, nor does any troublesome concern arise, causing declination to what is lower, such as to draw it down from its blessed contemplation of the higher, but it is always in contact with such objects, administering this universe with an effortless power.

§4.8.3.[30] But let us now turn to speak of the human soul, which is said [by Plato] to suffer all sorts of misfortune in the body and to 'experience distress'[31] through falling into follies and appetites and fears and all sorts of other evil states, and for which the body is a 'bond'
5 and a 'tomb',[32] and the world its 'cave' and 'cavern',[33] and inquire what view he has of its descent that will not be discordant with itself because the causes [he indicates] for the descent are not identical.[34]

---

25. See Pl., *Tim.* 38C7–8.

26. See Pl., *Phd.* 65C5–9.

27. See Pl., *Phd.* 65A10.

28. See Pl., *Phd.* 66C2–3.

29. Cf. 4.3.9.34–36; 6.4.16.16.

30. See Appendix II I.

31. See Pl., *Phd.* 95D3.

32. Cf. *supra* 1.30–34. A composite reference to Pl., *Phd.* 62D1 and *Crat.* 400C2.

33. A conjunction of the 'Cave' of Pl., *Rep.* Bk. 7 with the 'cavern' of Empedocles, fr. 31 B 120, also mentioned *supra* 1.34–35.

34. I.e., the cause for the descent of the human soul is not identical to the causes for the descent of soul of the cosmos and the soul of the stars.

So, accepting that universal Intellect dwells in the place of intellection whole and entire, which we indeed posit as the intelligible cosmos, and that there are comprised within it intellectual powers and particular intellects—for it is not one only, but one and many[35]—there are necessarily also both a multiplicity of souls and one Soul, and the many distinct from the one, like species derived from one genus, some better and some worse, some more intellectually active, while others are such to a lesser extent. For indeed there in the world of Intellect we have on the one hand Intellect itself embracing virtually all others, like a great Living Being[36] and, on the other, individual intellects, each actualizing one of those which the other embraced virtually.[37]

For example, if a city were to possess a soul embracing all the other ensouled beings within it, the soul of the city would be more perfect and more powerful, but would not preclude the other souls also being of the identical nature as it; or, if from fire as a whole one were to imagine there deriving on the one hand a big fire, and on the other many little fires; but the total substance will be that of fire as a whole—or rather that from which the substantiality of fire as a whole also derives.[38]

It is the role of the more rational soul to think,[39] but not solely that; otherwise, how would it differ from Intellect itself? For, by taking on in addition to its intellectual activity something else, it did not remain static in the manner of Intellect; it has its own proper role, after all, if indeed this is the case with all members of the intelligible world. When it looks toward what is prior to it, it thinks, but when it looks to itself, it turns to ordering and administering and ruling what is below it; because it was not possible for all things to remain fixed in the intelligible world, when the capacity existed for something else to arise in succession—of lesser status than it, certainly, but necessary nonetheless, if indeed that what comes before it is necessary also.

§4.8.4.[40] As for particular souls, they actually employ an intellectual desire in their reversion to that from which they derive, but they also possess a power directed toward this world, like a light which is attached on its upper side to the sun, but which on its lower side does

---

35. Cf. 5.1.8.23–27; 5.4.1.21. See Pl., *Parm.* 155E5. Intellect is usually said to be a one-many and Soul a one and many.
36. See Pl., *Tim.* 30C3–8.
37. Cf. 5.9.6.9–15.
38. Presumably, this would be the Form of Fire.
39. Referring to the rational part of the embodied soul or to the soul of the cosmos.
40. See Appendix II D; II I.

5   not begrudge what service it can provide;[41] they are free from care as long as they remain with universal soul in the intelligible world, while in heaven they share with the universal soul in its administration,[42] like those who associate with a king of universal power and assist in his administration without descending themselves from the royal

10   premises; for they are all together then in the identical place.

But, then, transposing themselves from the universal plane to existing as a part and to being on their own, and becoming in a way weary of existing with another, they retreat each into themselves.[43] When the soul actually does this over a period of time, and shunning the totality of things and standing apart in self-distinction, it ceases to look

15   toward the intelligible; having become a part, it falls into isolation and weakness, and busies itself with trivialities and takes a partial view, and due to its separation from the whole, it fastens upon some individual body and shuns the rest of the totality, coming and directing itself toward that one individual; battered as it is in every way by the totality of things, it severs itself from the whole and turns to administering the

20   particular with all the trouble that involves, fastening now upon this and putting itself in thrall to externals through its presence in it, and plunging itself deep into the interior of it.

It is here that there befalls it the so-called molting of feathers[44] and its coming to be in the bonds of the body, once it has failed of its blameless cooperation in the administration of the better alternative,

25   which involved remaining with the universal soul; that previous situation was altogether better for it, as it was tending upward. Consequent on its fall, then, it has been caught down here, and is in its prison, and is active at the level of sense-perception, because it is impeded from the outset from activating itself intellectually, and it is said to be 'buried' and 'in a cave';[45] whereas once it has turned itself back toward

30   intellection, it is said to be freed from its bonds and to 'ascend', when it has taken its start in 'contemplating Beings'[46] from its exercise of

---

41. Cf. 5.3.6.5–6, 40–41; 8.30–31; 6.9.2.35–36 on reversion to the One as reversion to the true self.

42. Plotinus seems here to be obscuring his own distinction between the hypostasis Soul and the soul of the cosmos, with the term 'universal soul' used for both. Cf. *infra* 7.10–11; 4.3.2.55–56.

43. The words 'existing as a part' indicate the individuality or particularity of an embodied soul as distinct from the individuality of an undescended intellect. Cf. 4.7.13.9–14; 6.4.16.32–37.

44. See Pl., *Phdr.* 246C2, 248C9.

45. See Pl., *Rep.* 7.514A5.

46. See Pl., *Phdr.* 249E5–250A1.

recollection; for despite everything it always retains some element of the transcendent.

Souls, then, come to be, in a way, amphibious, as of necessity they live part of their lives in the intelligible world and part of their lives in the sensible world;[47] those who are able to connect more with Intellect spending more time at the former level, while those in the contrary state whether by nature or misfortune are more engaged at this level. Plato actually gives a discreet hint of this when he divides in turn[48] the contents of the second mixing bowl and makes them 'parts',[49] and then declares that it is necessary that they proceed into the world of generation,[50] since they have become 'parts' of this sort. But if he speaks of the god 'sowing' them,[51] that is to be understood in the same sense as when he presents him as 'speaking' and, in a way, 'addressing an assembly';[52] for his mode of procedure requires him to depict as generated and created what is eternally existent in the nature of the cosmos, for the purposes of exposition presenting in sequence things that are always becoming and things there are eternally Beings.

§4.8.5. So, there is no discordance between the 'sowing into the world of generation' and the concept of descent for the perfection of the universe, the judgment and the cave, necessity and the voluntary—seeing as the necessity includes the voluntary—and the entry into body as something evil; nor yet is there a discordance in the 'flight from god' of Empedocles, nor the moral error, on which follows the judgment, nor the 'respite in flight' of Heraclitus,[53] nor, in general, that between the voluntariness and the involuntariness of the descent. After all, every process toward the worse is involuntary, but if something goes there by its own motion, in suffering the worse it is said to suffer punishment for its actions.[54]

But when the doing and experiencing of these things becomes necessitated eternally by a law of nature, that soul which unites itself to

---

47. Cf. 1.1.10.7–11, 11.2–8; 2.9.2.4–10; 4.3.12.3–8.
48. Reading αὖ τά with HS³, following Igal.
49. See Pl., *Tim.* 41D5–8. There is, however, in Plato's account only one mixing bowl, and two mixings. Plotinus is here adopting an aberrant interpretation of his Middle Platonic predecessor Atticus.
50. See Pl., *Tim.* 42A3–5.
51. See Pl., *Tim.* 41E1–4, where the Demiurge is said to 'sow' the souls into the organs of time, that is, the planets.
52. See Pl., *Tim.* 41A7–D4.
53. Cf. *supra* 11–19.
54. Cf. 1.4.4.15–19; 4.3.24.15–16.

a body in descending from a world superior to the human, accommodating itself to the needs of another. If one says that it is a god who has sent it down, one would not be in contradiction either with the truth,
15   or with oneself. For each class of things, albeit of the lowest status, even if there be many intermediate stages, is to be referred back to the principle from which it sprang.

Now, accepting that there are two stages of moral error, the one connected with the cause of the initial descent, the other with whatever vicious deeds one might commit when down here,[55] the first is punished precisely by that very thing, what it experiences in the initial descent, while the nature of the second, when less serious, causes it
20   to enter one body after another and the more quickly to proceed to judgment according to its due—the fact that it indeed comes about by divine ordinance is indicated by its very name, 'judgment'—while the immoderate type of vice merits punishment of a more serious nature, under the supervision of avenging daemons.[56]

In this way, then, though soul is a divine being and derives from
25   the places above, it comes to be encased in a body, and though being a god, albeit of low rank, it comes thus into this world by an autonomous inclination and at the bidding of its own power, with the purpose of bringing order to what is inferior to it. And if it extricates itself promptly,[57] it suffers no harm, acquiring a knowledge of evil and learn-
30   ing the nature of vice, while bringing its own powers into the light and exhibiting deeds and productions which, if it had remained inactive in the incorporeal world, would have been useless, as never coming to actuality; and the soul itself would never have known what capacities it had, since they would never have been revealed or developed. This is so, if indeed in all cases actualization reveals the potentiality that
35   would otherwise have been entirely hidden and in a way blotted out and non-existent, since it never would truly exist. As it is, however, everyone is brought to wonder at what is inside it by reason of the variegation of what is outside, reflecting on what sort of a thing it is from the observation of its sophisticated acts.

§4.8.6. If, then, it indeed had to be the case that there should not be just one thing only—for all things would then have remained hidden, since they would not possess form in the One, nor would any one of

---

55. See Pl., *Phdr.* 248C3–D2, 248E5–7.

56. Cf. 3.4.6.10–17. See Pl., *Phd.* 113D1–114C6; *Rep.* 10.615E4–616A4.

57. This presumably does not imply premature physical death, but rather a spiritual 'death' to the physical world and its attractions.

all things have come to exist, since the One would have stood fast in itself, nor would there have been the multiplicity of these Beings which have been generated from the One, if the things after them had not proceeded such that they assumed the position of souls in the order[58]— in the identical manner it had to be that there should not only be souls without the appearance of those entities which have come into being through their agency; if indeed it is inherent in each nature to produce what comes after it, and to unfold itself like a seed, developing from a partless principle to a sensible end product. The higher element remains always in its proper seat, while what follows it is, in a way, generated from an inexpressible power[59] such as is characteristic of those higher levels of being, for whom it is not an option to remain in a way inactive out of grudging;[60] rather, it always proceeds, until all things so far as possible reach their final state, under the impulsion of an immense power that extends from itself over all things, and can overlook nothing so as to leave it without a share in itself.

For there is actually nothing that prevents anything from having a part in the nature of the Good, insofar as each thing is capable of participating in it. So, either the nature of matter existed from all eternity, in which case it was not possible for it, as existing, not to participate in that which provides the good to all things insofar as they are competent to receive it; or its generation followed of necessity on the causes which preceded it, in which case not even so is it possible for it to stand apart, as if that which granted it its existence by a sort of gift came to a halt through lack of power before it reached it.[61]

That, then, which is finest in the sensible world is a manifestation of what is best in the intelligible world, both of its power and of its goodness, and all things are held together forever, both in the intelligible world and in the sensible world, the former existing of themselves, while the latter assume their eternal existence by participation in these, imitating their intelligible nature insofar as they can.[62]

§4.8.7. Given that soul's nature is twofold, intelligible and sensible, it is better for the soul to be in the intelligible, but it is necessary nonetheless for it to partake also of the sensible, possessing such a nature as it does; and it must not be discontented with itself if it cannot

58. Cf. 1.7.1.20–26; 2.9.3.7–12; 3.8.10.1–4; 5.1.6.38–39.
59. Cf. *supra* 3.19–22.
60. See Pl., *Tim.* 29E1–3, 42E5–6.
61. Cf. 1.8.14.51–54; 3.4.1.5–12.
62. Cf. 2.9.8.10–20, 16.48–56; 3.2.13.18–14.6.

in all respects adhere to the better, seeing as it holds a median position among things that exist.[63] Though belonging to the 'divine portion,'[64] it is yet situated at the outer limit of the intelligible, such that, sharing as it does a common border with the sensible nature, it gives something to this from what is proper to it, while apprehending something from that provided that it does not impose this arrangement at the cost of

10   preserving its own security, and plunges in with an excessive degree of enthusiasm, without remaining as a whole in contact with the universal soul.[65] This is especially so when it is possible for it to rise up again, after acquiring a record of what it saw and experienced in the sensible world and, therefore, having learned what it is like to be in the intelligible world, and by the comparison of what are in a way opposites, in a way learning more clearly of the better.

15   For the experience of evil results in a clearer knowledge of the Good in those whose power is too weak to attain knowledge of evil prior to experiencing it.[66] And just as the intellectual procession is a descent into the limits of that which is worst—for it is not feasible to ascend to what transcends it[67]—it must, then, because it is activating itself from

20   itself and is not able to remain in itself, proceed as far as soul by what is indeed a necessary law of nature[68]—that being its goal—hand over to soul that which comes next to it before ascending again,[69] such also is the activity of soul; one part is that which comes after it, namely, the contents of this world, while the other part is the contemplation of the Beings that are prior to it.

25   For some souls such an experience takes place little by little, and in a temporal sequence, and their reversion toward the better takes place in a milieu which is worse, while for that which we call the soul of the universe there has never actually come about an involvement in what is worse, but from a position unaffected by evils it is able to observe by contemplation the things that are below it, while remaining constantly in touch with what precedes it.

30   In fact, the two things are possible at the same time: that the soul should be in receipt of what comes from the intelligible world, while ministering to the needs of the sensible world, because there is no way that, being a soul, it can escape contact with these beings, too.

---

63. Cf. 3.3.3.9–19; 4.4.3.11–12.
64. See Pl., *Phdr.* 230A6.
65. Cf. *supra* 4.5–6.
66. See Pl., *Tht.* 149C1–2.
67. See Pl., *Rep.* 6.509B9.
68. Cf. 5.2.1.17–18; 6.2.22.23–32.
69. That is, governance of bodies.

§4.8.8. And if, against the general run of belief, one is to venture to express more clearly one's own view, the fact is that even our own soul does not descend in its entirety, but there is something of it always in the intelligible world.[70] However, if that part which is in the sensible world becomes dominant, or rather if it is dominated and subjected to disturbance, it does not permit there to be self-awareness[71] in us of   5
that of which the upper part of the soul is in contemplation. For that which is the object of intellection by the upper part only impinges on us when, in its descent, it reaches our self-awareness; it is not the case, after all, that we take cognizance of everything which happens in every part of the soul, before it comes to the whole soul; as, for example, an appetite that remains in the soul's faculty of appetite is not cognized   10
by us, except when we come to grasp it with the internal power of self-awareness, or with that of our discursive thinking, or both.

For every soul possesses an element which inclines downward toward body, and another which inclines upward toward Intellect. Now the universal soul or the soul of the universe[72] imposes order upon the whole universe with that part of it which inclines toward body while remaining above it free from any effort, because it does not   15
have to employ calculative reasoning as do we, but rather intellect, in order to administer what is below it as a whole—even as they say, 'craft does not deliberate'.[73]

Souls, on the other hand, which are particular and preside over a part, while they, too, possess a transcendent element, are yet very much taken up with sense-perception, and with the faculty of apprehension apprehend much that is unnatural and painful and disturbing,   20
inasmuch as the part that they are concerned with is both defective and beset on all sides by alien forces, while having at the same time many things that it aspires to; it is steeped in pleasure, and pleasure is its snare. The other soul is exempt from such fleeting pleasures, and its way of life is concordant with its abode.[74]

---

70. Cf. 2.9.2.5; 3.4.3.24–27; 4.3.12.1–3; 5.1.10.13–19; 6.4.14.16–22; 6.7.5.26.
71. The term αἴσθησις here seems to be used synonymously with the term συναίσθησις, 'awareness' and is translated accordingly.
72. Here Plotinus again seems intentionally to blur the distinction between the hypostasis Soul and the soul of the universe.
73. See Ar., *Phys.* 2.8.199b28. The syntax here is obscure, and probably corrupt, but this seems to be the sense.
74. See Ar., *Meta.* 12.7.1072b14–15.

5.1 (10)

On the Three Primary Hypostases

Introduction

The present treatise is, in a way, a continuation of the chronologically previous treatise 6.9 (9) 'On the Good or the One'. Given the perfection of the first principle of all, the question may be raised as to why there is any separation from it, including the separation of embodied souls. This treatise attempts to answer that question by situating the embodied lives of individuals into the larger metaphysical framework. This framework is a hierarchy of principles, beginning with the One, followed by the Intellect, and then Soul. Plotinus aims to show how from the unqualifiedly simple first principle of all anything non-simple can arise and how the process of unfolding or emanating is one of increasing complexity or ontological separation from the One. Here Plotinus also argues that his systematic representation of Plato's philosophy is accurate.

Summary

§1. Souls are separated from their father. The means of reconciliation are twofold: cultivation of disdain for that which is contaminated with matter and a technique for the recollection of one's authentic heritage. The need for self-knowledge in order to know this.

§2. The familial relation between the individual soul and the soul of the cosmos. Soul is the source of the life and motion of all things.

§3. Soul is an image of Intellect, the intelligible matter for the form that is an expressed principle of Intellect.

§4. The paradigmatic status of Intellect, containing all intelligible reality. The identity of Intellect and Forms.

§5. The absolutely simple One is above Intellect and is its cause. Number is generated by the operation of the One on the Indefinite Dyad, which is inchoate Intellect.

§6. How the One produces Intellect without itself changing. How Intellect reverts to the One and in so doing thinks all intelligibles and generates Soul.

§7. Intellect is like the One but not vice versa. The complete transcendence of the One. The generation of Soul by Intellect is the last generation within intelligible reality.

§8. The Platonic provenance of the three hypostases. Parmenidean antecedents and the superiority of the account of Parmenides in the dialogue of that name.

§9. The contributions of Anaxagoras, Heraclitus, Empedocles, and Aristotle to the doctrine of three hypostases.

§10. In what way the three hypostases are in us. The need to separate from the body.

§11. It is owing to the presence of Intellect that the embodied soul can think and with the presence of Intellect comes the One, its cause.

§12. The need to turn from the exterior to the interior and to ascend to the intelligible world.

---

§5.1.1. What can it be, therefore,[1] that has made the souls forget the god who is their father[2] and be ignorant of themselves and him even though they are parts of the intelligible world and completely belong to it?

The starting point for their evil[3] is, then, audacity, generation, primary difference,[4] and their willing that they belong to themselves.[5]   5
Since they appeared actually to take pleasure in their autonomy, and to have made much use of their self-motion, running in the opposite direction and getting as far away from home as possible, they came not to know even that they themselves were from the intelligible world. They were like children who at birth are separated from their fathers   10
and, being raised for a long time far away, are ignorant both of themselves and of their fathers. They can, then, no longer see their father or themselves, and they dishonor themselves, due to their ignorance of their lineage, honoring instead other things, in fact, everything more than themselves. They marvel at these things and are awestruck by them; they love them and are dependent on them; they severed them-   15
selves as much as possible from the things from which they turned away and which they dishonored.

---

1. Indicating a continuation of the line of thought in the previous treatise, 6.9 (9).

2. Probably a reference to Intellect, not to the One. Cf. 6.9.5.10–15.

3. The word κακόν, translated throughout as 'evil,' here has a connotation that extends beyond the moral to include all 'badness'.

4. I.e., the difference from the 'father' that results from 'willing that they belong to themselves'. Cf. 3.7.11.15; 4.8.4.11.

5. Cf. 4.4.3.1–3; 4.7.13.9–13; 4.8.4.13–18; 4.8.5.28; 6.9.8.31–32. See Pl., *Phdr.* 248D1–2; *Tim.* 41E3.

So, it follows that it is honoring these things and [thereby] dishonoring themselves that is the cause of their absolute ignorance of god. For to pursue and marvel at something is at the same time to accept that one is inferior to that which one is pursuing and to that at which one is marveling. If one supposes oneself inferior to things that come

20 to be and perish and assumes oneself to be the most dishonored and mortal of the things one does honor, neither the nature nor the power of god could ever 'be impressed in one's heart'.[6]

For this reason, the way of arguing with those so disposed should be twofold—that is, if one is indeed going to turn them around in the opposite direction and toward the things that are primary and lead

25 them up to that which is highest or first, that is, the One. What, then, are the two ways?

The first is to show how the things now honored by the soul are in fact dishonorable; we will discuss this further elsewhere.[7] The second is to teach the soul to remember the sort of lineage it has and what its worth is—a line of reasoning that is prior to the other one and, once it is clear, makes that other one evident, too. This is what needs to

30 be spoken of now; it is close to what we are seeking and provides the groundwork for it. For what is doing the seeking is a soul, and it ought to know what it is that is doing the seeking, so that it should first of all learn about itself; whether it has the ability for seeking such things, whether it has the right sort of 'eye' that is able to see,[8] and whether it is fitting for it to seek these things. For if the things sought are alien to it,

35 why should it seek them? But if they are of the same lineage, it is fitting for it to seek them, and it is possible to find that which it is seeking.[9]

§5.1.2.[10] So, let every soul first consider that soul itself[11] made all living beings by breathing life into them, those that are nourished by the earth and the sea, those in the air, and the divine stars in heaven.

5 Soul itself made the sun and this great heaven, and it made it a cosmos, and makes it circulate in a regular way, being a nature different from that which it puts in order, from that which it moves, and from that which it makes to be alive.[12] And it is necessarily more honorable than

---

6. See Homer, *Il.* 15.566.
7. It is difficult to know exactly what, if any, texts Plotinus is alluding to. 2.4, 3.4, 3.6, and 6.4 have all been suggested.
8. Pl. [?], *Alc.* 1.133B–C; *Rep.* 7.533D2; *Soph.* 254A10.
9. See Pl., *Tim.* 35A ff. See also *Phd.* 79D3; *Rep.* 3.409B4, 10.611E1–2; *Lg.* 899D7.
10. See Appendix II I.
11. See Pl., *Tim.* 39E10–40A2. The soul of the cosmos is meant.
12. See Pl., *Phdr.* 246B6–7; *Lg.* 896E8–897A1.

these, since while these are generated and destroyed whenever soul departs from them or supplies them with life, soul itself exists forever by 'not departing from itself'.[13]

As for the actual manner in which it supplies life to the whole uni- 10
verse[14] and to each individual, this is how soul should reckon the matter: let it consider the great soul,[15] as being itself another soul of no small value having already been released from deception, and from the things that have enchanted other souls, and that it is in a state of tranquility. Let not only its encompassing body and its surging waves 15
be tranquil, but all that surrounds it;[16] let the earth be tranquil, the sea and the air be tranquil, and heaven itself, its better part.[17] Let this soul, then, think of the great soul as, in a way, flowing or pouring everywhere into immobile[18] heaven from 'outside',[19] inhabiting and completely illuminating it. Just as rays from the sun light up a dark cloud, make it 20
shine, and give it a golden appearance, so soul entered into the body of heaven and gave it life, gave it immortality, and wakened it from sleep.

And heaven, moved with an everlasting motion by the 'wise guidance'[20] of soul, became 'a happy living being',[21] and acquired its value 25
from soul's dwelling within it, before which it was a dead body, mere earth and water, or rather the darkness of matter or non-being[22] and 'that which the gods hate', as the poet says.[23] The power and nature of soul would be more apparent, or clearer, if one were to reflect here on how soul encompasses and directs heaven by its own acts of will. For 30
soul has given itself to the entire extent of heaven, however much that is, and every interval both great and small is ensouled, even as one body lies apart from another, one here and one there, some separated by the contraries of which they are composed, and some separated in other ways.

The soul is, however, not like that, and it does not make something 35
alive by a part of itself being broken up and put into each individual, but all things are alive by the whole of it, and all soul, being the same

---

13. Cf. 4.7.9.6–13. See *Phdr.* 245C5–246A2; *Phd.* 105C9–107A1.

14. See Pl., *Tim.* 30B5, 31B2–3.

15. I.e., the soul of the cosmos.

16. See Pl., *Tim.* 43B5.

17. Presumably, 'the better part' is the soul.

18. Correcting ἑστῶσα to ἑστῶτα as per HS[4].

19. See Pl., *Tim.* 36E3.

20. Cf. 5.9.3.30–32. See Pl., *Tim.* 30B8, 36E4; *Lg.* 897B7–899B9.

21. See Pl., *Tim.* 34B8.

22. Cf. 1.8.3–5; 2.4.16.3, 11–13.

23. Homer, *Il.* 20.65, said of Hades.

as the father who begat it,[24] is present everywhere in each thing and in
40 everything. And though heaven is multiple and diverse, it is one by the
power of soul, and this cosmos is a god due to this.[25] The sun is also
a god—because it is ensouled—and the other stars; and we, if indeed
anything [is a god], for this reason, 'for corpses are more apt for dis-
posal than dung'.[26]

But the explanation for gods being gods must necessarily be a god
older than they. Our soul is of the same kind, and when you examine
45 it without the accretions, taking it in its 'purified condition',[27] you will
find that it has the identical value that soul was found to have, more
valuable than everything that is corporeal. For all corporeal things
are earth. But even if they were fire, what would be the cause of its
burning? And so, too, for everything composed of these, even if you
add water and air. But if the body is worth pursuing just because it is
50 ensouled, why would one[28] ignore oneself to pursue another? If you
love the soul in another, then love yourself.

§5.1.3.[29] Since the soul is indeed such an honorable and divine
thing, you should by now already be confident in your pursuit of a god
like this, and with this explanation in mind, ascend to him. You will
certainly not have to cast far, 'nor are the intermediary steps many'.[30] So,
5 understand soul's higher 'neighboring region',[31] which is more divine
than the divine soul, after which and from which the soul comes. For
even though soul is the kind of thing shown by the argument, it is an
image of Intellect.[32] Just as spoken words are an expressed principle of
thinking, so, too, Soul is an expressed principle of Intellect,[33] and its
whole activity, and the life which it sends forth to make something else
10 really exist.[34] It is just like fire that has both internal heat and radiant

---

24. Father, Demiurge, and Intellect are here identified. Cf. *infra* 8.5; 2.1.5.5; 2.3.18.15;
5.9.3.26. See Pl., *Tim.* 37C7.
25. Cf. 3.5.6.14–24. See Pl., *Tim.* 92C6–7.
26. See Heraclitus, fr. 22 B 96 DK.
27. Cf. 1.1.10.6; 6.4.14.23. See Pl., *Rep.* 10.611C3–4.
28. Reading τις with HS⁵.
29. See Appendix III A 3.
30. See Homer, *Il.* 1.56.
31. This is Intellect. See Pl., *Lg.* 705A4.
32. Cf. *infra* 7.1; also, 2.9.4.25; 5.3.4.15–21; 5.3.8.45–56; 5.9.3.30–37.
33. Λόγος ('expressed principle') is the manifestation or expression of that which is
hierarchically inferior in relation to that which is superior. The intelligible content of
the higher is maintained in the lower. Cf. 1.2.3.27–30; 4.3.5.8–18.
34. The discursive intellectual part of the embodied soul. Cf. 5.3.4.15–21. See Pl., *Tht.*
189E6–7; *Soph.* 263E3–9; Ar., *AP* 1.10.76b24–25.

heat.[35] But in the intelligible world, one should understand that the internal activity does not flow out of it; rather, one activity remains in it, and the other is that which comes into existence.

Since, then, Soul is derived from Intellect, it is intellectual, and its own intellect is found in its acts of calculative reasoning,[36] and its perfection, too, comes from Intellect, like a father raising a child whom he begat as imperfect in relation to himself. Its real existence, then, comes from Intellect, and its actuality as an expressed principle derived from Intellect occurs when Intellect is seen in it. For whenever Soul looks into Intellect, what it thinks and actualizes are objects that belong to it and come from within itself. And these alone should be called activities of Soul, namely, those that are intellectual and those that belong to it. The inferior activities come from elsewhere, and are states of an inferior soul.[37]

Intellect, then, makes Soul even more divine by being its father and by being present to it. For there is nothing in between them but the fact of their being different, Soul as next in order and as receptive, and Intellect as form. Even the matter of Intellect is beautiful,[38] since it is like Intellect and simple.[39] What Intellect is like, then, is clear from the above, namely, that it is superior to Soul thus described.

§5.1.4.[40] One could also see this from the following. Take someone who starts by marveling at this sensible cosmos, looking at its expanse and its beauty and its everlasting motion and the gods in it, both the visible and the invisible ones, and the daemons, and all the animals and plants; let him then ascend to the archetype of this cosmos and the truer reality, and in the intelligible world let him see all that is intelligible and eternal in it with its own comprehension and life,[41] and 'pure Intellect' presiding over these, and indescribable wisdom, and the life that is truly that under the reign of Kronos, a god of 'fullness'

---

35. Ar., *Meta.* 2.1.993b25.

36. Soul will include both individual souls and the soul of the cosmos. The intellectual activity of these is discursive; that of Intellect itself (and undescended intellects) will be non-discursive. Cf. 4.7.10.32–37.

37. Referring to embodied souls or to their lower parts. Cf. 3.6.4.30–38.

38. I.e., intelligible matter. Cf. *infra* 5.6–9, 13–17; 2.4.2–5; 3.8.11.4; 5.3.8.48. It is also possible that Soul itself is here taken to be the matter for Intellect. Cf. 3.5.7.4–9; 3.9.5.1–3.

39. See Ar., *DA* 3.5.430a10–15.

40. See Appendix II I; III B 1.

41. Cf. 3.7.3.9–17; 5.3.5.31–37; 6.7.17.12–26. See Pl., *Tim.* 37D1, 39E1; *Soph.* 248E6–249A2; Ar., *Meta.* 12.7.1072a26, 1072b20–31, 9.1074b34–35.

and intellect.[42] For it encompasses every immortal within itself, that is, every intellect, every god, every soul, and is always stable.[43] For why should it seek to change from its happy condition?[44] Where could it go, when it has all things within itself? It does not even seek to enlarge itself, since it is absolutely perfect.

15   For this reason, in addition, all the things in it are perfect so as to be perfect in every way, having nothing which is not like this, nothing in it that it does not think and it thinks not by way of inquiring but by having what it thinks.[45] Its blessedness is not acquired; rather, everything is in it eternally, and it is true eternity, which time imitates, moving around it[46] along with Soul, dropping some things and picking up oth-
20 ers. For at the level of Soul, thoughts are always changing; now it thinks of Socrates, now of a horse—always some particular being—whereas Intellect just is everything. It has, then, all Beings stable in it,[47] and it alone is, and the 'is' is always,[48] and the future is nothing to it—for it 'is' then, too—nor is there a past for it—for nothing in the intelligible
25 world has passed away—but all Beings are set within it always inasmuch as they are identical and in a way pleased to be in this condition.

Each of them is Intellect and Being,[49] that is, the totality consists of all Intellect and all Being—Intellect, insofar as it thinks, making Being come to exist, and Being, by its being thought, giving to Intellect its thinking, which is its existence.[50] But the cause of thinking is something else, something that is also the cause of Being:[51] in other words,
30 the cause of both is something else. For those coexist simultaneously and do not abandon each other, but this one thing is nevertheless two: Intellect and Being, thinking and what is being thought—Intellect, insofar as it is thinking, Being insofar as it is what is being thought.[52]

---

42. The fanciful etymology of Κρόνος, κόρος ('fullness') plus νοῦς ('intellect'), comes from Pl., *Crat.* 396B6–7.

43. Cf. 3.7.2.31–33.

44. See Ar., *Meta.* 12.7.1072b22–24, 9.1074b25–27.

45. See Pl., *Tht.* 197B8–10; Ar., *Meta.* 12.7.1072b22–24, 9.1074b25–27.

46. Reading παραθεών with Atkinson. HS⁵ suggests deleting ψυχὴν. Cf. 3.7.11.35–59. See Pl., *Tim.* 37D1–7.

47. Reading in ll. 21–22: ἐν [τῷ] αὐτῷ ἐν τῷ <αἰῶνι> with Atkinson. The whole line is then: ἔχει οὖν ἐν αὐτῷ πάντα ἑστῶτα ἐν τῷ αἰῶνι.

48. See Pl., *Tim.* 37E6.

49. 'Being' refers to the μέγιστον γένος Being and all the intelligibles that share in it as seen from the following lines. Cf. 5.3.5.26ff.; 5.5.3.1; 5.9.5.13; 5.9.8.2–4; 6.7.41.12. See Pl., *Soph.* 254B–D.

50. Cf. 5.5.1.51–58; 5.3.5.18–25; 5.9.5.1–8, 12–13.

51. I.e., the One. Cf. 6.7.16.22–31.

52. Cf. 5.3.1.1–12, 5.1–3; 6.7.1.7–9, 12–13, 39.12–13.

For thinking could not occur if there was not Difference as well as Identity.

Intellect, then, becomes these first: Being, Difference, and Identity.   35
And one should include Motion and Stability—Motion if Intellect is thinking, and Stability so that it remains the identical thing.[53] There must be Difference, so that there can be both thinking and what is being thought; in fact, if you were to remove Difference, it would become one and fall silent. It also must be that things that are thought are different from each other.[54] There must also be Identity, since Intellect is one   40
with itself, that is, there is a certain commonality in[55] all its objects, but 'differentiation is Difference'.[56] And in becoming many, they produce Number and quantity, and quality is the unique character of each of these, and from these as principles all the other things arise.[57]

§5.1.5. The god, then, who is above Soul is multiple, and it is possible for Soul to exist within this, connected to it, so long as it does not want to be 'separated' from it.[58] When it, then, approaches Intellect and in a way becomes one with it, it seeks to know who it is that produced it.[59] It is that which is simple and prior to this multiplicity, which is the   5
cause of this god's existence and its being multiple;[60] it is the producer of Number. For Number is not primary.

Before the Dyad is the One; the Dyad is second and, having come from the One, the One imposes definiteness on it, whereas it is in itself indefinite.[61] When it has been made definite, it is henceforth Number, Number as Substance.[62] Soul, too, is Number;[63] for the first things are   10
neither masses nor magnitudes. The things that have thickness, those

---

53. Cf. 6.2.7–8. See Pl., *Soph.* 254D4–5, 254E5–255A1; *Parm.* 145E. On the motion of Intellect, cf. 6.7.13.16. See Pl., *Lg.* 897D3.
54. Cf. 5.3.10.30–32, 40–42.
55. Reading ἐν in line 40 with Kirchhoff, not ἕν with HS².
56. See Ar., *Meta.* 4.2.1004a21, 9.1018a12–13.
57. Cf. 6.2.21.11–32. See Pl., *Parm.* 142D1–143A3.
58. See Pl., *Parm.* 144B2.
59. Reading ζητεῖ in l. 3 with the mss followed by a comma with HS⁵.
60. Cf. 3.8.9.3; 5.3.16.10–16.
61. Cf. 5.4.2.4–10; 6.6.3.12–15 for the identification of the Indefinite Dyad with Intellect in its initial 'phase' as derived from the One. That the One imposes definiteness does not mean that it itself is definite. Cf. 5.2.1.7–13; 5.3.11.1–12; 6.7.16.13–22, 17.15–16.
62. Cf. 5.4.2.7–8; 5.5.4.16–17; 6.6.1.1–2. See Ar., *Meta.* 1.6.987b14; 13.7.1081a14; Alex. Aphr., *In Meta.* 55.20–56.35. Substantial Numbers (i.e., Form-Numbers) are different from quantiative numbers.
63. Cf. 6.6.16.44–45. See Xenocrates, fr. 60 Heinze.

things that sense-perception takes to be beings, come later. Nor is it the moist part in seeds that is valuable, but the part that is not seen. This is number and an expressed principle.⁶⁴ What are, then, called Number and the Dyad in the intelligible world are expressed principles

15   and Intellect. But whereas the Dyad, understood as a sort of substrate, is indefinite,⁶⁵ each Number that comes from it and the One is a Form, Intellect in a way having been shaped by the Forms that come to be in it.⁶⁶ In one manner, it is shaped by the One, and in another by itself, as in the way the power of sight is actualized.⁶⁷ For intellection is a vision in which seeing and what is seen are one.⁶⁸

§5.1.6. How, then, does Intellect see, and what does it see, and how in general did it get to exist or come to be from the One in such a way that it can see? For the soul now grasps that these things must of necessity be, but in addition it longs to grasp the answer to the question much discussed indeed among the ancient wise men, too, of

5   how from a unity, such as we say the One is, anything acquired real existence, whether multiplicity or duality or number;⁶⁹ why it did not remain by itself, but why instead such a multiplicity flowed from it—a multiplicity which, though seen among Beings, we judge appropriate to refer back to it.

Let us speak of this matter, then, in the following manner, calling
10   to god himself, not with spoken words, but by stretching our arms in prayer to him in our soul, in this way being able to pray as solitary to him who is solitary.⁷⁰ So, since god is by himself, as if inside a temple, remaining tranquil while transcending everything,⁷¹ the contemplator should contemplate the statues which are in a way fixed outside the
15   temple already—or rather the first statue displayed, revealed to sight in the following manner.

It must be that for everything in motion there is something toward which it moves.⁷² Since the One has nothing toward which it moves, let us not suppose that it is moving. But if something comes to be after

64. Cf. 3.8.2.20–30; 6.7.11.17–28.
65. Cf. 2.4.5.22–23; 5.4.2.7–8. See Ar., *Meta.* 13.7.1081a14–5.
66. Cf. *infra* 7.5–18.
67. Cf. 3.8.11.1–8; 5.2.1.7–13; 5.3.11.4–6; 6.7.15.21–22, 16.10–13. See Ar., *DA* 3.2.426a13–4; 3.3.428a6–7.
68. See Ar., *Meta.* 12.9.1074b29–1075a10.
69. Cf. 5.2.1.3–5; 5.9.14.2–6.
70. Cf. 1.6.7.9; 6.7.34.7–8; 6.9.11.51.
71. Cf. 5.5.6.9–13. See Pl., *Rep.* 6.509B9.
72. See Ar., *Phys.* 4.11.219a10–11; 5.1.224b1–10.

it, it has necessarily come to be by being eternally turned toward it [the One].[73] Let the sort of coming to be that is in time not get in our way,   20
since our discussion is concerned with things that are eternal. When in our discussion we attribute 'coming to be' to them, we are doing so in order to give their causal order.[74] We should say, then, that that which comes to be from the One in the intelligible world does so without the One being moved. For if something came to be as a result of its having moved, then that which came to be would be third in line from it,   25
after the motion, and not second. It must be, then, that if something was second in line from it, that thing came to exist while the One was unmoved, neither inclining, nor having willed anything, nor moving in any way.[75]

How, then, does this happen, and what should we think about what is near to the One while it reposes? A radiation of light comes from it, though it reposes, like the light from the sun, in a way encircling it,   30
eternally coming from it while it reposes. And all beings, so long as they persist, necessarily, due to the power present in them, produce from their own substantiality a real, though dependent, existent around themselves directed to their exterior, a sort of image of the archetypes from which it was generated.[76] Fire produces the heat that comes from it, and snow does not only hold its coldness inside itself. Perfumes   35
especially witness to this, for so long as they exist, something flows from them around them, the existence of which a bystander enjoys. Further, all things, as soon as they are perfected, generate.[77] That which is always perfect always generates something everlasting, and it generates something inferior to itself.

What, then, must we say about that which is most perfect? Nothing   40
can come from it except what is next greatest after it. And the greatest thing after it, the second greatest thing, is Intellect. For Intellect sees the One and is in need of it alone. But the One has no need of Intellect. And that which is generated from something greater than Intellect is Intellect;[78] and Intellect is greater than all other things, because other

---

73. Reading αὐτὸ with Atkinson instead of αὐτὸ ('itself') in HS. With the latter, the end of the sentence reads 'while that [the One] is always turned toward itself'. In support of the former, cf. *supra* 5.17–19 and *infra* 7.5–18; for the latter, cf. 6.8.8.11–13; 6.8.15.1.
74. Reading αἰτίας <τι> τάξεως αὐτοῖς ἀποδώσειν with Atkinson thus enabling us to understand αἰτίας as genitive singular.
75. Cf. 5.3.12.28–31.
76. Cf. 4.6.8.8–12; 5.3.7.23–24; 5.45.2.27–33; 6.7.18.5–6; 6.7.21.4–6; 6.7.40.21–24.
77. See Ar., *DA* 2.4.415a26–28.
78. Cf. 5.3.16.10–16; 5.5.9.9–10; 6.8.18.3.

45   things come after it. For example, Soul is an expressed principle derived from Intellect and a certain activity, just as Intellect is an activity of the One. But Soul's expressed principle is murky, for it is a reflection of Intellect and, due to this, it must look to Intellect. Similarly, Intellect has to look to the One, so that it can be Intellect. It sees it not as having been separated from it, but because it comes after it and there is nothing in between, as there is nothing in between Soul and Intellect.

50   Everything longs for that which generated it and loves this, especially when there is just generator and that which is generated. And 'whenever what is best is the generator',[79] that which is generated must necessarily be found with it, since they are only separated by being different.

§5.1.7. We are saying that Intellect is an image of the One,[80] first—for we should express ourselves more clearly—because that which is produced must somehow be the One and preserve many of its properties, that is, be the same as it, just like the light that comes

5   from the sun. But the One is not Intellect. How, then, does it generate Intellect?

In fact, by its reversion to it, Intellect saw the One, and this seeing is Intellect.[81] For that which grasps anything other than itself is either[82] sense-perception or intellect. Sense-perception is a line, etc.[83] But the circle is the sort of thing that can be divided, and Intellect is not like that.

10   In fact, there is unity here, but the One is the productive power of all things.[84] Intellection observes those things of which the One is the productive power, in a way cutting itself off from that power. Otherwise, it would not have become Intellect—since as soon as it is generated, it has from itself, in a way, its self-awareness of this power, the power to produce Substance. For Intellect, by means of itself, also defines its own existence by the power that comes from the One.[85]

15   And, because it is, in a way, a unitary part of what belongs to the One and is the Substance that comes from it, it is strengthened by it and brought to perfection as Substance by it and as derived from it. It

---

79. See Ar., *Meta.* 14.4.1091b10.

80. Cf. *supra* 6.30–34, 43–46; 5.4.2.25–26.

81. Cf. 5.3.11.1–5, 9–13; 6.7.15.12–14.

82. Reading ἣ as per HS⁴.

83. I.e., sense-perception is comparable to a line, Intellect to a circle, and the One to the center of the circle. The text of this line, αἴσθησιν γραμμὴν καὶ τὰ ἄλλα is taken by HS² as corrupt.

84. Cf. 3.8.10.1; 4.8.6.11; 5.3.15.31; 5.4.1.23–26, 2.38; 6.7.32.31; 6.9.5.36–37.

85. With the puncuation from HS⁵. Cf. 6.7.15.18–22.

sees what is in the intelligible world within itself, a sort of division of the indivisible, and is life and thinking and all things, none of which the One is.[86]

For in this way everything comes from it, because it is not constrained by some shape, for it is one alone. If it were everything, it 20 would be among the Beings. This is why the One is none of the Beings in Intellect, although everything comes from it.[87] For this reason, these things are Substances, for each has already been defined, and each has a sort of shape. Being should not be suspended, in a way, in the indefinite, but fixed by definition and stability. Stability among intelligibles is 25 definition and shape, by means of which they acquire real existence.[88]

'This is the lineage'[89] of this Intellect, worthy of the purest Intellect, born from nowhere else than from the first principle, and, having been generated, at once generating all Beings which are with itself,[90] both all the beauty of the Ideas and all the intelligible gods. And it is full of the 30 Beings it has generated and, in a way, swallows them again by having them in itself and neither letting them fall into matter nor be reared by Rhea[91]—as the mysteries and myths about the gods enigmatically say that Kronos, the wisest god, before the birth of Zeus, holds back 35 in himself what he generates, so that he is full and is like Intellect in satiety.

After this, so they say, being already sated, he generates Zeus, for Intellect, being perfect, generates Soul. For since it is perfect, it had to generate and since it was such a great power, it could not be barren. That which was generated by it could, in this case as well, not be superior to it but had to be an inferior reflection of it, first similarly 40 undefined, and then defined and made a kind of image by that which generated it. The offspring of Intellect is an expressed principle and a real existent, that which thinks discursively.[92] This is what moves around Intellect and is a light and trace of Intellect,[93] dependent on it, on one side attached to Intellect and filled up with it and enjoying it 45 and sharing in it and thinking, and on the other side, attached to the things that came after it, or rather itself generating what is necessarily

86. Cf. 5.2.1.5–7; 6.9.3.36–40.
87. Cf. 3.8.9.40; 6.9.2.44–45.
88. Cf. 5.5.6.1–13. See Pl., *Parm.* 142B5–6.
89. See Pl., *Rep.* 8.547A4–5, quoting Homer, *Il.* 6.211.
90. Cf. 5.2.1.11–13; 6.7.17.33–34. Intellect is itself actualized when it is cognitively identical with all Being.
91. The wife of Kronos.
92. Referring to Soul and individual souls. Cf. 4.3.5.9–11.
93. Cf. 5.3.9.15–17; 5.5.5.14; 6.8.18.15, 23.

inferior to Soul. These matters should be discussed later.[94] This is as far as the divine Beings go.

§5.1.8.[95] And it is also because of this that we get Plato's threefold division: the things 'around the king of all'—he says this, meaning the primary things—'second around the secondary things,' and 'third
5   around the tertiary things'.[96] And he says 'father of the cause'[97] meaning by 'cause' Intellect.[98] For the Intellect is his Demiurge. And he says that the Demiurge makes the Soul in that 'mixing bowl'.[99] And since the Intellect is cause, he means by 'father' the Good, or that which transcends Intellect and 'transcends Substantiality'.[100] Often he calls Being and the Intellect 'Idea',[101] which shows that Plato understood
10   that the Intellect comes from the Good, and the Soul comes from the Intellect. And these statements of ours are not new nor even recent, but rather were made a long time ago, though not explicitly. The things we are saying now comprise exegeses of those, relying on the writings of Plato himself as evidence that these are ancient views.[102]
15   Parmenides previously touched on this doctrine to the extent that he identified Being and Intellect, that is, he did not place Being among sensibles, saying 'for thinking and Existence are identical'.[103] And he says that Being is 'immobile',[104] though he does attach thinking to it,
20   eliminating all corporeal motion from it so that it would remain as it is, likening it to a 'spherical mass',[105] because it encompasses all things and because thinking is not external to it, but rather within itself. Saying that it was 'one' in his own writings,[106] he got blamed for saying that this one thing was found to be many.[107]

---

94. No particular treatise is clearly indicated here. 2.4 is the most likely possibility.
95. See Appendix I B; II E; II F; II J.
96. See Pl. [?], *2nd Ep.* 312E1–4.
97. Cf. 6.8.14.37–38. See Pl. [?], *6th Ep.* 323D4.
98. See Pl., *Phd.* 97C1–2, quoting Anaxagoras fr. 59 B 12 DK. Also, *Tim.* 39B7, 47E4; *Phil.* 30C6–D8; *Rep.* 6.507C7–8, 530A6; *Soph.* 265C4; *Sts.* 270A5.
99. See Pl., *Tim.* 34B3–35B7, 41D4–5.
100. Cf. 5.3.17.13–14; 5.4.1.10; 5.6.6.30; 6.7.40.26; 6.9.11.42. See Pl., *Rep.* 6.509B8–9; Ar. *apud* Simplicius, *In DC* 485.22 (= fr. 1, p. 57 Ross).
101. See Pl., *Rep.* 6.507B5–10; *Soph.* 246B6–7.
102. Cf. 3.7.1.8–16.
103. Cf. 1.4.10.6; 3.8.8.8; 5.1.8.17–18; 5.6.6.22–23; 5.9.5.29–30; 6.7.41.18. See Parmenides, fr. 28 B 3 DK.
104. See Parmenides, fr. 28 B 8, 26 DK.
105. Parmenides, fr. 28 B 8, 43 DK.
106. Parmenides, fr. 28 B 8, 6 DK.
107. See Pl., *Soph.* 245A5–B1.

Plato's *Parmenides* speaks more accurately when he distinguishes   25
from among each other the primary One, which is one in a more
proper sense, a second one, which he calls 'one-many', and a third one,
'one and many'.[108] In this way, too, he is in harmony with our account of
the three natures.

§5.1.9.[109] Anaxagoras, too, in saying that 'Intellect is pure and
unmixed', is himself positing the first principle as simple and the One
as separate, although he neglects to give an accurate account due to
his antiquity.[110] In addition, Heraclitus knew the One to be everlasting
and intelligible, since bodies are always coming into being and are 'in   5
flux'.[111] And for Empedocles, 'Strife' divides and 'Love' is the One—he
himself makes this incorporeal, too—and the elements are posited as
matter.[112]

Aristotle later said that the first principle was 'separate'[113] and 'intelligible',[114] but when he says that 'it thinks itself',[115] he no longer makes
it the first principle.[116] Further, he makes many other things intelligi-   10
ble—as many as there are spheres in heaven, so that each intelligible
moves each sphere[117]—but by doing so he describes intelligibles in a
way different from Plato, proposing an argument from plausibility,
since he did not have an argument from necessity. One might pause
to consider whether it is even plausible, for it is more plausible that all
the spheres, contributing to one system, should look to one thing that
is the first principle.

And one might inquire if the many intelligibles are, according to   15
him, derived from one first principle, or whether he holds that there
are many principles among the intelligibles.[118] And if they are derived

---

108. Cf. 4.8.3.10; 5.3.15.10–22; 5.4.1.20–21; 6.7.14.1–18 on Intellect as one-many. See
Pl., *Parm.* 137C–142A, 144E5, 155E5.

109. See Appendix I C; I D; III B 1.

110. See Anaxagoras, fr. 59 B 12 DK, which Plotinus is quoting inexactly; Pl., *Phd.*
97B8–C2; Ar., *Meta.* 1.3.984B15–19.

111. See Heraclitus, fr. 22 A 1 DK; Pl., *Tht.* 152D2–E9, 179D6–183B5; *Crat.* 402A4–
C3, 439B10–440E2; Ar., *Meta.* 1.6.987a33–34.

112. Cf. 4.4.40.5–6; 6.7.14.19–20. See Empedocles, fr. 31 B 17.7–8 DK (= 26.5–6); Ar.,
Meta. 1.8.989a20–21; 12.10.1075b3.

113. See Ar., *DA* 3.430a17; *Meta.* 12.7.1073a4.

114. See Ar., *Meta.* 12.7.1072a26.

115. See Ar., *Meta.* 12.7.1072b20.

116. Supplying the negative οὐ, which is missing from HS². Cf. *supra* 4.31–33, 37–39;
5.6; 6.7.37–41.

117. See Ar., *Meta.* 12.8.1073a28–b1.

118. See Ar., *Meta.* 12.7.1072a23–26, 1072b14, 1074a36–38, 10.1074a36–38.

from one, it will be clear that it is analogous to the way that, among sensibles, one sphere encompasses another until you reach the outermost one that is dominant. So, in the intelligible world what is first will
20   also encompass everything, that is, there will be an intelligible cosmos. And just as in the sensible world the spheres are not empty, but the first is full of stars, and the others also have stars, so, too, in the intelligible world the movers will have many things within themselves, and the truer Beings will be there. But if each one is a principle, the principles will be an arbitrary collection.

And what will be the explanation for their functioning together[119]
25   and agreeing on a single task, namely, the concord of the entire universe? How can there be equality in number of the sensible spheres in heaven in relation to the intelligibles or movers? And how can these incorporeals be many in this way, without matter to separate them?[120]

So, among the ancients, those who adhered most closely to the doc-
30   trines of Pythagoras and his followers, and to those of Pherecydes, held to this account of the nature of things. But some of them worked out this view among themselves in their own writings, while some did not do so in writings but demonstrated it in unwritten discussions[121] or altogether left it alone.

§5.1.10.[122] It has already been shown that it is necessary to believe that things are this way: that there is the One which transcends Being, which is such as the argument strove to show to the extent that it is possible to demonstrate anything about these matters; that next in line is Being and Intellect; and that third is the nature that is Soul.[123]
5   And just as in nature these aforementioned three are found, so it is necessary to believe as well that these are in us. I do not mean that they are among sensibles—for these three are separate from sensibles—but that they are in things that are outside the sensible order, using the term 'outside' in the same manner in which it is used to refer to those things that are outside the whole of heaven. In saying that they belong
10   to a human being, I mean exactly what Plato means by 'the inner human being'.[124]

---

119. Reading συνεργήσει in l. 24 with Harder.
120. Cf. 2.4.4.2–7, 14–17. See Ar., *Meta.* 12.8.1074a31; 14.2.1088b14–28.
121. Probably a reference to Plato's 'unwritten teachings'. See Ar., *Phys.* 4.2.209b11–17, the only explicit reference to such teachings.
122. See Appendix II B; III A 2.
123. Cf. *supra* 3.1–16; 4.26–30; 6.12–41.
124. Cf. 4.8.1.1–11. See Pl., *Rep.* 9.589A7–B1.

So, our soul is something divine and of another nature [i.e., other than sensibles], like the nature of all soul; it is perfect by having intellect. One part of intellect is that which engages in calculative reasoning and one part is that which makes calculative reasoning possible.[125] The calculative reasoning part of soul is actually in need of no corporeal organ for its calculative reasoning,[126] having its own activity in purity in order that it also be possible for it to reason purely. Someone who supposed it to be separate and not mixed with body and in the primary intelligible world would not be mistaken. For we should not search for a place in which to situate it; rather, we should make it outside all place. For this is how it is for that which is by itself, outside and immaterial, whenever it is alone, retaining nothing from the nature of the body. Because of this, Plato says that the Demiurge 'in addition' encircled the soul of the universe from 'outside', pointing to the part of the soul that abides in the intelligible world.[127] In our case, he hid his meaning when he said that it is 'at the top of our head'.[128]

And his exhortation 'to be separate'[129] is not meant spatially—for our intellect is separate by nature—but is an exhortation not to incline to the body even by acts of imagination, and to alienate ourselves from the body, if somehow one could lead the remaining part of the soul upward, or even carry upward that which is situated in the sensible world, that part that alone acts demiurgically on the body and has the job of shaping it and caring for it.[130]

§5.1.11. Since, then, there is soul that engages in calculative reasoning about just and beautiful things, that is, calculative reasoning that seeks to know if this is just or if this is beautiful, it is necessary that there exist permanently something that is just, from which the calculative reasoning in the soul arises.[131] How else could it engage in calculative reasoning? And if soul sometimes engages in calculative reasoning about these things and sometimes does not, there must be Intellect that does not engage in calculative reasoning, but always possesses Justice, and there must be also the principle of Intellect and

---

125. Cf. *supra* 3.13. The distinction is between intellect in us and Intellect.

126. See Ar., *DA* 3.4.429a24–27; Alex. Aphr., *De an.* 84.10–12.

127. Cf. 2.9.2.5; 3.4.3.24–27; 4.3.121.1–3; 4.8.8.2–3; 6.4.14.16–22; 6.7.5.26. See Pl., *Tim.* 34B4, 36D9–E1.

128. See Pl., *Tim.* 90A5.

129. Cf. 1.8.6.10–12. See Pl., *Phd.* 67C6, 79C2–D7, 83A3–B4.

130. Cf. 1.1.3.21–25. See Pl. [?], *Epin.* 981B7–8.

131. See Pl., *Parm.* 132A1–4.

its cause and god.[132] And it must be indivisible and unchanging; and
10   while not changing place, it is seen in each of the many things that can
receive it, in a way, as something other.[133] Just as the center of the circle
exists in its own right, but each of the points on the circle contains it in
itself, the radii add their unique character to it. For it is by something
like this in ourselves that we are in contact with [the One] and are with
15   it and depend on it. And if we converge on it, we would be settled in
the intelligible world.[134]

§5.1.12. How, then, given that we have such great things in us, do
we not grasp them, but rather are mostly inactive with respect to these
activities; indeed, some people are altogether inactive?

They are always involved with their own activities—I mean, Intel-
5   lect and that which is prior to Intellect and eternally in itself, and Soul
as well, which is thus 'always moving'.[135] For not everything in soul is
immediately sensible, but it comes to us whenever it comes to our
sense-perception.[136] But whenever there is activity that is not being
transmitted to the faculty of sense-perception, it has not yet reached
the entire soul. We do not yet know it, then, inasmuch as we are the
10   whole soul, including the faculty of sense-perception, not just a part of
it. Further, each of the parts of the soul, always alive, is always acting
by itself with its own object. But cognizing occurs whenever transmission, that is, apprehension, occurs.

So, if there is going to be apprehension of things present in this
15   way, then that which is to apprehend must revert inward, and focus
its attention there. Just as if someone were waiting to hear a voice that
he wanted to hear, and, distancing himself from other voices, were to
prick up his ears to hear the best of sounds, waiting for the time when
it will come—so, too, in this case one must let go of sensible sounds,
except insofar as they are necessary, and guard the soul's pure power of
apprehension and be ready to listen to the sounds from above.

132. See Ar., *DA* 3.5.430a22.
133. Cf. 3.8.9.23–26.
134. Cf. 1.6.11.10–12; 5.6.5.1–2; 6.9.8.18–22.
135. See Pl., *Phdr.* 245C5.
136. Cf.1.1.11.2–8; 4.3.30.15–16; 4.8.8.6–7; 4.9.2.13–22.

ON THE GENERATION AND ORDER OF THE THINGS WHICH COME AFTER THE FIRST

Introduction

This brief treatise is a sort of appendix to the previous one, treating of the continuity of the three hypostastes. Plotinus here wants to show that the hierarchy beginning with the One and ending with the souls of plants is continuous, meaning primarily that there is nothing that could be that is not and that there could not be another arrangement of the hierarchy from first to last. The threefold principle of generation within the hierarchy is the stability of the higher, its procession to the lower, and the reversion of the lower to the higher.

Summary

§1. The One is all things and no thing. How Intellect comes from the One and Soul from Intellect. How from Soul come individual souls including the lowest types of souls, those of plants.

§2. The superiority of the higher to the lower. The hierarchy of psychical powers from rational beings to animals to plants.

§5.2.1. The One is all things and is not one thing.[1] For it is the principle of all things,[2] but is not those things, though all things are like it, for they did, in a way, find their way back to the intelligible world, or rather they are not there yet but will be.

How, then, do they arise out of a simple One, given that there is neither apparent variegation nor any doubleness whatsoever in that which is self-identical?[3]

In fact, it is because there was nothing in it that all things came from it; and, in order that Being should exist, it is itself not Being, but the generator of it. Indeed, this is, in a way, the first act of generation. Since it is perfect, due to its neither seeking anything, nor having anything, nor needing anything, it in a way overflows and its superabundance

5

---

1. Cf. 3.8.9.39–54; 3.9.4.3–9; 5.3.11.14–21, 13.2–3; 5.4.2.39–42. See Pl., *Parm.* 160B2–3.
2. Cf. 6.8.8.8–9.
3. Cf. 5.1.6.3–8; 5.4.1.23–28.

10   has made something else.[4] That which was generated reverted to it and
was filled up and became what it is by looking at it, and this is Intellect.
The positioning of it in relation to the One produced Being; its gazing
upon the One produced Intellect. Since, then, it positions itself in relation to the One in order that it may see, it becomes Intellect and Being
at the same time. Intellect, then, being in a way the One[5] and pouring
15   forth abundant power, produces things that are the same as it—Intellect is, after all, an image of the One—just as that which is prior to it in
turn pours forth.

And this activity, arising from the Substantiality of Intellect, belongs
to Soul, which becomes this while Intellect remains still. For Intellect
also came to be while that which was before it remained still.[6] But Soul
does not remain still when it produces; rather, being moved, it generated a reflection of itself. It looked to the intelligible world from where
20   it came to be, it was filled up, and it proceeded to another and contrary
motion, generating a reflection of itself, namely, sense-perception and
nature as it is found in plants.[7] Nothing of what is before it is separated
or cut off. For this reason, the Soul from above also seems to extend
down to plants, for Soul does, after all, extend down in a definite man-
25   ner, since there is life in plants. Of course, not all of Soul is in plants,
but it comes to be in them because of the way it is; it advanced all the
way down to them, producing another real existent by its procession
and its desire for what is inferior to it. And since the part of Soul prior
to this was dependent on Intellect, it leaves Intellect alone to remain
by itself.

§5.2.2. There is a procession, then, from the beginning to the end,
in which each thing is left in its own place for eternity, and each thing
that is generated takes a new inferior rank.[8] And yet each one becomes
identical with that upon which it follows, so long as it connects itself
5   with it. Whenever, then, Soul comes to be in a plant, it is like another
part of it, a part that is most audacious and unintelligent, having
proceeded such a long way. And, then, whenever Soul comes to be in a
non-rational animal, the power of sense-perception becomes dominant
and brings it there. But whenever Soul comes to be in a human being,
Soul's motion is either entirely in the faculty of calculative reasoning,

---

4. Cf. 3.8.10.4–19. See Pl., *Rep.* 6.508B6–7.

5. Cf. 6.4.11.16; 6.7.3; 6.7.17.41–42.

6. Cf. 5.1.6.40–46, 7.9–17.

7. Soul generates all psychical functions in living beings other than the higher function of discursive reasoning. Cf. 3.4.1.1–3; 4.4.13.1–8; 5.9.6.20.

8. Cf. 3.8.10.4–19; 4.8.6.10. See Pl., *Tim.* 42E5–6.

or it comes from Intellect, since an individual soul has its own intellect
and a will of its own to think or, generally, to move itself.   10

Let us look into the matter more closely. Whenever someone cuts
off the shoots or the tops of plants, where has the soul of the plant
gone? Where did it come from? For it has not separated itself spatially.
It is, then, in its source. But if you were to cut off or burn the root,
where would the soul in the root go? In the soul, for it has not changed   15
place. It could be in the identical place or in another, if it ran back to
its source. Otherwise, it is in another plant, for it is not constrained
to a place. If it were to go back to its source, it would go back to the
power preceding it. But where is that power? In the power preceding
it. That takes us back to Intellect, not to a place, for Soul was not in
place. And Intellect is even more not in place than Soul, which is not   20
in place either. It is, then, nowhere but in that which is nowhere, and
at the same time it is also everywhere. If it proceeded in this way to the
upper region, it would pause in the middle before arriving altogether
at the highest, and it has a life in a middle position and has rested in
that part of itself.

These things are and are not the One; they are the One, because they   25
are from it; they are not the One, because it endowed them with what
they have while remaining in itself. It is, then, in a way like a long life
stretched far out, each of its parts different from those that come next,
though it makes a continuous whole. The parts are distinguished by
being different one from the other, not because the first is destroyed
with the appearance of the second. What, then, is the soul that comes
to be in plants? Does it generate nothing?   30

In fact, it generates in that in which it is. We should examine how by
taking another starting point.[9]

---

9. Cf. 3.4.1–2; 4.4.22.

5.3 (49)

ON THE KNOWING HYPOSTASIS AND ON THAT WHICH IS TRANSCENDENT

Introduction

In this treatise, Plotinus explores the connection between our embodied intellects and the hypostasis Intellect. Following his own general metaphysical principles, but making extensive use of Peripatetic thought, Plotinus argues that intellection in general must be understood according to the paradigmatic activity of Intellect. Plotinus argues that intellection is primarily self-intellection or self-knowledge. Our embodied intellects are images or inferior versions of this. Plotinus will use this principle to respond to the profound attacks of Skeptics on the possibility of knowledge. If Intellect engages in the paradigmatic act of intellection, the question arises regarding intellection in the One. Plotinus will argue that the One is beyond intellection or cognition in general, although this is not a mark of deficiency in it.

Summary

§1. Thinking is primarily self-thinking. Primary self-thinking is identical with thinking of intelligibles.

§§2–3. The nature of embodied discursive reasoning in relation to sense-perception and intellection.

§4. The ascent from embodied discursive thinking to identification with our disembodied undescended intellect and hence with Intellect itself.

§5. The identification of intellect and intelligibles and how this is self-knowledge.

§6. The dialectical steps leading to the recognition that discursive thinking is an image of disembodied intellection.

§7. The connection between knowledge of the first principle and self-knowledge.

§8. The nature of Intellect's intellection and how this affects embodied thinking.

§9. Strategies for ascent through the hierarchy of cognition.

§10. Self-knowledge implies complexity in the knower identical with the objects of knowledge. Hence, the first principle of all, since it is absolutely simple, cannot have self-knowledge.

§11. How Intellect tries to cognize the One but can necessarily only cognize a multiplicity of its images, namely, all intelligibles.

§12. The absolute priority of the simple to the complex, including the complex self-thinking of Intellect.

§13. The One does not think itself nor can it be the object of thinking.

§14. Although it is not possible to think the One, it is possible to have a sort of awareness of its existence and presence.

§15. How the One produces that which it is not.

§16. The self-sufficiency of the One and its productive power.

§17. The relative self-sufficiency of Intellect. The ascent of the embodied individual to the One or Good.

---

§5.3.1. Must that which thinks itself be variegated in order that, with some one part of itself contemplating the others, it could indeed be said to think itself, the idea being that, were it altogether simple, it would not be able to revert to itself—that is, there could be no grasping of itself?[1] Or is it possible for that which is not composite to have   5 intellection of itself, too?

In fact, that which is said to think itself for the reason that it is a composite, just because some one part of itself actually thinks the others—as if we were to grasp in sense-perception our own shape and the rest of our corporeal nature—would not be able truly to think itself. For in this case, it will not be the whole that is known, since the   10 part which thinks all the rest has not also been thinking itself. This will not be a case of 'self-thinking'[2] which is what was wanted, but a case of one thing thinking another.

So, one should suppose that a grasping of itself belongs to something simple, and seek to discover, if one possibly can, how this occurs, or else relinquish the belief that anything really thinks itself. But relinquishing   15 this belief is completely impossible given that so many absurdities would follow. For even if we should refuse to allow self-thinking to the soul on the grounds that that would be quite absurd, still it would be altogether absurd not to give it to the nature of Intellect, and to claim that, although it has knowledge of other things, it will not be counted as having knowledge or scientific understanding of itself.[3]

---

1. See Sext. Emp., M. 7.283–287; 310–313 for the argument set out in full. Also, Ar., DA 3.4.429b9, 6.430b25–26.

2. See Ar., Meta. 12.7.1072b19–28, 9.1074b21–23.

3. Cf. 2.9.1.46–51. Throughout this treatise Plotinus uses the generic terms γνῶσις γιγνώσκω, in referring to the mode of cognition that belongs to Intellect. This mode of cognition will be, in fact, the highest mode, elsewhere usually called νόησις or ἐπιστήμη.

20   Now it is sense-perception and, if you like, discursive thinking and
belief that apprehend externals, but not Intellect, though whether
Intellect has knowledge of them or not should be examined. Clearly,
though, everything that is intelligible will be known by Intellect.[4] So,
will that which knows these know only these, or itself as well? Or will
25   it, then, know itself in the sense that it knows these things, although
it will not know itself? That is to say, will it know that it knows things
that belong to it, but have no further knowledge of who it is? Or rather
will it know both that which is its own and itself? In what manner this
occurs and to what extent is something that must be investigated.

§5.3.2. First, however, we must examine whether we ought to endow
the soul with knowledge of itself, and what in it knows, and how it does
it. We should start by saying that its faculty of sense-perception is only
of externals, for even if there were some self-awareness of what occurs
5   inside the body, the apprehension would still be of what is outside
itself, for it is itself the means by which it perceives states in the body.
      As for the part of the soul that engages in calculative reasoning: it
makes discriminatory judgments about the semblances presented to it
by sense-perception, organizing and distinguishing them.[5]
10   In fact, in regard to what comes from Intellect, it even considers
something like impressions of these, and has the identical power of
discrimination in relation to them.[6] And it acquires further comprehension as if by recognizing and matching up those impressions that
have been in it from before with new ones recently arrived. And we
would certainly call these acts the soul's 'recollections'.[7]
15   And does the intellect which is a part of the soul stop at this point in
its power, or does it turn to and know itself? Or is this to be attributed
[only] to Intellect? For if we grant self-knowledge to this part of the
soul—we shall now call it 'intellect'—we shall find ourselves investigating in what way it differs from the higher Intellect. But if we do not give
20   self-knowledge to intellect, the argument will lead us to Intellect, and
we shall have to investigate there what 'self-thinking' means.
      Further, if we should grant it to the intellect in the sensible world,
we shall have to investigate the difference between its 'self-thinking'
and Intellect's, for if there is none, this intellect will straightaway be the

---

4. Because intelligibles are not 'outside of' Intellect. Cf. 5.5.
5. Cf. 1.1.7.9–14, 9.15–23.
6. Cf.1.1.7.9–14; 4.3.30.1–15.
7. Cf. *infra* 16.45–47. See Pl., *Phd.* 72E5; *Men.* 81E4; Alcinous, *Didask.* 154.40–155.12.

'unmixed' Intellect.[8] So, does the soul's faculty of discursive thinking itself revert to itself? It does not. Rather, it acquires comprehension from the impressions it receives from each of its sources.[9] And how it   25
acquires comprehension is the matter that should be first investigated.

§**5.3.3.**[10] So, then, sense-perception saw a human being and gave the impression to discursive thinking.[11] What does discursive thinking say?[12]

In fact, it says nothing yet, but rather just became cognizant and stopped at that. Unless, that is, it were to converse with itself and say, 'Who is this?' assuming it had met this human being before, and would then say, relying on its memory, that this is Socrates. And if it analyzes   5
the shape, it is dividing up what the imagination has given it. And if it should say whether he is good, it says this based on what it has become cognizant of through sense-perception, but what it says about these things it would already have in itself, since it has a rule about the Good in itself. How does it have the Good in itself?   10

In fact, it is Good-like,[13] and is fortified for the sense-perception of this sort of thing by Intellect illuminating it. For this is the purified part of the soul, and it receives the traces of Intellect that have been impressed on it.

Why, then, is this not what Intellect is, and all the other faculties, starting with the perceptual, are what soul is? Is it not because soul has to be involved in acts of calculative reasoning? For all of these acts are the functions of a faculty of calculative reasoning. But, then, why   15
should we not just put an end to the matter by endowing this part with self-thinking? Is it not because we already endowed it with the job of examining externals and busying itself with them, whereas we judge that it belongs to Intellect to examine and busy itself with its own affairs, that is, the things that are internal to it? But if someone says, 'What, then, prevents this part from examining things internal to   20
it by another power?' he is not asking about the faculty of discursive thinking or calculative reasoning; rather, he has in view pure Intellect.

What, then, prevents pure Intellect from being in soul? We will say, 'Nothing'. But should we say in addition that Intellect belongs to soul? What we will say is that it does not belong to soul, though we will say

---

8. See Anaxagoras, fr. 59 A 15 DK; Ar., *DA* 1.2.405a16–7.
9. I.e., sense-perception and Intellect.
10. See Appendix III A 3.
11. The 'impression' is identical to the 'semblance' of 2.8 *supra*.
12. See Pl., *Tht.* 189E6–7; *Soph.* 263E4.
13. Cf. 1.8.11.16; 3.8.11.16; 6.7.15.9. See Pl., *Rep.* 6.509A3.

that it is our intellect;[14] and though it is other than the faculty of dis-
25   cursive thinking, having gone upward, nevertheless it is ours even if we
were not to count it among the parts of the soul.

In fact, it is ours and not ours. For this reason, we use it and do not
use it, though we always make use of discursive thinking. It is ours
when we use it and not ours when we do not.[15]

30   What, then, does 'using it' actually mean? Is it when we ourselves
become it or speak as Intellect does? Or is it rather when we do so in
accord with Intellect? For we are not Intellect. We are, then, in accord
with it by the faculty of calculative reasoning that is first receptive of
Intellect. For we perceive by means of sense-perception even if we are
not ourselves perceivers. Is it, then, that we think discursively in this
35   way, that is, we think by means of Intellect in this way?

In fact, we ourselves are the ones engaged in calculative reasoning,
and we ourselves think the thoughts by our faculty of discursive thinking. For this is what we are.[16]

The results of the acts of Intellect are from above just as the acts arising from sense-perception are from below. We are this—the sovereign
part of the soul[17]—in the middle between two powers,[18] a worse and
40   a better one, the worse being that of sense-perception and the better
being Intellect. But it has been conceded that sense-perception seems
to be always ours, for we are always perceiving; whereas Intellect is
disputed, because we do not always use it, and because it is separate.[19]
And it is separate due to its not inclining toward us, whereas we rather
are looking upward to it. Sense-perception is our messenger, but Intellect 'is our king'.[20]

§5.3.4. But we are kings, too, whenever we are in accord with
Intellect. We can be in accord with it in two ways: either by, in a way,
having its writings written in us like laws[21] or by being in a way filled
up with it and then being able to see it or perceive it as being present.

---

14. See Alex. Aphr., *De an.* 112.18.

15. Cf. 1.1.11.2–8; 2.9.2.4–10; 6.4.14.25–26.

16. Cf. 1.1.7.9–17, 11.5–8.

17. See Ar., *EN* 10.7.1178a2.

18. The word δύναμις ('power') could well be translated as 'faculty' when applied to
sense-perception. It could also be used for a faculty of embodied intellect, but is awk-
wardly applied to Intellect itself which is not a faculty of anything.

19. See Ar., *DA* 3.5.430a17.

20. See Pl., *Phil.* 28C7.

21. See Ar., *DA* 3.4.430a1.

And, due to this vision,[22] we know ourselves when we learn about   5
other things, either through the faculty of knowledge itself, because we
learn about other things by means of it, or because we become what we
learn, so that one who knows himself is double, one part knowing the
nature of the soul's faculty of discursive thinking, the other knowing
that which is above this, namely, the part which knows itself according   10
to the Intellect that it has become.

Further, in thinking himself again, due to Intellect, it is not as a
human being that he does so, but as having become something else
completely and dragging himself into the higher region, drawing up
only the better part of the soul, which alone can acquire the wings for
intellection,[23] in order that there be someone who could be entrusted
with what he sees in the intelligible world.

Is it actually the case that the faculty of discursive thinking does not   15
see[24] that it is the faculty of discursive thinking, and that it acquires
comprehension of externals, and that it discerns what it discerns, and
that it does so by internal rules, rules which it derives from Intellect,
and that there is something better than it that seeks nothing but rather,
in fact, has everything? But after all, does it not know what it itself is
just when it has scientific understanding of what sort of thing it is and   20
what its functions are? If, then, it were to say that it comes from Intellect and is second after Intellect and an image of Intellect,[25] having in
itself in a way all its writings, since the one who writes and has written
is in the intelligible world, will one who knows himself in this way
halt at these, but we, by using another faculty, observe again Intellect   25
knowing itself; or, by sharing in Intellect,[26] since it belongs to us and we
to it, shall we in this way know Intellect and ourselves?

In fact, it is necessary that we know it in this way, if indeed we
are going to know what 'self-thinking' is for the Intellect.[27] Someone has himself indeed become Intellect when he lets go of the other
things that belong to him, and looks at Intellect with Intellect; he then   30
looks at himself with himself. It is, then, actually as Intellect that he
sees himself.

---

22. Eliminating HS²'s <τῷ>.

23. See Pl., *Phdr.* 246B7–C2. The reference to the *Phaedrus* myth suggests that the
'better part of the soul' is the faculty of discursive thinking.

24. Reading εἶδε as per HS¹ and the mss.

25. Cf. *infra* 9.8; 5.1.3.7.

26. See Ar., *Meta.* 12.7.1072b20.

27. I.e., in knowing what Intellect is, we know what it is to be Intellect.

§5.3.5.[28] Does Intellect, then, with one part of itself observe another part of itself?[29] But in that case, one part will be seeing, and one part will be seen; this is not, however, 'self-thinking'. What if, then, the whole is comprised of parts that are, in a way, of the same kind, so that
5   the part that sees does not differ at all from the part that is seen? For in this way the part of itself that is seeing that which is identical with it sees itself—since that which sees does not differ from that which is seen.

In fact, first of all, the division of itself is absurd, for how does it divide? Indeed, it does not do so by chance. And what is it that is doing the dividing anyway? Is it the part that assigns to itself the task of see-
10   ing or the part that belongs to what is seen?

Next, how will that which is seeing know itself in that which is seen when it is undertaking for itself the task of seeing? For the seeing was not in that which is seen.

In fact, if it knows itself in this way, it will think itself as that which is being seen and not as that which sees, so that it will neither know all of itself nor know itself as a whole. For what it saw was what was seen;
15   it did not see the seeing. And in this way it will be something else, and not itself, that it is seeing.

Or perhaps it will add from itself that which has seen, too, in order that it would be thinking of itself perfectly. But if it adds that which has seen, at the same time it also adds the things seen. If, then, the things that have been seen exist in the seeing, either they are impressions of
20   them, and it does not have them themselves; or it has them, but not by the seeing that is a result of a division of itself; rather, it was prior to dividing itself that it saw and had them. If this is so, the seeing must be identical with the seen, that is, Intellect must be identical with the intelligible,[30] because if they are not identical, there will not be truth, for that which possesses things different from Beings will have an
25   impression, which is not truth.[31] The truth, therefore, should not be about something different from itself; rather, what it says is what it is. In this way, therefore, Intellect and that which is intelligible are one; and this is primary Being and indeed primary Intellect which has the Beings, or rather which is identical with them.[32]

---

28. See Appendix III B 1; III B 2; IV A; V A.
29. Returning to the problem raised by Sext. Emp., *M.* 7.310–312.
30. Cf. 5.5.2.18–20, 3.50–54. See Ar., *Meta.* 12.7.1072b21; *DA.* 3.4.429b9, 6.430b25–26.
31. Cf. 5.5.1.18–25.
32. Cf. 1.4.6.10; 5.1.8.17; 3.8.8.8; 5.9.5.6–10; 6.7.41.18; 6.9.2.36–37. See Parmenides, fr. 28 B 3 DK.

But if intellection and that which is intelligible are one, how will this be the explanation for the fact that that which thinks, thinks itself? For though intellection will, in a way, encompass that which is intelligible, or will be identical with that which is intelligible, it is not yet clear how Intellect will be thinking itself. But if intellection and that which is intelligible are identical[33]—for the intelligible is a certain kind of actuality; it is neither a potency nor something without thought, nor is it separated from life,[34] nor are life and thinking added to it by something that is other than it in the way that they might be added to a stone or to something inanimate[35]—then the intelligible is primary Substantiality. If, then, it is actuality, that is, the primary actuality and indeed the most beautiful, it would be intellection, that is, Substantial intellection.[36] For it is most true. And such intellection, actually being primary and primarily Intellect, would be the primary Intellect, for neither is this Intellect in potency nor is it one thing and its intellection another.[37] For if it were, again, the Substantial part of it would be in potency.

If, then, it is actuality, that is, the Substantiality of it is actuality, it would be one and identical with its actuality. But Being, or that which is intelligible, is also one with that actuality. All will be simultaneously one; Intellect, intellection, and intelligible. If, then, its intellection is that which is intelligible, and the intelligible is it, it will, therefore, be thinking itself, for it will think by its intellection, which it is, and it will think that which is intelligible, which it is. In both ways, therefore, it will think itself; because it is intellection and because it is that which is intelligible—that which it thinks by the intellection—which is what it itself is.

§5.3.6. The argument has indeed demonstrated that 'self-thinking' in the proper sense exists. Thinking, then, does occur in the soul, though it more properly occurs in Intellect. The soul thought itself because it belongs to something else, whereas Intellect thought because it is itself, that is, because it is the sort of thing it is or whatever it is, starting from its own nature and then reverting upon itself. For seeing Beings, it saw itself; and in seeing, it was in actuality, and the actuality was it. For Intellect and intellection are one. And the whole thinks by means of the whole, not one part by means of another.

---

33. See Ar., *DA* 3.4.430a2–9.
34. See Ar., *Meta.* 12.7.1072b27.
35. Cf. 4.7.3.23–29. See Pl., *Soph.* 246A8.
36. The phrase οὐσιώδης νόησις ('Substantial intellection') could be glossed as 'the kind of intellection belonging to Substantial Being'.
37. See Ar., *Meta.* 12. 9.1074b33–35.

Has this argument shown itself also to have, in some way, persuasive force?

In fact, it has the force of necessity, though it is not persuasive. For necessity is in Intellect, but persuasion is in soul.[38] But it does seem as if we are actually seeking more to persuade ourselves than to see the truth by means of pure Intellect, for while we were up in the nature of Intellect, we were content, and we were thinking, and, gathering all things into one, we saw.[39] For it was Intellect doing the thinking and speaking about itself, whereas the soul was tranquil and ceded to the result of the actualization of Intellect. But since we have come to be in the sensible world again in soul, we are seeking for some kind of persuasion to arise, wanting to see the archetype in a sort of image.[40] Perhaps, then, we ought to teach this soul of ours how Intellect sees itself, and to teach this part of soul that is somehow intellectual, supposing it to be a 'faculty of discursive thinking', a term which signals that it is some sort of intellect or that soul has this faculty due to Intellect and from Intellect.[41]

So, it belongs to the faculty of discursive thinking to know that it knows the things which it sees by itself and that it knows what it is speaking about. And if it were itself what it is speaking about, it would know itself in this way. And since the things it is speaking about are above or come to it from the intelligible world, where it came from itself, it might also happen that it would know itself by its being an expressed principle and receiving things that are akin to it and fitting them to the traces in itself.

So, let us transfer the image to the true Intellect, which was identified with the truths being thought, those that are really Beings and primary, both because it is not possible that something like this could be outside itself[42]—so that if it is indeed in itself and with itself and just what it is, it is Intellect—for an Intellect without thought could not exist—and it is necessary that the knowledge of itself accompanies it—and because it is in itself and the function and Substantiality for it is nothing other than to be Intellect alone. For it is, of course, not practical intellect, which looks to externals and does not remain in itself, and has a kind of knowledge of externals. If it were indeed entirely practical, it would not be necessary for it to know itself. But in that in which there is no

---

38. Cf. 6.8.13.4. See Pl., *Lg.* 903B1.
39. See Anaxagoras, fr. 59 B 12 DK.
40. See Pl., *Phdr.* 244B–C, 266B.
41. That the soul is 'discursive' (διανοητικόν) is 'due to Intellect' (διὰ νοῦ).
42. Cf. *supra* 5.21–23.

action—for pure Intellect has no desire for that which is absent from   40
it—the reversion to itself demonstrates not only that it is reasonable
but also that it is necessary that it should have knowledge of itself. For
if action is removed from it, what else would the life of that which is in
Intellect be?[43]

§5.3.7. We could say that Intellect contemplates god. But if someone
will agree that it knows god, he will be compelled to concede that in
this way it also knows itself. For it will know all such things as it has
from god, that is, what he has given and what he has the power to
do.[44] Learning these and knowing them, it will in this way know itself,   5
because it is itself one of the things that has been given—or, rather,
it is all the things that have been given. If, then, it will know god by
learning his powers,[45] it will also know itself, since it comes from the
intelligible world and has been provided from there with what it has
the power to do. But if it is powerless to see god clearly, since seeing   10
is, perhaps, the very thing that is seen, in this way especially it would
be left to it to see and know itself, if this seeing is identical with that
which is seen.

What else could we give to it? Stillness, by Zeus. But for Intellect,
stillness is not a self-transcending experience; rather, the stillness of   15
Intellect is an activity free from occupation with other things. In the
case of other things, too, which have stillness when they are apart from
the rest, their own proper activity remains, especially those things
whose existence is not potential but actual.[46] The existence of Intellect, then, is activity,[47] and there is nothing else to which the activity is
directed. It is, therefore, directed to itself. In thinking itself, therefore,
it is in this way directed to itself and has its activity within itself. For   20
if something comes from it, this will be due to its being in itself and
directed toward itself. For it first had to be in itself and next directed
toward something else, or something else must have come from it, having been made the same as it. Similarly, fire, which is first fire within
itself and, having the activity of fire, is able to produce a trace of itself   25
in another.[48]

43. See Ar., *EN* 10.8.1078b20–21; *Meta.* 12.9.1074b18.
44. The One is δύναμις τῶν πάντων. Cf. *infra* 15.32–33, 16.2–3; 5.1.7.9–10; 5.4.2.38–39;
6.9.5.36–37.
45. Reading αὐτοῦ with HS¹.
46. ἐνέργεια is translated as 'actuality' when it is used in contrast to 'potentiality' or
'potency' but 'activity' when there is no such implied contrast.
47. Cf. 6.7.40.14; 6.8.4.26–28.
48. Cf. 5.1.6.30–34; 5.4.2.27–33; 6.7.18.5–6, 21.4–6, 40.21–24.

And, again, Intellect is an activity within itself, whereas for soul, as much of it as is directed to Intellect is in a way inside, but as much as is outside Intellect is directed to what is outside it. One part of soul is made into a likeness of that from which it comes, whereas the other, not being a likeness, is nevertheless made to be a likeness of that from which it comes even while it is in the sensible world, whether it be by
30   acting or doing; for when it does something it is, nevertheless, con-templating, and in doing something it makes forms, which are, in a way, detached[49] acts of intellection, so that all things are traces of intellection and of Intellect proceeding according to the archetype and imitating it; the ones closer more so, while the ones furthest away pre-serve a murky image.[50]

§5.3.8.[51] What sort of thing does Intellect see when it sees the intelligible, and what sort of thing when it sees itself?

In fact, one should not seek the intelligible as if it were the color or the shape of a body, for the intelligibles exist prior to these. And the
5   expressed principle in the seeds that produce these colors or shapes is not identical with them. For by nature even these are invisible; even more so are the intelligibles. And the nature of the intelligibles and of those things which have them[52] is identical, as is the expressed principle in the seeds and the soul that has them.

The soul, however, does not see what it has, for it did not generate them but is itself a reflection, as are the expressed principles, whereas
10   that from which the soul came is clear and true and primary and belongs to itself and is for itself. But this reflection, if it did not come to be from another thing and exist in another thing, does not even last: 'for it belongs to an image, as coming from something else, to be in something else',[53] unless it is dependent on that from which it came. For this reason, soul does not see, inasmuch as it actually does not
15   have enough light, and even if it does see, it sees another thing that is realized in another, and it does not see itself.

But there is, then, nothing of these things in the intelligible world; rather, seeing and the object of sight are together in it, and the object of sight is the same sort of thing as the seeing, and the seeing is the same sort of thing as the object of sight. Who, then, will say what sort

---

49. Reading ἀπηρτημένας with Theiler.
50. Cf. 3.8.3.3–23.
51. See Appendix III B 1.
52. I.e., Intellect and intellects.
53. See Pl., *Tim.* 52C2–4.

of thing it is? The one who sees. But it is Intellect that sees. Even in the
sensible world, seeing, since it is light or, rather, united with light, sees   20
light, for it sees colors. But in the intelligible world, seeing is not by
means of something different; rather, it is by means of itself, because
it is not of what is outside it. Intellect thus sees one light with another,
not by means of another. Light, therefore, sees another light; therefore,
it sees itself.

And this light shined in the soul and illuminated it, that is, made it
intellectual; that is, it made it to be a likeness of itself by means of the   25
upper light. This is, then, in a way, the trace of light that came to be
in the soul, and if you believe that it is like this and even more beautiful and greater and clearer, you would come closer to the nature of
Intellect and of the intelligible. And again, having illuminated this, it
gave the soul a clearer life, but not a generative one.[54] On the contrary,   30
it made the soul revert to itself and did not allow it to be scattered;
rather, it made it love the splendor in itself. It is surely not a life of
sense-perception, for sense-perception looks outside itself and perceives, whereas that which acquires the light of true Beings sees visible
beings better but in the opposite sense of 'visible'.[55]   35

So, what remains is for it to have acquired an intellectual life, a trace
of the life of Intellect. For the intelligible world is where the true Beings
are. But the life or activity in Intellect[56] is the primary light, being an
illumination primarily for itself and gleaming for itself, illuminating
and being illuminated at the same time, that which is truly intelligible, that is, thinker and what is thought, seeing by itself and in need   40
of nothing else in order to see, sufficient to itself for seeing—for what
it sees is itself—known even by us due to that light, since the knowledge of it has come to us by means of that. How else could we speak
about it? Intellect is such that while it apprehends itself more clearly,   45
we apprehend it by means of it.

By means of these arguments, our soul, too, goes back up to it,
supposing itself to be an image of it, so that its life is a reflection and
likeness of it, and whenever it thinks, it becomes god-like, that is, 'Intel-
lect-like'.[57] And if one were to ask the soul, 'What sort of thing is the   50
Intellect that is perfect and complete and that knows itself primarily?',
it would actually use itself as evidence, referring to things of which it
possessed memories, since it was originally in Intellect, or ceded its

---

54. The faculty of generation comes from nature.
55. Eliminating the οὐ of HS². The 'non-visible' is more 'visible' to Intellect.
56. See Ar., *Meta.* 12.7.1072b27.
57. Cf. 1.2.3.11–30. See Pl., *Phd.* 95C5; *Tht.* 176B.

activity to Intellect. So, it is in some way able to see Intellect because it
55 is a kind of image of it, an image which is likened to it as closely as any
part of the soul can come to being like Intellect.

§5.3.9. It appears, then, that one who intends to know what Intellect
is should observe soul, especially the most divine part of it. This could
perhaps occur in the following way: if you first separated in thought
5 the body from the human being, I mean, from yourself, and next the
[lower] soul that shapes the body and, of course, all sense-perception,
appetites, and passions and other such irrelevancies,[58] since these all
tend toward the mortal, what actually remains of soul is this: that
which we called an image of Intellect,[59] preserving something of its
light—in a way, like the light of the sun which shines around it and out
of it, beyond its spherical mass.
10 Now no one would allow that the light of the sun exists on its own
around the sun, emitted and then remaining around it, and that successive rays of light proceed from the ones before until the light reaches us
on earth. Rather, one would suppose everything that is around the sun
15 is in something else, so that one did not allow there to be an interval
empty of body beyond the sun. But the soul, having arisen from Intellect as a light around it, is dependent on it and is neither in something
else, but rather is around Intellect, nor in place, for Intellect is not.
Hence, the sun's light is in air, whereas such a soul is pure, so that it is
20 able to see itself by itself and by any other soul of the same kind.
And soul ought to draw conclusions about Intellect, starting its
investigation from itself, though Intellect itself knows itself without drawing conclusions about itself, for it is always present to itself,
whereas we are only so when we are directed toward it. For our life has
been fragmented, that is, we have many lives, whereas Intellect has no
25 need of another life or of other lives, since what it provides it provides
to others, not to itself. For it neither has need of what is inferior to it,
nor does it provide to itself that which is less when it has everything,
nor does it have traces of primary Beings, since it has the originals.
More precisely, it does not have them, but is them itself.
If, however, someone is unable to grasp a soul such as this, one that
30 thinks purely,[60] let him grasp a soul which has beliefs, and next let him
ascend from this. But if he cannot do even this, let him take sense-perception, which provides the forms in the broader sense, but sense-per-

---

58. Cf. 1.1.12.13–21. See Pl., *Phd.* 66B8–E1.
59. Cf. *supra* 4.22–24; 8.46; 2.9.4.25; 5.1.3.7; 6.1.7.1.
60. I.e., the activity of embodied intellection. See Alcinous, *Didask.* 165.16–19.

ception in itself with its powers and already immersed in the forms.[61]
Or if someone wants, let him descend to the generative soul and keep
going until he arrives at the things it produces. Then, when he is there,
let him ascend from the forms that are at one extreme to the Forms   35
that are at the other extreme, or rather to the primary ones.

§5.3.13.[62] For this reason,[63] the One is, in truth, ineffable, for
whatever you might say about it, you will be saying something. But to
say 'transcends all things and transcends the majesty of Intellect'[64] is,
among all other ways of speaking of it, the only true one, not because
that is its name, but because it indicates that it is not 'something' among
all things, it having itself no designation.[65] But, as far as possible, we try   5
to give ourselves indications about it.

But if we raise as a problem that it has, then, no perception of itself
and is not consciously aware of itself and does not know itself, we
ought to consider that in saying this we are turning ourselves around
to the opposite claim.[66] For we make it many if we make it knowable   10
and knowledge, and, if we endow it with thinking, we put it in need of
thinking. But even if thinking were to belong to it, it will be superflu-
ous for it to think. And this is because, in general, thinking seems to
be a self-awareness of the whole when many parts come together in
the identical thing, that is, whenever something thinks itself, which is
actually thinking in the principal sense. Each part of this whole is itself   15
some one thing and seeks nothing, whereas if intellection is to be of
that which is outside it, it will be deficient and will not be thinking in
the principal sense.

Now that which is completely simple and self-sufficient is really in
need of nothing.[67] That which is self-sufficient in a secondary sense,
needing itself, needs this for thinking itself. And that which is deficient
in regard to itself has produced self-sufficiency in the whole with an   20
adequacy arising from all the parts, being present to itself and inclining toward itself, for self-awareness is a perception of something that is
many; even the word is a witness to this.[68]

---

61. Cf. 4.4.23.32; 4.5.2.48–49.
62. See Appendix II E.
63. In the previous chapter, Plotinus argued that the One is absolutely simple.
64. See Pl., *Rep.* 6.509B9.
65. Cf. 5.5.6.1–8, 24; 6.9.4.11–12. See Pl., *Parm.* 142A3; [?], *7th Ep.* 341C5–6.
66. Cf. 6.7.38.10.
67. Cf. 6.9.6.16–26.
68. The Greek word is συναίσθησις where the prefix συν indicates a complex act,
something beyond mere perception.

And intellection, being prior, reverts inward to Intellect, which is
25 clearly many. For even if it says only this, 'I am Being', it says it as one
discovering something—and it says it with good reason, for Being is
many. This is so, since if it were to focus on itself as something simple
and say 'I am Being', it would hit upon neither itself nor Being. For it
is not saying it is Being in the way it speaks the truth when it says a
stone has being, but it has said many things in one word. For this Being
30 which is said to be real Being and not to have a mere trace of Being—
which would not even be said to be a being because of this, but as an
image in relation to an archetype—has many things.

What, then? Will not each of these Beings be thought? Now if you
want to grasp the 'isolated and alone',[69] you will not be thinking. On
the contrary, Being itself is many within itself, and if you should mention something else, Being includes that. But if this is so, then if there
35 is something that is the simplest of all, it will not have intellection of
itself. For if it is, it will do it by being many. Neither, then, is the One
thinking, nor will it have intellection of itself.[70]

§5.3.14. How, then, do we speak about it?

In fact, we do speak in some measure about it, but we do not speak
it, nor do we have knowledge or intellection of it.

How, then, do we speak about it if we do not have knowledge or
intellection of it?[71]

5 In fact, if we do not have knowledge of it, does it follow as well that
we do not have it at all?[72] But we have it in such a way that we can speak
about it, though we cannot speak it. For we say what it is not; what it
is, we do not say, so that we are speaking about it on the basis of things
posterior to it. We are not prevented from having it, even if we do not
say it.

But just as those who are inspired and possessed have knowledge
10 to the extent that they know that they have something greater than
themselves in themselves[73]—even if they do not know what it is, and
from the things by which they are moved[74] and speak they acquire a
certain perception of that which moved them although their motions
are different from what moved them—in this way we, too, are related

---

69. Cf. 6.7.40.28. See Pl., *Phil.* 63B7–8.
70. Alternatively: 'nor is there intellection of it'.
71. See Pl., *Parm.* 142A5–6.
72. 'Have it' perhaps indicates some cognitive relation to the One. See *infra* ll. 13–14.
73. See Pl., *Ion* 533E6–7.
74. Correcting the typographical error κεκίνηται το κεκίνηνται.

to the One, whenever we possess purified Intellect.[75] We thereby have
it revealed to us not only that this is the inner Intellect, which gives   15
Substantiality and whatever else belongs to this level of Being, but also
that the One is, therefore, such as not to be those Beings; it is something more powerful than that which we call 'Being', but it is also more
and greater than what can be said about it, because it is more powerful than speech and intellect and sense-perception, and because it
provides these, not being them itself.[76]

§5.3.15. But how does it provide these? Either by having them or by
not having them.[77] But how can it provide what it does not have? But
if it has them, it is not simple. If, on the other hand, it does not have
them, how can the multiplicity of things come from it? Someone might
perhaps grant that one simple thing came from it—though even then   5
one should inquire into how this could come from what is absolutely
one. But nevertheless, even if it is possible to speak about how it comes
from the One in something like the way that radiance comes from
light—still, how do many things come from it?[78]

In fact, that which was to come from the One is not identical with
it. If, then, it is not identical, it is not better either. For what could be
better than the One or transcend it entirely? It is, therefore, worse. And
this means that it is more in need. What, then, is more in need than   10
the One?

In fact, it is that which is not one. It is, therefore, many, though,
nevertheless, desirous of the One. It is, therefore, a 'one-many'.[79] For
everything that is not one is preserved by the One and is whatever it is
due to this.[80] For if it has not become one, even if it is composed out of
many parts, it is not yet that which someone could speak of as 'itself'.[81]
And even if someone were able to say what each part is, they would be   15
saying this due to the fact that each is one, that is, due to its being itself.

But that which, not having many parts in itself, is thereby not one
by participation in the One, but is itself the One, and it is not one due

---

75. See Anaxagoras, fr. 59 B 12 DK.
76. Cf. 3.8.9.22–26; 6.9.3.22–36.
77. The mss have ἢ τῷ ἔχειν ('either by having'), while HS² add the words <ἢ τῷ μὴ
ἔχειν> ('or by not having'). The reason for the conjectured change is that without the
addition, Plotinus seems to contradict his claim that the One does not have any of the
things that it gives.
78. Cf. 5.1.7.21–22; 6.7.17.1–18.
79. Cf. 5.1.8.26; 6.2.15.14–15; 6.4.11.15–16. See Pl., *Parm.* 137C–142A, 144E5, 155E5.
80. Or 'that which is one', meaning whatever unity it has. Cf. 6.9.1.1–4.
81. Following de Strycker's suggestion and reading ὃ ἂν εἴποι. Cf. 3.8.10.20–28.

to something else but because it is the One, that from which other things somehow also come, some by being near and some by being far. For that itself which comes after it makes clear that it comes after

20   it due to its multiplicity, being a 'one-everywhere'. For even though it is a multiplicity, nevertheless it is self-identical and you could not divide it because 'all things are together'.[82] Since each of the things that come from it, so long as it partakes of life, is a 'one-many', each cannot show itself to be a 'one-everything'. But Intellect is a 'one-everything', because it comes after the principle.[83] For that principle really is one, and 'truly

25   is one'.[84] That which comes after the principle is, somehow, by the influence of the One, all things partaking of the One, and any part of it is all things besides being also one.

What, then, are 'all things'?

In fact, they are those things of which the One is the principle. But how is the One the principle of all things?[85] Is it because by producing each of them as one it preserves them in existence?[86]

In fact, it is also because it made them to exist. How did it actually do this?

30   In fact, it was by having them prior to their existence. But it has been said that in this way it will be a multiplicity. We must, therefore, say that it had them in such a way that they were not distinct, whereas the things in the second principle are made distinct by an expressed principle, for this is at once actuality, whereas the One is the productive power of all things.[87]

But what manner of power is this? For it is not what is meant when matter is said to be in potency, namely, because it is receptive. For mat-

35   ter is passive, and this type of being in potency is the opposite of producing.[88] How, then, does it produce what it does not have? Indeed, it does so neither by chance nor by having reflected on what it will produce yet it produces nevertheless. It has been said, then, that if there is something that comes from the One, it should be something other than it; being other, it is not one. For if this were one, it would be the One. But if it is not one, but two, it is at once necessary that it also be

---

82. See Anaxagoras, fr. 59 B 1 DK.
83. Reading μετὰ τὴν ἀρχὴν with Igal and HS⁴.
84. See Pl., *Soph.* 245A8.
85. See Pl., *Parm.* 153C3.
86. Cf. 6.7.23.22.
87. Cf. 3.8.10.1; 4.8.6.11; 5.1.7.9; 5.4.1.23–26, 36; 5.4.2.38; 6.7.32.31; 6.9.5.36.
88. Cf. 2.5.1.21–26.

a multiplicity, for it is at once different and identical and of some kind,   40
and the rest.[89]

It has been shown that that which comes from the One is actually
not one. But it is worth puzzling over the fact that this is a multiplicity
and the sort of multiplicity that has been observed to be in that which
comes after the One. And the necessity of there being something that
comes after the One is yet to be examined.

§5.3.16.[90] That there must be something after that which is first
has been said elsewhere and, generally, that the first is power, that
is, incredible power—this, too, has been said, namely, that this claim
should be trusted on the basis of all the other things we observe,
because there is nothing, not even at the extremes, that does not have
the power to generate.[91]   5

But as for those things, the point should now be made that, since
things that are generated cannot go upward, but can only proceed
downward, that is, in the direction of multiplicity, the principle of each
of them is simpler than they are. So, what makes the sensible cosmos
cannot itself be a sensible cosmos, but is rather Intellect and an intelligible cosmos. So, what is before this that which generates it, could not   10
be Intellect or an intelligible cosmos; rather, it must be simpler than
Intellect and simpler than an intelligible cosmos. For a many does not
come from many, but that which is many comes from that which is not
many. For if the intelligible cosmos is many, this is not a principle; the
principle is that which is before this. If indeed this is to be really simple, there must, then, be a coalescing into what is really one, outside of   15
any multiplicity and any qualified simplicity.

But how can that which is generated from the really simple be a multiple and comprehensive expressed principle, while that from which it
came is clearly not an expressed principle? And if it is not this, how,
then, can an expressed principle come from what is not an expressed
principle? And how does that which is 'Good-like' come from the
Good?[92] What indeed does it have in itself due to which it is said to be
Good-like?[93] Is it, then, because it has 'its identity in a stable manner'?[94]   20
And what does this mean in relation to the Good? For we seek out that
which is always stable just because it is one of the things that is good.

---

89. See Pl., *Soph.* 254E5–255A1.
90. See Appendix II E.
91. Cf. 2.9.3; 4.8.2.26–38, 6.1–18; 5.1.6.30–34; 5.2.1.7–28; 5.4.1.37.
92. Cf. 1.7.1.14–16. See Pl., *Rep.* 6.508E6–509A5.
93. Cf. *supra* 3.10; 3.8.11.16; 6.7.15, 18.1.
94. See Pl., *Soph.* 248A12.

In fact, we seek that which is prior to stability, which we should not leave, because it is the Good. If it were not, it would be better to be separated from it.

25 So, is living in a stable manner and willingly remaining like this what we are seeking? If, then, living like this is what it loves, it is clear that it seeks nothing. It would seem, then, that it lives like this for this reason, namely, because its present life is sufficient for it. But it loves its life because all things are at once actually present to it, that is, present but not as other than it. And if its entire life is a life of clarity and

30 perfection, then every soul and every intellect is in it, and nothing of life or of intellect is absent from it. It is, then, self-sufficient and seeks nothing. And if it seeks nothing, it has in itself what it would have sought, had that not been present to it. It has, then, in itself that which is good, whether we say life and intellect are actually that or something else that is accidental to these.

35 But if this is the Good, there would be nothing that transcends Life and Intellect. But if the Good transcends them, it is clear that Intellect's life is directed to it and dependent on it and has its real existence from it and lives directed to it. For that is its principle. So, the Good must be better than Life and Intellect, for this is why Intellect will revert to

40 it—both to the Life that is in the Good, as a kind of imitation of what is in it, in it insofar as what is in it is Life, and the Intellect in it, as a kind of imitation of what is in it, whatever this is.

§5.3.17.[95] What, then, is better than the wisest life, without a fault, unerring, that is, the life of Intellect, which has all things, and is all Life and all Intellect? If we respond, then, 'that which produced these' we should also ask 'how did it produce these?' And, should there not

5 appear something better, our calculative reasoning will not go on to something else but will stop at Intellect. But, still, one should go upward for many reasons, but especially because the self-sufficiency of Intellect, since that is due to all the things of which it is composed, is [from] outside it, for each of these is clearly deficient. And because each of these has partaken of and partakes of the One itself, it is not

10 the One itself. What, then, is that of which Intellect partakes, which makes it exist and all things together?[96] If it makes each exist, and it is by the presence of the One that the multiplicity of Intellect and Intellect itself are self-sufficient, it is clear that that which is productive

---

95. See Appendix II E; II J.
96. See Anaxagoras, fr. 59 A 60–61, B 1 DK.

of Substantiality and of self-sufficiency is itself not Substantiality but 'transcends this' and transcends self-sufficiency.[97]

Is it enough, then, having said these things, to leave off?   15

In fact, the soul is still in labor and even more so than before. Perhaps, then, she must now give birth, having both longed for the One and been consumed with labor.[98] But we must sing another charm if we are to find one to relieve her labor. Perhaps it would come from what has already been said, and if someone were to sing it over and   20 over, it would happen. What other fresh charm, then, is there? For she has run through all the truths, truths in which we participate, yet still flees them if someone wants to speak and think through them, since discursive thinking must, if it is to say something, go from one thing to the other. It is, in this way, successive. But what sort of succession is there for that which is completely simple?   25

But it is sufficient if one grasps it intellectually. And having grasped it, so long as one does, it is quite impossible to speak nor is there time to speak; later, one can reason about it. But at that moment, one cannot but be confident that one has seen, whenever the soul suddenly makes contact with light,[99] for this comes from the One and is it. And   30 at that moment, one cannot but believe that the One is present, just as when another god, called to someone's house, comes bringing light. If the god had not come, he would not have brought the light. Thus, the unilluminated soul, bereft of god, is without light. When she is illuminated, she has what she sought, and this is the soul's true goal: to make contact with that light and to see it by itself, not by the light   35 of something else; to see that very thing through which it sees. For the means of its illumination is what the soul ought to see; we do not see the sun by the light of something else. How, then, can this come about? Abstract from everything.[100]

---

97. See Pl., *Rep.* 6.509B8–9.
98. See Pl., *Rep.* 6.490B; Pl. [?], *2nd Ep.* 313A4–5.
99. See Pl., *Symp.* 210E4; Pl. [?], *7th Ep.* 341C7–D1.
100. Cf. 5.5.13.7–13; 6.7.34.1–4; 6.8.21.25–28.

5.5 (32)

THAT THE INTELLIGIBLES ARE NOT OUTSIDE THE INTELLECT, AND ON THE GOOD

Introduction

This treatise is really a part of the treatise that precedes it chronologically, 5.8 (31). That treatise may also include 3.8 (30) and 2.9 (33). Their separation is owing to Porphyry's non-chronological ordering. The task of 5.5 is to show that the intelligibles or Forms cannot be external to Intellect; rather, they must be constitutive of Intellect's identity. This claim must be established not only to properly understand Intellect, but also since Intellect is engaged in the paradigm of thinking, if Intellect is not cognitively identical with Forms, then the possibility of thinking even for us is eliminated. From the internal complexity of Intellect, Plotinus shows the necessity of an absolutely simple first principle of all.

Summary

§1. The necessity of the internality of Forms to Intellect. The identity of Forms and Intellect means that Forms are alive and are not separable from each other.

§2. Intellect is cognitively identical with Forms and so possesses them, or more exactly is them. Intellect's cognition of Forms is non-inferential and non-propositional.

§3. Intellect, the second god, is the locus of Being and derived from the first god.

§4. The unity of Intellect is inferior to the unity of the One. The One is not a number.

§5. The One is productive of all things. It produces Intellect first. The One is not participated in.

§6. The transcendence of the One. It is beyond Being. The requirement of negative theology.

§7. Analogy of intellection to sight.

§8. The omnipresence of the One.

§9. The 'containment' of Soul within Intellect and Intellect within the One. The One is itself within nothing.

§10. The One is unlimited in power and is identical with the Good. The One must be unlike everything of which it is the cause.

§11. The unqualified unlimitedness of the One. The immateriality of the first principle of all.

§12. The priority of the Good to that which is beautiful. The desire for the Good is prior to the desire for the beautiful.

§13. The absolute simplicity and transcendence of the Good. The Good is not good nor does it possess any other predicates.

---

§5.5.1. Might, then, one say that Intellect—the true and real Intellect—will ever be in error and have beliefs about non-beings?[1] Not at all. For how would Intellect still be what it is if it is unthinking?[2] It must, therefore, always know and not ever forget, and its knowledge   5
must not be conjecture, or uncertain, or like something heard at second hand. So, its knowledge is not acquired by means of demonstration either.[3] For even if someone were to say that some of what it knows it knows by means of demonstration, in that case there would still be something self-evident to it. Actually, our argument maintains that everything is self-evident to it. For how could someone distinguish the things that are self-evident to it from those that are not?

But as for those things they concede are self-evident to it—from   10
where will they say their being self-evident comes?[4] And from where will Intellect derive the conviction that things are self-evident to it? For even sensibles, which certainly seem to bring with them the most self-evident conviction, do not, in fact, convince us that their seem-ingly real existence is in substrates rather than in our experiences, and   15
that they are not in need of intellect or discursive thinking to make judgments about them. For even if it is agreed that the sensibles are in their substrates, the apprehension of which sense-perception will bring about, what is known by means of sense-perception of the object is a reflection of the thing; it is not the thing itself that sense-perception receives, for that object remains outside it.

Given that when Intellect knows, it knows intelligibles, how, if these   20
are different from it, would it connect with them?[5] For it is possible that it does not, so that it is possible that it does not know, or knows

---

1. This treatise is continuous with 5.8. The last sentence of that treatise is: 'So, is what has been said sufficient to lead to a clear understanding of the intelligible world, or should we go back and take another path like this one?'

2. I.e., since Intellect's activity is eternal cognitive identification with Beings, its having beliefs about that which is not would be equivalent to 'unthinking' for it.

3. Cf. 5.8.7.43.

4. The Epicureans. See D.L., 10.32; Sext. Emp., *PH* 2.169–170; *M.* 7.203, 364; 8.9.

5. See Pl., *Tht.* 186C7–10; Ar., *DA* 3.4.4430a4–5, 5.430a19–20, 6.430b25–26, 7.4430b17, 8.431a22–23.

them only at the time when it connected with them and will not always have the knowledge. But if they are going to say that they are linked to it, what does the term 'linked' mean?[6] In that case, acts of intellection 25 will be impressions.[7] And if this is so, they act externally, that is, they are impacts.[8] But how will these impressions be made, and what will be the shape of such things? And in that case, an act of intellection will be of what is outside it just like sense-perception. And in what way will it differ from sense-perception other than by apprehending something smaller? And how will it know that it really apprehended them? And 30 how will it know that something is good or beautiful or just? For each of these will be other than the object, and the principles of judgment by which it will attain conviction will not be in it, but rather these will be outside it, and the truth will be there.

Next, either intelligibles are themselves without perception and without any portion of life and intellect, or they do have intellect. And if they have intellect, both are simultaneously here—this truth and this 35 primary Intellect—and we shall investigate in addition what the truth here is like, and whether the intelligible and Intellect are identical and occur simultaneously, and yet are still two and different—or how are they related?[9]

But if the intelligibles are without thought or without life, what sort of Beings are they?[10] For they are certainly not 'premises' or 'axioms' or 'sayables';[11] if they were, straightaway they would be referring to things 40 different from themselves, and they would not then be the Beings themselves. For example, if they will say 'that which is just is beautiful', that which is just and that which is beautiful are in fact other than what is said.

But if they say that these are 'simples', Justice being separate from Beauty, then, first, the intelligible will not be some one thing nor in one thing, but each intelligible will be dispersed.[12] And where and in what

---

6. The term συνεζεῦχθαι ('linked') is attributed to the Epicureans by Sext. Emp., M. 7.203.

7. The term τύποι ('impressions') is Stoic. See D.L., 7.45.

8. The term is πληγαί. Cf. 3.1.2, 11; 3.6.6.35, 62. See Alex. Aphr., De an. 72.5–11.

9. Cf. infra 2.1–13; 3.8.9.5–11.

10. Cf. 6.7.8.25–27. See Pl., Rep. 5.477A3; Soph. 248E6–249A2.

11. Cf. 5.8.5.20–25. The premises are the supposedly self-evident propositional truths that form the basis of Aristotelian demonstrations. See Ar., Pr. An. 1.1.24a16–b15. The axioms and 'sayables' are Stoic. See SVF 2.132 (= Sext. Emp., M. 7.38). Plotinus may also be responding to Longinus, who reputedly held that Forms are outside the intellect and are identical to 'sayables'. See Syrianus, In Meta. 105.25–30.

12. See Pl., Soph. 259E4–6.

places will they be dispersed? And how will Intellect hit upon them,   45
meandering through these places? How will it remain undisturbed—
rather, how will it remain in the identical place? In general, what sort of
shape or impression will it have of them? Or are we to assume that they
are like constructed golden images or some other matter produced by
some sculptor or engraver? But if they are like this, the contemplating
of Intellect will in fact be sense-perception.[13] Further, why is one of
these things Justice and another something else?   50

But the greatest objection is this. If indeed one were to grant that
these intelligibles are totally outside Intellect, and then claim that
Intellect contemplates them as such, it necessarily follows that it does
not itself have the truth of these things and that it is deceived in all
that it contemplates; for it is those intelligibles that would be the true
reality.[14] So, it will contemplate them though it does not have them,   55
instead receiving reflections of them in a kind of cognition like this.
Not having true reality, then, but rather receiving for itself reflections
of the truth, it will have falsities and nothing true. So, if it knows that
it has falsities, it will agree that it has no share in truth. But if it is
ignorant of this as well, and thinks that it has the truth when it does   60
not, the falsity that is generated in it is double, and that will separate it
considerably from the truth.

This is the reason, I think, that in acts of sense-perception, too, truth
is not found, but only belief, because belief is receptive,[15] and for this
reason, being belief, it receives something other than that from which   65
it receives what it has. If, then, there is no truth in Intellect, an intellect
of this sort will not be truth nor will it be truly Intellect, nor will it be
Intellect at all. But there is nowhere else for the truth to be.

§5.5.2. So, one should not seek for intelligibles outside Intellect, nor
assert that there are impressions of Beings in it, nor, depriving it of
truth, make it ignorant of intelligibles and make them non-existent,
and even eliminate Intellect itself. But if indeed one must also bring in   5
knowledge and truth, that is, preserve Beings and knowledge of what
each of them is—but not of their qualities,[16] inasmuch as in having
these, we would have only a reflection and a trace of real Beings,
and we would not have or be present with or mixed with the Beings
themselves—all Beings should be given to true Intellect. For in this way

---

13. Cf. 3.7.3.36–38.
14. Cf. *supra* 2.18–20; 5.3.5.22–23.
15. Taking the word for 'belief', δόξα, from the word for 'receive,' δέχομαι.
16. Cf. 2.6.1.43–44. See Pl. [?], *7th Ep.* 342E2–343A1.

10 it would know, that is, truly know, and not forget, nor would it meander seeking them, and the truth will be in it, and it will be the foundation[17] for these Beings, and they will be alive and will be thinking.

All of this must belong to the most blessed nature anyway; otherwise, where will its honor and dignity be? Indeed, again, this being the case, it will also have no need of demonstration or of conviction that these

15 things are so—because it is itself the way that it is and it is self-evident to itself that it is this way; and if there is something prior to it, that is because it is self-evident to it that it comes from that; and if something comes after what is prior to it, that is because it is self-evident to it that that is itself—and no one can be more convinced of this than it is—and because in the intelligible world it is this and really so.

So, the real truth is also not its being in harmony with something

20 else, but with itself, and it expresses nothing else beside itself, but what it expresses, it is, and what it is, this is also what it expresses.[18] Who, then, could refute it? And from where would one draw the refutation? For the refutation adduced would rely on the identical thing said before, and even if you were to provide something else, it is brought in line with that which was said originally and it is one with that. For you could not find anything truer than the truth.

---

17. The term ἕδρα ('foundation') is used by Pl., *Tim.* 52B1, for the receptacle of becoming Intellect, as intelligible matter, plays an analogous role for Beings.
18. Cf. 5.3.5.22–23.

6.4 (22)

THAT BEING, ONE AND IDENTICAL, IS SIMULTANEOUSLY EVERYWHERE WHOLE[1] 1

Introduction

6.4–5 (22–23) comprise a single work on the omnipresence of the intelligible: it preserves its unity in its presence to all sensible things. Any restriction on its presence lies with the sensible, and not the intelligible.

Summary

§1. Discussion of how soul is present throughout the cosmos, first with two solutions from the *Timaeus*, and then brings up the fundamental puzzle of how something without extension can extend throughout the sensible world.

§§2–6. A first explanation. **§2** explains that the sensible world is in the intelligible, and is an imitation of it. **§3** argues that the intelligible is everywhere, in that it does not belong to any of the things which receive it imperfectly; in any case it is not in a place. **§4** shows that there are a multiplicity of intellects and souls because multiplicity and unity are both present in the intelligible. **§5** argues the soul is great, but not in such a way as to have mass and size. Soul belongs to the body that advances toward it. **§6** explains how many bodies share in one soul.

§§7–14. A second explanation. **§7** offers two images to aid understanding, that of the hand and that of the luminous sphere. **§8** argues that since the intelligible is incorporeal it possesses none of the properties of bodies, especially place, divisibility, and passivity. Of itself, the intelligible does not enter the sensible. **§§9–10** Sensible powers are images of the intelligible, and hence depend on their model. **§11** Each being only participates in the intelligible insofar as it is able to. **§12** offers a series of images—ears and eyes, and the presence of sound and sight in the air. While the soul remains in itself, body approaches it, and receives it. **§13** The sensible can only participate in the intelligible, that is, in something non-corporeal. **§14** Soul itself suffices for all living things in that it is unlimited, in containing all souls and intellects.

---

1. See Pl., *Parm.* 131B1–2, 144C8–D1.

§15–16. When a body approaches the intelligible it receives only what is appropriate to it. In living things, body may dominate intellect. **§16** explains the terms used by the decree of Adrastus (Plato, *Phaedrus* 248C–249B).

---

§6.4.1. Is Soul really present everywhere to the universe, because the body of the universe has a determinate size, and because soul naturally divided in bodies?[2]

In fact, no, no soul in itself is everywhere, and not just where it would
5   be extended to by body. Indeed, does body not find that soul is everywhere prior to body?[3] The result is that wherever body happens to be placed, it finds that Soul is already there prior to body's being placed in any part of the universe, and the whole body of the universe is placed in Soul which is already there.

But if Soul extends so far that, prior to reaching a body of a deter-
10   minate size, it filled up all extension, how will it not have a magnitude? Or in what manner would it exist in the universe prior to the universe coming to be, when the universe was not? How would anyone accept that Soul, said to be without parts and without magnitude, is everywhere, if it does not have magnitude?[4] And if Soul were said to be extended along with body, though it is not a body, in this way one
15   would not avoid the problem of giving it magnitude accidentally.[5]

Similarly, someone could reasonably inquire here how it acquired magnitude accidentally, for Soul actually does not, like a quality such as sweetness or color, belong to the whole body.[6] For these are affec-
20   tions of bodies, so that the whole of that which is affected has the affection, and the affection is nothing in itself, belonging as it does to a body and apprehended along with body. For this reason, the affection necessarily has the magnitude of the body, and the pale of one part of the body is not affected along with the pale of another part.

Furthermore, in the case of pale, the pale in the one part and the pale in another are identical in form though not in number,[7] whereas

---

2. Cf. *infra* l. 27; 4.1; 4.2.1.17–41; 4.3.20.41–51; 6.7.13.20–21. See Pl., *Tim.* 35A2–3.

3. Cf. 4.7.8⁵·42–43; 6.5.9.41.

4. Cf. 4.7. 8.1–3.

5. See Numenius, fr. 4b (= Nemesius, *De nat. hom.* 2.8–14). The view that the soul is accidentally a body was attributed to Plotinus's teacher, Ammonius Saccas, and to Numenius.

6. Cf. 4.2.1.47–59.

7. Cf. 4.2.1.33–40. See Ar., *Meta.* 5.6.1016b31–32.

in the case of Soul, the soul in the foot is numerically identical to the   25
soul in the hand, as our acts of apprehension[8] make clear.[9] And, universally, with qualities, the identical thing is understood to be divided into
parts, whereas, in the case of Soul, the identical thing is not divided
into parts,[10] but is said to be divided because it is everywhere.

Let us, then, give an account of these things beginning with their
principle, to establish whether there is something clear and acceptable   30
about the way soul can be incorporeal and without magnitude and yet
reach the greatest extent, either prior to bodies or in bodies. Presumably,
if it were also to appear to be able to do this before there are bodies, it
would be easier to accept also that this kind of thing happens in bodies.

§6.4.2. Certainly, there is both the true universe and the imitation
of the universe,[11] that is, the nature of the visible universe.[12] The true
universe is, then, in nothing, for there is nothing prior to it. Anything
posterior to this is at once necessarily in the [true] universe, if indeed
it is at all, and is completely dependent on that; it cannot either persist   5
or move without it. And indeed even if someone were to posit such a
thing [the universe] not to be in it [the true universe] as in a place—
because he thinks that place is 'the limit of a surrounding body' insofar
as it surrounds body, or an interval that was prior to the nature of the
void and still is[13]—and if he were rather to suppose it [the universe]   10
to be in the [true] universe, as if it were supported by and resting on
the [true] universe, which is everywhere and holds the visible universe
together, still he should set aside the predication of the name, and
grasp with his mind what is being said.

This, however, was said to make another point, namely, that the
[true] universe, the primary Being, neither looks for a place nor is it in
anything at all. Actually, the [true] universe, being all, is not such that   15
it falls short of itself; rather, it has both completed itself and is equal to
itself. And where the universe is, it is there, for it is itself the universe.[14]

Universally, if something other than the universe settles in it, that
thing participates in the [true] universe, and comes together with it
and gets its strength from it, without dividing it. Instead, it finds the   20

8. Cf. 4.5.1.6; 5.3.1.20.
9. Cf. 4.2.2.1–11.
10. Cf. 4.2.1.64–66.
11. Cf. 2.9.8.16–29.
12. See Pl., *Tim.* 48E6–49A1.
13. See Ar., *Phys.* 4.4.212a6, 11.
14. I.e., the intelligible world is present wherever the sensible world is present and the
former is really or truly what the latter is.

[true] universe in itself as it approaches it, without the [true] universe thereby coming to be outside itself. For it is not possible for Being to be in non-being, but rather, if anything, for non-being to be in Being.[15] Non-being, then, encounters Being as a whole. For it was not possible for Being to be severed from itself, and to say that it is everywhere clearly means that it is in being, with the result that it is in itself.[16]

And there is nothing to be astonished at if that which is everywhere is in being and in itself. For that which comes to be everywhere is already in unity [of Being]. For in positing being in the sensible world, we also posit that that which is everywhere is there. Because we think that the sensible is large, we are puzzled how that nature is extended in something of such a largeness. But that which is said to be large is, in fact, small, whereas that which is believed to be small is large, at least if it extends as a whole to every part of the sensible;[17] rather, this, proceeding from everywhere with its parts to that, finds everywhere [true] universe larger than itself.

Hence, since nothing more would be gained by its having extension—for in that case, it would come to be outside even the [true] universe—it [the universe] wanted to circle around it [the true universe],[18] and having been able neither to encompass it nor again to come to be inside it, it was satisfied to have a place and a rank where it would be preserved, neighboring on that which is present and again, not present.[19] For that [true] universe is in itself, even if something should want to be present to it. Actually, wherever the body of the universe comes together with it, it finds the [true] universe, so that it no longer has a need to go further, but it turns in the identical place,[20] since it is this universe, where it is, that enjoys in every part the whole of that [true] universe.

If that universe were in place, then the sensible universe would have had to approach it there and proceed in a straight line, to touch one part with another part of that and to be both far and near. But if there is neither distance nor nearness, that universe must be entirely present, if indeed it is present at all. And it is wholly there for each of those things for which it is neither from afar nor from nearby. It is there for things able to receive it.

---

15. See Pl., *Soph.* 256D.
16. That is, intelligible Being is present to sensible being, so that Being is present to itself.
17. Cf. *infra* 4.5.
18. Cf. 2.2.
19. Cf. 6.5.3.12.
20. See Pl., *Tim.* 34A3–4.

§6.4.3. Will we, then, say that the true universe is itself present or that, while it is by itself, the powers that come from it extend to everything, and it can be said to exist everywhere in this way?[21] For this is how they[22] say that souls are like rays, so that while it is settled in itself, the rays that are sent out come to one living being and then to another.

In fact, in living beings in which there is that unity, because it does not preserve all the nature that is in that [true universe], here a power is present in anything it is present to. Still, one cannot say [the true universe] is not wholly present, since it is not cut off from that one of its powers, which it bestowed on that living being. But the receiver was able to receive just so much, though it was all present.

But where all the powers are, it is itself clearly present, despite being nonetheless separate.[23] For if it had become the form of this one thing, it would cease being everything and being in itself everywhere, while being the form of something else accidentally. Since it belongs to nothing that wants to belong to it, it approaches, as far as possible, whatever might want it,[24] not coming to belong to that, or indeed to anything else, but because that thing desires it.

There is, then, nothing amazing in its thus being in all things, because it is in none of them in such a way as to belong to them. For this reason, it is perhaps not absurd to claim that, in this way, even Soul accompanies body accidentally, that is, if the soul were said to exist on its own, not belonging to matter or body, and the whole body is in a way illuminated wholly by it.

One should also not be amazed if the [true] universe, while not being in place, is present to everything that is in place. The contrary would be amazing, in fact, not just amazing, but impossible, if it also had its own place and were present to something else that was in place, or was present wholly, namely, in the way we say it is present.[25] As things are, the argument asserts that it is necessary for it, since it has occupied no place, to be wholly present to anything it is present to, and

---

21. See Ar. [?], *De mun.* 6.397b32–398a6, b6–10.

22. See Plutarch, *De fac. orb.* 943D8; Hippolytus, *Refutations* 5.19.4, both referring to a Gnostic position. In Plutarch, the word for 'ray' is ἀκτίς, not βολή as here.

23. See Ar., *Phys.* 3.3.202b8.

24. The text has not been satisfactorily emended: the restriction of the power must lie in the recipient, not in the true universe. Cf. *infra* 8.37–45. The translation follows Ficino's emendation as understood by MacKenna and Igal: ᾧ ἂν αὐτὸ ἐθέλῃ ὡς δύναται.

25. See *SVF* 2.463 (= Galen, *In Hippocr. De nat. hom. lib.* 1.15.32), 465 (= Plutarch, *De comm. not.* 37 1077e), 466 (= Alex. Aphr., *De mixt.* 219.16), 467 (= Simplicius, *In Phys.* 530.9), on 'total mixture' of bodies, the position Plotinus is here rejecting.

30   to be present to all just as it is also wholly present to each. If this is not
      so, part of it will be here and part elsewhere. The result is that it will be
      divisible and a body.[26]

      [But that is impossible.] For how will you actually divide it? Will
      you divide its life? But if the whole of it is life, part of it will not be life.
      Or will you divide its intellect, so that part of it is in one thing and
      another in another? But neither of these parts will be intellect. What
35   about its being? But the part will not be being, if the whole was being.[27]
      What if someone were to say, then, that the body is divided, and it has
      parts that are bodies?

      In fact, it was not a division of body, but of a certain quantity of
      body, and each body is called a body due to its form. But this form did
40   not have a determinate quantity, since it did not have any quantity.

      §6.4.4. How, then, is there Being and beings and many intellects
      and many souls, if Being is everywhere one and not just the same in
      form,[28] and Intellect is one and Soul is one?[29] There is the soul of the
5   universe, and there are other souls.[30] This seems to contradict what
      we have said, but even if it has a kind of necessity, it is not persuasive,
      in that the soul thinks it unconvincing that that which is one can be
      identical everywhere in this way.

      Perhaps it would be better to divide the whole [universe] without
      diminishing that from which the division has come about or else, hav-
      ing come to be from it—indeed, to put it in better terms—thus allow
10   one thing to exist on the basis of it,[31] and the rest, coming to be like its
      parts, the souls, complete all things.

      But if that Being remains in itself, because it seems paradoxical that
      that which is a whole is at the same time present everywhere, the iden-
      tical argument will apply to souls. For they will not be in the whole
15   bodies they are said to be in as wholes: either they will be divided or,
      while remaining whole, they will just bestow their power to somewhere
      in the body. And the identical puzzle of the whole being everywhere
      will arise in the case of the souls and their powers. Furthermore, some
      part of the body will have soul and some part only a power.

      ---

      26. Cf. *infra* 8.18–19; 4.2.1.11–12; 6.5.4.10.
      27. Cf. 6.6.18.35; 6.7.13.41; 6.9.2.24–26. See Pl., *Soph.* 248E–249A.
      28. Cf. *supra* 1.24–26.
      29. On the unity of soul, cf. 4.3 and 4.9.
      30. See Pl., *Tim.* 41D5–8. These are the souls of the stars.
      31. The soul of the universe.

But how are there many souls and many intellects and Being and beings? Moreover, in proceeding from the prior entities as numbers,[32] and not as magnitudes, they will likewise give rise to a puzzle, namely, how they fill the universe. In our view, then, nothing in a multiplicity proceeding in this way has been discovered to lead to a solution, since we will agree that Being is many, due to difference, and not to place, for Being is all together, even if it is thus many; 'being borders on being'[33] and 'everything is together'.[34] And Intellect is many due to Difference, not place, and [is many] all together.

And souls, too? Indeed, souls too, since 'that which is divided when in bodies'[35] is said to be naturally partless, but since the bodies have magnitude, and the nature of soul is present to them—or rather, bodies come to be present to it—to the extent that they are divided, and this nature is reflected in every part, it was believed to be divisible in this way among bodies.

Since it was not divided along with the parts but is whole everywhere, this makes clear that unity and indivisibility really belong to its nature. The fact, then, that Soul is one does not cancel out the many souls, just as Being does not cancel out beings, nor does multiplicity in the intelligible world contradict its unity, nor must we fill bodies with life by means of multiplicity, nor must we believe that the multiplicity of souls arises because of the magnitude of body; rather, souls were both many and one prior to bodies. For the many souls are already in the whole, not potentially, but each one is there actually. For the one, whole Soul does not prevent there being many souls in it, nor do the many prevent the unity. They are distinct without being distinct; they are present to one another without being alienated from themselves. They are not divided by limits, any more than are the many sciences in the soul. And Soul is a unity such that it has in it all souls.[36] It is in this way that this kind of nature is limitless.

§6.4.5. And Soul's largeness should be understood like that, and not in terms of mass. For this is small, proceeding to nothingness, if one subtracts from it. But in the intelligible world, it is not possible to take anything away, nor, if you did take anything away, would it give out. And if it will indeed not give out, why should one fear that it will be

---

32. For souls as numbers, cf. 5.1.5.9; 6.5.9.14; 6.6.16.45.
33. See Parmenides, frs. 28 B 8.5 DK.
34. See Anaxagoras, fr. 59 B 1 DK.
35. Cf. 6.9.8.30–32. See Pl., *Tim.* 35A2–3.
36. Cf. *infra* 11.10–12; 4.3.2.13–57; 6.5.10.48–52. See Pl., *Phil.* 13E9ff.

5   absent from anything?[37] For how could it be absent when it does not give out? Instead, it is a nature that eternally wells up, without being in flux. For if it were in flux, it would go as far as it could flow. But it is not in flux, for were it so, there is nowhere for it to flow to, for it has taken hold of the universe; indeed, it is the [true] universe. And, since it is

10   greater than the nature of body, it is reasonably believed to give little of itself to the universe, to wit, just as much as this can bear.

      One should neither say that Soul is less nor, if we do posit it as less in mass, then be mistrustful, on the grounds that the lesser cannot cover something greater. For 'less' should not be predicated of it at all,[38] nor, in measuring, should mass be set beside something without

15   mass—this would be as if someone were to say that the craft of medicine is smaller than the doctor's body. Nor should one believe that the universe is, in this way, larger by measurement of its quantity, since this does not apply to Soul. Rather, that is how the large and the small belong to body. There is evidence of the largeness of Soul in the fact

20   that, the identical soul, which was in the lesser mass, extends to the whole body when the mass of a body increases. For it would be ridiculous in many ways if one were also to attribute mass to the soul.

     §6.4.6. Why, then, does [one] soul not also enter another body?

     In fact, the body must come to the soul, if it can, and the body that has come to it and has received it possesses it.

     What, then? Does another body possess the identical soul when it possesses the soul that it possesses? What differentiates [between the souls]?

5   In fact, it lies in the additions.[39]

     Next, how is it that there is the identical soul in the foot and the hand, whereas that soul which is in this part of the universe is not identical to the soul in another part? But if sense-perceptions differ, the affections that go along with these should be said to differ as well.[40] But, then, it is not that which judges that differs but the things judged.

10   The one who judges is the same judge who comes to be in different affections. Yet the judge is not identical to that which undergoes these affections; that is the nature of a body. It is like the case where the identical judge judges both the pleasure in a finger and the pain in the head.

---

37. See Pl., *Parm.* 144B3–4.
38. Soul has no quantity or mass. Cf. 4.7.5.50–53; 4.9.1.7–8.
39. I.e., to the soul through the body; see the immediately following lines, 6–11. Cf. 1.1.12.18–20; 6.5.12.21. And contrast *supra* 4.39–46.
40. Cf. 3.6.1.1–4; 4.4.22.30–33.

Why, then, is one soul not also aware of the judgment of another? In fact, because it is a judgment, not an affection.

Next, the identical soul that judges does not also say 'I have judged'; it only judged. Not even in us does sight say 'I have judged' to hearing, though both have judged; calculative reasoning judges in both cases, and is different from both.[41] Frequently, calculative reasoning also knows the judgment made in one who is different from it and has comprehension of the state that the other is in. But we have spoken about these matters elsewhere.[42]

§6.4.7. But let us explain again how the identical thing extends over all things. This is the identical question as to how each of the many sensibles is not without a share in the identical thing, even though they are situated in many places.[43] For, from what has been said,[44] it is not correct to divide up that thing into the many things; instead, one should refer back the divided many to one. That one has not come to them; rather, they, because they are scattered, make us believe that one thing has indeed been divided among them, as if one were to separate the controlling and cohesive thing into parts equal to what is controlled.

A hand, however, could well control a whole body, for example, a piece of wood many cubits in length, or something else, and, while controlling the thing entirely, it is nonetheless not separated into parts equal to what is in its control. The power may seem to extend as far as what is grasped, but nonetheless the hand is limited by its own quantity, not by that of the body that it lifts and controls. And if you were to add another length to the body that is controlled, and if the hand had the power to carry that, too, that power would control it and would not be separated into the number of parts that the body has. Then, what would be the case, if one supposed the corporeal mass of the hand removed, but left the identical power that was in the hand, and which held the thing beforehand? Would it not, in that case, be the identical indivisible power in the whole thing in the same way as it is in each part?

And what if one were actually to make a small luminous mass, in a way, the center of a larger transparent spherical body, so that the light from the inside is revealed in all the surrounding parts without any radiance reaching the outer mass from anywhere else? Will we not

---

41. Cf. 4.7.6.9–15; 5.3.2.8–11.
42. Cf. 4.9.2–3.
43. See Pl., *Parm.* 131A–C.
44. Cf. *supra* 2.1–25.

then say that the inside remains unaffected, but has extended itself to every part of the exterior of the mass while remaining fixed itself, and that light seen in the small mass has taken hold of the exterior? So, since that light does not come from the small corporeal mass—for it is not insofar as it is a body that it possesses the light—but as a body which is luminous because of an incorporeal power,[45] so, then, if one were to remove the mass of the body, while keeping the power of the light, would you then still say that the light was somewhere, and not that it was equally throughout the exterior sphere? You would no longer rest in the thought where the light was situated beforehand, and you could not say anymore where it came from and where it is going, but, having been puzzled, you would then be amazed, when, attending simultaneously to here and there in the spherical body, you would yourself see the light in both places.

This is also the case with the sun, since you are able to say where the light illuminating all the air comes from by looking toward the sun's body. Nonetheless, you see the identical light everywhere,[46] and it is not divided. In addition, the segments of the sun in eclipse make this clear, since they neither allow the light to pass over to the other side to that from which the light has come nor do they divide it. So, if the sun were, moreover, only a power separated from body and providing light, light would still not originate from the sun, and you would not be able to say where it does come from. Instead, there would be light everywhere, one and identical, without having originated there or indeed having any origin anywhere.

§6.4.8. Given, then, that light belongs to body,[47] you are able to say where it came from by saying which body it came from. But if there is something immaterial and in need of no body, since it is naturally prior to everybody and set in itself, or rather not needing a seat of this sort, but actually having a nature such that it has neither an origin which it started from nor a place from which it came nor a body to which it belongs, how will you say some of it is here and some of it there? For if you could say this, you could say both where it started and to what it belonged.

So, it remains to explain how, if something participates in [the true universe], it participates in the power of the whole of it, since it is neither affected in any other way, nor has it been divided. For being

---

45. Cf. 4.5.7.13–17.
46. See Pl., *Parm.* 131B3–C8.
47. Cf. 4.5.7.41.

affected belongs to something with a body, even if it has a body accidentally, and in that way it could be said to be subject to affection and
divisible, since this is a kind of affection or form of body.[48] That which   15
does not belong to body but which a body wants to belong to, necessarily cannot undergo any other affection of the body and cannot possibly be divided. For this [division] primarily belongs to body, namely,
its primary affection, and a property of a body as such. If, then, the
divisible is indeed such insofar as it is a body, then the indivisible is
such insofar it is not body. For how will you divide something which   20
does not have magnitude?[49] If, then, something which has magnitude in
any way participates in that which does not have magnitude, it would
not participate in it by that being divided. Otherwise, it will again have
magnitude.

Whenever, then, you say that [the true universe] is in many things,
you are not saying that it has become many. Instead, you are attributing
the affection belonging to the many things to that one, because you see   25
it simultaneously in many things. But the words 'in [the many]' should
not be taken to indicate that it has come to belong either to each of the
many things or to all of them, but that it belongs to itself and it exists
itself and that it does not leave itself behind.

Nor, again, is it of the same size as the sensible universe, nor as some
part of the universe. For it does not have a quantity at all. How then   30
could it have a size? For size belongs to body, whereas one should in
no way attribute size to anything which is not body but is of a different nature; not even such and such a quality belongs to it. So, neither
should a term such as 'where' be used of it. So, neither, should 'here'
and 'there' be used of it, for in that case it would be in many 'wheres'.

So, if the division is by places, whenever part of it is here, and part   35
of it is there, how could you divide something with no here in it at
all? It must, therefore, be undivided and with itself, even if the many
should happen to desire it. If, then, the many do desire it, it is clear
that they desire it as a whole, so that, if they are able to participate in
it, they would participate in the whole of it, insofar as they can.[50] The   40
things that participate in it, then, must possess a part of it such that
they participate in something[51] not proper to them. For in this way, it
would remain itself whole in itself, and whole in the things in which it
is seen. For if it is not whole, it is not itself, nor will the participation

---

48. Cf. 4.7.8².6–43.
49. Cf. 2.4.9.3–12.
50. Cf. *supra* 2.48, 3.16, 5.10; *infra* 11.3–9.
51. Reading οὐ μετέλαβε with Igal.

45   be in the thing desired but in something else, which was not what the
desire was for.

§6.4.9. For indeed if the part that has come to be in each thing were
a whole, and each one was like the primary thing,[52] each one always
being cut off, then, the primary things would be many, and each of
these would be primary.[53]

Next, what would hold apart these many primary things, so that
5   they were not all together one? It certainly couldn't be their bodies,
since it would not be possible for them to be forms of bodies, if indeed
these, too, are to be the same as the primary thing from which they
derive.

If the parts said to be in the many things are its powers, then in the
first place, each is no longer a whole.

Next, how did they come to the many, having been cut off and
10   having left behind the primary thing? For if they actually did leave it
behind, they clearly left it behind by going somewhere.

Next, are the powers that have come to be in the sensible world still
in the [intelligible world] or not? If they are not, it is absurd for that
to be diminished and to have become powerless by being deprived of
15   the powers that it previously had. And how would it be possible for the
powers to be separate or to be cut off from their being? But if the powers are both in it and elsewhere, too, either the wholes or parts of them
will be in the sensible world. If parts of them are in the sensible world,
the rest of the parts will be in the intelligible world. If the wholes are
in the sensible world, either what is both in the intelligible world and
in the sensible world is not divided, and again the identical thing will
20   be everywhere, without being divided, or the powers will each be one
whole that has become many, and they will be the same as each other,
so that the power will be with each substance. Or else there will only
be one power that goes with substance, and the others will be powers
only.

But just as it is not possible to have substance without power, so it is
25   not possible to have power without substance, for power in the intelligible world is real existence and Substance, or greater than Substance.[54]

But if the powers that come from the intelligible world are different,
since they are diminished and faint, like the light that is faint when it
comes from a brighter light, then indeed so, too, are the substances

---

52. I.e., the intelligible Being participated in.
53. See Pl., *Parm.* 142D–E.
54. See Pl., *Rep.* 6.509B5–9.

that go along with these powers, in order that a power does not come to be without substance.

First, in the case of such powers, it is necessary—since they come to be entirely of the same form as each other—either to agree that they are the identical power everywhere[55] or else, if they are not identical everywhere, then they are each the identical whole power at the same time in each place, not divided, as if it were in one identical body.[56] But if this is the case, why is it not in the whole universe? But if it is divided, each power is divided indefinitely and would no longer be a whole in itself, and it will be powerlessness, because of the division.

Next, if one power is here and another there, that will not allow for self-awareness.[57]

Next, like the image of something, like a weaker light, too, it exists no longer when it has been cut off from its source; universally, it is not possible either to make something exist that has its existence from another and is an image of that, once it is cut off. Nor could these powers, coming from there, exist, once they are cut off from that. But if this is so, then that from which they originate will be there at the same time [as they are], and the result would be that again the identical whole will be everywhere undivided at the same time.

§6.4.10. But if someone should say that it is not necessary for a reflection to be joined to its archetype, since it is possible for there to be an image when the archetype from which the image is derived is not there, just as something heated by fire can be hot when the fire is removed; first, in the case of the archetype and image, if one is speaking about the image made by the painter, we will say that it was not the archetype that produced the image, but the painter, given that even if someone paints himself, it is not an image of him. For what does the painting is not the body of the painter, nor the imitated form. It is not the painter but the arrangement of these colors thus and so that should be said to produce this kind of image.

Nor is this the making of the image or reflection in the strict sense, such as occurs in water, mirrors, or shadows.[58] For in these cases, images come to exist strictly as derived from that which was prior to them, and they come to be from it, and it is not possible for them,

---

55. Cf. 4.9.4–5.
56. Cf. *supra* 1.25–27; 4.3.8.47–49.
57. Cf. 1.1.9.20–22; 5.4.2.15–20; 5.6.5.1–8; 6.7.16.19–22, 41.26–27.
58. See Pl., *Soph.* 239D6–7; *Rep.* 6.510E2–3.

once they have come to be, to be when they are cut off from that.[59] But [our opponents] will acknowledge that this is the manner in which the weaker powers come from the prior powers.

In the case of the fire, the heat should not be said to be an image of the fire, unless one were also to say that the fire is in the heat. But if 20   one does not put the fire in the heat, one will make heat apart from fire.

Next, even if not immediately, the heated thing will stop being heated, and the body will cool down, once the fire is removed. But if these people[60] were to extinguish these powers, in the first place they will assert that only one thing is indestructible, and they will be making souls and Intellect destructible.

25   Next, they will produce things in flux from Substance that is not in flux. And indeed if the sun were to remain, being situated somewhere, it would provide the identical light to the identical places. But if some-one were to say that it is not identical, by this he would confirm that the body of the sun is in flux. But that the things that come from that 30   [the One] are not destructible; rather, that the souls and every intellect are immortal has been shown elsewhere using many arguments.[61]

§6.4.11.[62] But why, if [the true universe] is indeed a whole everywhere, does not everything participate in it as a whole? And in what way is there a primary thing in the intelligible world and then a secondary thing and all the others that come after that?

In fact, one should believe that that which is present is present 5   because of the fitness of the recipient,[63] and Being is everywhere in Being, without leaving itself behind;[64] what can be present to it is pres-ent. It is present as far as it can be, but not in place, in the way the trans-parent is present to light, whereas the participation for turbid stuff is otherwise.

Moreover, the primary, secondary, and tertiary things are deter-10   mined by rank, power, and differentiae, not by their places,[65] for noth-ing prevents different things from being all together, such as soul and intellect and all sciences, both the major and the derived ones. For the eye sees the color, and the nose smells the scent, and the other senses

---

59. Reading ἀπ᾽ αὐτοῦ with Kirchhoff. Cf. 5.8.12.19–20.
60. The Gnostics. Cf. 2.9.6.57–58.
61. Cf. 4.7.11.9–18; 5.1.6.27–39; 6.9.9.3–7.
62. See Appendix II J.
63. Cf. *supra* 8.41.
64. I.e., everything in the intelligible world remains there despite being received by their participants.
65. Cf. 6.7.42. See Pl. [?], *Ep.* 2.312E.

sense their different objects that all come from the identical thing, although they are all together, and not separate from each other.

Does this, then, make the intelligible world variegated and multiple? 15

In fact, the variegated is simple, too, and the many are one,[66] for an expressed principle is one and many,[67] and all Being is one. For that which is different is in it itself, and Difference belongs to it, since it certainly could not belong to non-being.[68] And Being belongs to unity, which is not separated from Being, and wherever Being may be, its unity is present to it, and the One-Being is again in itself,[69] for it is 20 possible to be present while being separate.

But the way that sensibles are present to intelligibles—those that are present, and those they are present to—is different from the way that intelligibles are present to themselves. And the way that body is present to soul is different from the way that science is present to the soul and science is present to science, when each is in the identical intellect. And body is present to body in a way different from these. 25

---

66. Cf. 5.1.8.26; 5.3.15.10, 22; 6.2.15.14–15.
67. Cf. 6.7.14.
68. Cf. *supra* 4.23–26, 39–46; 6.2.8; 5.1.4.33–41. See Pl., *Soph.* 255C–D. Here, Difference (= relative 'non-being') refers to one of the μέγιστα γένη ('greatest genera'), which is 'part' of real Being; non-being, then, must refer to what has no real Being or even that which has no being altogether, namely, τὸ μηδαμῶς ὄν.
69. Cf. 6.9.1.1–17. See Pl., *Parm.* 144E1–2.

6.7 (38)

How the Multiplicity of the Ideas Came to Exist and on the Good

Introduction

6.7 is among the longest of the treatises, and it evinces a long development of its theme: basically, what happens when soul is directed by the Good. To this end, we move in the course of the work from Intellect to the Good, beginning with the relation between sensible things and Intellect. A core claim is that being directed by the Good requires being directed by nothing else.

Summary

§§1–14. Explains the relation between sensible things and the forms. Intellect is the collection of Forms, complete Life.

The Good as cause or explanation:

§1. Did the gods give sensations to sensible living things, so that they can live? No, sense-perception was not given to living things by reasoning workmen gods, since god does not reason discursively.

§2. Intellect explains all of sensible life.

§3. But how can there be sensible living things in the intelligible, for they must have the capacity for sense-perception?

§4. Answering this question requires investigation of what the definition of human being includes.

§5. The definition is a mixture of two expressed principles, that for growth and that for intellect. Three human beings are to be distinguished: the first illuminates the second, the second the third.

§6. In Intellect, there is sense-perception of sensibles, such as they are in Intellect.

§7. Sense-perception in the intelligible is clear, in the sensible, faint.

The Good in rational choice:

§§8–14. All of the kinds of life can be in Intellect, since there is a hierarchy among them, and each of them represents Intellect in its own way.

§8. Intellect is the complete living being, containing all intellects and all souls.

§9. The powers unfold hierarchically, the lower from the higher, but the lower ones do not include all the power before them, but they make up for these deficiencies with their own peculiar attributes.

§10. Intellect is a unitary perfect Living Being; and this precludes it possessing differentiating attributes.

§11. The elements in matter derive from their veritable living counterparts in intellect, being expressed principles like plants and animals.

§12. All living things are necessarily in the Living Being. In turn, all life is derived from one source.

§13. Intellect is variegated, indeed it comprises all life, since it fulfills its own nature as Substance.

§14. Intellect is a structured 'one-many', such that all things have their place in it.

§§15–42. The nature of the Good and its relation to Intellect.

The Forms are Good-like:

§§15–23. What does it mean to say that Forms and hence Intellect are Good-like? The Intellect turns toward the Good, but only in receiving the Good is there actual thought of the Forms. Only in this way does the soul desire Intellect. The paradox is that Forms resemble something without form.

§15. Intellect is complete Life, whereas life in the sensible world is merely trace of the archetype. Intellect is Good-like, because it contains the Good in the Forms, so it is a variegated good.

§16. Intellect does not see the Good but lives in accordance with it, hence the Good explains the forms, 'substantial being', and their being seen.

§17. Intellect acquires boundaries on having seen the Good, hence the Forms are in Intellect, and are themselves intellects. Intellect makes Soul rational by passing on a trace of what it itself receives from the Good.

§18. Life is only good when it comes from the Good; life is not in the Good itself.

§19. But each thing is not good because of desire, and because of each thing's virtue in the sensible world, but not in Intellect, since there nothing is bad. Reason still needs to understand in what way the Good is in the Forms.

§20. Intellect is not the Good, since, although soul desires it, not everything does.

§21. The activity of Intellect and its contents are Good-like insofar as they are derived from the Good, and bounded. Soul desires the life of Intellect insofar as this is derived from the Good.

§22. Each thing is what it is in itself, but it becomes desired when the Good itself colors it, because this gives it grace and love in the eyes of those desiring it.

§23. There must be the Good, otherwise there would be no vice either. The Good produces Intellect, Life, and Soul.

Nine questions about defining the Good:

§§24–30. Is the Good all that the soul desires? Is the Good a mixture of pleasure and knowledge?

§24. The Good is what everything desires; that is how we know there is the Good. The objection is then raised that in and of themselves Life and Intellect, and anything beyond them, are not good.

§25. Our good includes joy, but the Good itself is desired because it is good, not vice versa. The good of the body is soul, that of the soul is virtue. Then comes Intellect, and finally, the Good. It provides 'light' to Intellect.

§26. One can tell that one has hit on the Good when things improve, there is fulfillment and no regrets. Pleasure, in contrast, always requires continuation with something new.

§27. Appropriation occurs for each thing when it attains its own fulfillment, which is determined by something superior to itself. This leaves the question of what the primary Good is.

§28. Matter has awareness of the Good, that is, being formed, and so being something. The Good is as far from matter as possible.

§29. Pleasure is not characteristic of the primary Good, since it consists in filling a need.

§30. We have a portion of the Good because of a mixture of truth, measurement, and beauty.

The soul's return to its origin in the Good:

§§31–36. The Good goes beyond the truth, beauty, and proportion of Intellect. When the soul is directed by the Good alone, this means that it is not directed by any Form whatever.

§31. On account of the love of the Good in the soul, it moves beyond sensible things, and Intellect, and desires to make itself like the thing it loves.

§32. The principle of the beauty of the Forms lies in something formless, namely, in the Good.

§33. Form is measured, but Beauty itself is without measure, and without form: Beauty is the nature of the Good itself.

§34. When the soul arrives at Beauty itself, it sheds all other properties, and has a contentment that cannot be surpassed.

§35. When soul arrives at the Good, all motion, and thought, ceases. Intellect can both think its own contents, and is also receptive for the Good. The Good unifies soul and intellect when it is present to them.

§36. Cognizing the Good is 'the most important subject of learning'. In its case, seeing and light are one.

The Good and thought:

§§37–42. The separation of Intellect from the Good, and the hierarchy of existence.

§37. The Good does not think, and so does not think itself, as the Peripatetics claim.

§38. The Good is not, has no predicates, and does not think itself.

§39. Thinking and Substantiality requires Difference, so that the Good cannot think itself, on pain of not being simple.

§40. Persuasion is added to the arguments: the Good is unmixed with thinking, and is only attained when one moves beyond thought.

§41. Since the Good is perfectly one, primary and independent, it cannot think, since thinking requires an object.

§42. The hierarchy: all beings are for the sake of the Good. Intelligibles follow the Good directly, Soul in Intellect produces the sensible things.

---

§6.7.1. When the god or a god[1] sent the souls to come to be, he put 'light-bearing eyes'[2] in their faces, and gave them the other sense-organs, foreseeing that like this they would be preserved, if they looked ahead, and heard beforehand and, having touched things, could pursue one and avoid another.   5

How could the god actually foresee these things? For it was certainly not because other things had previously come to be, then perished for want of perceptual capacities, that he then gave these to human beings and other animals, which would be preserved in this way from suffering by them.

In fact, someone might say that he knew that the living being would   10
be amid hot and cold and the other affections of bodies,[3] and that, knowing this, he gave living beings sense-perception and the organs for these so that their bodies might not easily perish; and through these organs the sense-perceptions are actualized. But he gave them either the organs when they already had the capacities or he gave them both at once. But if he gave them the senses as well, then although they were   15
souls beforehand, they did not have the potency for sense-perception.

---

1. See Pl., *Tim.* 44E5: it is the younger gods made by the Demiurge who make the human body.
2. See Pl., *Phd.* 113A4–5; *Tim.* 34BC, 41DE.
3. As Plato does, *Tim.* 33A.

If they already had the potency for sense-perception when they became souls, and if they became souls so that they might enter the realm of becoming, then it would be natural for them to do so. Therefore, being apart from the realm of becoming, that is, being in the intelligible world, would then be contrary to their nature. And in that case, they would have been produced so as to belong to another thing, and to be amid evil. And providence would see to it that they might be

20 preserved amid this evil; and this would be the calculation of god, that is, comprehensive calculation.

What are the principles of these calculations? For even if they come from previous calculations, they must aim at something prior to the calculation, or at some things in any case. So what are the principles? They must [belong] either to sense-perception or intellect. But sense-perception did not yet exist; therefore, intellect. But if the prem-

25 ises [belong to] intellect, then the conclusion must be scientific knowledge. It does not, therefore, concern anything sensible. For since that of which the starting point is in the intelligible reaches its conclusion in the intelligible, too, how is it possible that this disposition[4] should arrive at discursive thinking regarding the sensible? Given that this is so, neither providence for the living being, nor indeed for this universe, could come about on the basis of calculation since there is no

30 calculation in the intelligible world; one speaks of calculation[5] only to indicate that things are arranged as though they were the consequences of calculation; and of foresight, because they are as a wise man would have foreseen.[6] For in things which do not come to be without prior calculation, calculation is useful because of an absence of the power before the calculation, and foresight is useful because the human being

35 who foresees does not possess the power which would mean that he would have no need of foresight.

For foresight is so that this and not that occurs; and it fears, in a way, that such and such does not occur. But it is not foresight, where only this is the case. For calculation also takes one thing instead of another; for what could one calculate if only one of the alternatives is the case?

40 How can what is alone, one, and simple contain, in a developed state, 'this, so that this does not happen', or 'this had to be, if not that', 'this appeared useful, and this was preservative when it came about'? He who says these things, therefore, foresaw something and, therefore,

---

4. I.e., the disposition (ἕξις) of Intellect which is exclusively for intellection.
5. See Pl., *Tim.* 34A8.
6. Cf. 4.3.25.20–27; 5.8.7.36–47; 6.2.21.32–35.

calculated it beforehand, certainly in the case we started from, too;[7] the god bestowed the senses, even if this gift is most puzzling. Nonetheless, if no activity can be incomplete,[8] and if it is not lawful to think that anything belonging to god is other than whole and total, then everything must be present in anything that belongs to him.

So, anything that is going to be exists already. There is certainly nothing which only occurs later in the intelligible world; rather, something that is already present in the intelligible world comes to be later in something else.[9] If, then, what is to be is already present, it must be present in such a way that it has been thought in advance for the later event; that is, because it requires nothing then, that is, there is no deficiency. All things, therefore, already were and were always, and were in such a way that one later says this is after that. For when something is extended and, in a way, developed, then it can display this after that, though while it is together, it is all this.[10] This is what it means [for something] to contain its explanation in itself.

§6.7.2. For this reason, one can even discover in the sensible world the nature of Intellect, which we see better than we do other things; still, we do not see the dimensions of the need for Intellect; we grant that it contains the 'that', but not yet the 'why'.[11] Or, if we were to grant it the 'why', then it is only as something separate. We see a human being or an eye, as it may be, like a statue or as belonging to a statue. In the intelligible world, there is the 'that' of human being,[12] and the 'why' there is human being, if indeed human being in the intelligible world has to be intellectual; so, too, with the eye and its 'why'. For it would not be at all, were there no 'why'. In the sensible world, just as each of its parts is separate, so, too, is the 'why'. In the intelligible world, all are in one, with the result that the thing [the 'that'] and the 'why' of the thing are identical.

---

7. Cf. *supra* ll. 1–17.
8. See Ar., *Meta.* 9.6.1048b34–35.
9. Cf. 3.7.3.28.
10. Cf. 5.3.15.21; 5.8.9.3; 5.9.6.3–8. See Anaxagoras, fr. 59 B 1 DK.
11. For the distinction between the 'that' something is the case and the 'why' something is the case, see Ar., *AP* 1.13. The 'why' here is the explanation of 1.57 *supra*, and in 2.4–9.
12. Or: 'Human Being' indicating the Form. Throughout this chapter and the following Plotinus does not distinguish between the Form of Human Being which is identical with Intellect and the individual undescended intellect. The ambiguity is preserved using lower case throughout.

Often in the sensible world, too, the thing and its 'why' are identical, for example, in answer to the question what is an eclipse?[13] What, then, prevents each thing being a 'why' in the other cases, too, and this being the substantiality of each thing? Rather, this is necessary. And for any-
15   one trying to grasp the 'what it was to be',[14] this is the right approach. For what each thing is is why it is. I do not mean that the Form is the explanation for each thing's existence,[15] although that is true, but that if you unravel each Form in itself, you will find the 'why' in it. Anything
20   inactive and without life quite simply does not have the 'why' in it; whereas for something that is Form and belongs to Intellect, where else is it meant to take the 'why' from? If someone says that it gets it from Intellect, then the Form is not separate from it, if indeed it is Intellect. If, then, the thing must have no deficiency in anything, then neither does it have a deficiency in the 'why'.
25   This is how Intellect has the 'why' of each of the things in it. It is each of those things in it, so that each of them has no need of 'why' it came to be; all at once it comes to be and possesses the explanation for its real existence. Since it has not come to be by chance, it cannot be missing any of the 'why'; instead, since it possesses everything it also possesses the beautiful togetherness of its explanation. And it bestows
30   this in such a way on the things that partake of it, so that they possess the 'why'.

Further, just as in this universe here, which consists of many things, all things are strung together, and each 'why' also depends on the being of all—just as the part in each case is seen as relating to the whole—it is
35   not the case then when this has come to be, then that comes to be after this; rather, explanation and explanandum are together, standing in relation to one another. So, too, in fact, even more so in the intelligible world must all things stand in relation to the whole, and each thing in relation to itself.

If, then, the real existence[16] of all things hangs together, and is not a matter of chance and if they must not be separated, the explananda
40   would have the explanations in themselves; and each thing is such that it has its explanation in a non-explanatory fashion.

If, then, they do not have an explanation for their existence, they are self-sufficient, and bereft of explanation; they must have the

---

13. See Ar., *Meta.* 8.4.1044b14; *AP* 2.2.90a15.
14. Τὸ τί ἦν εἶναι, the Aristotelian technical term for the essence of something.
15. I.e., its existence as the kind of thing it is. See Pl., *Phd.* 99D4ff. on the Form as αἰτία.
16. Cf. *infra* 40.48.

explanation in themselves, and with themselves. For indeed if nothing in the intelligible world is in vain, and many things are in each thing, you should be able to say why each thing contains all the things it does   45 contain.[17] The 'why' is prior, and existed together with the other things in the intelligible world, without being 'why', but just being the 'that'.[18] It would be better to say that both of these are one. For what would [an intelligible] have above and beyond Intellect, such that a thought of Intellect is not just that, a perfect product?

If, then, it is perfect, it is not possible to say where it is deficient, nor that it is not present because of such and such a reason. You can, therefore, say it is present because it is present. The 'why', therefore, is   50 in its real existence [the 'that']. So, in each thought and in the result of each act, in a way, the whole of human being appeared, human being bringing all of itself with it, possessing altogether all it has possessed from the start, and altogether available.

Next, if it is not everything, if, that is, one needs to add something to it, then it belongs to the product of a coming to be. But it is always;   55 so it is everything, whereas the human being that has come to be is generated.

§6.7.3. What, then, prevents god from deliberating in advance about the generated human being?

In fact, he must correspond to that human being in Intellect, so one may not take any part away or add it:[19] deliberation and calculation occur because of the hypothesis; for Plato hypothesized things as having come to be. Thus, deliberation and calculation [are found   5 in the dialogue]. But in indicating that 'these things always come to be',[20] Plato cancelled out the calculation. For there is no calculation in eternity. For calculation belongs to someone forgetful of how things were beforehand. Then, if it is better afterward, it must have been worse beforehand. And if they were beautiful beforehand, then they are similarly beautiful now. They are beautiful together with their explanation.[21]

---

17. See Ar., *DC* 1.4.271a33.
18. Cf. *supra* 2.3–4, and l. 40.
19. See Theognis, 809–810.
20. See Pl., *Tim.* 27D6–28A1.
21. The word is αἰτία which can also be translated 'cause'. The translation 'cause' seems better when speaking about Intellect or the One, and 'explanation' when speaking about the Forms or intelligibles generally.

10   Even in the sensible world, too, something is beautiful because it
contains all that belong to it[22]—for a form also contains everything
belonging to it—and because it dominates the matter, and it dominates
matter if nothing is left unshaped. And it leaves it unshaped if some
shape is missing, an eye or some such. So, when giving the explanation,
you will recount all these things. Why, then, are there eyes? So that
15   everything may be there. And why eyebrows? So that everything may
be there. And were you to say, 'for the sake of protecting the eyes,'[23]
you would be saying there is something safeguarding the substantiality present in it, that is, that it contributes to the substantiality. The
substantiality, therefore, was before this, and therefore the explanation
is part of the substantiality.[24] So, there is something else belonging to
the substantiality, namely, what it is. So, all things are for one another;
20   and the whole and complete substance, in total, as well as its being
beautiful comes with the explanation and lies in the explanation: the
substantiality, or the 'what it was to be', and the 'why' are one.

So, if having the faculty of sense-perception, and being able to perceive in this way is included in the Form, on the grounds of eternal
25   necessity and the perfection of Intellect, which possesses the explanations in itself, if indeed it is perfect, such that we only see afterward that
things are right this way—for in the intelligible world, the explanation
is one and complete, and the human being in the intelligible world
is not just intellect[25] with the faculty of sense-perception added when
he was sent to birth—how could that intellect not incline to things in
the sensible world? For what would the faculty of sense-perception be
30   other than the grasping of sensibles? How would it not be strange if the
faculty of sense-perception is in the intelligible world from eternity,
whereas actual sense-perception is in the sensible world, that is, for the
actualization of the potency in the intelligible world to be fulfilled in
the sensible world just at the time when the soul becomes worse?

§6.7.4.[26] In view of this puzzle, then, we must return to the question
of what that human being in the intelligible world is. Presumably, we
should say first just what the human being in the sensible world is,
5   so that we do not investigate that one, as though we had him in our

---

22. Cf. 6.5.10. See Pl., *Rep.* 4.420C–421B; *Tim.* 87D.
23. Cf. 1.6.2.18–28. See Ar., *PA* 4.9.685b14.
24. Cf. 6.2.4–5; 6.3.15.24–38.
25. I.e., the undescended intellect. Cf. *infra* 5.26–29, 17.26–27; 3.4.3.24; 4.3.5.6;
4.3.12.3–4; 4.8.8; 6.8.6.41–43.
26. See Appendix II A.

possession, whereas we do not know him accurately at all. Perhaps it would seem to some that this human being and that one are identical.

The inquiry begins from this point: is the human being [in the sensible world] an expressed principle other than the soul which produces this human being, providing him with life and reasoning? Or is such and such a soul the human being? Or the soul using a body of such a kind?[27] But if human being is a rational animal,[28] and an animal consists of body and soul, then this expressed principle would not be identical with the soul. But if the expressed principle of human being consisted of rational soul and body, how could it be an eternal real existent, if this kind of expressed principle of human being only comes into being when body and soul come together? For then this expressed principle will reveal the future human being, but not such a one as we call the human being itself; it will be more like a definition indeed like the kind which does not make the 'what it was to be' clear.[29] For it does not make the enmattered form clear, but the form-matter complex, which is already. If this is the case, then the [intelligible] human being has not yet been discovered. For it was the one corresponding to the expressed principle.[30]

If someone were to say, the expressed principle of such things must be [of] a complex, a 'this in a this',[31] he does not think it worthwhile to mention that according to which each thing is. But one has to say this, for even if it is necessary to say that the expressed principles belong to the enmattered forms, and are themselves with matter, one must grasp as far as possible the expressed principle itself which has produced, for example, a human being; this is especially so for anyone who thinks that in each case the 'what it was to be' has to be defined, when you define properly.[32]

What, then, is it to be a human being?[33] Is this the inherent factor which has made this human being, and which is not separable? This expressed principle itself, then, will be a rational living being. Or is the complex the rational animal, while the expressed principle itself is productive of the rational living being? What, then, is it itself? Or does 'living being' take the place of 'rational life' in the definition?[34] So,

27. See Pl. [?], *Alc.* 1.129E–130A; *Phd.* 79C2–3.
28. See Ar., *Pol.* 1.2.1253a9; fr. 192 Rose[3] (= Ross, p. 132).
29. See Ar., *AP* 2.3.90b30, 10.94a11.
30. Cf. *infra* 5.1–6, 23–31.
31. See Ar., *Meta.* 7.5.1030b18.
32. See Ar., *Meta.* 7.4.1029b14.
33. Cf. 1.1.
34. Adding a question mark to the sentence.

the human being is rational life. Is the human being, then, life without soul?

35   In fact, soul provides rational life; and the human being will then be the activity of soul, and not a substance; or else the soul will be the human being. But if the rational soul is to be the human being, then how is it not a human being when it enters another animal?

§6.7.5.[35] So, the human being must be an expressed principle other than soul.[36] What prevents the human being from being some complex: a soul in such an expressed principle, given that the expressed principle is, in a way, such and such an activity, and given that the activity cannot
5   exist without the agent?[37] This is the way the expressed principles are in seeds. For they are neither without souls nor just souls. The expressed principles that produce them are not inanimate, and there is nothing surprising if these kinds of substances are expressed principles.

The expressed principles, then, which actually produce the human
10   being are the activities of what kind of soul? Of the soul responsible for growth?

In fact, they are of the soul which produces the living being, a clearer soul,[38] and hence more alive.

A soul of this kind, when it has come to be in such and such matter, inasmuch as it is this, that is, being disposed this way, and without the body, is the human being; when in itself shaped in the body, it made
15   another image of human being such as the body can take on, just as the painter will produce a human being lesser even than this one;[39] it has the shape, the principles or characters, the dispositions, the capacities, but they are all faint because this human being is not the primary one.
20   Moreover, this soul has other senses which are held to be clear, but are fainter relative to those prior to them and images.

But the human being above this one belongs to a more divine soul, containing a better human being and clearer senses. This must be the human being Plato defines when he adds that the soul 'uses a body';[40]
25   it supervenes on that soul which primarily uses a body, and the soul which uses body at one remove is more divine. Once a human being

---

35. See Appendix II A.
36. This is an exceptionally clear use of the core meaning of λόγος for a Form contained in Intellect and 'expressed' in souls. The composite human being cannot be soul alone.
37. I.e., the soul.
38. 'Clearer' means higher in the intelligible hierarchy. Cf. 3.8.8.18; 6.3.7.22; 6.6.18.16.
39. See Pl., *Rep.*10.595A–598C.
40. I.e., the intellect. See Pl. [?], *Alc.* 1.129E11; *Phd.* 79C2–3.

with a faculty of sense-perception had come to be, this soul followed
and bestowed a clearer life on the human being. It would be better to
say, not that it followed, but that it added itself, in a way. For it does
not step outside the intelligible world, but, bound together with the
lower soul, it holds the lower soul depending on it itself, having mixed   30
itself, an expressed principle, with an expressed principle. Hence, this
human being, although he is murky, becomes clear by illumination.[41]

§6.7.6. How, then, is there the faculty of sense-perception in the
better soul?

In fact, it is a potency for sense-perception of the sensibles in the
intelligible world as they exist there. For this reason, it also perceives
the sensible harmony in this way,[42] whereas the human being [in the
sensible world] has a receptive perceptual potency, and is attuned to   5
the last degree to the harmony in the intelligible world, for example,
when the fire in the sensible world is attuned to the Fire in the intelligible world, the sense-perception of this fire belongs to that soul corresponding to the nature of Fire there.

Insofar as there are these bodies in the intelligible world, there
would be acts of sense-perception and acts of apprehension of them
by the soul. And the human being in the intelligible world, the soul of   10
such and such a kind, would be capable of apprehending them. This is
why the posterior human being, the imitation, contains their expressed
principles in an imitative form. The human being in the Intellect is the
human being prior to all human beings.

The first illuminates the second, and the second the third. The last
human being contains all of them in a certain sense, not by becoming
them but because it is close to them. One of us acts according to the   15
last human being, another has something of the one before the last
one, and yet another has his activity from the third [the human being
in Intellect]. Each of them is the human being according to which he
is active; and yet each both does and does not contain them all. Given
that the third life, that is, the third human being, is separated from the   20
body, if the second[43] continues to be connected with the body, it would
be connected while not separated from things above, where it and the
[first] are said to belong.

---

41. Cf. 4.4.18.4–15.
42. The 'sensible harmony' is the mathematical proportions of the elements.
43. Reading ἡ δευτέρα with the mss.

When it [the second soul] takes hold of a beast's body, one is filled with wonder, as to how the expressed principle of this is the expressed principle of a human being.

In fact, it is everything, and it acts at different times in accordance
25 with different things; and before it has gone bad, it wants to be the human being and is a human being. For this is more beautiful, and it produces what is more beautiful. It produces also the prior daemons,[44] which have the same form as human beings. And the human being before this soul is even more of a daemon, or better, a god, for the daemon that depends on god, as the human being does on the daemon, is an imitation of god.

30 What the human being depends on in fact is not called a god. For there is a distinction, namely, the one that souls have toward one another, even if they belong to the identical rank. One should also call 'daemons' that kind of daemon that Plato calls 'intelligences'.[45] But when the soul connected to the daemon it had when it was human being follows a soul that chose 'the nature of a beast',[46] it gives the expressed principle that it had in itself to the animal. For this contains it, and this is an inferior activity for it.

§6.7.7. But if the soul only informs a bestial nature on going to the bad, and being degraded, there was not anything originally in it which would have produced an ox or a horse. Thus, the expressed principle of horse, that is, the horse, would have been contrary to nature.

In fact, it is something lesser, not really contrary to nature; that
5 which produced them was in some way originally a horse or a dog. And if the soul contains the means, then it produces something better, and if not, then it produces what it can, which at any rate was what it was preordained to produce. It is like creators who know how to produce many forms, and then either produce these, or what they were ordered to, or what the matter was suited to.

10 For what prevents the power of the soul of the universe from producing a sketch beforehand, inasmuch as it is the expressed principle of everything, even before the psychical powers deriving from it? And what prevents the sketch produced beforehand from being like illuminations anticipating matter, and soul from carrying out the work,

---

44. Cf. 3.4.2.16–30; 3.4.3.13–22; 3.5.6.37.
45. See Pl., *Symp.* 202D13–E1; *Tim.* 90A2–4. At *Crat.* 398B, Plato says that δαίμονες ('daemons') are δαήμονες ('intelligences'). Accordingly, Harder is followed in reading δαημόνων. This is accepted by HS[1] but not by HS[2].
46. See Pl., *Tim.* 42C3–4.

following these traces, articulating the traces part for part?[47] Each soul   15
becomes then what it draws near, shaping itself, just as the dancer fits
himself to the role assigned to him.

We have reached this point by following one continuous line of
thought. Our argument was how the faculty of sense-perception
belongs to the [intelligible] human being, and how those things [sensi-
bles] in the intelligible world do not look in the direction of generation.
And it seemed to us, and the argument showed, that those things in the   20
intelligible world do not look in the direction of things [sensibles] in
the sensible world, but these things here are dependent upon those
things there, and imitate them. And this human being has its powers
from that human being, in relation to those things [sensibles]: the sensibles in the sensible world are coupled with this human being, and the
sensibles in the intelligible world are coupled with that human being.

We called the latter 'sensibles'[48] because, though they are incorpo-   25
real, they are apprehended in a different way[49]—and in the sensible
world we called it 'sense-perception' because it is of bodies, though
this apprehension is fainter than that in the intelligible world, where,
because it is of incorporeals,[50] it was said to be clearer. Because of this,
the human being in the sensible world has a faculty of sense-perception,
too, because he has a lesser apprehension of lesser images than those   30
in the intelligible world. The upshot is that these acts of sense-perception
are faint acts of intellection, whereas the acts of intellection in the
intelligible world are clear acts of sense-perception.

§6.7.8. So much for the faculty of sense-perception. But how are
horse and each of the animals in the intelligible world really there in
the intelligible world? And how did the [Demiurge] not want to look at
the things in the sensible world when he produced the animals?[51] But
what if it were the case that, in order that a horse or another animal
may come to be in the sensible world, he invented the thought of a

---

47. Cf. 4.3.6.13–15.
48. Cf. *supra* 6.2, 8.
49. The logic of this troubled text, as translated, suggests that the 'sensibles' in the
intelligible world are apprehended in a way differently from the apprehension of those
intelligibles that do not have sensible imitations. Alternatively, with a slightly different
text, Plotinus is making the predictable claim that all intelligibles are apprehended
differently from the way sensibles are apprehended.
50. Reading αἴσθησιν ὅτι <ἀ>σωμάτων with Hadot.
51. Following Hadot, we read ὅλως with the mss and adding a question mark in the
first sentence and then adding <πῶς> at the beginning of the second sentence. Cf.
supra 7.18–20.

5   horse? Still, how was it possible, when wanting to produce a horse,
to think it up? For clearly the thought of a horse was there already, if
indeed he wanted to produce a horse.

The upshot is that it is not possible to have the thought, in order that
he can produce the horse; instead, the horse that does not come to be
exists in the intelligible world before the one that will exist after that.
If, then, the horse in the intelligible world existed before the generation
[of the other one], and was not thought so that the horse in the sensible
world could come to be, then he who possesses in himself the horse in
10   the intelligible world does not possess it with a view to the horses here.
Nor did he possess the horse—and other [intelligibles]—so that he
could produce the horses in the sensible world; rather, they were in the
intelligible world, and the ones in the sensible world followed them of
necessity.[52] For it was not possible for things to stop with the things in
the intelligible world. For who could have stopped a power that could
both remain and proceed?[53]

15   But why are the animals [in the sensible world] in the intelligible
world?[54] What are they in god? Rational animals are there, so be it. But
the vast number of non-rational animals—what is holy about them?
And why not the opposite? Because it is clear that the One-Being also
has to be many, since it is posterior to that which is absolutely One.[55]
Otherwise, it would not be posterior to the One, but would be the
20   One itself. And since it is posterior to that, it was not possible for it to
exceed that One in unity; it had to fall short of it. Since the best was
the One, it had to be more than one. For multiplicity lies in deficiency.

So what prevents it from being a Dyad?

In fact, it was not possible for either of the two parts in the Dyad to
25   be absolutely one; rather, they had to be at least two, and so, too, their
parts in turn.[56]

Next, there was Motion and Stability in the primary Dyad, there
was Intellect and Life in it—that is, perfect Intellect and perfect Life.[57]
So, it was not as one Intellect, but as all Intellect, that is, Intellect containing all the individual intellects; Intellect as many as these are, and
30   more. And it was alive not as one soul, but as all souls, containing more

---

52. Cf. 5.9.7–8.
53. Cf. 5.1.6.37–39.
54. Cf. 5.5.1–3; 5.9.7–8.
55. Cf. 5.1.8; 6.9.1–4. See Pl., *Parm.* 145A2.
56. See Pl., *Parm.* 142E3–143A1.
57. Cf. 5.1.4.30–43; 5.9.10.10–15; 6.9.2.24–25. See Pl., *Soph.* 249A–C on the μέγιστα
γένη ('greatest genera'), including Motion and Stability.

power to produce the individual souls. And it was a 'complete Living Being',[58] containing not only the human being in itself; otherwise, human being would be only in the sensible world.

§6.7.9.[59] Let us admit, someone may say, the more honorable animals, but what about the lower animals and the non-rational ones? Their lowness comes from their being non-rational, clearly, if honor belongs to that which is rational. And if animals are honorable due to their intellectual quality, they are the opposite by their lack of it. Yet how can something without thought[60] or non-rational belong to that   5
Intellect in which each thing exists or from which they came?

Before we actually approach these questions, let us grasp that the human being in the sensible world is not such as the one in the intelligible world; so, then, other animals are not in the intelligible world as they are in the sensible world—they have to be understood in a superior sense.

Next, neither is there rationality there. The human being is presum-   10
ably rational in the sensible world; in the intelligible world, he is prior to calculative reasoning.[61] Why, then, would the human being calculate in the intelligible world, and not the other animals?

In fact, since thinking in the intelligible world is different in human beings and in other animals, then so, too, is calculating different. Many products of discursive thinking are in other animals as well; why, then, are they not equally rational? And why are not human beings among   15
themselves equally rational?

One should bear in mind that the many lives are, in a way, motions, and the many acts of intellection need not be the same: both lives and acts of intellection are different. The distinctions differ in luminosity and clarity, first, second and third, depending on the proximity to the   20
first principles. This is why some of these acts of intellection are gods, others a second kind, which has here the designation 'rational', and the one coming after that is called 'non-rational'. In the intelligible world, what is called here 'non-rational' is an expressed principle, and what is

---

58. See Pl., *Tim.* 31B1.

59. See Appendix III B 2.

60. The word is ἀνόητον ('without thought'), which would normally be translated as 'non-intelligible' but is here used to mean 'non-intellectual' since the hypothetical Greek word for the latter, ἀνόερος, does not seem to exist.

61. Cf. 4.8.1.4–8; 6.2.21.27–37. The words λογικός ('rational') and λογίζεσθαι ('calculating') are quite close. Plotinus is thinking of rationality as discursive as opposed to intellection (νόησις) which is not.

without Intellect is Intellect; for it is Intellect that is thinking Horse—
25 and the intellection of Horse is Intellect.

But if it was intellection alone, there would be nothing absurd in it being the intellection of that which is without thought. But, as it is, if intellection is identical with the thing, then, how can there be intellection, with the thing being without thought?[62] For in that way, Intellect would make itself be without thought.

In fact, then, it is not without thought, but Intellect with such and such a nature; for it has such and such a life.[63]

30 For just as such and such a life does not cease to be life, Intellect does not cease to be Intellect; since the intellect in any living being, including a human being, does not cease to be the Intellect of all things, if indeed each and every part is a part of the Intellect of all things, each, presumably, in a different sense.[64] In actuality it is that one thing, but 35 it has the potency for everything. We grasp what is actualized in the particular. And what is actualized is the last thing, for example, the last thing of [the actuality of] Intellect is being horse: it is a horse insofar as it ceases proceeding to ever inferior life forms, and another form if it ceases lower down.

As the powers unfold, they always leave something above. In pro-
40 ceeding, they lose something at each step, and different powers, by losing different things because of the inadequacy of the animal which appears, find different additions coming out of the deficiency, for example, because the animal no longer had what was sufficient for living, nails appeared, claws, with fitting teeth, or horns. The result is that wherever Intellect has descended to, it bounces back because of the self-sufficiency in its nature; it finds in itself the cure for the deficiency.

§6.7.10. But how did it come to be deficient in the intelligible world? Why are there horns for defense in the intelligible world?

In fact, for the self-sufficiency and completeness of the Living Being. For as Living Being it must be complete, and as Intellect, it must be complete, and so, too, as Life. The result is that if it is not this, well, 5 then it is that.[65] And the differentia comes from this [property] being substituted for that, so that from all things there may ensue the most

---

62. See Ar., *Meta.* 12.9.1075a1–5.
63. Here employing the ambiguity of ἀνόητον as 'without thought' or 'non-intelligible'. Intellect is not without thought because its life is actively thinking, and so identical with, all that is intelligible.
64. Each individual intellect and each intelligible thing is a part of Intellect.
65. I.e., a putatively deficient A is really a complete or perfect B.

complete Living Being, complete Intellect, and the most complete Life: each thing is perfect as the thing it is.

Further, if the Living Being consists of many things, it must still be one; in fact, it is not possible that it consists of many things and that these are all identical.

In fact, it would then be a self-sufficient unity. So, it must consist of things that are specifically different, like any composite, and where   10
each thing, that is, the shapes[66] and definitions of the ingredients, are preserved. For the shapes, for example, of a human being, come from such differences, and yet there is one that stands over all. And they are better and worse than one another, eye, and finger, but they all belong to the one thing. But the universe is not worse; indeed, it is better that   15
it is this way. The expressed principle is living being, plus something else [the differentiating property] which is not identical with living being. And 'virtue' refers to what is common [the genus] and to what is unique [the differentiating property]; and what is beautiful is the whole [genus plus differentiating property], while what is common is indifferent [neither beautiful nor ugly].

§6.7.11. But it is said that heaven itself does not disdain the nature of all animals—and many animals do actually appear in it— since the universe contains them all. Where, then, does it have them from? Are there all things such as are in the sensible world also in the intelligible world?

In fact, it has all those that are produced by an expressed principle and in accordance with form. But when[67] it contains fire, then it   5
contains earth, too; and, in any case, it contains plants. And how are there plants in the intelligible world? And how does fire live there? And earth? Indeed, either it lives or it is like a corpse in the intelligible world; then, the result would be that not everything in the intelligible world is alive.

And, generally, what are these things in the intelligible world?

In fact, plants can be fitted into the argument since even in the sen-   10
sible world, a plant is an expressed principle based in life. If the enmat- tered expressed principle of the plant, in accordance to which the plant is, is indeed such and such a life, and a kind of soul, and the expressed principle is some one thing, then this expressed principle is either the primary plant or it is not; and in the latter case, the primary plant [the Form of the Plant] is before it, that is, the one this plant derives from.

---

66. The μορφαί ('shapes') are the sensible counterparts of the intelligible Forms.
67. 'When' in the sense of 'if'.

15   And that primary plant is one, whereas these ones here are many, and
      necessarily derive from one. And if this is indeed so, then the primary
      one must live more and be itself a plant; and in derivation from this, the
      others live secondarily and at a third remove, following in its footsteps.

      And what about earth? And what is it for earth to exist? And what
      is the earth in the intelligible world in possession of life? Or, first, what
      is earth in the sensible world, that is, what is it to be earth? Certainly,
20   it must, even in the sensible world, have some shape and an expressed
      principle. And in the case of the plant in the intelligible world it was
      alive, as its expressed principle is alive in the sensible world. So, too, for
      this earth in the sensible world?

      In fact, if we grasp whatever has most become earthen and been
      shaped in it, then we would find the nature of earth.

      So, consider the growth and formation of stones, the inner shap-
25   ing of growing mountains. In these cases, we are bound to think of
      these coming from an animate expressed principle which creates them
      inwardly and gives them form. And this is the productive form of
      earth, just as in trees their so-called nature,[68] and so-called earth is
30   analogous to the wood in the tree; and when a stone is cut off it is thus
      like when one cuts a bit from the tree; but if this does not happen to it,
      it is still fitted together, like something not cut from the living plant.

      When we have indeed discovered nature creating as a creator situ-
      ated in earth, a life in an expressed principle, we will believe all the more
35   that earth in the intelligible world is much more alive, the expressed
      principle of life, earth itself, primary earth, from which earth in the
      sensible world originates.

      If fire, too, is an expressed principle in matter, as with the other
      things like this, it is not spontaneously fire; for then where does it
      come from? Not from rubbing as one might think. For rubbing is of
40   the bodies being rubbed together which already contain fire, and there
      is already fire in the universe.[69] Nor is the matter fire in potency in such
      a way that it is in it, if, that is, the productive factor actually has to work
      according to an expressed principle, as it gives shape to the product.
      So, what would this be other than the soul that is able to produce fire?
      This is life and an expressed principle, both being one and identical in
      both.

---

68. Cf. 5.9.6.20. This is the Stoic use of the term φύσις. See *SVF* 2.743 (= Galen, *De foet. form.* 4.699).
69. See Ar., *DC* 2.7.289a20.

For this reason, Plato says that soul is in each of the elements,[70] actu-   45
ally producing the sensible fire. So, what produces fire in the sensible
world is also a kind of fiery life, a truer fire. And fire in the intelligible
world, being more fire, must be more alive. The fire, therefore, itself
lives as well.

The identical argument applies to the others, that is, to water and air.   50
But why are these not ensouled like the earth? It is anyway clear that
these elements are in the whole Living Being, that is, that they are parts
of a Living Being. But life does not appear in these elements any more
than it does in earth. However, it was possible to deduce its presence
in the intelligible world[71] from the things which come to be in it. Still,
living beings come to be in fire, too, and most clearly in water. And the   55
composition of some living beings is airy.[72]

Each fire, in coming to be and in being extinguished quickly, passes
by the soul in all fire, and has not come to be a persisting mass, such
that it would manifest its soul. Similarly with air and water, for if they
did naturally coagulate, they would manifest it, but since they needed
to be flowing, they do not manifest the soul they have.   60

It is, presumably, the same with the fluids in us such as blood. For
flesh, and anything that becomes flesh, is held to have soul from the
blood,[73] while blood, not providing sense-perception,[74] does not seem
to have soul; but there is necessarily soul in it, too. Without anything
violent happening to it, it is ready to separate itself from the soul pres-   65
ent in it. This is just as one has to conceive of it in the case of the three
elements; for the living beings consisting above all of air do not perceive what they undergo.[75] Like air passing by intense and steady light,
as long as it persists,[76] this is how air both passes by its soul in a circle
and does not pass by. And likewise for the other elements.

§6.7.12. However, let us say the following: since we assert that this
universe stands in relation to that one [the intelligible world] as to
what is, in a way, its model, the whole Living Being must exist prior in
the intelligible world, too, and if its existence is to be complete,[77] then

---

70. See Pl. [?], *Epin.* 981B–C, 984BC.
71. Cf. *supra* ll. 21–36.
72. I.e., daemons. Cf. *infra* ll. 67–68; 4.5.7.26–27. See Pl. [?], *Epinomis* 984E5.
73. See Pl., *Tim.* 80D–81B; Ar., *PA* 2.3.650a34.
74. Because, whereas we perceive our flesh being touched, we do not perceive our
blood being touched. See Ar., *PA* 2.3.650b5.
75. These are daemons. Cf. 3.5.6.31.
76. For what happens when a current of air passes through a ray of light, cf. 4.3.22.4–8.
77. See Pl., *Tim.* 31B1.

it must be all living beings. And the sky must actually be a living being
5   in the intelligible world, too, not of course a sky empty of stars, as we
call them in the sensible world; that is what being sky is. And clearly
the earth is not empty in the intelligible world either, but much more
alive than in the sensible world: all animals are in it—those that we
call footed and land animals in the sensible world, and, clearly, plants
10   settled in life. And there is sea in the intelligible world, and all water in
flux and persisting life; and all the living beings in water. And air is part
of the universe in the intelligible world, and the airy animals are in it
analogous to the air itself. How can things in what is living [the Living
Being] not be living, as they actually are even in the sensible world?[78]

How, then, could not all living beings be in the intelligible world of
15   necessity? As each of the great parts of the cosmos are in the intelligible
world, so, too, there is necessarily the nature of living beings in them.
In the manner, then, in which heaven is in the intelligible world, so,
too, all the living beings in heaven are in the intelligible world; it is not
possible for them not to be. Otherwise, the great parts would not be in
the intelligible world either.[79]

Who, then, inquires where living beings come from, inquires where
20   heaven in the intelligible world comes from? This is to inquire where
the Living Being comes from, and this is identical to inquiring where
life, that is, universal Life, soul, that is, universal Soul, and intellect,
that is, universal Intellect, come from, because there is no poverty or
lack in the intelligible world; instead, everything is filled with life, and
25   in a way boiling.[80] There is, in a way, a flowing of all things from one
spring, not as from a single breath or heat, but as though there were
one quality which contains all qualities in itself, and preserves them,
sweetness with sweet-odor, a vinous quality, the powers of all tastes,
the sights of all colors, all that touch can know, all that hearing can
hear, all tunes and all rhythms.[81]

§6.7.13.[82] For neither Intellect, nor the Soul arising from it is
something simple, but they are all[83] variegated according to their
simplicity, that is, according to their lack of composition, and insofar
as they are principles and activities. At the bottom end, the activity is

---

78. Cf. 5.9.9.8–14.
79. Cf. 5.8.4.4–11.
80. Cf. 6.5.12–9. See Ar., *DA* 1.2.405a28 for the conjectured etymological connection between ζεῖν ('boiling') and ζῆν ('living').
81. Cf. 3.8.10.5–19.
82. See Appendix II H; III B 2.
83. Including intellects that partake of Intellect and souls that partake of Soul.

simple because it is where things come to a stop; and all the activities of the first are simple. Intellect in motion is moved [always] in the same manner, that is, in identical respects, and always [as] the same things, since it is not one identical thing in particular, but all things.[84] For even the one particular is not one thing but unlimited when it is divided.[85]

Where should we assert it starts from, and where does it finally end? Is all that lies in between like a line, or like another uniform and unvariegated body? But what would be so august about that? For if there is no radical alteration in it, if no Difference wakes it into life, then it would not be activity.[86] For a condition like that would be no different from non-activity. And if the Intellect's motion were like this, then its life would not be multifarious, but monotonous. But it must live entirely, and in every aspect everywhere, and nothing of it may not live. It must, then, move itself in all directions, or rather to have moved itself in all directions.

Indeed, if it were to move itself simply, it would only contain that one motion. And either it is itself, and has not proceeded to anything further, or if it has proceeded, some other [part] of it remained. The result is, then, that it is two. And if this is identical with that [part], it remains one, and has not proceeded; and if this is different from that, it proceeded with difference, and produced a third one from that which is identical and different.[87] Since it has indeed come to be from Identity and Difference, the thing that comes to be has the nature of Identity and Difference. But it is another something, another whole. For that which is identical is the whole of that which is identical. Since it is the whole of Identity and the whole of Difference, it leaves out none of the different things. It, therefore, has the nature to be made wholly different.

If, then, all the different Beings are prior to it, it would have already undergone motion under their influence. If they are not, then this Intellect generated all things, or indeed better, was all of them. It is not possible, therefore, for Beings to be if Intellect does not activate them, and it activates one thing after another, and in a way wandering all wanderings, wandering in itself, just as it is the nature of true Intellect

---

84. Cf. *infra* l. 50.

85. Cf. 5.3.10.23–29. See Pl., *Parm.* 144B1–E7; *Soph.* 248A12.

86. See Ar., *Meta.* 12.9.1074b17–18.

87. See Pl., *Tim.* 35A3–5. In this passage, the 'third one' refers to the soul of the cosmos. Here, Plotinus uses 'third one' to refer to Intellect in its identity with all intelligibles. The 'first one' is the One; the second, Intellect in its initial phase as generated by the One.

to wander[88] in itself. It naturally wanders among Substances, as the Substances run along its wanderings with it. Intellect is everywhere itself. It, then, has a constant wandering. Its wandering is on 'the plain
35   of truth',[89] which it does not leave.

It has taken it all into its possession, and has made it in a way a place for its motion; the place is identical with that of which it is the place. This plain is variegated, so that it may traverse it. Were it not in every respect and always variegated, it would come to a standstill insofar as it is not variegated. If it comes to a standstill, it does not think. The result
40   is that if it ever came to a standstill, then it was not thinking. And if so, then it does not exist. It is, then, intellection.[90]

All motion fulfills all Substance, and all Substance is all intellection, embracing all Life, one thing after another. And whatever belonging to Intellect is identical with and also different from it; it makes another thing always appear for anyone who analyzes the Intellect. The path
45   goes through life, and past all living beings, just as for someone going over the earth all he passes is earth, even if the earth has differences.

And the Life in the intelligible world, through which the path leads is identical, but because it is always different, it is not identical. For the Intellect always has the identical traversal running through things that are not identical, because it does not swap one thing for another, but is with the other things in the same way and in the identical respects. If
50   the same way and the identical respects did not apply to other things, the Intellect would be entirely idle; being active and activity would be nowhere.[91] For the Intellect itself is the other things, too, such that it is itself all. If indeed it is itself, it is all; if it were not, then it would not be itself. If it is itself all, and it is all because it is all things, and there is nothing which does not contribute to the completion of all things, then
55   there is nothing belonging to Intellect which is not another thing, so that it may by being another thing also complete this thing. For if it is not another thing, but identical with another thing, it will diminish its own substantiality by not providing for the completion of its nature.[92]

§6.7.14. It is possible by the use of intellectual models to know what manner of thing Intellect is, that is, how it does not stand not being other than it is, in the fashion of a unit. You would not want to take the

---

88. See Pl., *Parm.* 136E2; *Lg.* 683A.
89. See Pl., *Phdr.* 248B6.
90. See Ar., *Meta.* 12.9.1074b33–35.
91. See Pl., *Soph.* 248A12.
92. Cf. 5.3.7.18–25.

expressed principle of plant or animal as a model. For if it was some
one being, and not a variegated one, then it would not be an expressed   5
principle; rather, the thing that has come to be would be matter, since
the expressed principle would not have become it all, by entering in
everywhere in the matter and letting none of it be itself.

For example, a face[93] is not one mass; it is also nostrils and eyes, and
the nose is not merely one thing, but there are several parts of it, if it is   10
to be a nose. For if it were one simple being, then it would be merely a
mass. In the same way, the unlimited is also one in the Intellect, in the
sense of a 'one-many',[94] not in the way a mass is one, but as an expressed
principle in it which is multiple; in one figure of the Intellect, like an
outline, it contains outlines inside, and configurations inside also, and
powers and acts of intellection, not according to a linear division, but   15
eternally inward, like that of the whole Living Being into the natures of
living beings it embraces, and again a division into fairly small living
beings, and into the weaker power, where it finally comes to a stop at
the individual form.[95]

But the division lying in Intellect is not a jumble, even if it is of
Beings that are one; rather, this is, in the universe, what is called 'Love
in the universe',[96] not of course the love in the sensible universe, in that   20
this is an imitation of being friendly arising out of disparate things.
True love is for all things to be one and never dispersed. Empedocles
does, however, claim that it is dispersed within our universe.[97]

§6.7.15.[98] Who, then, would not delight in this life, if he saw it—
plentiful, whole, of the first order and one, and disdain all other life?
For the other lives are in darkness, the lives down below, that are
small and faint, cheap, not pure, and dirtying the pure lives. And if   5
you should look toward these lives, then you will no longer see the
pure lives, nor will you live all those lives all together in which there is
nothing which does not live, and in which one lives purely without any

93. Cf. 6.4.1.24.
94. On Intellect as 'one-many', cf. 4.8.3.10; 5.1.8.26; 5.3.15.11, 22; 6.2.15.14–15, etc.
See Pl., *Parm.* 144E5, 155E5.
95. See Ar., *Top.* 3.6.120a35; *Phys.* 5.4.227b7.
96. Love or Friendship, in Empedocles the ordering principle. See fr. 31 B 17.7, 26.5
DK. In lines 22–23 where Empedocles's theory is also mentioned, he is not named.
97. The word here is οὐρανός, usually translated as 'heaven' but evidently referring to
all that is under the 'dome' of heaven, that is, the sensible cosmos. See Empedocles,
fr. 31 A 52 DK (= Simplicius, *In DC* 293.22–23; *In Phys.* 31.23).
98. See Appendix II E.

evil. For evils are in the sensible world, because here is just a trace of Life and a trace of Intellect.

In the intelligible world, Plato says, the archetype is Good-like,[99]
10   because it contains the Good in the Forms. On the one hand, there is the Good, and on the other Intellect is good because its life consists in contemplation. It contemplates the objects of contemplation themselves which are Good-like, and which it obtained when it contemplated the nature of the Good.[100] They came to it, not as they were there [i.e., in the Good], but as Intellect itself came to possess them. For that
15   [the Good] is the principle, and from that the Forms come to be in Intellect; this Intellect is what produced these things from that Good. For it was not licit for Intellect, in looking toward the Good, either to think nothing or to think them in the Good. For in that case, Intellect would not have generated them.

For the Intellect acquired the power to generate from the Good, and to be filled with its offspring, because the Good granted them, which
20   it itself did not have. But out of one thing many come about for this Intellect. For it broke up the power which it was unable to contain, and made many out of the one power, so that it could bear it part by part. Whatever it generated came from the power of the Good and was Good-like, and Intellect itself was good from the things Good-like—a variegated good.

25   For this reason, if someone liken the Good to a living variegated sphere,[101] and either imagine it a thing all face, radiant with living faces, or as all pure souls congregated together without lack having all that belongs to them, with the whole Intellect settled on their tops, so as to illuminate the place with intellectual light—if you imagine it like this, then you would be seeing it from outside as one looking at another; but one should become that itself, and make oneself the vision.[102]

§6.7.16. But it is necessary not always to rest in this multiple beauty; one must make the transition, rushing upward, leaving this [Intellect], too, behind, not starting from this heaven, but from that one,[103] filled with wonderment at who engendered it and how.

---

99. Cf. 1.8.11.16; 3.8.11.16–17; 5.3.16.19; 6.8.18.27, where the Good is the archetype. See Pl., *Rep.* 6.509A3.

100. See Pl., *Phil.* 60B10.

101. Cf. 6.5.4.22. See Pl., *Phd.* 110B7.

102. Cf. 1.6.9.22; 5.8.10.40, 11.20–21; 6.9.10.19–21, 11.43.

103. The intelligible heaven. Cf. *supra* 15.20–22.

Each thing, then, is a Form, and each is, in a way, a unique impres-   5
sion. Since they are Good-like,[104] they all contain in common the thing
that runs through them all; so they all have in them Being, they all have
the Living Being, since a life in common is present in all; and, presumably, other things, too.

But what can they be good in accordance with and because of? Actually, for this kind of inquiry it is probably helpful to start as follows: 10
Did Intellect, when it was looking toward the Good, conceive of that
One as a many and, being one itself, conceive of the Good as a many,
in portioning up the Good, because it was not capable of thinking it
whole all together? But looking at the Good it was not yet Intellect; it
looked non-intellectually.

In fact, we should assert that Intellect was never seeing the Good;   15
rather, it was living relative to it; it was dependent on it, and was turned
toward it. The motion itself was actually fulfilled by being motion in
the intelligible world, and it was fulfilled in relation to the Good itself;
it was no longer mere motion, but satiated and full motion. Intellect
next became all things and knew this in its self-awareness;[105] and now   20
it was Intellect, having been fulfilled, so that it possessed what it saw; it
looks on them with light, since it is provided both with them and the
light by the bestower of them.

Because of this the Good is said[106] to be the cause not only of the
Substance but also of the Substance being seen; just as the sun, in being   25
the cause of sensible things being seen and coming to be, and so of
seeing in a way, too—and so it is neither seeing nor the things coming
to be—so, too, the nature of the Good, being the cause of Substance
and Intellect, is light, according to the analogy, for the visible things in
the intelligible world and the seeing things there, although it is neither
Beings nor Intellect, but is the cause of them, and, with its light, makes   30
possible thinking and being thought for Beings and Intellect. Intellect
came into being by being fulfilled, and fulfilled it was, and brought all
things to completion together and saw it. Its principle was before Intellect was fulfilled; it is another principle which, in a way, from outside
fulfilled it, and which stamped it with its mark in fulfilling it.

§6.7.17.[107] But how are the Forms in Intellect, and how are they
identical with it, although they are not there in the Good which fulfils

---

104. Cf. *infra* 18.1.
105. Cf. 5.3.11.12; 13.13, 21. See Ar., *EE* 7.12.1244b26, 1245b24.
106. See Pl., *Rep.* 6.509B2–8; 509A1, B2, B4.
107. See Appendix II E.

it, nor in the Intellect as it is being fulfilled? For when it was not yet fulfilled, it did not contain them.[108]

In fact, it is not really necessary for something that gives something
5   to possess what it gives, but in such cases the giver is to be considered as greater, and what is given is lesser than the giver.[109] Such is coming to be in Beings. For first there has to be something in actuality,[110] whereas the later stages are potentially what came before them. That is, the primary transcends the secondary, and the giver transcends the given.[111] For it is better.

10   If, then, anything is prior to actuality, then it transcends actuality; and thus transcends Life, too. If Life is in Intellect, then the giver gave Life, and is itself beautiful and more honorable than Life. So, Intellect had Life, and was in no need of a variegated giver. Life was a kind of trace of the Good, not the Life of the Good.

15   Life, then, while it was looking to the Good, was indefinite, but once it had looked, it was bounded in the intelligible world, although the Good has no boundary. For straightaway on having looked toward something that is one, it is bounded by it, and has in itself boundary, limit, and form. And the form is in the thing shaped, while the thing that shapes is without shape. The boundary was not external, as though
20   it had been set around a magnitude, but was a boundary belonging to all that Life, which was itself multiple and unlimited, because it shines out of such a great nature. And it was not life of just something, for then it would have been, as belonging to an individual, bounded already. But, nonetheless, bounded it was; it was, therefore, the bounded Life of a 'one-many'—and indeed each of the many was also bounded[112]—and
25   while it was bounded as many, because of the multitude of its Life, it was still one because of its boundary.

What, then, does it mean to say 'life was bounded as one'? That it is Intellect, for bounded Life is Intellect. And what are these many things? Many intellects. All things, then, are intellects; the whole is Intellect, and each is an intellect.

Does the whole Intellect, including each intellect, include each as identical to it? If it did, then it would include only one.[113] And if they

---

108. Cf. 3.8.11.6–8; 5.3.15.1–7.
109. Cf. 5.3.15.33–40; 6.9.6.54–55.
110. See Ar., *Meta.* 9.8.1049b5.
111. See Pl., *Rep.* 6.509B3.
112. Cf. *infra* l. 26. See Pl., *Parm.* 145A2.
113. Cf. 6.2.22.10–11.

are many intellects, there must be some differentiation[114] among them.   30
Again, then, how does each intellect acquire some differentiation?

In fact, it possessed a difference by becoming entirely one. For the
totality of Intellect is not identical with any one intellect.

The Life of Intellect, then, was all power, whereas the seeing coming from the Good was the potentiality for being all things. And the
Intellect that came to be appeared as all things themselves. The Good
is enthroned over them, not so that it has a foundation, but so that it   35
may found the Form of the primary Forms,[115] while remaining form-
less itself.

Intellect comes to be in relation to Soul as light for it, just as that Good
is for Intellect. And when Intellect bounds Soul, it makes it rational
by giving it a trace of what it acquired. Intellect, then, is also a trace of
the Good. Since Intellect is also Form, both in extent and multiplic-   40
ity, that Good is shapeless and formless: for it produces Forms in this
way.

If that Good were Form, then Intellect would be an expressed
principle. But that which is first may not be multiple in any way; its
multiplicity would again depend on another prior to it.

§6.7.18. But on account of what are the things in Intellect Good-like?
Is it that each is a Form or insofar as each is beautiful or what? Indeed,
if all that comes from the Good possesses a trace or impression of it, or
a trace of that which derives from it, just as what comes from fire is the
trace of fire or what comes from the sweet is a trace of sweetness, and
if Life, too, has come from the Good to Intellect—for it comes to really   5
exist from the activity from the Good[116]—and if Intellect really exists
on account of that, and that is where the beauty of the Forms comes
from, then everything is Good-like, both Life, and Intellect and Idea.

But what did they have in common? For being derived from the
Good does not actually suffice for their identity. For a common feature must be in them. For things that are not identical may come to   10
be out of one and identical thing, or something given in the same way
may become other in the things receiving it. Since it is one thing that

---

114. The word is διαφορά, which can refer to a differentia among species within a
genus or to a difference among individuals within a species. The translation 'differentiation' is neutral between the two.

115. Cf. 5.5.6.4–5. See Ar., *DA* 3.8.432a2 where Aristotle identifies intellect as 'form
of forms'.

116. The 'external' activity of the Good distinct from the 'internal' activity. Cf. *infra*
21.4–6, 40.21–24; 2.9.8.22–25; 4.5.7.15–17, 51–55; 5.1.6.34; 5.3.7.23–24; 5.4.2.27–33;
5.9.8.13–15; 6.2.22.24–29.

pertains to primary activity, another that is given by the primary activity, that which comes from these is at once, thereby, another.

In fact, nothing prevents each [Intellect, Idea, Life] being Good-like
15   though rather differently in each case.[117] What, then, is it especially that makes them identical?

First, we have to consider this: Is Life a good, as such, Life viewed as bare and entirely stripped?

In fact, Life is a good when considered as coming from the Good. Is this 'from the Good' not just a qualification? What, then, is this Life
20   with this qualification? Is it the life of the Good?[118] It was not its life, but Life that comes from the Good.[119] But if true Life flows from the Good into the Life in the intelligible world, and nothing dishonorable comes from it, and if it should be called good insofar as it is Life, then about true Intellect, that primary one, one should say, too, that it is good.

25   And clearly each Form is good and Good-like, in that it thus possesses a good, either a good in common, or with one thing having it more than another, or with one having it primarily and another in succession and secondarily.[120]

Since we have grasped that each Form already has a good in its Substance,[121] and is good because of this—for even if Life was not sim-
30   ply good, but good because it was said to be true Life, and because it derives from the Good, whereas Intellect is truly good—something identical has to be seen in all of them. Since they are different, when the identical thing is predicated of them, nothing prevents this being in their Substantiality, though it is still possible to grasp this identical thing apart from the account, just as animal belongs to both human
35   being and horse, and hot belongs to water and fire, the first as the genus, the second as the primary holder of the predicate as opposed to the secondary holder of the predicate. Otherwise, either one member of these pairs would be said to be good equivocally, or each thing would be homonymously good.

So is the Good in their Substantiality?

---

117. Cf. 1.4.3.18–40.
118. Taking the words ἢ ἀγαθοῦ as a question raised by an interlocutor.
119. Cf. 1.6.7.11–12; 3.8.10.1–4; 5.3.16.35–38.
120. The alternatives refer to the ways in which the Forms, Intellect, and Life may be said to be good or Good-like.
121. Cf. *supra* ll. 20–25.

In fact, each is a whole good, and Good is not applied just with respect to one thing. How does it, then, apply? As parts? But the Good is without parts.   40

In fact, it is one itself, but one thing is good in one way, and another thing in another. For the primary activity [of Intellect] is a good, and that which is bounded by that is good, and indeed both of them together are good; the primary activity is good because it comes to be under the influence of the Good, the good bounded by activity is good because its order comes from the Good; and both of them together are good for both reasons.

They, then, come from the Good, yet they are not identical, just as   45
voice, walking, and anything else coming from the identical source are all good because correctly accomplished.

In fact, in the sensible world this is because of order and rhythm; and what about in the intelligible world?

In fact, you might say that in the sensible world the factors come from outside to make up the beautiful state of something, and they differ, whereas in the intelligible world they are identical. But how are they identical? We should not just trust in the fact that they come from the Good and leave it at that. For we have to agree that they are honor-   50
able because they come from the Good; but reason longs to grasp just how they are good.

§6.7.19. Shall we, then, hand over the judgment to desire, that is, to the soul, and because we trust in its affection, will we assert that what is desirable to the soul is good, and not bother to inquire why it desires it? Are we going to provide demonstrations of what each thing is, but in this case, just hand over the good to desire?   5

Many absurdities appear to follow from this. First, the good would become a relative.

Next, there are many desired things, and different things are desired by different beings. How, then, will we judge by the one desiring if what is desired is better than something else? Presumably, we would not know the better if we do not know that which is good.

Will we define the good according to the excellence[122] of each thing?   10
Of course, if we referred this to the Form and the account of it, we would be proceeding correctly. But when we arrive at the intelligible world, what will we say when we investigate why these Forms themselves are good? For, quite reasonably, we recognize such a nature when it is in inferior things, even if it is there not in a pure state, since it is not pri-   15

---

122. See Ar., *EN* 1.6.1098a15–16.

marily there, but only by conjunction with inferior things. But where nothing is bad, and the good things are themselves in themselves, we will be at a loss. Is the problem, then, since reason is seeking the 'why' for things that are in themselves, it is puzzled that, in this case, the 'why' is the 'that'?[123] Even if we claim that the explanation is something else, namely, god,[124] still the problem is the same, since reason has not yet attained that [explanation].

We should not leave off the inquiry,[125] to see if there is not another way we can go so that a solution appears to us.

§6.7.20.[126] Since, then, we put no faith at present[127] in our desires as determining what something is or what kind of thing it is, is it necessary that we have recourse to the judgments and to the oppositions between things such as order-disorder, symmetry-asymmetry, health-disease, form-shapelessness, substantiality-destruction [i.e., loss of substantiality], and in general, constitution-obliteration?[128]

Who could doubt that the first of each of these pairs is in the form of good?[129] If this is the case, then we should rank the things that produce them in the 'portion of good'.[130] And indeed virtue, and intellect, life and soul, at least a rational soul, lie within the form of good. And thus, too, anything the rational life[131] desires.

But, then, someone will say, why do we not stop at Intellect and postulate this as the Good? For both Soul and Life are traces of Intellect, and soul desires it. Soul judges and thereby desires Intellect, judging justice better than injustice, and putting every form of excellence before every form of vice, and it honors the identical things it chooses. But if it desires only Intellect, it would presumably need more argument to show that Intellect is not the ultimate thing; and while not everything desires Intellect, everything desires the Good.[132]

---

123. Cf. *supra* 2.2.
124. See Pl., *Rep.* 2.379C2–3.
125. Cf. *supra* 18.50.
126. See Appendix III C 1.
127. Cf. *infra* 24.4–5.
128. See Ar., *Meta.* 1.5.986a23, 12.1072a31; Stob., *Ecl.* 4.1.49, p. 15.20–21.
129. The words ἐν ἀγαθοῦ εἴδει ('in the form of good') can also indicate 'Good-like' as above. Plotinus is no doubt taking advantage of the ambiguity.
130. See Pl., *Phil.* 54C10; also 20D1, 60B4.
131. See Pl., *Rep.*7.521A4.
132. See Pl., *Rep.* 6.505D5–9; *Phil.* 20D8; Ar., *EN* 1.1.1094a3.

And even among things without intellect, not all try to come to possess it, and those who do have it do not stop there, but go on to look for   20
the Good; they look for Intellect on the basis of calculative reasoning, whereas they look for the Good prior to reason as well.[133] But if they desire life and eternal existence and activity, then the object desired is not desired as Intellect, but as Good, as deriving from the Good and leading to the Good; for that is the way life is.

§6.7.21. What, then, is that one factor in all these things that makes each thing good? Let us venture to say that Intellect and its life are Good-like, and that desire is for these, insofar as they are Good-like. I call them 'Good-like' insofar as Life is the activity of the Good, or   5
rather the activity from the Good, an activity which is bounded.[134] They [Intellect and Life] are full of radiance, and are pursued by the soul, since it comes from them and relates back to them.

So, does it pursue them as belonging to the soul, and not as good?[135]

In fact, even if they are just Good-like, they are not to be cast aside for this reason. For what belongs to them, even if it were not good, can be avoided, even if it does belong. For things which are distant and   10
inferior can also move the soul.

Intense love for them [Intellect and Life] comes about not when they are what they are but when they are what they are and, in addition, acquire something from the Good. Just as with bodies, even when they have their own light mixed with them, still they need a light from elsewhere, so that the light makes the color in them appear, so, too,   15
although they have much light, they need a better light, so they can be seen by themselves and by another.[136]

§6.7.22. Then, when someone sees this light, he is indeed at that moment moved toward these things, and he is greedily delighted by the light which accompanies them; just as in the case of bodies in the sensible world love is not for the material substrates, but for the beauty   5
which appears in them. Each thing is what it is in itself, but it becomes desired when the Good itself colors it, because this gives it grace and love in the eyes of those desiring it. So, the soul, when it takes in the

---

133. See Pl., *Symp.* 206A12.

134. The two types of activity 'of a principle' and 'from a principle'. Cf. *supra* 18.5–6; *infra* 40.21–24. Since the Good is uniquely unbounded, whatever comes from the Good is, thereby, bounded.

135. Making the sentence into a question with Hadot.

136. I.e., the soul.

10

'outpouring from the intelligible world',[137] is moved and dances, and is pricked by desire, it becomes love.

Prior to this, it is not moved toward Intellect, even if it is beautiful. For its beauty is inactive until it grasps the light of the Good, and the soul 'falls backwards'[138] in itself, and is inactive in every respect, and despite the presence of the Intellect, remains blind to it. But when

15

the Intellect gets to it, a sort of warming from the intelligible world, it gains strength, is wakened and truly becomes winged.[139] Although it is struck by things close by, it is lifted more toward something else greater by, in a way, a sort of memory.[140] And it is raised by the giver of love naturally upward. It can go beyond even Intellect, on the one

20

hand, but it cannot go beyond the Good, since there is nothing lying beyond it. If it stays within Intellect, it contemplates beautiful and holy things—and still does not have all it seeks. It approaches it like a beautiful face, but one which is unable to activate sight, since that grace is not in it which accompanies beauty.

25

For this reason, here beauty is rather that which shines from symmetry, rather than the symmetry itself; this is what is loveable. For why is there more light of beauty in a living face, and just its trace in a dead face, even if the face has not decayed in its flesh and symmetry? And

30

living beings are more beautiful than statues, even if the latter are more symmetrical.[141] And is not an uglier living being more beautiful than the beautiful living being in the statue?

In fact, it is because the living being is more desirable, and this because it has a soul, and this because it is more Good-like, and this because it is colored by the light of the Good in some way. And because

35

it is colored, it has been awakened and lifted up, and has lifted up what it possesses—and makes it good and wakes it up, as far as is in its power.

§6.7.23. Actually, in the intelligible world, what the soul pursues is also what provides light to the Intellect, and when it enters, it leaves a trace of itself. And there is no need to wonder why it has such power that it drags the soul to itself, and calls the soul back from all its

5

wandering,[142] so it can come to rest with it. For if all things come from

---

137. See Pl., *Phdr.* 251B2.
138. See Pl., *Phdr.* 254B8.
139. See Pl., *Phdr.* 251B2–3.
140. See Pl., *Phdr.* 251D6.
141. Cf. 1.6.1.20–25; 5.8.1.12–26.
142. See Pl., *Phd.* 81A6.

something, then there is nothing more powerful than that; everything else is inferior. In what way is the Good not the best of Beings?[143]

Further, if the nature of the Good has to be the most self-sufficient, and in need of nothing else whatever, what else apart from this nature could one discover that was what it was before all else, when there was no vice at all? If there were evils posterior to the Good, in things which had no part in it at all, that is, in the very uttermost things, than which there is nothing worse, evils would relate to it contrarily without having a middle in their contrariety.

This, therefore, would be the Good. For either there is no Good at all, or else, if there has to be, it must be this and nothing else. If someone says the Good does not exist, then there is no evil either. In that case, things would be by nature indifferent as a basis for our choice.[144] But this is impossible. They call other things good with reference to this, but the Good is related to nothing.[145]

What, then, does it produce by being of this kind?

In fact, it produced Intellect, Life, and souls from this, and all other things which partake of reason, Intellect, or Life. As for the actual source or principle[146] of these things: who could say how good and great it is?

But what does it now produce?

In fact, it now preserves these things,[147] and makes thinking things think, living beings live, filling intellect and life with breath, and if something is incapable of life, at least it makes it exist.

§6.7.37.[148] Those thinkers, then, who attribute intellection to the Good in their account[149] did not attribute to it intellection of the lesser things, or of what is derived from it. Some[150] say, however, that it is absurd if it does not know other things.

The first group, then, finding nothing more worthy than it, attribute to it the intellection of itself, as though it would be made more

---

143. The phrase το' ἄριστον τῶν ὄντων ('the best of Beings') is a strong affirmation that, although the Good is above the οὐσία ('Substantiality') and εἶναι ('Existence') of all composite Beings, it itself exists. Cf. *infra* 32.10–14; 1.8.2.4–5; 2.9.1.8–9; 5.3.13.16–17. See Pl., *Rep.* 7.518C9, 526E3–4; *Phil.* 20E6, 60B10–C4.
144. See *SVF* 3.117 (= D.L., 7.102).
145. Cf. 6.8.8.22, 11.32, 17.27–28.
146. See Pl., *Phdr.* 245C9.
147. Cf. 1.6.7.10–12; 5.3.15.11–12, 28.
148. See Appendix III B 1; III B 2.
149. See Ar., *Meta.* 12.9.1074b17–35.
150. The Stoics, with their theory of providence. Cf. 5.6.6.31.

beautiful by intellection, as though intellection is better than being the Good in itself, and it was not it that made thinking beautiful.

From what will it acquire its honorable state?[151] From thinking or from itself? If from thinking, then in itself it is not honorable, or less so. But if it is honorable in itself, then it is perfect before thinking, and
10   is not perfected by thinking.

If it has to think because it is actuality, and not potency,[152] then if it is a Substance that always thinks,[153] and they say that it is thereby actuality, then they are saying that two things are together, Substance and intellection; and they are not saying it is simple—they add something else to it, like adding the actual seeing to eyes, even if they always
15   see. But if they say that it is in actuality because it is both activity and intellection,[154] then it would not think due to its being intellection,[155] just as motion does not move. So, then, what shall we say?

Do you[156] not say yourselves that the intelligibles are Substances and actuality? But we agree that these are many and different from one another, whereas the first thing is simple, and we grant intellection to
20   what derives from something else, and [we grant] in a way the investigation of its own Substantiality and what produces it, and assert that it is in turning inward in contemplation and recognizing itself that it is now Intellect in the proper sense.[157]

But in the case of something that does not come to be nor has anything prior to itself, but is always what it is, what explanation will there
25   be for its thinking? It is for this reason that Plato is right to say that it is beyond thinking.[158]

Now Intellect that does not think is without thought.[159] For in the case of something whose nature includes thinking, if it were not to do this, it would be without thought. But in the case of that which has no function, how could anyone give it a function, and then predicate the privation of this in it, because it does not perform its function? It is as though someone were to label the Good 'devoid of medical science'.

The fact is that no function belongs to it, in that nothing is ordained
30   for it to do. For it is sufficient to itself. One should not look for anything

---

151. See Ar., *Meta.* 12.9.1074b21.
152. See Ar., *Meta.* 12.6.1071b20, 7.1072b28, 9.1074b20.
153. See Ar., *Meta.* 12.7.1073a4, 9.1074b20.
154. See Ar., *Meta.* 12.7.1072b28.
155. Cf. 6.9.6.53–55.
156. The Peripatetic is speaking to the Platonist.
157. Cf. 5.3.5.28–48.
158. See Pl., *Rep.* 6.509A7, B9.
159. Cf. *supra* 9.26–29.

besides, since it is above all Beings. For it is enough for itself and other things in being what it itself is.

§6.7.38. There is no 'is' either in it, for it has no need of this.[160] For neither can you say of it that it is good. You can say this only of something of which you can say 'is'. 'Is' is not said as one thing of another, but as meaning what something is.

We use the words 'the Good' of it, not intending to say its name or   5 predicating 'good' as belonging to it, but because it is the Good itself.[161]

Next, we do not think it right to say 'it is good', nor even to add 'the' to it—we are unable to make ourselves clear, if someone were to take it away entirely—so that in order not to make it one thing and then another, and so not to have need of 'is', we say 'the Good'.[162]

But who will accept a nature which does not perceive or know itself?   10 What would it know about itself? 'I am'? But it is not! Why, then, will it not say 'I am good'?

In fact, again, the 'is' is predicated of it. Or it will say only 'good', adding something—for one can think 'good' without 'is' as long as it is   15 not predicated of something else.[163]

That which thinks of itself that it is good will always be thinking 'I am that which is good'. If not, it will think 'good', but it will not be present to it to think that it is this. There must, then, be the thinking 'I am good'. But if the thinking itself is the Good, then the thinking is not of itself,[164] but thinking of the Good; and the Good will not be itself,   20 but the thinking. And if the thinking of the Good is other than the Good, then there is the Good before the thinking of it. If the Good is self-sufficient before the thinking, since it is in itself self-sufficient for being good, it would need no thinking of itself. The upshot is: as good,   25 it does not think itself.[165]

§6.7.39.[166] But then, as what does it think itself?

In fact, nothing else is present to it and it will have a simple act of apprehension in regard to itself. Since there is nothing such as distance

---

160. See Pl., *Parm.* 141E9–11.

161. See Pl., *Soph.* 244B–C.

162. In Greek, the definite article and the nominalized adjective 'good' here are joined together to make a single word, thus avoiding the appearance that the definite article is something other than the Good itself.

163. Cf. 3.8.11.13–16.

164. See the Aristotelian formulation 'the thinking of thinking', referred to *supra* 37.1.

165. Cf. 3.9.9.12–17; 5.3.12.47–52.

166. See Appendix III B 1.

or difference in respect of itself, what else would this act of apprehension
5   be except itself? For this reason, Plato rightly understands difference
where there is Intellect and Substance.[167] For Intellect must always grasp
difference and identity if it is indeed going to think. It cannot distinguish itself from the intelligible by the relation of difference it has to that,
nor will it contemplate all things, unless difference comes about, such
that all things can exist. Otherwise, there would not even be two things.

10   Next, if indeed the Good does think, it will never, I suppose, think
only itself, if it is going to think at all. For why will it not think all
things? Or is it because it is incapable of doing so? Generally speaking, it will not be simple, if it thinks itself; the thinking of itself has to
be something different, if anything can think itself at all. But we said[168]
that there is no thinking by the Good, even if it wants to see itself as
15   something else. For in thinking itself it becomes many—intelligible,
thinking, moved, and all else it befits Intellect to be.

In addition, it befits us to see, as has been said elsewhere already,[169]
that each act of thinking, if indeed it is going to qualify as thinking, has
to be something variegated,[170] whereas the simple and entirely itself—in
20   a way like motion if it were like an act of contact[171]—will contain nothing intellectual.

What, then? Will the Good know neither other things nor itself?
The other things are posterior to it; it was what it was before them, and
its thinking of them would be something acquired, and in that case, it
would not always be identical, nor would its thinking be of stable things.

Even if it did think of things that are stable, it would be many. For
25   it will certainly not be possible that the posterior things will have their
substantiality along with the thinking while the acts of thinking by
the Good will be only empty contemplation. Providence is sufficiently
guaranteed by its being itself, from which all things come to be.

How does it stand in relation to itself, if it does not [know][172] itself?
It rests 'in majestic immobility'. Plato said,[173] on the subject of Sub-
30   stance, that it will think but will not rest majestically, on the grounds
that Substance thinks, while the thing that does not think will rest 'in
majestic immobility'; he says that it rests because he could not put it

---

167. Cf. 6.2.8.32–43. See Pl., *Soph.* 254E5–255A1; *Parm.* 146A–D.
168. Cf. *supra* 38.21–24.
169. Cf. *supra* 13.2.37, 14.5, 15.24, 17.13, 32.3, 33.10, 35.8.
170. Cf. 5.3.10.30, 41; 6.9.2.44. See Alex. Aphr., *De an.* 85.23.
171. Cf. 5.3.10.42.
172. Cf. *infra* 39.21 following Hadot.
173. See Pl., *Soph.* 249A1–2.

any other way, and because he considers that which surpasses thinking to be more majestic, or truly majestic.

§6.7.40. Those who have had any contact of this sort will know that there can be no question of thinking in connection with it. But we should add some words of encouragement to what has been said, to the extent it is possible for argument to make such a thing clear. For persuasion must be mixed with the necessity of proof.[174]   5

So, anyone who is aiming to acquire scientific understanding must realize that thinking originates from something and is of something. And one type of thinking, which is together with that from which it originates, has as a substrate that of which there is thinking, and is itself superimposed on the object of thinking because it is its actuality; it fulfills what was potentially, but without engendering it. For it is the   10
thinking of the thing it is of, only in the sense of being its completion.

The other type of thinking, which is accompanied by Substantiality, and which makes Substantiality really exist, cannot be in that from which it came to be.[175] For it would not have engendered anything, had it been in that. But since this thinking is a power of engendering, it engendered in itself; its actuality is Substantiality, and is in Substanti-   15
ality, too.[176] Thinking and Substantiality itself are not different. Insofar as its nature thinks itself, thinking and that which is thought are not different, except in definition, while being a multiplicity, as has been often shown.[177] This thinking is the primary actuality, in making Substantiality really exist: it is the image of something else so great that   20
this image became Substantiality.

If thinking belonged to the Good, rather than deriving from it, then thinking would not have been different from it, and would not have had real existence in itself. For indeed in being primary actuality and primary thinking, it would have neither actuality nor thinking prior to it.

So, then, when someone moves beyond this Substantiality and   25
thinking, he would reach neither Substantiality nor thinking; he reaches what 'transcends' Substantiality'[178] and thinking, 'something wonderful',[179] which has neither Substantiality nor thinking in itself, which is 'alone',[180] in itself, and in no way needing any of the things

174. Cf. 1.2.1.52; 5.3.6.9–10; 6.5.11.5–7. See Pl., *Lg.* 903B1.
175. I.e., the Good.
176. Cf. 5.3.7.18, 12.1–7; 6.8.4.26–28.
177. Cf. *supra* 17.39–40; 3.8.9.3–4; 3.9.1.13; 6.9.5.16.
178. Pl., *Rep.* 6.509B9.
179. Pl., *Symp.* 210E5.
180. Pl., *Phil.* 63B8.

30   originating in it. For it is not by being active beforehand that it pro-
       duced actuality. For, then, there would have to be actuality before it
       was engendered. And it is not by thinking that it produced intellec-
       tion, for it would already have been thinking before thinking came
       to be.

           For generally, if thinking is of the Good, then it is inferior to the
       Good. So, thinking cannot belong to the Good. I say that it does not
       belong to the Good, but I do not mean one cannot think the Good—let
35   us assume that is possible—but that there is no thinking in the Good
       itself. If that were the case, the Good and what is inferior to it—that
       is, its thinking—would be one. If thinking is inferior to the Good, it
       is thinking and being that are together. If thinking were better than
       Substantiality, then the intelligible would be inferior.

           So, thinking is actually not in the Good, but because thinking is
40   inferior and gains value through the Good itself, it must be in a dif-
       ferent place, *leaving the Good unmixed with thinking and all else.* The
       Good is *unmixed with* thinking and is purely what it is, unimpeded by
       the presence of thinking from being pure and one.

           But if someone were to make the Good at once thinking and object
45   of thinking, as well as Substance and thinking conjoined with Sub-
       stance—wanting in this way to make it self-thinking—then the Good
       would be in need of something prior to it, if the actuality, that is, think-
       ing, is either the perfection of another substrate or the co-production
       of its own real existence, and so itself has another nature prior to it by
       which thinking happens as it should.

50   For it has something to think of because something is before it. And
       when thinking thinks itself, then it is as though it recognizes what
       it acquired from the vision of other things in itself. As for anything
       which has nothing prior to it, or is not mixed with anything taken from
       elsewhere, why and how could it think itself? What would it look for or
       desire? Or would it seek to know how great its power is, since it comes
55   from outside itself, to the extent which it conceives of it? I mean, if it
       were one power that it gets to know, and another by which it gets to
       know it. If it were one power, what is it seeking?

       §6.7.41. As it happens, thinking was bestowed on the more divine
       natures, which are nonetheless inferior to the Good, as a means of
       preservation, in a way like an eye for the blind. But why would an eye
       need to see Being, since it is itself light? And anything that does need
5   to do this, because it has darkness in itself, looks for light using the eye.
       If thinking is light, and light does not look for light, then that splendor,
       in not looking for light, would not look to think either, nor to add

thinking to itself. For why would it do that? And why would it add it to itself, when Intellect itself is also in need, so that it may think?

So, the Good does not perceive itself—it has no need to—nor is it 10 two, or rather many—it and its intellection—for it itself is actually not its thinking—so, what is thought of must be a third thing. If Intellect, thinking, and intelligible are identical, by becoming one they would make themselves disappear in themselves. If they are distinguished by being other than each other, then they are not the Good either.

So, leave all else entirely out of the best nature, since it needs no 15 assistance. For whatever you add will diminish by its addition the nature that needs nothing. For us, thinking is beautiful, because the soul needs to have intellect, and also for Intellect, since Existence is identical with it,[181] and thinking has produced Intellect.[182]

Intellect, then, must be together with thinking, and always attain a 20 comprehension of itself, that this is this, and that these two are one. If they were only one, then it would have been self-sufficient and there would be no need for it to grasp itself. For 'know thyself' is directed at those who because of their inner multiplicity have a job to count their parts, and to understand that they do not know, either entirely or at all, 25 how many parts and what kinds of parts they have, nor what rules over them, or in what respect they are themselves.

If the Good were something for itself,[183] then that would be in a way superior to knowledge, thinking, and self-awareness. But it is not anything for itself, for it takes in nothing; 'it' suffices for it. It, then, is not good for itself, but for other things. For they are in need of it, and 30 it is not in need of itself; that would be ridiculous. For, then, it would indeed be lacking itself, too. Nor does it actually see itself; for it would have to be something and to become something in looking.

It has left all these Beings to the Beings posterior to itself; and as it happens, nothing that is present with other Beings is present with the Good, not even Substantiality.[184] So, neither is it thinking, if indeed 35 that is where Substantiality is, and, taken together, primary thinking, thinking in a strict sense, and Existence. For this reason, it is neither 'reason, nor sense-perception nor scientific understanding,'[185] because it is not possible to predicate of it that anything is present in it.

---

181. Cf. 1.4.10.6; 3.8.8.8; 5.1.8.17–18; 5.6.6.22–23; 5.9.5.29–30. See Parmenides, fr. 28 B 3 DK.

182. I.e., thinking is of intelligibles and Intellect is identical with intelligibles.

183. Reading αὐτῷ with ms X, Theiler, and Hadot.

184. See Pl., *Parm.* 141E9.

185. Cf. 5.6.2. See Pl., *Parm.* 142A3–4.

§6.7.42.[186] But when you are puzzled at such a point and so investigate where one should posit these things, once reason has brought you to them, place those things you consider venerable in the second rank[187]— neither add things of the second rank to the first, nor things of the third rank to the second. Place the second rank around the first, and the third around the second.[188] In this way, you will allow each to relate to the others as they do. You will be making the last things depend on the superior ones: the last things encircle the superior ones, which remain in themselves.

For this reason, it is said, and quite rightly, too, that all Beings encircle the king of all and all Beings are for the sake of him.[189] Plato means Beings by 'all things', and he adds 'for his sake', in that he is the cause of their existence: they in a way desire him, since he is different from all Beings, and possesses nothing that is present in them.

In fact, they would not be all Beings, if anything of what comes after him belonged to him. If, then Intellect, too, is one of all Beings, then Intellect does not belong to the king of all things.

In saying he is the cause of all beautiful things, Plato is obviously positing the Beauty among Forms, and to posit the Good above all Beauty.

In actually positing these Forms as Beings of second rank, he asserts that the beings which come from them are suspended as beings of the third rank. And in positing that around the beings of third rank there are beings engendered by beings of third rank, he asserts that this cosmos depends on Soul. Since Soul is suspended from Intellect, and Intellect from the Good, in this way all beings relate to the Good through intermediaries, some nearer, some neighbors to the near ones. These last are sensible things suspended from Soul at the greatest distance from it.[190]

---

186. See Appendix II J.
187. See Ar., *Meta.* 12.9.1074b18.
188. Cf. 5.1.8.1–4; 6.9.8.40–45. See Pl. [?], *Ep.* 2.312E3–4.
189. See Pl. [?], *Ep.* 2.312E1–2. Plotinus now shifts to the metaphorical representation of the Good.
190. Cf. 5.4.1.1–4.

6.8 (39)

ON THE VOLUNTARY AND THE ONE'S WISHING[1]

Introduction

Is the One free? Anything explained by the Good is as it should be, rational. The definition of freedom when applied to the human soul and intellect is the starting point for the whole inquiry. This treatise tackles, as part of its subject, the problems of attributing any predicates to the Good.

Summary

§1. 'What depends on us': can this expression be extended from humans to intelligibles and the One? We have to ask how 'what depends on us' is distinguished from the voluntary.

§2. Which faculty of the soul does 'what depends on us' relate to—desire, spirit, or a combination of desire and reason? No action depends entirely on us.

§3. Does true freedom lie in opinion or representation? No, in the intellect.

§4. Is it not impossible to attribute freedom to intelligible beings? For they are subject to their own natures. In the case of intelligible beings, one should not distinguish between activity and substance—so one is not subject to the other.

§5. Can virtue be free? It is like a second intellect.

§6. Only freedom in the activity of the intellect is freedom in the full sense. It is the will for the Good that makes the intellect free.

§7. The 'reckless argument': the Good is not free since it does not control its own nature. However, a consequence would be to make the expression 'what depends on us' meaningless.

§8. The predicates which cannot be applied to the Good.

§9. The principle of all things cannot be by accident; it is prior to necessity in being what it is.

§10. The cause of Intellect cannot be by accident; the Good is above all necessity because of its boundless power.

§11. The Good is not, and so cannot be the object of inquiry; it is none of the predicates collected in the genera of Being.

---

1. Porphyry's title. The word θέλημα ('wishing') is Porphyry's. Plotinus uses θέλησις. Cf. *infra* 16.22–23.

§12. We are aware of our own freedom, so the principle that makes us free must also be free.

§13. Predicates used of the Good are used to persuade: the Good's activity is not subservient to its being, since the two are identical. Only the Good satisfies itself. Still, all predicates hold only 'as it were' of the Good.

§14. If each being is the cause of itself, the good must be *a fortiori* cause of itself.

§15. The awareness of our own freedom allows us to approach the true life of the Good.

§16. The positive attributes of the Good.

§17. Neither intelligible nor sensible being is accidental; only the Good relates solely to itself.

§18. We should look for the Good in ourselves; images of the Good.

§19. Contemplation of the Good itself is better than mere images of it; it is 'beyond substantiality'.

§20. Is the Good not prior to itself if it produces itself?

§21. The Good is will entirely; it cannot produce itself other than it does. There is identity between the Substantiality of the Good and its will. To contemplate the Good, one has to do away with all other predicates.

---

§6.8.1. Can one so much as raise the question whether, in the case of the gods, too, there is anything that is up to[2] them, or is it really only appropriate to look for such a thing among the frailties and ambiguous powers[3] of human beings, whereas we should grant

5   omnipotence to gods, so that it is not merely something that is up to them, but everything? Or is omnipotence indeed only to be granted to one [god],[4] and, as to the other gods, some are actually disposed in one way, and some in another way, and there are some gods of which either is true?

---

2. Up to it, or us or them, that is, to do something or its opposite, indicating, minimally, moral or legal responsibility but also equivalent to what is indicated by the words 'free will'. These phrases translate τὸ ἐφ᾽ἡμῖν, which is an important term in Aristotle and then Stoic discussions of action. Alternative translations are 'dependent on us', 'in our power', 'authority over ourselves'. However, asking whether anything depends on the god(s) or is in their power would be strange. Cf. 3.1.7.14–16. See Ar., *EN* 3.1.1110a17–18, 4.1111b30, 5,1112a31, 7.1113b5; *SVF* 2.35 (= Aëtius, *Plac.* 1. Prooem. 2), 298 (= Plutarch, *De St. repug.* 1047b); Epictetus, *Disc.* 1.1.

3. Cf. *infra* 21.1–8. See Alex. Aphr., *De fato* 204.12–16.

4. I.e., the One.

In fact, we should investigate these things, too, and we should dare
to investigate these things both in the case of the primary Beings[5] and
in the case of what is above all [the One], how anything is up to it, even
if we agree that it is omnipotent.[6] Yet what this very power means has
to be investigated, so long as we do not take it to mean a potency in
relation to an actuality, that is, to a future actuality.

Let us postpone these questions for the moment, and first look at
ourselves, where one anyway usually looks,[7] to see if anything happens
to be up to us. The first thing to be investigated is how we should define
something being up to us, that is, what is the conception of such a
thing. In this way, we may come to know if it may be transferred to the
gods, too, and even more so to god [the One], or not.

In fact, it should be transferred, but we have to investigate just how
it applies to the other things, and to the primary Beings.

So, what do we think when we say something is up to us? And why
do we investigate it? It is my view that because we are subject to motion
in the midst of opposing fortunes and necessities, and the assaults of
violent passions attacking the soul, and because we consider all these
to be dominant, and because we are subservient to them, and are led
where they drive us, we are puzzled as to whether we are nothing after
all, and as to whether in fact nothing is up to us.

The upshot is that something that is up to us is as follows: something we do without being enslaved to fortunes or necessities or violent
passions, because we will it, when nothing opposes our willing. If this
is so, then the conception of being up to us is that which is subservient to our willing and will occur or not, depending on the extent of
our willing it.[8] Everything is voluntary that occurs without force[9] and
with knowledge [of the circumstances]; in contrast, anything is up to
us over which we are in charge.

In many cases, the voluntary and what is up to us may coincide,[10]
even if their definitions are distinct, though there are cases where they
diverge. For example, if someone has the power to kill someone else,
it would not be voluntary for him when he did it, if he did not know

10

15

20

25

30

35

---

5. I.e., Intellect, Soul, undescended intellects, and intelligibles, here and *infra* in l.
21.
6. Cf. 5.3.15.33; 6.7.39.26–27, etc.
7. I.e., looking to ourselves rather than to the gods. See, e.g., Ar., *EN* 3.5.1113b5; *SVF*
2.285 (= Cicero, *Acad. Pr.* 2.143), 295 (= D.L., 7.42).
8. See Ar., *Meta.* 8.5.1048a13–21.
9. See Ar., *Meta.* 5.5.1015a26–28; *EN* 5.10.1135a33.
10. Cf. 3.1.9.11–13.

that it was his father.[11] And that[12] would perhaps diverge from what is
40   up to him.[13] And, certainly, knowledge relating to what is voluntary
must include not only particulars, but also universals. For why is it
involuntary if you do not know it is a friend, but not involuntary if you
do not know that you should not kill generally?[14] Because you should
have learned that this is so? Not knowing that one should have learned
these things is not voluntary, nor is anything voluntary that drives you
away from learning them.

§6.8.2. But we have to investigate which factor in us we should
actually attribute something to, when we explain it by saying it is up
to us. Should we attribute it to impulse or some kind of desire? For
example, attributing what is done or not to spiritedness or to appetite
5   or to calculative reasoning about the benefit along with desire?[15]

In fact, if it were explained through spiritedness or desire we would
say that things are up to children and beasts,[16] also to mad people, and
those beside themselves, and those under the influence of drugs or
adventitious imaginative representations,[17] over which they have no
control.[18]

If we attribute something's being up to us to calculative reasoning
10   coupled with desire, then the question arises if we should attribute it to
calculative reasoning even when it goes wrong.

In fact, it should be attributed to correct calculative reasoning and
correct desire.[19] But even then one should investigate whether calculative reasoning moves the desire or the desire the calculative reasoning.[20] For even if the desires are natural, the soul would follow the
necessity of nature, if they belong to the animal, that is, the composite.
15   If the desires belong to the soul alone, then many of the things which
at present we say are up to us would fall outside this range.

---

11. E.g., Oedipus. See Ar., *EN* 5.8.1135a28–30; Alex. Aphr., *De fato* 14.183.27–30,
15.185.13.
12. Reading κἀκεῖνο with HS¹.
13. See Ar., *EN* 3.1.1110b33–1111a2, 5.1113b30–1114a3.
14. See Ar., *EN* 3.2.1110b30–33; 5.8.1135a23–33.
15. See Pl., *Rep.* 4.435C–441C; Ar., *EN* 3.3.1111a25–34.
16. See Ar., *EN* 3.4.1111b8–9. Plotinus, unlike Aristotle, does not use 'voluntary'
for children and animals. He wants to restrict the voluntary to the actions of rational
animals.
17. Cf. 3.1.7.14, 6.15.18.
18. See Ar., *EN* 3.4.1111b8–9, 1114a32, 7.1149b35–1150a1; Alex. Aphr., *De fato*
14.183.30–184.9.
19. See Ar., *EN* 3.5.1114b29.
20. See Ar., *DA* 3.10.433a18–20.

Next, what bare calculative reasoning would precede the [bodily and mental] states? And how, when imagination compels us and desire drags us toward wherever it leads, does that put us in control of these actions?[21] How, generally, are we in control of that to which we are driven? For something in need, desirous of a necessary replenishment, is not in control of the thing to which it is in every way driven.

                            20

How, generally, is something an origin for itself, when it originates from another thing, that is, has its origin in something other, which in turn explains why the thing has come to be such as it is? For it lives due to that other thing, that is, as it has been formed by it.[22]

In fact, in that case even inanimate things will be able to have something up to them.[23] For even fire produces effects in line with the way it was produced.

                            25

If the animal, that is, the soul, has things up to it because it knows what it does, and if this knowledge is through sense-perception, then what contribution does this make toward its having something up to it? For sense-perception does not give the soul control of the effect merely by its seeing. If it is through knowledge, and if this knowledge is of what has been done, and it merely knows this, well then, something else drives it to the action. If reason or knowledge acts, that is, prevails over desire, then we have to investigate by what this is to be explained; and, quite generally, where this occurs. And if reason itself produces another desire, how is this to be understood? If reason halts the desire, and comes to a standstill, and being up to us lies at this point, then being up to us will not lie in the action; rather, it will come to a stop in the intellect,[24] since everything in action, even if reason prevails, is mixed and is not purely up to us.

                            30

                            35

§6.8.3. For this reason, these things have to be looked into, too. For we now are once more[25] close to the argument about the gods. So, we have now attributed what is up to us to willing, and next posited this as lying in reason, and next in correct reason.[26] Perhaps we should now add the correctness of scientific understanding. For it is not the case that, if someone has the right belief and acts on it, he would

                            5

---

21. See *SVF* 3.177 (= Plutarch, *De St. repug.* 1057A).

22. Cf. 3.3.4.31–34.

23. See Alex. Aphr., *De fato* 14.184.15–19.

24. See the Stoic view that what is up to us is assent to a representation, e.g., *SVF* 2.285 (= Cicero, *Acad. Pr.* 2.143).

25. Cf. *supra* 1.18.

26. Cf. *supra* 2.10.

really, uncontroversially, have autonomy,[27] unless he knows why it is right, and is not driven toward his duty by chance or imagination. Since we deny that imagination is up to us, how could we rank those

10 acting in accordance with imagination as having autonomy? Indeed, by 'imagination properly speaking' I mean that imagination roused from bodily states[28]—for states of emptiness with respect to food and drink in a way shape the imagination as does being full of seed—the

15 kind of imaginative representations depending on the qualities of the moistures in the body.[29] And we do not rank those who are active in ways corresponding to these imaginative representations under the principle of autonomy.

For this reason, we do not designate the actions of bad people, who do many things according to their imaginative representations, as

20 being up to them or voluntary.[30] But we will designate as autonomous those who, due to intellect, are free of the affections of the body. In explaining what is up to us by reference to the most beautiful principle, we will grant that the activity of intellect and the premises[31] arising from it are truly free, and we shall say that the desires roused from the

25 intellect, which are not involuntary, are present in the gods living in this manner, that is, those who live by intellect and strive according to intellect.[32]

§6.8.4. Still, one should investigate how something occurring in accordance with desire will fall under the autonomy of the agent, because desire drives the agent toward something external, and contains a deficiency. The thing desiring is driven, even if it is driven toward the Good.

5 Moreover, a problem about Intellect itself arises: Since it acts by nature based on what it is by nature, should it be said to be free and are things up to it when it is not up to it not to produce some result?

Next, one should investigate if, generally, one can say 'up to them' in the proper sense for those beings in which no action is present.[33]

---

27. The word is αὐτεξούσιον. Alternative translations are: self-determination, sovereignty. See *SVF* 2.975 (= Hippolytus, *Philos.* 21), 2.990 (= Origen, *De princ.* 3.110 Delarue); Alex. Aphr., *De fato.* 182.24.
28. Cf. 1.1.3.4; 2.3.9.10; 3.6.1.2; 4.2.2.23; 5.3.2.6.
29. Cf. 3.1.7.13–15.
30. Cf. 1.8.14.21–27; 4.8.4.12–21.
31. I.e., used in arguments about how to act.
32. Following HS¹ in preserving the last line which is bracketed by HS².
33. I.e., Beings in the intelligible world.

But even for those things which possess the potency for action, the necessity comes from outside.[34] For they will not act for no reason. But, then, how will freedom apply also to those enslaved to their own nature?

In fact, if something is not forced to follow another, how then is 'enslaved' meant? How can something borne toward the Good be forced, when the desire is voluntary, and if it knows, in moving toward it as good, that it is good? For the involuntary is a diversion from the Good and toward something forced, when one is borne toward something not good for one. And that is enslaved which is not free and which does not have the power to move toward the Good; rather, because something else better has a commanding position over it, it is driven away from its own goods, in serving the other thing. Slavery is blamed, not because one has[35] power to move toward the bad, but where one has no power to move toward one's own good because one is driven to the good of another.

One can speak of slavery to one's own nature if you distinguish between the thing enslaved and what it is enslaved to.[36] For how could a simple nature, that is, one activity, which is not different potentially and actually, not be free? For you could not say that it acts according to its nature, such that its substantiality is one thing and its activity is another, if indeed in the intelligible world existence and acting are identical.[37] If, then, the activity is not because of another thing nor up to another thing, how can it not be free? It must be free, even if 'up to itself' does not fit, but something more than 'up to itself' is here, and up to itself in such a way that it is not conditional on another, and nothing else is master of its activity. For neither is anything else master of its substantiality, if indeed the substantiality is a principle.

Even if Intellect has another principle, still, this is not outside Intellect, but in the Good.[38] Even if Intellect conforms to that Good, it will be all the more up to itself and something free. For one seeks freedom and what is up to it for the sake of the Good. If, then, Intellect is active in conformity to the Good, then its activity is more up to it. For

---

34. See Ar., *EN* 3.1.1110a2.

35. Omitting the οὐκ ἔχει as due to dittography after οὐχ οὖ: blame does not attach to slavery because it is a positive power for the bad, but because slaves perform someone else's good.

36. See Pl., *Rep.* 4.443D4; *Tim.* 89D3–4; *Lg.* 645B1–2.

37. Cf. 5.3.7.18; 6.7.40.14.

38. Because the Good is not outside anything. All things are in it.

Intellect already has an orientation[39] toward that from itself and has in itself what it is better for it to be in itself if indeed it is orientated toward the Good.

§6.8.5. Then, is autonomy or the 'up to it'[40] in Intellect only when it is thinking alone, that is, in pure Intellect, or are they also in the soul when it is intellectually active and acting according to virtue?[41] If indeed we grant these attributes to a soul engaged in action, first we
5 should not grant it to the soul in respect of what is accomplished in the action. For we do not possess the mastery over bringing actions to completion.[42]

But if we grant it to acting beautifully and bringing about everything in our power, then that would be said correctly. But how is even that up to us? For example, if we are courageous because there is war. I mean
10 how is the activity then up to us, when, if war had not taken control of the situation, we would not have engaged in this activity? Likewise with all other actions in accordance with virtue, when virtue is always forced to bring about this or that. Indeed, if one were to grant choice to
15 virtue itself, we can ask if it would want there to be wars, so that it can act and be courageous and want for there to be injustice, so that it can determine and organize what is just, or poverty, so that it can manifest liberality, or, when everything is still and going well, would it choose stillness over action, since no one needs their service, just as a doctor,
20 for example, Hippocrates, wants no one to need his skill.

If, then, virtue, being active in actions, were to be forced to help, how would it have the 'up to it' in a pure fashion? Would we call the actions necessary, but the willing, and the reasoning before the actions not necessary?
25 In fact, if so, then, in positing these attributes in the bare factor[43] prior to the thing done, we will posit autonomy and being up to virtue itself outside the action.

---

39. The term is τὸ ὁρμώμενον ('an orientation') which is a correction by Kirchhoff followed by HS² for τὸ ὁρμώμενον ('that which is seen'). Either reading is difficult to construe.

40. The terms τὸ αὐτεξούσιον ('autonomy') and τὸ ἐπ' αὐτῷ ('up to it') are being used synonymously.

41. There is no virtue in Intellect. Cf. 1.2.6.15–27. See Ar., *EN* 4.2.1120a23; 10.8.1178b6; Alcinous, *Didask.* 152.33–153.4.

42. Plotinus here agrees with the Stoics. Cf. *supra* 2.35. See Plutarch, *De comm. not.* 27.1071C–D.

43. I.e., the willing and reasoning preceding the action; these are up to us, not the action itself.

What is, then, up to virtue itself, as a habit or disposition?[44] Should we not say it comes to order the badly disposed soul, by bringing measure to affective states and desires?[45] How, then, will we say being good   30
and 'virtue without a master'[46] are up to us?

In fact, insofar as it is willed and chosen. Or, because, when it has come about in us, it constitutes freedom and the 'up to us', and does not permit us still to be the slaves of what we were slaves to before. If, then, virtue is in a way another intellect[47] and a habit which makes the soul   35
rational, then again being up to us does not belong to us in action, but to intellect detached from actions.

§6.8.6. How, then, did we explain something being up to us earlier by reference to willing, in saying 'this would occur in accordance with my willing', and also adding 'or would not occur'?[48]

If, then, this was said correctly, and if the following remarks are to agree with what has been said, we will say that virtue and intellect are   5
authoritative, and that one should explain what is up to us and freedom by these.[49] And we will say that, since they are without a master,[50] intellect wills to be on its own, and virtue wills to be in charge of itself, being in charge of the soul, such that it is good and, to this extent, wills to render themselves and the soul free. But when unavoidable feelings   10
and actions befall it, the good soul, rendered such by virtue, does not want them to occur, and nonetheless, even amid them, preserves what is up to it, by returning to itself even in the sensible world. And we will say that it will not simply obey the demands of the situation, for example, when saving someone in danger; rather, should it think right,   15
even in abandoning him, it orders him to abandon life, possessions, children, and his country itself, and, in so doing, it has its own beauty as aim, not the existence of those subordinate to it.

The result is, we will say that autonomy and what is up to us are   20
not to be referred back to acting,[51] not to the external situation, but to the internal activity and intellection and the contemplative activity of virtue itself. This virtue must be called a kind of intellect, not reckoning with it those affective states enslaved to or moderated by

---

44. See Pl., *Phil.* 11D4; Ar., *EN* 2.5.1106a22–24.
45. Cf. 1.2.2.13–19. See Pl., *Phil.* 45D–E.
46. Cf. 2.3.9.17; 4.4.38.25. See Pl., *Rep.* 10.617E3.
47. Cf. 1.2.6.11–15; 6.7.35.5.
48. Cf. *supra* 1.32–33.
49. See Ar., *EN* 3.7.1113b6.
50. See Pl., *Rep.* 10.617E3.
51. See Pl., *Rep.* 4.443C10–D1.

reason. For those, Plato says,[52] when corrected 'by habits and exer-
25   cises' belong 'close to the body.' And, as a result, we will say that it is
quite clear that what is immaterial is what is free,[53] and it is by this that
what is up to us must be explained, and willing itself, which is in control and on its own,[54] even if something, of necessity, directs it toward
something external. Those things, then, which originate in willing and
30   occur because of it are up to us, both externally and in itself. Whatever
the will itself wills and accomplishes without hindrance, is indeed the
prime case of something being up to us.

     Theoretical intellect, that is, primary Intellect,[55] is in this way up to
itself, since its function is never up to something else. On the contrary,
35   it reverted entirely toward itself and its function,[56] lying itself in the
Good with no deficiency, existing complete and living in a way in conformity with will. Its will is intellection, but it is called 'will' because
its [activity] accords with Intellect. So-called will[57] imitates what is in
accord with Intellect, for will wants the Good, while thinking lies truly
40   in the Good. Intellect, then, possesses what will wants, and, when will
attains it, will becomes intellection. If we, then, posit what is up to us in
the will for the Good, how can something which already has what will
wants to attain[58] not have what is up to it?

     In fact, it must be assumed to be something greater, if one does not
want to make 'what is up to itself' ascend to this level.

     §6.8.7.[59] Soul, then, becomes free when it hastens without hindrance
toward the Good because of Intellect. And what it does because of
Intellect is up to it, while Intellect does what it does because of itself.
The nature of the Good is that which is to be desired for itself, and
5   is that because of which other things have what is up to themselves,
when they have the power to attain it without hindrance, or when
Intellect has it.[60]

---

52. See Pl., *Rep.* 7.518D10–E2.
53. Cf. 5.1.10.19–21.
54. The words ἐφ᾽ ἑαυτῆς ('on its own') indicate relative causal independence. Cf. *supra*
l. 7; 4.3.3.26; 6.4.2.39; 6.5.1.18.
55. See Ar., *DA* 3.9.432b26–7.
56. Cf. 5.1.7.5, 12–13; 5.2.1.10.
57. I.e., the will involved in actions of the body-soul composite.
58. I.e., the Good. Plotinus has now discussed the 'up to it' in Intellect and Soul. Now,
on this basis, he turns to the Good.
59. See Appendix III C 1.
60. Cf. *supra* 5.29. See Pl., *Phil.* 20D8–9.

The Good is master of all things lesser in honor, being in the primary abode,[61] toward which other things want to ascend, and on which they depend,[62] and from which they have their powers, such that some things are up to them. How could one bring the Good under the concept 'up to it' when that concept is properly used [only] of me and you? Intellect was just barely, albeit violently, dragged under this concept.[63]

We could do this only if we follow a reckless argument.[64] This argument uses a different premise, and claims that, since the nature of the Good is disposed as it is by chance, and is not master of what is, and since it is not what it is on account of itself, it will have neither freedom nor what is up to it, whether or not it produces the effects which it is forced to produce or not to produce.

This argument is certainly repellent and without support; it does away with the nature of the voluntary and of autonomy, and the conception of what is up to us, in that, on this assumption, it would be fruitless to say these things, being mere sounds referring to nonexistent things. For the argument must not just claim that nothing is up to anything; it must also say that this phrase cannot be thought or comprehended. If the argument admits that it can be comprehended, then it would already be refuted with ease, since the conception of what is up to us fits those things which the argument claims it does not fit.[65]

But this conception neither has anything to do with substantiality nor does it include it, since it is impossible for a thing to produce itself or to bring itself into real existence.[66] Rather, our thought wants to consider which beings are slaves of others, and which have autonomy, and which are subordinate to other beings, and which are master of their own activity, a feature which belongs purely both to eternal Beings insofar as they are eternal, and to those who pursue or possess the Good without hindrance. Indeed, since the Good is above these, it is absurd to look for some other sort of good, beside it, since it is also not correct to say that the Good exists according to chance.

---

61. See Pl., *Rep.* 7.519D1; Ar., *EN* 1.1.1094a3.
62. Cf. *infra* 9.35; 1.8.2.3; 6.5.10.2; 6.6.18.48; 6.7.42. See Ar., *Meta.* 12.7.1072b13.
63. These very compressed lines are translated *ad sensum*.
64. Intellect was 'dragged' to the sensible world where things were up to human beings with intellect. Perhaps what follows is a reference to a Gnostic argument (cf. 2.9.15.10), although other targets have been suggested, including Epicurus, certain Christian theologians, and the Peripatetic Alexander of Aphrodisias.
65. I.e., the Idea of the Good as first principle of all.
66. I.e., the conception of autonomy or what is up to something is not about self-creation.

35   For chance occurs in things that are posterior and plural.[67] We should
      not say that the first thing conforms to chance, nor that it is not the
      master of its own coming to be, because it never did come to be.

           It is absurd to say that it produces effects corresponding to what it
      is, if one were to think that freedom then exists when something pro-
      duces effects or is active contrary to its nature.[68] Nor may something
      solitary[69] actually be deprived of power, if it is solitary not through
40   being prevented by another thing, but because it is just that thing itself
      and, in a way, is self-sufficient, and has nothing better than itself.[70]
      Otherwise, one would be removing autonomy from that which attains
      the Good to the greatest degree.

           If this is absurd, it would be even more absurd to deprive the
45   Good of autonomy, because it is good and remains by itself, in not
      needing to be moved toward any of those things moving toward it,
      and being deficient in nothing. Its sort of existence is actually its sort
      of activity—for these are not two distinct things indeed any more
      than they are in the case of Intellect, since its activity does not[71]
50   conform to Existence, any more than vice versa—which means that
      the Good cannot be active in conformity with its nature, nor can
      its activity and its sort of life be explained by reference to its sort
      of substantiality.[72] Rather, its sort of substantiality co-exists with its
      activity and, sort of coming about with it from eternity, produces
      it itself out of both, for its own sake and belonging to nothing else.

      §6.8.8. We see that autonomy is not an accident of the Good; rather,
      we see that it has this autonomy by stripping away the contraries
      from things with autonomy in other respects.[73] In transferring
      lesser attributes from lesser beings to the Good, on account of our
5   inability to grasp those things which should be said of it, we would
      like to say the following about it; yet we are in no position to find
      anything to say about it, let alone anything properly applicable to

---

67. See Ar., *Phys.* 2.6.198a9–10.
68. See Pl., *Parm.* 153B8–D3.
69. See Ar., *Meta.* 7.15.1040a29.
70. Cf. 1.8.2.4–5, 3.12–18; 2.9.1.8–9; 5.3.13.16–17; 6.7.23.7–10.
71. Reading οὔτι with Kirchhoff rather than the ὅτι of HS². On the latter reading,
either Plotinus would have to be saying what he denies, namely, that activity follows
being more than being follows activity or else the questionable claim would have to
be put in the mouth of an objector. But this sentence does not otherwise indicate that.
72. The expression οἷον ('sort of', 'in a way') indicates that the terms 'being', 'activity',
'life' and so on only apply to the Good analogously. Cf. *infra* 8.4–5, 13.48–51; 5.5.3.23.
73. Cf. 5.3.13.1, 14.1; 5.5.6.12; 6.7.36.7.

it.[74] Both all beautiful and all holy attributes are posterior to it, for it is their principle.[75] Nonetheless, it is not their principle in another respect. Indeed, if you take everything away from it, then you take away the 'up to it', as posterior, and 'autonomy', since this means an activity in relation to another; so, too, 'unhindered', and also 'without impediment toward others', insofar as there are others. Generally, you should not speak of it in relation to another thing.[76] It is just what it is, and is prior to them.

Since we strip away 'is' as well,[77] so, too, we strip away anything relative to beings. Nor may we actually say 'it has grown to be naturally'.[78] For this is posterior also. Even if this phrase were used of intelligibles, it would be said of things coming from something else, and thus primarily of Substantiality, because this grew naturally out of the Good.[79] But if nature is in temporal things, then it is not said of Substantiality.[80] Nor indeed should 'not being from itself' be said of this nature. For we stripped away 'is', and 'not from itself' might be said when something is by the agency of another thing. Is it, then, accidentally thus?

In fact, not even 'it is accidentally' is to be applied to the Good, for no attribute is accidental to it, nor is it in relation to another thing.[81]

'It is accidentally' is said, of many things, when some things are, and they are other things accidentally; so how could the first thing of all be accidentally? Nor did it come here, so you cannot investigate how it did come, or which chance brought it or gave it real existence. For chance did not yet exist, nor did spontaneity.[82] For spontaneity also is both derived from something else and occurs among things that come to be.

§6.8.12. What, then? Is the Good not what it is? Is it at least master of being what it is or of transcending Existence?[83] For the soul, not persuaded[84] by anything we have said, finds itself at an impasse. So, this is what is to be said in response to these objections, namely, that

---

74. I.e., non-metaphorical.
75. Cf. 5.2.1.1.
76. Cf. *infra* l. 22.
77. See Pl., *Parm.* 141E9–10.
78. Cf. *supra* 4.5, 4.26, 7.50–52.
79. Playing on the etymological connection between φύσις ('nature') and ἔφυ ('was born').
80. Cf. *supra* 7.3.
81. Cf. *infra* 11.32, 17.27–28; 6.7.23.18.
82. See Ar., *Phys.* 2.6.197a36ff.
83. Cf. *supra* 11.21. See Pl., *Rep.* 6.509B5.
84. Cf. *infra* 13.4.

5   each of us, in respect of the body, must be far from Substantiality but,
in respect of the soul and what we are most of all,[85] we participate in
Substantiality, and we are a substance, that is, in a way, a composite of
differentia and substantiality.[86]

We are, then, not Substance properly speaking, and not Substantiality itself.[87] For this reason, we are not masters of our own substantiality.
10   For the substantiality is, in a way, one thing and we are another, and we
are not masters of our substantiality; rather, the substantiality is master
over us if indeed it adds the 'differentia'.[88] Since, however, we are in a
way precisely what is master of us, we may thus be said to be in the
sensible world no less masters of ourselves.

But that[89] of which the substantiality itself is completely what it is—
15   and it is not one thing and its substantiality another—in this case, it is
what it is and is master of this, and is no longer to be related [to the
substantiality of] another insofar as it exists and insofar as it is substance. For it is again left to be master of itself insofar as it is primarily
related to its [own] substantiality.

As for the factor that actually has made the Substance [Intellect]
free, and which is naturally such as to make it free,[90] and which one
20   might call 'freedom-maker', what could that be slave to if indeed it is
licit to say such a thing at all? A slave to its own substantiality? But Substance is free because of the Good and is posterior to the Good, which
has no substantiality. If, then, there is activity in it, and we posit it to
consist in the activity, this would not be grounds for it being different
from itself, nor for it not being master of itself, from whom the activity
25   derives, because the activity is not different from it. But if we generally
do not admit actuality to be in it,[91] but claim instead that other things

---

85. Cf. 1.1; 1.4.14.1; 4.7.1.24–25. See Pl. [?], *Alc.* 130C; Ar., *EN* 9.8.1169a35, 10.1178a2-3.
86. Cf. 6.2.14.21, 19.4. The 'difference' is due to embodiment.
87. I.e., the Form of Humanity or perhaps the undescended intellect of each person.
88. Cf. 4.3.10.20–22. This is so if the embodied soul is necessarily what it is due to the
Form of Humanity or the undescended intellect of each person.
89. I.e., Intellect.
90. I.e., the Good.
91. Plotinus denies ἐνέργεια to the Good in several places. Cf. 3.8.11.8–10; 3.9.9.8–12;
5.3.12.16; 6.7.17.10. But he also affirms ἐνέργεια of it. Cf. *supra* 12.25; *infra* 16.16–17;
20.9–15; 6.7.18.6. Given l. 22 *supra*, it seems that it is because the Good has no οὐσία that
it has no ἐνέργεια. This allows Plotinus to distinguish the ἐνέργεια that it does not have
from the ἐνέργεια that it does have. In the first sense, ἐνέργεια implies a δύναμις ('potentiality'); in the second sense it does not. Everything other than the Good, including Intellect, is actualizing a potency in relation to the Good as object of desire. The one word
ἐνέργεια should be understood as 'actuality' in the first case and 'activity' in the second.

have their real existence by their actuality in relation to it, then all the less will we grant that master and mastered are in the intelligible world.

But neither will we grant it to be master of itself, not because something else is master of it, but because we have attributed being master 30 of itself to Substance,[92] and we posit the Good to be at a greater level of honor than is in conformity with being master of itself. What, then, is there at a greater level of honor than something which is master of itself?

In fact, it is because in the intelligible world, Substance and actuality, although two things in a way, provide the conception of 'master' from the actuality, although this was identical to the Substance; because of this, being master became separate and Substance was said 35 to be master of itself. But where it is not two taken together as one but just one—for the Good is activity alone, or it is not activity at all—then it is not correct to speak of it being master of itself.

§6.8.13. But even if these names must be applied to the object of the investigation, let it be said once more that these names are not correctly applied because one should not make the Good two even in conception; but now we need to deviate from strict accuracy in our arguments for 5 the sake of persuasion. For if we were to attribute activities to it, and attribute its activities to what is in a way its willing—for it is not active unwillingly—and its activities are in a way its substantiality, then its willing and its substantiality will be identical. If this holds, therefore, as it will, so it is. It is, therefore, not the case that it wills and is active according to its nature rather than its substantiality controlling the 10 way it wills and is active. It, therefore, is entirely master of itself, in possessing existence in itself.

Actually, consider this. Each being, in desiring the Good,[93] wills to be that rather than what it itself is; and it thinks it is most of all that, when it participates in the Good. In such a case, each thing chooses 15 for itself existence insofar as it can come to possess it from the Good. The grounds for this are that, for the Good, the nature of the Good is clearly more choice worthy[94] for itself, if indeed any portion of the Good in another thing is most choice worthy for that thing and, for the Good, substantiality is voluntary, and comes to it by wishing, and since it is one and identical with its wishing, and exists because of 20 wishing. And as long as each thing has not come to have the Good,

---

92. Cf. *supra* ll. 13–17.
93. Cf. 1.6.7.1; 6.5.1.12; 6.7.26.6.
94. See Pl., *Phil.* 20D1, 54C10, 60B4–10.

it wants something other than itself, and insofar as it has the Good, it at once wants itself already and is; and presence like this is not by chance, nor is its substantiality outside willing. And it is defined by this, and belongs to itself by this.

25   If, then, each thing produces itself by the Good, clearly it then becomes such as the Good would be toward itself primarily, by which other things, too, are being for themselves. And its wishing to be such as the Good is, goes together with its sort of substantiality. It is not possible for anyone to grasp the Good without its wanting for
30   itself to be such as it is. Its wanting to exist itself coincides with[95] its being itself that which it wants, and the wishing and itself are one, and it is not less one because it did not happen to be and that which it willed to be another. For what else would it want to be other than what it is?

Indeed, if we were to suppose it to choose for itself what it wanted
35   to become, and that it is possible for it to alter its nature into another thing, neither would it will to become another thing, nor would it blame itself for being that which it is by necessity, since this is 'being itself', which it always wanted and wants. For in truth the nature of the Good is wishing for itself, without being bribed by, or slavishly follow-
40   ing, its own nature, but in choosing itself, because there was nothing else such that it could be dragged toward it.

Further, one could also say that everything other than the Good does not include in the account of its substantiality the principle of self-satisfaction; for it might be dissatisfied with itself. But the choice
45   of and wishing of itself is necessarily included in the real existence of the Good; otherwise, it would scarcely be possible for another thing to be satisfied with itself, since things are satisfied with themselves by partaking of the Good or by their imagining themselves doing so.

We must go along with the names, should someone use them of necessity in talking about the Good just by way of indication, although
50   we are not allowed to say them in all strictness. Add 'in a way' to each of them!

If, then, the Good has been established as really existing, and choice and willing together comprise its existence—it cannot be without them—then choice and willing will not be many, and willing, sub-stantiality, and wanting[96] must be drawn together into one. If wanting
55   comes from it, then necessarily its existence comes from it, and the

---

95. Cf *supra* 6.8.20.26, *infra* 54, συνυφίστησιν.
96. Retaining καὶ τὸ θέλειν which is bracketed by HS².

result is that the argument has shown that it has produced itself.[97] For if willing comes from it, and is in a way a function of it, and willing is identical to its real existence, then in this way it will have brought itself into real existence. The result is that it is not any chance thing, but what it willed itself to be.

§6.8.14. Moreover, we should also regard the matter as follows. Everything that is said to exist can be identical with, or different from, its own essence. For example, this human being is one thing, and the essence of a human being something else, given that a human being partakes of the essence of a human being. Soul, in contrast, and the   5
essence of soul are identical,[98] if soul is something simple and not said of another thing, and human being is identical with the essence of a human being.[99] And though a human being can come to be by chance, insofar as he is different from the essence of a human being, the essence of a human being cannot come to be by chance. For Human Being itself comes from itself.

If indeed the essence of a human being comes from itself and not   10
by chance or accidentally, how can that which is above Human Being itself, and which is generative of Human Being itself indeed from which all Beings come, exist by chance?[100] It is after all a simpler nature than the essence of Human Being, and the essence of Being quite generally.

Furthermore, it is not possible, as one moves toward the simple, to take chance with you; the result is that it is impossible for chance to   15
ascend to the simplest thing.

Furthermore, we should recall something said elsewhere,[101] namely, each of the true Beings comes to have real existence through the agency of the nature of the Good, and if something among sensibles   20
is of a certain kind,[102] it is of a certain kind by coming from those true Beings. By 'being of a certain kind' I mean possessing, along with sub-stantiality, the explanation for the existence of such a substance,[103] such that the researcher in retrospect can express the reason why each of the features present in it is there—for example, why there is an eye, and why the feet of such and such an animal are as they are—and that

---

97. Cf. *supra* 10.36–37; *infra* 14.41, 16.14–15, 18.48–49, 20.2, 21.
98. See Ar., *Meta.* 8.3.1043b1–2.
99. See Ar., *Meta.* 7.6.1031a28–b3.
100. Cf. *infra* 18.40; 6.9.3.49.
101. Cf. 6.7.2.10, 25–30, 52–55; 16.24–35, 23.20–24. See Ar., *AP* 2.2.90a15.
102. Retaining τοιοῦτον with HS¹.
103. I.e., why an animal has the characteristics it has given that the substantiality of the animal is to be instantiated.

there is an explanation which pertains to each of the parts of each
25   thing, and that the parts are there because of one another. Why are the
feet elongated? Because this feature is such and such, and because
the face is such and such, the feet are such and such. And in general
the concord of all parts with each other is their reciprocal explanation;
and the explanation why this part is, is that this is what it is to be a
human being.

The result is that existence and explanation [of the parts] are one,
30   that is, identical. These come from one source in this way, a source
which did not engage in calculative reasoning but which provided
altogether the 'why' and the 'that'.[104] It, then, is the source of existence
and of the explanation for existence, because it provides both. But just
as in the case of things that come to be, the thing they derive from is
much more of an archetype, truer and, to a greater extent than in the
35 . case of things that come to be, related to the better. If, then, none of the
things which have their explanations in themselves are random or by
chance or accidental, it has everything from the Good, since it is the
'father of reason and of explanations', I mean, of explanatory Substantiality.[105] It must be the principle, like a paradigm for anything certainly
40   with no share in chance, truly the paradigm, the primary paradigm,
unmixed with chance events and spontaneity and accidents, itself
being the explanation for itself, from itself, and because of itself. For it
is primarily itself, and is itself above Being.[106]

§6.8.15.[107] And it is itself object of love and love, that is, love of itself,[108]
inasmuch as it is only beautiful[109] by reason of itself and in itself.[110] And
indeed whatever is present to itself would not be so if that which is
present and that to which it is present were not one or identical. If the
5   thing that is present is one with the thing to which it is present, and the
thing in a way desiring, one with the thing desired, but the thing desired
is in point of real existence even like a substrate, then once again[111] desire

---

104. Cf. 6.7.2.19, 19.18–19. Plotinus usually attributes operation without calculation
to Intellect. Cf. 3.2.2.8–9; 6.7.1.32–57.
105. See Pl. [?], *Ep.* 6. 323D4.
106. Cf. *infra* 16.33; 6.9.6.44–45.
107. See Appendix II E.
108. Cf. *infra* 16.13.
109. In this and in following chapters, Plotinus invests the Good with a number of
'personal' attributes. The impersonal pronouns are here retained on the grounds that
all of these personal attributes have to be understood οἷον ('in a way').
110. Cf. 6.7.33.22–27, 34.8–21. See Pl., *Phdr.* 250E1.
111. Cf. *supra* 13.19–20.

will have shown itself to be identical to substantiality. If that is so, then it is the identical being that produces itself, and is master of itself, and did   10
not come to be such as another wanted, but as it itself wanted.

Further, if we were to say that the Good takes nothing into itself, nor does anything take it into itself, we would make it such as to be outside the realm of chance, not only by making it isolated,[112] and pure of all else, but also for the following reason. If we ourselves were to see a nature like this in ourselves, with nothing in it of the other things   15
attached to us, due to which we undergo whatever happens and whatever is present by chance[113]—for all else in us is enslaved and exposed to chance events, dependent on us in a way according to chance—to this alone belongs our mastery of self and autonomy, by means of the activity of a light Good-like[114] and good, a light greater than that of   20
Intellect, in that this activity is so disposed that its being above Intellect is not an acquired attribute.

On actually ascending to this, and becoming this alone, casting aside all else, what could we say about it, except that we are more than free, and have more than autonomy? Who would connect us with chance events, either random or due to an accidental attribute, once we have become the true Life itself, or having come to be in it, which contains   25
nothing else, but is just itself?

Other things, then, which become isolated are not self-sufficient for their existence, whereas the Good is what it is even when it is isolated.[115] Primary real existence[116] does not depend on anything inanimate or on non-rational life. For non-rational life is weak in existence, since it is a   30
scattering of reason and indeterminate. To the extent that it progresses toward reason, it leaves chance behind. For if something accords with reason, then it is not by chance. For us, once we have made the ascent, the Good is not reason but more beautiful than reason. Such is the distance separating it from being a chance accident. For the root of reason originates in itself, and all things come to an end in it, like the principle and foundation of a very large plant living according to an expressed principle, resting in itself, and giving the plant that expressed principle which it itself receives.[117]

---

112. Cf. 5.3.13.18; 5.5.13.6; 6.7.23.7, 33.18; 6.9.11.51.
113. Retaining καὶ bracketed by HS².
114. See Pl., *Rep.* 6.509A3.
115. Cf. 2.9.1.9; 5.3.13.18; 5.6.2.15; 6.6.18.53; 6.7.23.7, 33.18.
116. Cf. *supra* 10.12.
117. Cf. 3.8.10.10–12.

§6.8.16.[118] Since we say, and it is generally admitted, that the Good is everywhere[119] and again nowhere,[120] we should ponder this, and consider what kind of thing those who look at it from this point of view should posit the objects of our inquiry to be. For if it is nowhere, then it is not accidentally anywhere, and if everywhere, then it is everywhere such as it is itself. The upshot is that being everywhere and in every way are it itself, not because it is in the 'everywhere', but because it is the 'everywhere' and gives being to others situated side by side everywhere. By possessing the topmost rank, or rather not possessing it, but being itself topmost, the Good possesses all things as subservient without itself being an accidental attribute of other things, but the other way around. It would be better to say that the other things are around it, while it does not regard them, but the other way around.[121] It is borne in a way inside itself, as though loving itself, in the pure radiance,[122] being itself that which it loved, that is, it has made itself exist,[123] if indeed it is persisting activity and the most loved thing, like Intellect.[124]

But Intellect is the result of actuality; hence, the Good is that, too, but not of anything else.[125] It is, therefore, the result of its own activity. It is, therefore, not as it is accidentally; rather, it is as it itself acts.

So, furthermore, if it exists most of all, because it fixes itself relative to itself, and in a way regards itself, and this being for itself, in a way, is its self-regard, as though it would produce itself, then, it is not as chance would have it, but the way it wants to be, nor is its wishing random, nor accidentally as it is. For because its wishing is of the best, it is not random.

But that this sort of inclination toward itself, being in a way an activity of itself, and a persistence in itself, produces what it is, is testified to by supposing the opposite. If its inclination were toward that which is outside itself, it would destroy what it is. Being, therefore, just what it is, it is activity relative to itself. This is one thing, namely, itself.

---

118. See Appendix III B 1.
119. Cf. 3.8.9.24–28; 3.9.4.3; 5.5.8.23; 6.4.3.18.
120. See Pl., *Parm.* 131A–C, 138A2–3.
121. Cf. 6.9.8.35–45.
122. See Pl., *Phdr.* 250C4.
123. Cf. *supra* 10.35–38, 11.1–5.
124. Cf. 2.5.3.6; 6.5.3.2; 6.7.27.18. See Ar., *Meta.* 7.1072b3.
125. The word is ἐνέργημα ('the result of actuality'), that is, the result of ἐνέργεια, which can be understood either as 'actuality' or 'activity'. Intellect, actualizing its potency, is ἐνέργημα according to the former sense (cf. 3.8.11.1–3); the Good, having no potency, is ἐνέργημα only according to the latter.

It, therefore, brings itself into existence, because its activity is
brought about along with it. If, then, its activity did not come to be, but   30
always was, and like a waking[126] when the being who is awake is not
something else than the waking, always a waking and super intellection,[127] then it is in such a way that it is awake. And the waking transcends[128] Substantiality and Intellect[129] and intelligent life, though it is   35
these. It, therefore, is activity beyond Intellect, intelligence, and Life.
These come from it and nowhere else. Its existence, therefore, originates in it, and comes from it. There it is not as it is accidentally, but as
it wanted itself to be.

---

126. See Ar., *Meta.* 12.7.1072b17.
127. The term is ὑπερνόησις, a *hapax* in Greek literature prior to Plotinus. Cf. the
related term κατανόησις, 5.3.1.4, 13; 5.4.2.17.
128. See Pl., *Rep.* 6.509B9, 7.521A4.
129. See Ar., *On Prayer apud* Simplicius, *In DC* 485.19–22 (= fr. 1, p. 57 Ross).

6.9 (9)

ON THE GOOD OR THE ONE

Introduction

All beings are beings because of the One. Here, Plotinus gives a brief but comprehensive treatise in which a system of dependence on the One or the Good is sketched. The One, especially understood as eternal presence, provides guidance and well-being to the soul.

Summary

§1. Everything is because of the One; while soul provides unity, it is not the One.

§2. Nor is Intellect the One, and nor are individuals.

§3. For the soul to be directed by the one requires the soul to leave off the variety it is accustomed to, and undergo habituation of character, and then use Intellect as a guide, while excluding all determinations from the One.

§4. The presence of the One is prior to that of science, and only direct vision, not teaching, provides contact with the One.

§5. The progress from awareness of body to that of the One leads via the possession of reason and virtue, then from the science to Intellect, and finally from Intellect to the One. The One is prior to the Intellect in that it has no parts.

§6. The One is not like a monad or a point because it is not in another thing. It is a maximum in being infinite in power; it has no need of anything. It has no good nor will, nor thought nor being with itself.

§7. The One is the object of investigation in that it may be present, not as a thing, and the presence is to be found in not knowing; the presence of the One is to be found within oneself.

§8. For we revolve around the center, or better making our center coincide with the center of all things; in that way the eternal presence is present to us.

§9. By turning around the One, we receive being, in turning toward the One we receive well-being. For the soul has innate love of the Good which makes us desire death, even if true contemplation is possible in this life.

§10. This contemplation is interrupted, although it is unity with the One.

§11. One only remembers being like the One. The soul needs not be afraid of proceeding to nothing. For virtue and contemplation take turns in guiding the soul.

---

§6.9.1. All beings are beings due to unity,[1] both those beings that are primarily Beings and those that are said to be among beings in any way. For what could be, if it were not a unity?[2] For if you take away the unity which they are said to be, then they are not those things. For an army[3] does not exist unless it is a unity, nor a choir, nor a herd, if it is not a unity.   5 Nor a house or a ship, if it does not have unity, since a house or a ship is a unity, and if it loses its unity, then it is no longer a house or a ship.

So, there cannot be continuous magnitudes unless unity is present in them; when divided, they alter their existence, insofar as their unity is   10 destroyed.[4] And indeed so, too, with the bodies of plants and animals, since each is a unity, if they lose their unity when they are divided into a multiplicity, they lose the substantiality they had, in that they are no longer what they were; they have become other things which in turn exist, insofar as they are each a unity.

There is health when the body is ordered into a unity, beauty, when   15 the nature of unity controls the parts, and virtue of the soul, when it is unified into a unity that is, into a single concord.

Turning, then, to soul, should we say that because it unifies all things, in creating, forming,[5] shaping, and ordering them, it is soul itself that bestows unity or that it is the One?[6]   20

In fact, just as soul is not the other things it provides to body, such as shape and form, which are different from it, so, too, we should think that in the case of unity, even if soul does provide unity, it bestows a unity which is different from itself; by looking toward the One it makes each thing a unity, just as it looks to Human Being in producing a   25 human being, grasping the unity inherent in the Form Human Being

---

1. Cf. 5.3.15.11–15; 6.6.1.4–8. The words τῷ ἑνί ('due to unity') could also be translated as 'due to the One', which, for Plotinus, is certainly no less true. But the wider, ambiguous claim seems to be here the starting point. When Plotinus is speaking dialectically, τὸ ἕν is translated 'unity'; when he speaking of the source of unity in anything, τὸ ἕν is translated as 'the One'. The adjective ἕν is translated 'one'.
2. Cf. 5.6.3.15–22.
3. Cf. 6.2.10.1–5.
4. See Ar., *Meta.* 10.11052a18–21.
5. See Pl. [?], *Epin.* 981B8, 984C3–4.
6. Because soul provides unity, it might be supposed to be the One itself. Either the hypostasis Soul or the soul of the cosmos is meant.

along with it. For each of the things which is said to be a unity in this way is a unity to the extent it possesses just what it is; the result is that things that are beings to a lesser degree have unity to a lesser degree, and so correspondingly with those that have being to a greater degree.

Moreover, since soul is different from the One, it has unity to a greater degree [than ensouled things] corresponding to the greater 30 degree of its real existence; but it is not the One itself. For soul is one, and unity is somehow an accident of soul, that is, soul and unity are two things, just as body and unity are. And something divided, like a choir, is further from the One, and continuous things are nearer to it, but soul shares its unity even more.

35 If someone were to claim that, because there would be no soul were it not one, soul and the One, therefore, should be viewed as identical, the reply is, first, that all other things are also what they are along with being one, and still the One is different from them. For body and the One are not identical; rather, body partakes of the One.

Next, one must reply that soul is many, even the unitary soul,[7] and 40 even if it does not consist of parts. For there are several faculties in it— calculative reasoning, desiring, perceiving[8]—which are held together by unity, as by a bond. So, soul bestows unity on other things, because it is one itself. But soul itself takes unity from elsewhere.[9]

§6.9.2. Is it the case, then, that for each of the things for which unity is one of their parts, their substantiality and unity are not identical, while, in general, for what is Being or Substance, Substantiality or Being and unity are identical?[10] The result would be that someone who has discovered Being would have discovered the One, that is, Substance 5 itself would be the One itself.[11] For example, if Substance is Intellect, then the One should be Intellect, too, given that it is primary being and

---

7. This is either the soul of the cosmos or the individual soul.

8. The word is ἀντιλαμβάνεσθαι ('perceiving') or, alternatively, 'apprehending'.

9. See *SVF* 2.366 (= Stob., *Ecl.* 2.107.14), 367 (= D.L., 7.129), 368 (= Origen, *Contra Celsum* 4.81 Vol. 1 p. 351, 7 Kö), whose doctrine of λόγος as the animating principle of the cosmos is perhaps Plotinus's target here. One of the types of λόγος is soul.

10. The proposed identity of τὸ ὄν ('real being'), οὐσία ('substantiality') is difficult to translate. Here, most clearly, οὐσία indicates the 'beingness' of a being, what explains its being, translated here as 'substantiality'. It may be thought that in the intelligible world, Beings and their 'substantiality' coincide, and so that is where the One is to be found.

11. I.e., the One is nothing but the unity of real being. See Ar., *Meta.* 10.2.1054a13. Alternatively, Plotinus could be referring to the intelligible Unity, distinguished from the One in the later treatise 6.6.

primary unity passing existence to other things to the extent it passes on unity to them.[12]

What else could anyone say the One is apart from them? For either it is identical with Being—'human being and one human being are identical'[13]—or unity[14] is a kind of number of each thing, just as when you say 'two things', so, too, unity applies to a single thing. If, then, Number is among Beings, it is clear that unity is, too. And we must investigate what it is.

If counting were an act of the soul passing through things in succession, then unity would not be among Beings.[15] But our argument above[16] concluded that if there were no unity, there would be nothing at all. We should, then, look to see whether, on the assumption that the unity and the being for each thing are identical, and unity in general and being in general are identical.

But if the being of each thing is a multiplicity, and unity cannot be a multiplicity, then being and unity in general will be different. The Form of Human Being combines animal, rational, and many parts by unity. Therefore, human being and unity are different, since the one is divisible and the other not. And indeed the whole of Being, because it contains all Beings in itself, is even more a many, and is different from unity, having unity by participation or partaking.

Being has life, too[17]— for it is certainly not a corpse—it is, therefore, a many. If Being is Intellect, then it, too, would have to be many, all the more so if it contained the Forms. For the Idea is not one; rather, it is a Number, both each Idea, and all of them together, and one in the way that the cosmos is one. Generally speaking, the One is primary, while Intellect, Forms, and Being are not primary. For each Form is a composite of many elements and is posterior to these.

The following considerations will also make clear that Intellect is not primary. Intellect necessarily consists in thinking; and the best intellect, that is, the one that does not look outside itself, necessarily thinks what is prior to itself.[18] For in reverting to itself, it reverts to its origin and if it is both thinking and object of thinking, it will be double, and

---

12. This is perhaps the position of Plotinus's classmate, Origen. See Proclus, *PT* 2.31.4–17. But it is also a position held by many so-called Middle Platonists. See, e.g., Alcinous, *Didask.* 10.22.18–23, Whittaker.
13. See Ar., *Meta.* 4.2.1003b25–27.
14. I.e., being one, oneness.
15. Cf. 6.6.16.32–46.
16. Cf. *supra* 1.3–14.
17. Cf. 5.9.10.10–15.
18. I.e., the One.

not simple nor will it be the One. But if it looks to something different from itself, it will be looking completely to what is better than and
40 prior to. But if it looks to itself and to what is better than it, then it is secondary in that way, too.

One must also take Intellect to be such that on the one hand it is present to the Good, that which is first, and looks to it, and on the other it is together with itself, and both thinks itself and thinks of itself as being all things. There is, therefore, no question of the One being
45 variegated. So, neither will the One be all things, for then it would not still be one; nor is the One Intellect, for in that case it would be all things because Intellect is all things.[19] Nor, finally, is the One Being. For Being is all things.

§6.9.3.[20] What, then, would the One be, what nature would it have?

In fact, it is no wonder it is not easy to say, when it is not easy to say what Being or Form is. Indeed, our cognition relies on Forms, and so the more the soul moves toward what is formless,[21] it glances off the object and is afraid it will have nothing,[22] since it is completely inca-
5 pable of comprehending the object on account of not being limited by, and, in a way, given an impression by, the variegation of the thing making the impression.[23] For this reason, in such a situation it gets weary, and takes pleasure in descending from all these things until it reaches sensible, solid[24] reality, which provides a kind of relief. This
10 resembles what happens when sight, wearied with small things, turns with pleasure to large things.

When the soul wants to see according to its own seeing, seeing merely by being self-absorbed,[25] and being one[26] the soul does not then think that it has what it seeks, on the grounds that it is then not different from what is being thought.[27]

---

19. Cf. 3.9.9.5–12; 5.3.5.26–28.
20. See Appendix II C; II F; II I.
21. I.e., the One. Cf. *infra* 39.43–44; 5.5.6.4; 6.7.17.40, 28.28, 32.9, 33.21.
22. I.e., grasp nothing. Cf. 6.7.17.36–43, 33.7–22.
23. Cf. 6.7.15.24, 33.10, 39.18.
24. See Pl., *Phdr.* 246C3.
25. συνεῖναι ('being self-absorbed') can also have the connotation of physical intimacy. The soul is the more intimate with itself the more it separates itself from the body. Cf. *infra* 7.23, 9.45, 10.10, 11.21. See Pl., *Phd.* 79D1, 4.
26. Cf. 5.5.4.1; 5.8.11.4; 6.8.17.14; 6.9.1.17.
27. When the soul thinks intelligibles, it identifies with them and so does not have what it seeks. Cf. *infra* l. 22; 6.7.35.4.

Still, that is what one actually has to do, if one is to philosophize about the One. So, since that which we seek is one, and we are searching for the principle of all things, the Good, that which is first, one should not, in falling to the extremes of all beings, move outside those Beings in the ambit of the primary Beings,[28] but in striving for the primary Beings, lift oneself up from sensible beings—which are the extreme— and free oneself from all vice inasmuch as one is aiming toward the Good. And one should ascend to the principle in oneself, and become one from being many,[29] if one is to be the spectator of a principle that is one.

So, becoming intellect,[30] one should entrust the soul to the intellect, and subordinate it to intellect, so that, being awakened, it may take in what the intellect sees. And it contemplates the One, not by adding any sense-perception, or by any of itself being taken up by the One; rather, it contemplates the purest thing by pure intellect, by the primary element in intellect.

So, whenever in preparing for contemplation of such a thing, one makes an image with size, shape, or mass relating to the nature of the One, then intellect is not the guide for this contemplation;[31] in that case, it is guided by the activity of sense-perception or by the belief following on sense-perception. But one should grasp the claims of intellect regarding what it is capable of. Intellect can see things that belong to it, or things prior to it. What is in intellect is pure,[32] but even purer and more simple are those things which come prior to it, or rather the thing prior to it.[33]

So the One is not Intellect, but prior to it. For Intellect is something, whereas the One is not something, because it is prior to every Being, since it is not Being. Indeed, Being has in a way the shape of Being, whereas the One is shapeless, without even an intellectual shape. For the nature of the One, being generative of all beings, is to be identified with none of them.[34] It is, then, not a 'this',[35] not quality or quantity, neither Intellect nor Soul. Neither is it in motion nor at a standstill, nor

---

28. I.e., the intelligibles. See Pl. [?], *Ep.* 2.312E1.
29. See Pl., *Rep.* 4.443E2; Pl. [?], *Epin.* 992B6.
30. Or 'Intellect'. Plotinus is here probably referring to our own intellects and their powers.
31. See Pl., *Lg.* 963A8.
32. See Anaxagoras, fr. 59 B 12 DK.
33. I.e., the Good. Cf. 3.8.9.1–3, 50–54.
34. Cf. 2.9.1.1; 5.5.13.20.
35. Ti ('something'), the first of the Aristotelian categories. Cf. 6.1.2–3.

in place or time,[36] but 'itself in itself, uniform';[37] rather, it is formless,[38] being prior to all Form, prior to Motion and Stability. All these things relate to Being, and make it into a many. But why, if it is not in motion, is it not stable? Because in the case of Being, one of these attributes or both of them necessarily apply; something stable is stable due to Stability, and is not identical to Stability, with the result that being stable is an accident, and the thing that is stable is not simple.[39]

Since this is so, to say that the One is a cause is not to predicate an accident of it, but of ourselves, because we grasp something of it, although it is in itself. If one is speaking precisely, one should not say either 'that thing' or 'being' of it, but of us.[40] It is us, in a way circling it from outside, who wish to interpret the affections we undergo, as we sometimes are closer to it and sometimes more distant to it, through the puzzles arising from it.

§6.9.11.[41] This is indeed what the injunction about the mysteries makes clear, not to communicate them to the uninitiated; since that[42] is not communicable, it forbids explaining the divine to anyone who has not had the good fortune to see for himself. So, since they were not two, but the seer was one with what is seen, as though it was not being seen by him, but was unified with him, if he remembers who he became when he mingled with the One, then he will have in himself an image of it.

He was a one, and contains no difference relative to himself, nor in any other respect. For nothing moved in him, neither spiritedness, nor appetite for anything else was present in him when he reverted to the One; but also not reason, nor intellection,[43] nor he himself, if one should say that. He was instead ravished or ecstatic in solitary quiet, in an unwobbling fixedness, unwavering from his own substantiality in any way, not rotating about himself, entirely stable, as if he were the stability itself. Nor had he any desire for beautiful things, having already surpassed beauty, having already outdone the chorus of

---

36. See Pl., *Parm.* 139B5, 138B5–6, 141A5.

37. See Pl., *Symp.* 211B1; *Phd.* 78D5–6.

38. Cf. 5.5.6.4–5; 6.7.17.26, 40.

39. Strictly speaking, there are no accidents in the intelligible world. However, the participation of one Form in another not identical with it entails the compositeness of the Form that participates.

40. Cf. 5.3.14.1–8.

41. See Appendix II E; II H.

42. I.e., the One.

43. See Pl., *Parm.* 142A3.

virtues.[44] It is like someone who enters the inner sanctum and leaves behind the statues of the gods in the temple.[45]

And these are the first things one sees on leaving the inner sanctum   20
after the vision within. The intimate contact within is not with a statue or an image, but with the One itself. The statue and the image are actually secondary visions, whereas the One itself is indeed not a vision, but another manner of seeing. It is ecstasy, simplification, and surrender of the self, an urging toward touch, a resting, concentration on   25
alignment, if one is to have a vision of what is in the sanctum. If indeed someone looks in a different way, then nothing is present to him.

These, then, are images; and yet they provide in a riddling manner a hint to wise interpreters of the way that god is seen. Once a wise priest has understood the riddle, he may, by coming to be in the intelligible world, make true the vision of the sanctum. And if he has not been   30
there, and thinks that the sanctum, that is, the source, and principle, is an invisible thing,[46] he will know that he sees the principle as principle,[47] things that are the same coming together. And, prior to the vision, he omits nothing divine that the soul can contain; the rest he will ask of the vision.

This rest comes to anyone who has gone beyond all things, namely,   35
what is prior to all things. For the nature of the soul will indeed not arrive at what entirely is non-being, but when it descends, it will come to evil, and thus into non-being, but not into what is entirely non-being.[48] Moving in the opposite direction, it will not come to something else, but to itself; thus in being in nothing else, it will not be in nothing, but   40
will be in itself,[49] that is, in itself alone, and not in that Being there.[50] For a self does not become Substantiality, but 'transcends Substantiality'[51] by this intimate contact.

If, then, one sees oneself having become this, then one has himself as a likeness of that;[52] and if one moves from oneself, as from the image

44. Cf. 4.7.10.44. See Pl., *Phdr.* 247D6.

45. Cf. 5.1.6.12–15.

46. See Pl., *Phdr.* 245C9.

47. Reading ὡς ἀρχὴ with ms Q. See Philolaus, fr. 44 A 29 DK; Empedocles, fr. 31 B 109 DK; Democritus, fr. 68 B 164 DK.

48. Cf. 2.4.14.21–24, 16.3.

49. Cf. 6.7.22.15–20.

50. I.e., among intelligibles.

51. See Pl., *Rep.* 6.509B9.

52. I.e., the One. Cf. *supra* ll. 4–8.

45　　to the archetype,[53] then he reaches 'journey's end'.[54] And when one drops out of the vision, then one wakens virtue in oneself again; and seeing oneself ordered by virtues one is again uplifted by virtue, in the direction of intellect, and wisdom; and through wisdom, toward oneself.[55] This is the way of life of gods, and divine, happy human beings, the release from everything here, a way of life that takes no pleasure in things here, the refuge of a solitary in the solitary.[56]

---

53. Cf. 6.8.18.27.
54. Cf. *supra* 8.43–44. See Pl., *Rep.* 7.532E3.
55. See Pl., *Phdr.* 248A1; *Tht.* 176A1–2.
56. Cf. 1.6.7.9; 3.1.10.10–12; 5.1.6.11–12; 6.7.34.7–8.

Appendix of Classical Sources

I. Pre-Socratics

(All selections from *Philosophy Before Socrates*, 2nd ed., edited and translated by Richard D. McKirahan, Hackett Publishing, 2010. The numbering is McKirahan's. For example, 10.33 (101) refers to his chapter 10, selection 33. The number in parentheses refers to the numbering of the fragments in the standard edition of the fragments of the Pre-Socratics, that of H. Diels and W. Kranz, *Die Fragmente der Vorsaktriker*, 6th ed., Berlin, 1951.)

A. Heraclitus [see 4.8.1]

10.33   (101) I searched myself.

10.41   (84b) It is weariness to labor at the same things and <always> to be beginning [or, "It is weariness to labor for the same <masters> and to be ruled"].

10.47   (50) Listening not to me but to the *Logos*, it is wise to agree that all things are one.

10.50   (54) An unapparent connection (*harmonia*) is stronger than an apparent one.

10.54   (13) Pigs rejoice in mud more than in pure water.

10.78   (84a) Changing [or, "by changing"], it is at rest.

10.80   (90) All things are an exchange for fire and fire for all things, as goods for gold and gold for goods [or, "as money for gold and gold for money"].

10.113 (45) You would not discover the limits of the soul although you traveled every road: so deep a *Logos* does it have.

B. Parmenides [see 3.8.8; 5.1.8]

11.3   (3) . . . For the same thing both can be thought of and can be. [Alternative translations: "For thinking and being are the same"; "The same thing is for thinking and for being."]

11.4   (4) But gaze upon things which although absent are securely
        present to the mind.
        For you will not cut off what-is from clinging to what-is,
        neither being scattered everywhere in every way in order
        nor being brought together.

11.5   (5) For me, it is indifferent where I am to begin from:
        for that is where I will arrive back again.

11.6   (6) It is right both to say and to think that it is what-is: for it is
        the case that it is,
        but nothing is not: these things I bid you to ponder.
        For this is the first route of investigation from which I hold you
        back,
        And then from that one on which mortals, knowing nothing,
        wander, two-headed: for helplessness in their
        breasts steers their wandering mind. They are borne along
        deaf and blind alike, dazed, hordes without judgment
        by whom it (namely, what-is) is thought both to be and not to
        be the same
        and not the same; but the path of all is backward-turning.

C. Anaxagoras [see 5.1.9]

13.1   (1) 1. All things were together, unlimited in both amount and
        smallness.
        2. For the small too was unlimited.
        3. And when [or, "since"] all things were together, nothing was
        manifest on account of smallness.
        4. For *aēr* and *aithēr* dominated all things, both being unlimited.
        5. For these are the greatest ingredients in the totality, both in
        amount and in magnitude.

13.12   (12) 1. The other things have a portion of everything, but Mind
        is unlimited and self-ruled and is mixed with no thing, but is
        alone and by itself.
        2. For if it were not by itself but were mixed with something
        else, it would have a share of all things, if it were mixed with
        anything.
        3. For in everything there is a portion of everything, as I have
        said before.

4. And the things mixed together with it would hinder it so that it would rule no thing in the same way as it does, being alone and by itself.

5. For it is the finest of all things and the purest, and it has all judgment about everything and the greatest strength.

6. And Mind rules all things that possess soul—both the larger and the smaller.

7. And Mind ruled the entire rotation, so that it rotated in the beginning.

8. And at first it began to rotate from a small region, but it is <now> rotating over a greater range, and it will rotate over a <still> greater one.

9. And Mind knew all the things that are being mixed together and those that are being separated off and those that are being separated apart.

10. And Mind set in order all things, whatever kinds of things were going to be—whatever were and are not now, and all that are now and whatever kinds of things will be—and also this rotation in which the things being separated off are now rotating—the stars and the sun and the moon, and the *aēr* and the *aithēr*.

11. This rotation caused them to separate off.

12. And the dense is being separated off from the rare and the hot from the cold and the bright from the dark and the dry from the wet.

13. But there are many portions of many things.

D. Empedocles [see 4.8.1; 5.1.9]

14.49 (11) Fools. For their thoughts are not far-reaching—
those who expect that there comes to be what previously was not,
or that anything perishes and is completely destroyed.

14.58 (17) I will tell a double story. For at one time they grew to be only one
out of many, but at another they grew apart to be many out of one.

II. Plato

(All selections from Plato, *Complete Works*, edited by John M. Cooper, Hackett Publishing, 1997.)

A. *Alcibiades* 129B1–131A1 (pp. 587–589)
[see 1.1.1, 5; 1.4.4; 4.7.1; 6.7.4, 5]

SOCRATES: Tell me, how can we find out what 'itself' is, in itself? Maybe this is the way to find out what we ourselves might be—maybe it's the only possible way.

ALCIBIADES: You're right.

SOCRATES: Hold on, by Zeus—who are you speaking with now? Anybody but me?

ALCIBIADES: No.

SOCRATES: And I'm speaking with you.

ALCIBIADES: Yes.

SOCRATES: Is Socrates doing the talking?

ALCIBIADES: He certainly is.

SOCRATES: And is Alcibiades doing the listening?

ALCIBIADES: Yes.

SOCRATES: And isn't Socrates talking with words?

ALCIBIADES: Of course.

SOCRATES: I suppose you'd say that talking is the same as using words?

ALCIBIADES: Certainly.

SOCRATES: But the thing being used and the person using it—they're different, aren't they?

ALCIBIADES: What do you mean?

SOCRATES: A shoemaker, for example, cuts with a knife and a scraper, I think, and with other tools.

ALCIBIADES: Yes, he does.

SOCRATES: So isn't the cutter who uses the tools different from the tools he's cutting with?

ALCIBIADES: Of course.

SOCRATES: And likewise isn't the lyre-player different from what he's playing with?

ALCIBIADES: Yes.

SOCRATES: This is what I was just asking—doesn't the user of a thing always seem to be different from what he's using?

ALCIBIADES: It seems so.

SOCRATES: Let's think about the shoemaker again. Does he cut with his tools only, or does he also cut with his hands?

ALCIBIADES: With his hands, too.

129B

129C

129D

SOCRATES: So he uses his hands, too.

ALCIBIADES: Yes.

SOCRATES: And doesn't he use his eyes, too, in shoemaking?

ALCIBIADES: Yes.

SOCRATES: Didn't we agree that the person who uses something is different from the thing that he uses?

ALCIBIADES: Yes.

SOCRATES: So the shoemaker and the lyre-player are different from the hands and eyes they use in their work.

129E

ALCIBIADES: So it seems.

SOCRATES: Doesn't a man use his whole body, too?

ALCIBIADES: Certainly.

SOCRATES: And we agreed that the user is different from the thing being used.

ALCIBIADES: Yes.

SOCRATES: So a man is different from his own body.

ALCIBIADES: So it seems.

SOCRATES: Then what *is* a man?

ALCIBIADES: I don't know what to say.

SOCRATES: Yes, you do—say that it's what uses the body.

ALCIBIADES: Yes.

130A

SOCRATES: What else uses it but the soul?

ALCIBIADES: Nothing else.

SOCRATES: And doesn't the soul rule the body?

ALCIBIADES: Yes.

SOCRATES: Now here's something I don't think anybody would disagree with.

ALCIBIADES: What?

SOCRATES: Man is one of three things.

ALCIBIADES: What things?

SOCRATES: The body, the soul, or the two of them together, the whole thing.

ALCIBIADES: Of course.

SOCRATES: But we agreed that man is that which rules the body.

130B

ALCIBIADES: Yes, we did agree to that.

SOCRATES: Does the body rule itself?

ALCIBIADES: It couldn't.

SOCRATES: Because we said it was ruled.

ALCIBIADES: Yes.

SOCRATES: So *this* can't be what we're looking for.

ALCIBIADES: Not likely.

SOCRATES: Well then, can the two of them together rule the body? Is this what man is?

ALCIBIADES: Yes, maybe that's it.

SOCRATES: No, that's the least likely of all. If one of them doesn't take part in ruling, then surely no combination of the two of them could rule.

ALCIBIADES: You're right.

130C SOCRATES: Since a man is neither his body, nor his body and soul together, what remains, I think, is either that he's nothing, or else, if he *is* something, he's nothing other than his soul.

ALCIBIADES: Quite so.

SOCRATES: Do you need any clearer proof that the soul is the man?

ALCIBIADES: No, by Zeus, I think you've given ample proof.

SOCRATES: Well, if we've proven it fairly well, although perhaps not rigorously, that will do for us. We'll have a rigorous proof when we find out what we skipped over, because it would have taken quite a lot of

130D study.

ALCIBIADES: What was that?

SOCRATES: What we mentioned just now, that we should first consider what 'itself' is, in itself. But in fact, we've been considering what an individual self is, instead of what 'itself' is. Perhaps that was enough for us, for surely nothing about us has more authority than the soul, wouldn't you agree?

ALCIBIADES: Certainly.

SOCRATES: So the right way of looking at it is that, when you and I talk to each other, one soul uses words to address another soul.

130E ALCIBIADES: Very true.

SOCRATES: That's just what we were saying a little while ago—that Socrates converses with Alcibiades not by saying words to his face, apparently, but by addressing his words to *Alcibiades*, in other words, to his soul.

ALCIBIADES: I see it now.

SOCRATES: So the command that we should know ourselves means that we should know our souls.

131A ALCIBIADES: So it seems.

B. *Phaedo* 64B4–69C2 (pp. 55–60)
[see 1.2.3, 5; 1.6.6, 7; 4.8.1, 2; 5.1.10]

Simmias laughed and said: By Zeus, Socrates, you made me laugh, though I was in no laughing mood just now. I think that the majority,

64B on hearing this, will think that it describes the philosophers very well, and our people in Thebes would thoroughly agree that philosophers are nearly dead and that the majority of men is well aware that they deserve to be.

And they would be telling the truth, Simmias, except for their being aware. They are not aware of the way true philosophers are nearly dead, nor of the way they deserve to be, nor of the sort of death they deserve. But never mind them, he said, let us talk among ourselves. Do we believe that there is such a thing as death?

Certainly, said Simmias.

Is it anything else than the separation of the soul from the body? Do we believe that death is this, namely, that the body comes to be separated by itself apart from the soul, and the soul comes to be separated by itself apart from the body? Is death anything else than that?

No, that is what it is, he said.

Consider then, my good sir, whether you share my opinion, for this will lead us to a better knowledge of what we are investigating. Do you think it is the part of a philosopher to be concerned with such so-called pleasures as those of food and drink?

By no means.

What about the pleasures of sex?

Not at all.

What of the other pleasures concerned with the service of the body? Do you think such a man prizes them greatly, the acquisition of distinguished clothes and shoes and the other bodily ornaments? Do you think he values these or despises them, except insofar as one cannot do without them?

I think the true philosopher despises them.

Do you not think, he said, that in general such a man's concern is not with the body but that, as far as he can, he turns away from the body towards the soul?

I do.

So in the first place, such things show clearly that the philosopher more than other men frees the soul from association with the body as much as possible?

Apparently.

A man who finds no pleasure in such things and has no part in them is thought by the majority not to deserve to live and to be close to death; the man, that is, who does not care for the pleasures of the body.

What you say is certainly true.

Then what about the actual acquiring of knowledge? Is the body an obstacle when one associates with it in the search for knowledge?

64C

64D

64E

65A

65B   I mean, for example, do men find any truth in sight or hearing, or are not even the poets forever telling us that we do not see or hear anything accurately, and surely if those two physical senses are not clear or precise, our other senses can hardly be accurate, as they are all inferior to these. Do you not think so?

I certainly do, he said.

When then, he asked, does the soul grasp the truth? For whenever it attempts to examine anything with the body, it is clearly deceived by it.

65C   True.

Is it not in reasoning if anywhere that any reality becomes clear to the soul?

Yes.

And indeed the soul reasons best when none of these senses troubles it, neither hearing nor sight, nor pain nor pleasure, but when it is most by itself, taking leave of the body and as far as possible having no contact or association with it in its search for reality.

That is so.

And it is then that the soul of the philosopher most disdains the body, flees from it and seeks to be by itself?

65D   It appears so.

What about the following, Simmias? Do we say that there is such a thing as the Just itself, or not?

We do say so, by Zeus.

And the Beautiful, and the Good?

Of course.

And have you ever seen any of these things with your eyes?

In no way, he said.

Or have you ever grasped them with any of your bodily senses? I am speaking of all things such as Bigness, Health, Strength, and, in a word, the reality of all other things, that which each of them essentially is. Is what is most true in them contemplated through the body, or is this the position: whoever of us prepares himself best and most

65E   accurately to grasp that thing itself which he is investigating will come closest to the knowledge of it?

Obviously.

Then he will do this most perfectly who approaches the object with thought alone, without associating any sight with his thought, or drag-

66A   ging in any sense perception with his reasoning, but who, using pure thought alone, tries to track down each reality pure and by itself, freeing himself as far as possible from eyes and ears and, in a word, from the whole body, because the body confuses the soul and does not allow it to acquire truth and wisdom whenever it is associated with it. Will not that man reach reality, Simmias, if anyone does?

What you say, said Simmias, is indeed true.

All these things will necessarily make the true philosophers believe and say to each other something like this: There is likely to be something such as a path to guide us out of our confusion, because as long as we have a body and our soul is fused with such an evil we shall never adequately attain what we desire, which we affirm to be the truth. The body keeps us busy in a thousand ways because of its need for nurture. Moreover, if certain diseases befall it, they impede our search for the truth. It fills us with wants, desires, fears, all sorts of illusions and much nonsense, so that, as it is said, in truth and in fact no thought of any kind ever comes to us from the body. Only the body and its desires cause war, civil discord and battles, for all wars are due to the desire to acquire wealth, and it is the body and the care of it, to which we are enslaved, which compel us to acquire wealth, and all this makes us too busy to practice philosophy. Worst of all, if we do get some respite from it and turn to some investigation, everywhere in our investigations the body is present and makes for confusion and fear, so that it prevents us from seeing the truth.

66B

66C

66D

It really has been shown to us that, if we are ever to have pure knowledge, we must escape from the body and observe things in themselves with the soul by itself. It seems likely that we shall, only then, when we are dead, attain that which we desire and of which we claim to be lovers, namely, wisdom, as our argument shows, not while we live; for if it is impossible to attain any pure knowledge with the body, then one of two things is true: either we can never attain knowledge or we can do so after death. Then and not before, the soul is by itself apart from the body. While we live, we shall be closest to knowledge if we refrain as much as possible from association with the body and do not join with it more than we must, if we are not infected with its nature but purify ourselves from it until the god himself frees us. In this way we shall escape the contamination of the body's folly; we shall be likely to be in the company of people of the same kind, and by our own efforts we shall know all that is pure, which is presumably the truth, for it is not permitted to the impure to attain the pure.

66E

67A

67B

Such are the things, Simmias, that all those who love learning in the proper manner must say to one another and believe. Or do you not think so?

I certainly do, Socrates.

And if this is true, my friend, said Socrates, there is good hope that on arriving where I am going, if anywhere, I shall acquire what has been our chief preoccupation in our past life, so that the journey that is now ordered for me is full of good hope, as it is also for any other man who believes that his mind has been prepared and, as it were, purified.

It certainly is, said Simmias.

And does purification not turn out to be what we mentioned in our argument some time ago, namely, to separate the soul as far as possible from the body and accustom it to gather itself and collect itself out of every part of the body and to dwell by itself as far as it can both now and in the future, freed, as it were, from the bonds of the body?

Certainly, he said.

And that freedom and separation of the soul from the body is called death?

That is altogether so.

It is only those who practice philosophy in the right way, we say, who always most want to free the soul; and this release and separation of the soul from the body is the preoccupation of the philosophers?

So it appears.

Therefore, as I said at the beginning, it would be ridiculous for a man to train himself in life to live in a state as close to death as possible, and then to resent it when it comes?

Ridiculous, of course.

In fact, Simmias, he said, those who practice philosophy in the right way are in training for dying and they fear death least of all men. Consider it from this point of view: if they are altogether estranged from the body and desire to have their soul by itself, would it not be quite absurd for them to be afraid and resentful when this happens? If they did not gladly set out for a place, where, on arrival, they may hope to attain that for which they had yearned during their lifetime, that is, wisdom, and where they would be rid of the presence of that from which they are estranged?

Many men, at the death of their lovers, wives, or sons, were willing to go to the underworld, driven by the hope of seeing there those for whose company they longed, and being with them. Will then a true lover of wisdom, who has a similar hope and knows that he will never find it to any extent except in Hades, be resentful of dying and not gladly undertake the journey thither? One must surely think so, my friend, if he is a true philosopher, for he is firmly convinced that he will not find pure knowledge anywhere except there. And if this is so, then, as I said just now, would it not be highly unreasonable for such a man to fear death?

It certainly would, by Zeus, he said.

Then you have sufficient indication, he said, that any man whom you see resenting death was not a lover of wisdom but a lover of the body, and also a lover of wealth or of honors, either or both. 68C

It is certainly as you say.

And, Simmias, he said, does not what is called courage belong especially to men of this disposition?

Most certainly.

And the quality of moderation which even the majority call by that name, that is, not to get swept off one's feet by one's passions, but to treat them with disdain and orderliness, is this not suited only to those 68D who do most of all despise the body and live the life of philosophy?

Necessarily so, he said.

If you are willing to reflect on the courage and moderation of other people, you will find them strange.

In what way, Socrates?

You know that they all consider death a great evil?

Definitely, he said.

And the brave among them face death, when they do, for fear of greater evils?

That is so.

Therefore, it is fear and terror that make all men brave, except the philosophers. Yet it is illogical to be brave through fear and cowardice.

It certainly is. 68E

What of the moderate among them? Is their experience not similar? Is it licentiousness of a kind that makes them moderate? We say this is impossible, yet their experience of this simple-minded moderation turns out to be similar: they fear to be deprived of other pleasures which they desire, so they keep away from some pleasures because they are overcome by others. Now to be mastered by pleasure is what they call licentiousness, but what happens to them is that they master 69A certain pleasures because they are mastered by others. This is like what we mentioned just now, that in some way it is a kind of licentiousness that has made them moderate.

That seems likely.

My good Simmias, I fear this is not the right exchange to attain virtue, to exchange pleasures for pleasures, pains for pains and fears for fears, the greater for the less like coins, but that the only valid currency 69B for which all these things should be exchanged is wisdom. With this we have real courage and moderation and justice and, in a word, true virtue, with wisdom, whether pleasures and fears and all such things be present or absent. When these are exchanged for one another in separation from wisdom, such virtue is only an illusory appearance of virtue; it is in fact fit for slaves, without soundness or truth, whereas, in truth, moderation and courage and justice are a purging away of all such things, and wisdom itself is a kind of cleansing or purification. It is likely that those who established the mystic rites for us were not inferior persons but were speaking in riddles long ago when they said that whoever arrives in the underworld uninitiated and unsanctified will wallow in the mire, whereas he who arrives there purified and initiated will dwell with the gods.

69C

C. *Symposium* 210A1–212B1 (pp. 492–494)
[see 1.6.1, 6, 7; 6.9.3]

210A

"Even you, Socrates, could probably come to be initiated into these rites of love. But as for the purpose of these rites when they are done correctly—that is the final and highest mystery, and I don't know if you are capable of it. I myself will tell you," she said, "and I won't stint any effort. And you must try to follow if you can.

"A lover who goes about this matter correctly must begin in his youth to devote himself to beautiful bodies. First, if the leader leads aright, he should love one body and beget beautiful ideas there; then he should realize that the beauty of any one body is brother to the beauty of any other and that if he is to pursue beauty of form he'd be very foolish not to think that the beauty of all bodies is one and the same. When he grasps this, he must become a lover of all beautiful bodies, and he must think that this wild gaping after just one body is a small thing and despise it.

210B

"After this he must think that the beauty of people's souls is more valuable than the beauty of their bodies, so that if someone is decent in his soul, even though he is scarcely blooming in his body, our lover must be content to love and care for him and to seek to give birth to such ideas as will make young men better. The result is that our lover will be forced to gaze at the beauty of activities and laws and to see that all this is akin to itself, with the result that he will think that the beauty of bodies is a thing of no importance. After customs he must move on to various kinds of knowledge. The result is that he will see the beauty of knowledge and be looking mainly not at beauty in a single example—as a servant would who favored the beauty of a little boy or a man or a single custom (being a slave, of course, he's low and

210C

210D

small-minded)—but the lover is turned to the great sea of beauty, and, gazing upon this, he gives birth to many gloriously beautiful ideas and theories, in unstinting love of wisdom, until, having grown and been strengthened there, he catches sight of such knowledge, and it is the 210E knowledge of such beauty. . . .

"Try to pay attention to me," she said, "as best you can. You see, the man who has been thus far guided in matters of Love, who has beheld beautiful things in the right order and correctly, is coming now to the goal of Loving: all of a sudden he will catch sight of something wonderfully beautiful in its nature; that, Socrates, is the reason for all his earlier labors:

"First, it always *is* and neither comes to be nor passes away, neither 211A waxes nor wanes. Second, it is not beautiful this way and ugly that way, nor beautiful at one time and ugly at another, nor beautiful in relation to one thing and ugly in relation to another; nor is it beautiful here but ugly there, as it would be if it were beautiful for some people and ugly for others. Nor will the beautiful appear to him in the guise of a face or hands or anything else that belongs to the body. It will not appear to him as one idea or one kind of knowledge. It is not anywhere in another thing, as in an animal, or in earth, or in heaven, or in anything 211B else, but itself by itself with itself, it is always one in form; and all the other beautiful things share in that, in such a way that when those others come to be or pass away, this does not become the least bit smaller or greater nor suffer any change. So when someone rises by these stages, through loving boys correctly, and begins to see this beauty, he has almost grasped his goal. This is what it is to go aright, or be led 211C by another, into the mystery of Love: one goes always upwards for the sake of this Beauty, starting out from beautiful things and using them like rising stairs: from one body to two and from two to all beautiful bodies, then from beautiful bodies to beautiful customs, and from customs to learning beautiful things, and from these lessons he arrives in the end at this lesson, which is learning of this very Beauty, so that in the end he comes to know just what it is to be beautiful. 211D

"And there in life, Socrates, my friend," said the woman from Mantinea, "there if anywhere should a person live his life, beholding that Beauty. If you once see that, it won't occur to you to measure beauty by gold or clothing or beautiful boys and youths—who, if you see them now, strike you out of your senses, and make you, you and many others, eager to be with the boys you love and look at them forever, if there were any way to do that, forgetting food and drink, everything but looking at them and being with them. But how would it be, in our 211E view," she said, "if someone got to see the Beautiful itself, absolute, pure, unmixed, not polluted by human flesh or colors or any other great nonsense of mortality, but if he could see the divine Beauty itself in its one form? Do you think it would be a poor life for a human being to look there and to behold it by that which he ought, and to be with it? Or haven't you remembered," she said, "that in that life alone, when he looks at Beauty in the only way that Beauty can be seen—only then will it become possible for him to give birth not to images of virtue (because he's in touch with no images), but to true virtue (because he is in touch with the true Beauty). The love of the gods belongs to anyone who has given birth to true virtue and nourished it, and if any human being could become immortal, it would be he."

D. *Phaedrus* 246B5–250C7 (pp. 524–528)
[see 1.2.6; 1.6.4, 5, 7; 3.8.5, 11; 4.8.1, 2, 4]

"And now I should try to tell you why living things are said to include both mortal and immortal beings. All soul looks after all that lacks a soul, and patrols all of heaven, taking different shapes at different times. So long as its wings are in perfect condition it flies high, and the entire universe is its dominion; but a soul that sheds its wings wanders until it lights on something solid, where it settles and takes on an earthly body, which then, owing to the power of this soul, seems to move itself. The whole combination of soul and body is called a living thing, or animal, and has the designation 'mortal' as well. Such a combination cannot be immortal, not on any reasonable account. In fact it is pure fiction, based neither on observation nor on adequate reasoning, that a god is an immortal living thing which has a body and a soul, and that these are bound together by nature for all time—but of course we must let this be as it may please the gods, and speak accordingly.

"Let us turn to what causes the shedding of the wings, what makes them fall away from a soul. It is something of this sort: By their nature wings have the power to lift up heavy things and raise them aloft where the gods all dwell, and so, more than anything that pertains to the body, they are akin to the divine, which has beauty, wisdom, goodness, and everything of that sort. These nourish the soul's wings, which grow best in their presence; but foulness and ugliness make the wings shrink and disappear.

"Now Zeus, the great commander in heaven, drives his winged chariot first in the procession, looking after everything and putting all things in order. Following him is an army of gods and spirits arranged in eleven sections. Hestia is the only one who remains at the home of the gods; all the rest of the twelve are lined up in formation, each god in command of the unit to which he is assigned. Inside heaven are many wonderful places from which to look and many aisles which the blessed gods take up and back, each seeing to his own work, while anyone who is able and wishes to do so follows along, since jealousy has no place in the gods' chorus. When they go to feast at the banquet they have a steep climb to the high tier at the rim of heaven; on this slope the gods' chariots move easily, since they are balanced and well under control, but the other chariots barely make it. The heaviness of the bad horse drags its charioteer toward the earth and weighs him down if he has failed to train it well, and this causes the most extreme toil and struggle that a soul will face. But when the souls we call immortals reach the top, they move outward and take their stand on the high ridge of heaven, where its circular motion carries them around as they stand while they gaze upon what is outside heaven.

247B

247C

"The place beyond heaven—none of our earthly poets has ever sung or ever will sing its praises enough! Still, this is the way it is—risky as it may be, you see, I must attempt to speak the truth, especially since the truth is my subject. What is in this place is without color and without shape and without solidity, a being that really is what it is, the subject of all true knowledge, visible only to intelligence, the soul's steersman. Now a god's mind is nourished by intelligence and pure knowledge, as is the mind of any soul that is concerned to take in what is appropriate to it, and so it is delighted at last to be seeing what is real and watching what is true, feeding on all this and feeling wonderful, until the circular motion brings it around to where it started. On the way around it has a view of Justice as it is; it has a view of Self-control; it has a view of Knowledge—not the knowledge that is close to change, that becomes different as it knows the different things which we consider real down here. No, it is the knowledge of what really is what it is. And when the soul has seen all the things that are as they are and feasted on them, it sinks back inside heaven and goes home. On its arrival, the charioteer stables the horses by the manger, throws in ambrosia, and gives them nectar to drink besides.

247D

247E

248A

"Now that is the life of the gods. As for the other souls, one that follows a god most closely, making itself most like that god, raises the head of its charioteer up to the place outside and is carried around in the circular motion with the others. Although distracted by the horses, this soul does have a view of Reality, just barely. Another soul rises at one time and falls at another, and because its horses pull it violently in different directions, it sees some real things and misses others. The remaining souls are all eagerly straining to keep up, but are unable to rise; they are carried around below the surface, trampling and striking

248B one another as each tries to get ahead of the others. The result is terribly noisy, very sweaty, and disorderly. Many souls are crippled by the incompetence of the drivers, and many wings break much of their plumage. After so much trouble, they all leave without having seen reality, uninitiated, and when they have gone they will depend on what they think is nourishment—their own opinions.

248C "The reason there is so much eagerness to see the plain where truth stands is that this pasture has the grass that is the right food for the best part of the soul, and it is the nature of the wings that lift up the soul to be nourished by it. Besides, the law of Destiny is this: If any soul becomes a companion to a god and catches sight of any true thing, it will be unharmed until the next circuit; and if it is able to do this every time, it will always be safe. If, on the other hand, it does not see anything true because it could not keep up, and by some accident takes on a burden of forgetfulness and wrongdoing, then it is weighed down,

248D sheds its wings and falls to earth. At that point, according to the law, the soul is not born into a wild animal in its first incarnation; but a soul that has seen the most will be planted in the seed of a man who will become a lover of wisdom or of beauty, or who will be cultivated in the arts and prone to erotic love. The second sort of soul will be put into someone who will be a lawful king or warlike commander; the third, a statesman, a manager of a household, or a financier; the fourth will be

248E a trainer who loves exercise or a doctor who cures the body; the fifth will lead the life of a prophet or priest of the mysteries. To the sixth the life of a poet or some other representational artist is properly assigned; to the seventh the life of a manual laborer or farmer; to the eighth the career of a sophist or demagogue, and to the ninth a tyrant.

"Of all these, any who have led their lives with justice will change to a better fate, and any who have led theirs with injustice, to a worse one. In fact, no soul returns to the place from which it came for ten

249A thousand years, since its wings will not grow before then, except for the soul of a man who practices philosophy without guile or who loves boys philosophically. If, after the third cycle of one thousand years, the last-mentioned souls have chosen such a life three times in a row, they grow their wings back, and they depart in the three-thousandth year. As for the rest, once their first life is over, they come to judgment; and, once judged, some are condemned to go to places of punishment beneath the earth and pay the full penalty for their injustice, while the others are lifted up by justice to a place in heaven where they live in the

249B manner the life they led in human form has earned them. In the thousandth year both groups arrive at a choice and allotment of second lives, and each soul chooses the life it wants. From there, a human soul can enter a wild animal, and a soul that was once human can move from an animal to a human being again. But a soul that never saw the truth cannot take a human shape, since a human being must understand speech in terms of general forms, proceeding to bring many perceptions together into a reasoned unity. That process is the recollection of the things our soul saw when it was traveling with god, when it disregarded the things we now call real and lifted up its head to what is truly real instead.

249C

"For just this reason it is fair that only a philosopher's mind grows wings, since its memory always keeps it as close as possible to those realities by being close to which the gods are divine. A man who uses reminders of these things correctly is always at the highest, most perfect level of initiation, and he is the only one who is perfect as perfect can be. He stands outside human concerns and draws close to the divine; ordinary people think he is disturbed and rebuke him for this, unaware that he is possessed by god. Now this takes me to the whole point of my discussion of the fourth kind of madness—that which someone shows when he sees the beauty we have down here and is reminded of true beauty; then he takes wing and flutters in his eagerness to rise up, but is unable to do so; and he gazes aloft, like a bird, paying no attention to what is down below—and that is what brings on him the charge that he has gone mad. This is the best and noblest of all the forms that possession by god can take for anyone who has it or is connected to it, and when someone who loves beautiful boys is touched by this madness he is called a lover. As I said, nature requires that the soul of every human being has seen reality; otherwise, no soul could have entered this sort of living thing. But not every soul is easily reminded of the reality there by what it finds here—not souls that got only a brief glance at the reality there, not souls who had such bad luck when they fell down here that they were twisted by bad company into lives of injustice so that they forgot the sacred objects they had seen before. Only a few remain whose memory is good enough; and they are startled when they see an image of what they saw up there. Then they are beside themselves, and their experience is beyond their comprehension because they cannot fully grasp what it is that they are seeing.

249D

249E

250A

"Justice and self-control do not shine out through their images down here, and neither do the other objects of the soul's admiration; the senses are so murky that only a few people are able to make out, with difficulty, the original of the likenesses they encounter here. But beauty was radiant to see at that time when the souls, along with the

250B

250C glorious chorus (we were with Zeus, while others followed other gods), saw that blessed and spectacular vision and were ushered into the mystery that we may rightly call the most blessed of all. And we who celebrated it were wholly perfect and free of all the troubles that awaited us in time to come, and we gazed in rapture at sacred revealed objects that were perfect, and simple, and unshakeable and blissful. That was the ultimate vision, and we saw it in pure light because we were pure ourselves, not buried in this thing we are carrying around now, which we call a body, locked in it like an oyster in its shell.

E. *Republic* 508B8–509C5 (pp. 1129–1130) [see 1.2.4; 1.6.8, 9; 3.8.9, 11; 5.1.8; 5.3.13, 16, 17; 6.7.15, 17; 6.8.15; 6.9.11]

The sun is not sight, but isn't it the cause of sight itself and seen by it? That's right.

Let's say, then, that this is what I called the offspring of the good, which the good begot as its analogue. What the good itself is in the intelligible realm, in relation to understanding and intelligible things,

508C the sun is in the visible realm, in relation to sight and visible things.

How? Explain a bit more.

You know that, when we turn our eyes to things whose colors are no longer illuminated by the light of day but by night lights, the eyes are dimmed and seem nearly blind, as if clear vision were no longer in them.

Of course.

Yet whenever one turns them on things illuminated by the sun, they

508D see clearly, and vision appears in those very same eyes?

Indeed.

Well, understand the soul in the same way: When it focuses on something illuminated by truth and what is, it understands, knows, and apparently possesses understanding, but when it focuses on what is mixed with obscurity, on what comes to be and passes away, it opines and is dimmed, changes its opinions this way and that, and seems bereft of understanding.

It does seem that way.

So that what gives truth to the things known and the power to know

508E to the knower is the form of the good. And though it is the cause of knowledge and truth, it is also an object of knowledge. Both knowledge and truth are beautiful things, but the good is other and more beautiful than they. In the visible realm, light and sight are rightly considered sunlike, but it is wrong to think that they are the sun, so here it is right to think of knowledge and truth as goodlike but wrong to think

509A that either of them is the good—for the good is yet more prized.

This is an inconceivably beautiful thing you're talking about, if it provides both knowledge and truth and is superior to them in beauty. You surely don't think that a thing like that could be pleasure.

Hush! Let's examine its image in more detail as follows.

How? 509B

You'll be willing to say, I think, that the sun not only provides visible things with the power to be seen but also with coming to be, growth, and nourishment, although it is not itself coming to be.

How could it be?

Therefore, you should also say that not only do the objects of knowledge owe their being known to the good, but their being is also due to it, although the good is not being, but superior to it in rank and power. 509C

And Glaucon comically said: By Apollo, what a daemonic superiority!

It's your own fault; you forced me to tell you my opinion about it.

And I don't want you to stop either. So continue to explain its similarity to the sun, if you've omitted anything.

I'm certainly omitting a lot.

F. *Parmenides* 137B1–142A8 (pp. 371–376) [see 5.1.8; 6.9.3]

"Well then, at what point shall we start? What shall we hypothesize 137B first? I know: since we have in fact decided to play this strenuous game, is it all right with you if I begin with myself and my own hypothesis? Shall I hypothesize about the one itself and consider what the consequences must be, if it is one or if it is not one?"

"By all means," said Zeno.

"Then who will answer my questions?" he asked. "The youngest, surely? For he would give the least trouble and would be the most likely to say what he thinks. At the same time his answer would allow me a breathing space."

"I'm ready to play this role for you, Parmenides," Aristotle said. "Because you mean me when you say the youngest. Ask away—you 137C can count on me to answer."

"Very good," he said. "If it is one, the one would not be many, would it?"—"No, how could it?"—"Then there cannot be a part of it nor can it be a whole."—"Why?"—"A part is surely part of a whole."—"Yes."— "But what is the whole? Wouldn't that from which no part is missing be a whole?"—"Certainly."—"In both cases, then, the one would be composed of parts, both if it is a whole and if it has parts."—"Necessarily."—"So in both cases the one would thus be many rather than one."— 137D "True."—"Yet it must be not many but one."—"It must."—"Therefore, if the one is to be one, it will neither be a whole nor have parts."—"No, it won't."

"Well, then, if it doesn't have a part, it could have neither a beginning nor an end nor a middle; for those would in fact be parts of it."—"That's right."—"Furthermore, end and beginning are limits of each thing."—"Doubtless."—"So the one is unlimited if it has neither beginning nor end."—"Unlimited."—"So it is also without shape; for it partakes of neither round nor straight."—"How so?"—"Round is surely that whose extremities are equidistant in every direction from the middle."—"Yes."—"Furthermore, straight is that whose middle stands in the way of the two extremities."—"Just so."—"So the one would have parts and be many if it partook of either a straight or a curved shape."—"Of course."—"Therefore it is neither straight nor curved, since in fact it doesn't have parts."—"That's right."

137E

138A

"Furthermore, being like that, it would be nowhere, because it could be neither in another nor in itself."—"How is that?"—"If it were in another, it would surely be contained all around by the thing it was in and would touch it in many places with many parts; but since it is one and without parts and does not partake of circularity, it cannot possibly touch in many places all around."—"It can't."—"Yet, on the other hand, if it were in itself, its container would be none other than itself, if in fact it were in itself; for a thing can't be in something that doesn't contain it."—"No, it can't."—"So the container itself would be one thing, and the thing contained something else, since the same thing will not, as a whole at any rate, undergo and do both at once. And in that case the one would be no longer one but two."—"Yes, you're quite right."—"Therefore, the one is not anywhere, if it is neither in itself nor in another."—"It isn't."

138B

"Then consider whether, since it is as we have said, it can be at rest or in motion."—"Yes, why not?"—"Because if it moves, it would either move spatially or be altered, since these are the only motions."—"Yes."—"But the one surely can't be altered from itself and still be one."—"It can't."—"Then it doesn't move by alteration at least."—"Apparently not."—"But by moving spatially?"—"Perhaps."—"And if the one moved spatially, it surely would either spin in a circle in the same location or change from one place to another."—"Necessarily."—"Well then, if it spins in a circle, it must be poised on its middle and have other parts of itself that move round the middle. But how will a thing that has nothing to do with middle or parts manage to be moved in a circle round its middle?"—"Not at all."—"But by changing places does it come to be here at one time, there at another, and move in this way?"—"If in fact it moves at all."—"Wasn't it shown that it cannot be anywhere in anything?"—"Yes."—"Then is it not even more impossible

138C

138D

for it to *come* to be?"—"I don't see why."—"If something comes to be in something, isn't it necessary that it not yet be in that thing—since it is still coming to be in it—and that it no longer be entirely outside it, if in fact it is already coming to be in it?"—"Necessarily."—"So if anything is to undergo this, only that which has parts could do so, because some of it would already be in that thing, while some, at the same time, would be outside. But a thing that doesn't have parts will not by any means be able to be, at the same time, neither wholly inside nor wholly outside something."—"True."—"But isn't it much more impossible still for a thing that has no parts and is not a whole to come to be in something somewhere, if it does so neither part by part nor as a whole?"—"Apparently."—"Therefore it doesn't change places by going somewhere and coming to be in something, nor does it move by spinning in the same location or by being altered."—"It seems not."—"The one, therefore, is unmoved by every sort of motion."—"Unmoved."

138E

139A

"Yet, on the other hand, we also say that it cannot be in anything."—"Yes, we do."—"Then it is also never in the *same* thing."—"Why?"—"Because it would then be *in* that—in that same thing it is in."—"Of course."—"But it was impossible for it to be either in itself or in another."—"Yes, you're quite right."—"So the one is never in the same thing."—"It seems not."—"But what is never in the same thing neither enjoys repose nor is at rest."—"No, it cannot."—"Therefore the one, as it seems, is neither at rest nor in motion."—"It certainly does appear not."

139B

"Furthermore, it won't be the same as another thing or itself; nor, again, could it be different from itself or another thing."—"Why is that?"—"If it were different from itself, it would surely be different from one, and would not be one."—"True."—"On the other hand, if it were the same as another, it would be that thing, and not itself. So in this way, too, it would not be just what it is—one—but would be different from one."—"Yes, you're quite right."—"Therefore, it won't be the same as another or different from itself."—"No, it won't."

139C

"And it won't be different from another, as long as it is one; for it is not proper to one to be different from something, but proper to different-from-another alone, and to nothing else."—"That's right."—"Therefore it won't be different by being one. Or do you think it will?"—"No indeed."—"Yet if it isn't different by being one, it will not be so by itself; and if it isn't so by itself, it will not itself be so. And if it is itself in no way different, it will be different from nothing."—"That's right."

"Nor will it be the same as itself."—"Why not?"—"The nature of the one is not, of course, also that of the same."—"Why?"—"Because it is

139D

not the case that, whenever a thing comes to be the same as something, it comes to be one."—"But why?"—"If it comes to be the same as the many, it must come to be many, not one."—"True."—"But if the one and the same in no way differ, whenever something came to be the same, it would always come to be one; and whenever it came to

139E   be one, it would always come to be the same."—"Certainly."—"Therefore, if the one is to be the same as itself, it won't be one with itself; and thus it will be one and not one. But this surely is impossible. Therefore the one can't be either different from another or the same as itself."—"It can't."—"Thus the one could neither be different from nor the same as itself or another."—"Yes, you're quite right."

"Furthermore, it will be neither like nor unlike anything, either itself or another."—"Why?"—"Because whatever has a property the same is surely like."—"Yes."—"But it was shown that the same is separate in its

140A   nature from the one."—"Yes, it was."—"But if the one has any property apart from being one, it would be more than one; and that is impossible."—"Yes."—"Therefore, the one can in no way have a property the same as another or itself."—"Apparently not."—"So it cannot be like another or itself either."—"It seems not."

"Nor does the one have the property of being different; for in this way too it would be more than one."—"Yes, it would be more."—"Surely that which has a property different from itself or another would be

140B   unlike itself or another, if in fact what has a property the same is like."—"That's right."—"But the one, as it seems, since it in no way has a property different, is in no way unlike itself or another thing."—"Yes, you're quite right."—"Therefore the one could be neither like nor unlike another or itself."—"Apparently not."

"Furthermore, being like that, it will be neither equal nor unequal to itself or another."—"How?"—"If it is equal, it will be of the same measures as that to which it is equal."—"Yes."—"But surely if it is greater or

140C   less, it will, in the case of things with which it is commensurate, have more measures than those that are less, and fewer than those that are greater."—"Yes."—"And in the case of things with which it is not commensurate, it will be of smaller measures in the one case, and of larger measures in the other."—"No doubt."—"Well, if a thing doesn't partake of the same, it can't be of the same measures or of the same anything else at all, can it?"—"It can't."—"So it couldn't be equal to itself or another, if it is not of the same measures."—"It certainly appears not."—"Yet

140D   if it is, on the other hand, of more measures or fewer, it would have as many parts as measures; and thus, again, it will be no longer one, but just as many as are its measures."—"That's right."—"And if it were of one measure, it would prove to be equal to its measure; but it was shown that it couldn't be equal to anything."—"Yes, it was."—"Therefore, since it doesn't partake of one measure or many or few, and since it doesn't partake of the same at all, it will, as it seems, never be equal to itself or another; nor again will it be greater or less than itself or another."—"That's absolutely so."

140E

"What about this? Do you think that the one can be older or younger than, or the same age as, anything?"—"Yes, why not?"—"Because if it is the same age as itself or another, it will surely partake of likeness and of equality of time, of which—likeness and equality—we said the one has no share."—"Yes, we did say that."—"And we also said that it does not partake of unlikeness and inequality."—"Of course."—"Then, being like that, how will it be able to be older or younger than, or the same age as, anything?"—"In no way."—"Therefore, the one could not be younger or older than, or the same age as, itself or another."—"Apparently not."

141A

"So if it is like that, the one could not even be in time at all, could it? Or isn't it necessary, if something is in time, that it always come to be older than itself?"—"Necessarily."—"Isn't the older always older than a younger?"—"To be sure."—"Therefore, that which comes to be older than itself comes to be, at the same time, younger than itself, if in fact it is to have something it comes to be older than."—"What do you mean?"—"I mean this: there is no need for a thing to come to be different from a thing that is already different; it must, rather, already be different from what is already different, have come to be different from what has come to be different, and be going to be different from what is going to be different; but it must not have come to be, be going to be, or be different from what comes to be different: it must come to be different, and nothing else."—"Yes, that's necessary."—"But surely older is a difference from younger and from nothing else."—"Yes, it is."—"So that which comes to be older than itself must also, at the same time, come to be younger than itself."—"So it seems."—"But it must also not come to be for more or less time than itself; it must come to be and be and have come to be and be going to be for a time equal to itself."—"Yes, that too is necessary."—"Therefore it is necessary, as it seems, that each thing that is in time and partakes of time be the same age as itself and, at the same time, come to be both older and younger than itself."—"It looks that way."—"But the one surely had no share of any of that."—"No, it didn't."—"Therefore, it has no share of time, nor is it *in* any time."—"It certainly isn't, as the argument proves."

141B

141C

141D

"Now, don't you think that 'was' and 'has come to be' and 'was coming to be' signify partaking of time past?"—"By all means."—"And again that 'will be' and 'will come to be' and 'will be coming to be' signify partaking of time hereafter?"—"Yes."—"And that 'is' and 'comes to be' signify partaking of time now present?"—"Of course."—"Therefore, if the one partakes of no time at all, it is not the case that it has at one time come to be, was coming to be, or was; or has now come to be, comes to be, or is; or will hereafter come to be, will be coming to be, or will be."—"Very true."—"Could something partake of being except in one of those ways?"—"It couldn't."—"Therefore the one in no way partakes of being."—"It seems not."—"Therefore the one in no way is."—"Apparently not."—"Therefore neither *is* it in such a way as to be one, because it would then, by being and partaking of being, be. But, as it seems, the one neither is one nor is, if we are obliged to trust this argument."—"It looks that way."

"If something is not, could anything belong *to* this thing that is not, or be *of* it?"—"How could it?"—"Therefore, no name belongs to it, nor is there an account or any knowledge or perception or opinion of it."—"Apparently not."—"Therefore it is not named or spoken of, nor is it the object of opinion or knowledge, nor does anything that is perceive it."—"It seems not."—"Is it possible that these things are so for the one?"—"I certainly don't think so."

G. *Theaetetus* 176C3–177A9 (pp. 195–196) [see 1.2.1, 3; 1.6.5]

[SOCRATES: . . .] Let us try to put the truth in this way. In God there is no sort of wrong whatsoever; he is supremely just, and the thing most like him is the man who has become as just as it lies in human nature to be. And it is here that we see whether a man is truly able, or truly a weakling and a nonentity; for it is the realization of this that is genuine wisdom and goodness, while the failure to realize it is manifest folly and wickedness. Everything else that passes for ability and wisdom has a sort of commonness—in those who wield political power a poor cheap show, in the manual workers a matter of mechanical routine. If, therefore, one meets a man who practices injustice and is blasphemous in his talk or in his life, the best thing for him by far is that one should never grant that there is any sort of ability about his unscrupulousness; such men are ready enough to glory in the reproach, and think that it means not that they are mere rubbish, cumbering the ground to no purpose, but that they have the kind of qualities that are necessary for survival in the community. We must therefore tell them the truth—that their very ignorance of their true state fixes them the more firmly therein. For they do not know what is

141E

142A

176D

the penalty of injustice, which is the last thing of which a man should be ignorant. It is not what they suppose—scourging and death—things which they may entirely evade in spite of their wrongdoing. It is a penalty from which there is no escape. 176E

THEODORUS: And what is that?

SOCRATES: My friend, there are two patterns set up in reality. One is divine and supremely happy; the other has nothing of God in it, and is the pattern of the deepest unhappiness. This truth the evildoer does not see; blinded by folly and utter lack of understanding, he fails to perceive that the effect of his unjust practices is to make him grow 177A more and more like the one, and less and less like the other. For this he pays the penalty of living the life that corresponds to the pattern he is coming to resemble. And if we tell him that, unless he is delivered from this 'ability' of his, when he dies the place that is pure of all evil will not receive him; that he will forever go on living in this world a life after his own likeness—a bad man tied to bad company: he will but think, 'This is the way fools talk to a clever rascal like me.'

H. *Sophist* 248A2–249D5 (pp. 269–271) [see 3.8.9; 6.7.13; 6.9.11]

THEAETETUS: All right.

VISITOR: Let's turn to the other people, the friends of the forms. You serve as their interpreter for us.

THEAETETUS: All right.

VISITOR: You people distinguish coming-to-be and being and say that they are separate? Is that right?

THEAETETUS: "Yes."

VISITOR: And you say that by our bodies and through perception we have dealings with coming-to-be, but we deal with real being by our souls and through reasoning. You say that being always stays the same and in the same state, but coming-to-be varies from one time to another.

THEAETETUS: "We do say that." 248B

VISITOR: And what shall we say this *dealing with* is that you apply in the two cases? Doesn't it mean what we said just now?

THEAETETUS: "What?"

VISITOR: What happens when two things come together, and by some capacity one does something to the other or has something done to it. Or maybe you don't hear their answer clearly, Theaetetus. But I do, probably because I'm used to them.

THEAETETUS: Then what account do they give?

VISITOR: They don't agree with what we just said to the earth people about being.

248C   THEAETETUS: What's that?

VISITOR: We took it as a sufficient definition of *beings* that the capacity be present in a thing to do something or have something done to it, to or by even the smallest thing or degree.

THEAETETUS: Yes.

VISITOR: In reply they say that coming-to-be has the capacity to do something or have something done to it, but that this capacity doesn't fit with being.

THEAETETUS: Is there anything to that?

248D   VISITOR: We have to reply that we need them to tell us more clearly whether they agree that the soul knows and also that *being* is known.

THEAETETUS: "Yes," they say.

VISITOR: Well then, do you say that knowing and being known are cases of doing, or having something done, or both? Is one of them doing and the other having something done? Or is neither a case of either?

THEAETETUS: Obviously that neither is a case of either, since otherwise they'd be saying something contrary to what they said before.

248E   VISITOR: Oh, I see. You mean that if knowing is doing something, then necessarily what is known has something done to it. When being is known by knowledge, according to this account, then insofar as it's known it's changed by having something done to it—which we say wouldn't happen to something that's at rest.

THEAETETUS: That's correct.

VISITOR: But for heaven's sake, are we going to be convinced that it's true that change, life, soul, and intelligence are not present in *that*
249A   *which wholly is*, and that it neither lives nor thinks, but stays changeless, solemn, and holy, without any understanding?

THEAETETUS: If we did, sir, we'd be admitting something frightening.

VISITOR: But are we going to say that it has understanding but doesn't have life?

THEAETETUS: Of course not.

VISITOR: But are we saying that it has both those things in it while denying that it has them in a soul?

THEAETETUS: How else would it have them?

VISITOR: And are we saying that it has intelligence, life, and soul, but that it's at rest and completely changeless even though it's alive?

249B   THEAETETUS: All that seems completely unreasonable.

VISITOR: Then both *that which changes* and also *change* have to be admitted as being.

THEAETETUS: Of course.

VISITOR: And so, Theaetetus, it turns out that if no beings change then nothing anywhere possesses any intelligence about anything.

THEAETETUS: Absolutely not.

VISITOR: But furthermore if we admit that everything is moving and changing, then on that account we take the very same thing away from those which are.

THEAETETUS: Why?

VISITOR: Do you think that without rest anything would be the same, in the same state in the same respects?   249C

THEAETETUS: Not at all.

VISITOR: Well then, do you see any case in which intelligence is or comes-to-be anywhere without these things?

THEAETETUS: Not in the least.

VISITOR: And we need to use every argument we can to fight against anyone who does away with knowledge, understanding, and intelligence but at the same time asserts anything at all about anything.

THEAETETUS: Definitely.

VISITOR: The philosopher—the person who values these things the most—absolutely has to refuse to accept the claim that everything is at rest, either from defenders of the one or from friends of the many forms. In addition he has to refuse to listen to people who make *that*   249D
which is change in every way. He has to be like a child begging for "both," and say that *that which is*—everything—is both the unchanging and that which changes.

I. *Timaeus* 27C4–31A2 (1234–1236)
[see 4.8.1, 2, 3, 4; 5.1.2; 6.9.3]

TIMAEUS: That I will, Socrates. Surely anyone with any sense at all will always call upon a god before setting out on any venture, whatever its importance. In our case, we are about to make speeches about the universe—whether it has an origin or even if it does not—and so if we're not to go completely astray we have no choice but to call upon the gods and goddesses, and pray that they above all will approve of all we have to say, and that in consequence we will, too. Let this, then, be our   27D
appeal to the gods; to ourselves we must appeal to make sure that you learn as easily as possible, and that I instruct you in the subject matter before us in the way that best conveys my intent.

As I see it, then, we must begin by making the following distinction: What is *that which always is* and has no becoming, and what is *that which becomes* but never is? The former is grasped by understand-   28A
ing, which involves a reasoned account. It is unchanging. The latter is grasped by opinion, which involves unreasoning sense perception. It

comes to be and passes away, but never really is. Now everything that comes to be must of necessity come to be by the agency of some cause, for it is impossible for anything to come to be without a cause. So whenever the craftsman looks at what is always changeless and, using a thing of that kind as his model, reproduces its form and character,
28B   then, of necessity, all that he so completes is beautiful. But were he to look at a thing that has come to be and use as his model something that has been begotten, his work will lack beauty.

Now as to the whole universe or world order [*kosmos*]—let's just call it by whatever name is most acceptable in a given context—there is a question we need to consider first. This is the sort of question one should begin with in inquiring into any subject. Has it always existed? Was there no origin from which it came to be? Or did it come to be and take its start from some origin? It has come to be. For it is both visible and tangible and it has a body—and all things of that kind are percepti-
28C   ble. And, as we have shown, perceptible things are grasped by opinion, which involves sense perception. As such, they are things that come to be, things that are begotten. Further, we maintain that, necessarily, that which comes to be must come to be by the agency of some cause. Now to find the maker and father of this universe [*to pan*] is hard enough, and even if I succeeded, to declare him to everyone is impossible. And so we must go back and raise this question about the universe: Which of the two models did the maker use when he fashioned it? Was it the
29A   one that does not change and stays the same, or the one that has come to be? Well, if this world of ours is beautiful and its craftsman good, then clearly he looked at the eternal model. But if what it's blasphemous to even say is the case, then he looked at one that has come to be. Now surely it's clear to all that it was the eternal model he looked at, for, of all the things that have come to be, our universe is the most beautiful, and of causes the craftsman is the most excellent. This, then, is how it has come to be: it is a work of craft, modeled after that which is changeless and is grasped by a rational account, that is, by wisdom.

Since these things are so, it follows by unquestionable necessity
29B   that this world is an image of something. Now in every subject it is of utmost importance to begin at the natural beginning, and so, on the subject of an image and its model, we must make the following specification: the accounts we give of things have the same character as the subjects they set forth. So accounts of what is stable and fixed and transparent to understanding are themselves stable and unshifting. We must do our very best to make these accounts as irrefutable and invincible as any account may be. On the other hand, accounts we

give of that which has been formed to be like that reality, since they   29C
are accounts of what is a likeness, are themselves likely, and stand in
proportion to the previous accounts, i.e., what being is to becoming,
truth is to convincingness. Don't be surprised then, Socrates, if it turns
out repeatedly that we won't be able to produce accounts on a great
many subjects—on gods or the coming to be of the universe—that are
completely and perfectly consistent and accurate. Instead, if we can
come up with accounts no less likely than any, we ought to be content, keeping in mind that both I, the speaker, and you, the judges, are
only human. So we should accept the likely tale on these matters. It   29D
behooves us not to look for anything beyond this.

SOCRATES: Bravo, Timaeus! By all means! We must accept it as you
say we should. This overture of yours was marvelous. Go on now and
let us have the work itself.

TIMAEUS: Very well then. Now why did he who framed this whole   29E
universe of becoming frame it? Let us state the reason why: He was
good, and one who is good can never become jealous of anything. And
so, being free of jealousy, he wanted everything to become as much
like himself as was possible. In fact, men of wisdom will tell you (and
you couldn't do better than to accept their claim) that this, more than   30A
anything else, was the most preeminent reason for the origin of the
world's coming to be. The god wanted everything to be good and nothing to be bad so far as that was possible, and so he took over all that
was visible—not at rest but in discordant and disorderly motion—and
brought it from a state of disorder to one of order, because he believed
that order was in every way better than disorder. Now it wasn't permitted (nor is it now) that one who is supremely good should do anything   30B
but what is best. Accordingly, the god reasoned and concluded that
in the realm of things naturally visible no unintelligent thing could as
a whole be better than anything which does possess intelligence as a
whole, and he further concluded that it is impossible for anything to
come to possess intelligence apart from soul. Guided by this reasoning,
he put intelligence in soul, and soul in body, and so he constructed
the universe. He wanted to produce a piece of work that would be as
excellent and supreme as its nature would allow. This, then, in keeping
with our likely account, is how we must say divine providence brought   30C
our world into being as a truly living thing, endowed with soul and
intelligence.

This being so, we have to go on to speak about what comes next.
When the maker made our world, what living thing did he make
it resemble? Let us not stoop to think that it was any of those that

have the natural character of a part, for nothing that is a likeness of anything incomplete could ever turn out beautiful. Rather, let us lay it down that the universe resembles more closely than anything else that Living Thing of which all other living things are parts, both individually and by kinds. For that Living Thing comprehends within itself all intelligible living things, just as our world is made up of us and all the other visible creatures. Since the god wanted nothing more than to make the world like the best of the intelligible things, complete in every way, he made it a single visible living thing, which contains within itself all the living things whose nature it is to share its kind.

30D

31A

37C6–D9 (p. 1241) [5.1.2, 4]

Now when the Father who had begotten the universe observed it set in motion and alive, a thing that had come to be as a shrine for the everlasting gods, he was well pleased, and in his delight he thought of making it more like its model still. So, as the model was itself an everlasting Living Thing, he set himself to bringing this universe to completion in such a way that it, too, would have that character to the extent that was possible. Now it was the Living Thing's nature to be eternal, but it isn't possible to bestow eternity fully upon anything that is begotten. And so he began to think of making a moving image of eternity: at the same time as he brought order to the universe, he would make an eternal image, moving according to number, of eternity remaining in unity. This number, of course, is what we now call "time."

37D

J. *Epistle* II. 312D1–313C3 (p. 1638)
[see 5.1.8; 5.3.17; 6.4.11; 6.7.42]

Enough of these matters. The sphere is not correct. Archedemus will explain it to you when he comes. And upon that other question of weightier and more sublime import about which you say you have difficulties, let him by all means enlighten you. According to his report, you say that the nature of "the first" has not been sufficiently explained. I must speak of this matter to you in enigmas, in order that if anything should happen to these tablets "in the recesses of the sea or land," whoever reads them may not understand our meaning. It is like this. Upon the king of all do all things turn; he is the end of all things and the cause of all good. Things of the second order turn upon the second principle, and those of the third order upon the third. Now the soul of man longs to understand what sort of things these principles are, and it looks toward the things that are akin to itself, though none of them is adequate; clearly the king and the other principles

312D

312E

313A

mentioned are not of that sort. The soul thereupon asks, What then is the nature of these principles? This is the question, O son of Dionysius and Doris, that causes all the trouble; or rather, this it is that produces in the soul the pains of childbirth, from which she must be delivered, or she will never really attain truth. You yourself once told me, under the laurel trees in your garden, that you understood this matter, having found the answer yourself; and I replied that if you thought so, you had spared me many words. I said, however, that I had never met anyone who had discovered this truth, and that most of my own study was devoted to it. Perhaps you once heard something from someone and providentially started on the track of the answer, but then, thinking you had it safe, neglected to fix fast the proofs of it, which now dart here and there about some object of your fancy, whereas the reality itself is quite different. You are not alone in this experience; I assure you that everyone at first hearing is affected in just this way, and though some have more difficulty than others, there is almost no one who escapes with but little effort.

313B

313C

K. *Epistle* VII. 341A7–343C8 (pp. 1658–1660) [see 1.6.9; 5.3.17]

It was in this fashion that I then spoke to Dionysius. I did not explain everything to him, nor did he ask me to, for he claimed to have already a sufficient knowledge of many, and the most important, points because of what he had heard others say about them. Later, I hear, he wrote a book on the matters we talked about, putting it forward as his own teaching, not what he had learned from me. Whether this is true I do not know. I know that certain others also have written on these same matters; but who they are they themselves do not know. So much at least I can affirm with confidence about any who have written or propose to write on these questions, pretending to a knowledge of the problems with which I am concerned, whether they claim to have learned from me or from others or to have made their discoveries for themselves: it is impossible, in my opinion, that they can have learned anything at all about the subject. There is no writing of mine about these matters, nor will there ever be one. For this knowledge is not something that can be put into words like other sciences; but after long-continued intercourse between teacher and pupil, in joint pursuit of the subject, suddenly, like light flashing forth when a fire is kindled, it is born in the soul and straightaway nourishes itself. And this too I know: if these matters are to be expounded at all in books or lectures, they would best come from me. Certainly I am harmed not least of all if they are misrepresented. If I thought they could be put into written words adequate for the multitude,

341B

341C

341D

what nobler work could I do in my life than to compose something of such great benefit to mankind and bring to light the nature of things for all to see? But I do not think that the "examination," as it is called, of these questions would be of any benefit to men, except to a few, i.e., to those who could with a little guidance discover the truth by themselves. Of the rest, some would be filled with an ill-founded and quite unbecoming disdain, and some with an exaggerated and foolish elation, as if they had learned something grand.

341E

Let me go into these matters at somewhat greater length, for perhaps what I am saying will become clearer when I have done so. There is a true doctrine that confutes anyone who has presumed to write anything whatever on such subjects, a doctrine that I have often before expounded, but it seems that it must now be said again. For every real being, there are three things that are necessary if knowledge of it is to be acquired: first, the name; second, the definition; third, the image; knowledge comes fourth, and in the fifth place we must put the object itself, the knowable and truly real being. To understand what this means, take a particular example, and think of all other objects as analogous to it. There is something called a circle, and its name is this very word we have just used. Second, there is its definition, composed of nouns and verbs. "The figure whose extremities are everywhere equally distant from its center" is the definition of precisely that to which the names "round," "circumference," and "circle" apply. Third is what we draw or rub out, what is turned or destroyed; but the circle itself to which they all refer remains unaffected, because it is different from them. In the fourth place are knowledge (*epistēmē*), reason (*nous*), and right opinion (which are in our minds, not in words or bodily shapes, and therefore must be taken together as something distinct both from the circle itself and from the three things previously mentioned); of these, reason is nearest the fifth in kinship and likeness, while the others are further away. The same thing is true of straight-lined as well as of circular figures; of color; of the good, the beautiful, the just; of body in general, whether artificial or natural; of fire, water, and all the elements; of all living beings and qualities of souls; of all actions and affections. For in each case, whoever does not somehow grasp the four things mentioned will never fully attain knowledge of the fifth.

342A

342B

342C

342D

342E

These things, moreover, because of the weakness of language, are just as much concerned with making clear the particular property of each object as the being of it. On this account no sensible man will venture to express his deepest thoughts in words, especially in a form which is

343A

unchangeable, as is true of written outlines. Let us go back and study again the illustration just given. Every circle that we make or draw in common life is full of characteristics that contradict the "fifth," for it everywhere touches a straight line, while the circle itself, we say, has in it not the slightest element belonging to a contrary nature. And we say that their names are by no means fixed; there is no reason why what we call "circles" might not be called "straight lines," and the straight lines "circles," and their natures will be none the less fixed despite this exchange of names. Indeed the same thing is true of the definition: since it is a combination of nouns and verbs, there is nothing surely fixed about it. Much more might be said to show that each of these four instruments is unclear, but the most important point is what I said earlier: that of the two objects of search—the particular quality and the being of an object—the soul seeks to know not the quality but the essence, whereas each of these four instruments presents to the soul, in discourse and in examples, what she is not seeking, and thus makes it easy to refute by sense perception anything that may be said or pointed out, and fills everyone, so to speak, with perplexity and confusion.

343B

343C

III. Aristotle

A. *De Anima* (Selections from Aristotle, *De Anima*, translated by C. D. C. Reeve, Hackett Publishing, 2017.)

1. 412a1–413a10 (pp. 21–22) [see 1.1.3, 4]

So much, then, for the views handed down by our predecessors con-
412a1   cerning the soul. Let us go back again and start afresh, as it were, and
try to determine what the soul is and what its most common account
5   would be.

We say, then, that one kind (*genos*) among the beings is substance, and
of this, one sort is substance as matter, which is intrinsically not a this
something, and another is shape and form, on the basis of which something is already said to be a this something, and a third, what is composed of these. And matter is potentiality, whereas form is actuality—and
10   this in two ways, as scientific knowledge is and as contemplating is.

It is bodies that seem most of all to be substances, and among these,
the natural ones. For these are starting-points for the others. Of natural bodies, some have life, while some do not have it. And by life we
mean self-nourishment, growth, and decay. So every natural body that
15   participates in life would be a substance, but a substance as a composite. But since it is also a body of such-and-such a sort, for it has life,
it would not be a body. For the body is not among the things that are
predicated of an underlying subject, but rather [is spoken of] as an
underlying subject and matter.

It is necessary, then, for the soul to be substance as form of a natural
20   body that has life potentially. But substance is actuality. Therefore, it
is the actualization of such a body. But something is said to be actual
in two ways, either as scientific knowledge is or as contemplating is.
And it is evident that it is as scientific knowledge is. For both sleep
and waking depend on the presence of the soul; waking is analogous
25   to contemplating, and sleep to having but not actualizing [scientific
knowledge]; and in the same individual scientific knowledge is prior in
coming to be. That is why the soul is the first actualization of a natural
body that has life potentially.

This sort of body would be one that is instrumental. For even the
412b1   parts of plants are instruments, although extremely simple ones—for
example, the leaf is a covering for the pod and the pod for the fruit, and
the roots are an analog of the mouth, since both take in nourishment.
5   If, then, we must state something that is common to every soul, it
would be that it is the first actualization of a natural instrumental body.
That is why we should not inquire whether the soul and the body are

one, any more than the wax and the shape, or, in general, the matter of a given thing and that of which it is the matter. For, since one and being are said of things in many ways, the controlling way is actuality.

It has now been stated in universal terms what the soul is. For the 10 soul is a substance in accord with the account. And this is the essence of this sort of body. It is just like this: if an instrument—for example, an axe—were a natural body, its substance would be the being for the axe, and this would be its soul. And if this were separated from it, it would not still be an axe, except homonymously. As things stand, though, it is an axe. For it is not of this sort of body that the essence and the account 15 is the soul, but of a certain sort of natural body that has a starting-point of movement and rest within itself.

We must get a theoretical grasp on how what has been said applies also in the case of the parts [of the body]. For if the eye were an animal, sight would be its soul. For that is the substance of an eye, the one in accord with the account. And the eye is matter for sight, and if this 20 fails, it is no longer an eye, except homonymously, like an eye in stone or in a picture. We must now apply what holds in the case of the part to the whole living body. For as the part is in relation to the part, so analogously is the whole of perception in relation to the whole body 25 that is perceptual, insofar as it is such. But it is not what has lost its soul that is potentially such as to live, but what has it. The seed and the fruit are potentially bodies of this sort.

As, then, are cutting and seeing, so too is being awake an actuality, 413a1 and as are sight and the capacity of the instrument, so is the soul, whereas the body is what is potentially [alive]. But just as the eye-jelly and sight are an eye, so in this case the soul and the body are an animal.

Hence that the soul is not separable from the body—or that certain parts of it are not, if it naturally has parts—is quite clear. For of some 5 parts the actuality is of the parts themselves. Nevertheless nothing prevents some of them at any rate from being separable, because of being the actualities of no body. Further, it is unclear whether the soul is the actualization of the body in this way or in the way that a sailor is of a ship.

So much, then, by way of making determinations in outline and 10 giving a sketch of the soul.

2. 429A10–23 (p. 53) [see 5.1.10]

Concerning the part of the soul by which the soul both knows and 10 thinks (whether this is separable or not separable as a spatial magnitude but only in account), we must investigate what its differentia (*diaphora*) is, and how on earth understanding comes about.

Now, if understanding is like perceiving, it would be either a sort of being affected by the intelligible object or something else of that sort. It
15   must be unaffectable, therefore, but receptive of the form, and potentially such as it is, although not the same as it, and as what is capable of perceiving is in relation to the perceptible objects, so the understanding must be in relation to the intelligible ones.

It must, therefore, since it understands all things, be unmixed, as Anaxagoras says, in order that it may master them—that is, in order that it may know them. For something foreign intruding into it
20   impedes and obstructs it. So too it has no other nature than this, that it is potentially something. That part of the soul, therefore, that is called the understanding (and I mean by the understanding that by which the soul thinks and grasps things) is actively none of the beings before it [actively] understands them.

3. 430a10–25 (p. 55) [see 5.1.3, 9; 5.3.3]

But since in the whole of nature there is something that is matter
10   for each genus (*genos*) (and this is what is potentially all those things [that are in the genus]), while there is something else that is causal and productive, because of producing them all (which, for example, is the role of a craft in relation to its matter), so in the soul too there must be these differences (*diaphora*). And in fact there is one sort of understanding that is such by becoming all things, while there is another
15   that is such by producing all things in the way that a sort of state, like light, does, since in a way light too makes potential colors into active colors.

And this [productive] understanding is separable, unaffectable, and unmixed, being in substance an activity (for the producer is always more estimable than the thing affected, and the starting-point than
20   the matter), not sometimes understanding and at other times not. But, when separated, this alone is just what it is. And it alone is immortal and eternal (but we do not remember because this is unaffectable, whereas the passive understanding is capable of passing away), and
25   without this it understands nothing.

B. *Metaphysics* (All selections from Aristotle, *Metaphysics*, translated by C. D. C. Reeve, Hackett Publishing, 2016.)

1. 1072a18–1073a13 (pp. 205–207) [see 1.6.7; 1.8.2; 5.1.4, 9; 5.3.5, 8; 6.7.37, 39; 6.8.16]

Since it is possible that things are this way, and if they are not this way, they would have come from night, or all things together, or from

not being, these issues may be taken as resolved. And there is some-   20
thing that is always moved with an unceasing movement, which is in
a circle (and this is clear not from argument alone but also from the
facts). So the primary heaven would be eternal. There is, therefore, also
something that moves it. But since what is moved and moves something is something medial, there is something that moves without
being moved, being eternal, substance, and activity.   25

This, though, is the way the object of desire and the intelligible
object move things: they move them without being moved. Of these
objects, the primary ones are the same. For the [primary] object of
appetite is the apparently noble, and the primary object of wish is the
really noble. But we desire something because it seems [noble] rather
than its seeming so because we desire it. For the starting-point is
the active understanding. And understanding is moved by intelligible objects, and what is intrinsically intelligible is the one column [of   30
opposites], and in this substance is primary, and in *this* the simple one
and an activity—oneness and simplicity are not the same, since unity
signifies a measure, whereas simplicity signifies that the thing itself is
a certain way. But the noble, too, and what is choiceworthy because
of itself are in the same column, and what is primary is always best or   35
analogous to the best.

That the for-the-sake-of-which does exist among the immovable   1072b1
things is made clear by a distinction. For the for-the-sake-of-which is
both the one *for whom* and *that toward which*, and of these the latter is
among the immovable things and the former is not. And it produces
movement insofar as it is loved, whereas it is by being moved that the
other things move.

Now if something is moved, it admits of being otherwise than it is,
so that if the primary spatial movement for its part is an activity, inso-   5
far as it is being moved, in this respect it admits of being otherwise—
with respect to place, even if not with respect to substance. But since
there is something that moves while it itself is immovable, though it
is in activity, it can in no way admit of being otherwise. For spatial
movement is primary among the sorts of change, and of these, that in a
circle is primary; and this it produces. Therefore, it [the prime mover]   10
of necessity is; and insofar as it is of necessity, it is in noble fashion,
and in this way a starting-point [of movement]. For something is said
to be necessary in a number of ways—as what is forced contrary to
natural impulse, as that without which what is good does not exist,
and as what does not admit of being otherwise, but is unconditionally
necessary.

This, therefore, is the sort of starting-point on which the heaven
and nature depend. And its pastime is like the best that we can have—
and have for a short time (for it is always in that state [of activity],
whereas we cannot be)—since its activity is also pleasure. And it is
because of this that waking, perceiving, and active understanding are
a very great pleasure, and expectation and memory because of these.
Active understanding, though, is intrinsically of what is intrinsically
best, and the sort that is to the highest degree best is of what is to
the highest degree best. And the understanding actively understands
itself by partaking of the intelligible object. (For it becomes an intelligible object by touching and understanding one, so that understanding and intelligible object are the same.) For what is receptive of the
intelligible object and of the substance is the understanding, and it
is active when it possesses it, so that this rather than that seems to
be the divine thing that understanding possesses, and contemplation
seems to be most pleasant and best. If, then, that good state [of activ-
ity], which we are sometimes in, the [primary] god is always in, that
is a wonderful thing, and if to a higher degree, that is yet more wonderful. But that is his state. And life too certainly belongs to him. For
the activity of understanding is life, and he is that activity; and his
intrinsic activity is life that is best and eternal. We say, indeed, that
the god is a living being who is eternal and best, so that living and a
continuous and everlasting eternity belong to the god, since this is
the god.

Those who take it, as the Pythagoreans and Speusippus do, that
the noblest and best is not present in the starting-point, because,
while the starting-points of plants and animals are causes too,
noble beauty and completeness are in what comes from these, are
not correct in their thinking. For the seed comes from other things
that are prior and complete, and the first thing is not seed but the
complete thing, as we might say "the human is prior to the seed"—
not the one who came to be from it but another one from whom
the seed came.

It is evident from what has been said, then, that there is a substance
that is eternal and immovable and separate from perceptible things.
And it has also been shown that this substance cannot have any
magnitude, but must be without parts and indivisible. For it moves
something for an unlimited time, and nothing finite has unlimited
capacity. And, since every magnitude is either unlimited or finite,
it cannot have a finite magnitude, because of what we said, and it
cannot have an unlimited magnitude because there is no unlimited
magnitude at all. But then it has also been shown that it is impassive

and inalterable. For all the other movements are posterior to that with respect to place.

It is clear, then, why things are this way.

2. 1074b14–1075a10 (pp. 210–211) [see 5.3.5; 6.7.9, 13, 37]

Issues concerning the [divine] understanding involve certain puzzles. For while it seems to be the most divine of the appearances, the question of how it can have that character involves certain difficulties. For if on the one hand it understands nothing, where is its dignity? It would be just like someone asleep. And if on the other hand it does understand something, but this other thing controls it (since what it is, its substance, is not active understanding, but a capacity), it would not be the best substance. For it is because of actively understanding that esteem belongs to it.

Further, whether it is understanding [as a capacity] or active understanding that is the substance of it, what does it understand? For it is either itself or something else. And if something else, then either always the same thing or sometimes this and sometimes that. Does it, then, make a difference or none at all whether it actively understands the noble or some random object? Or are there not certain things that it would be absurd for it to think of? It is clear, therefore, that it actively understands what is most divine and most estimable and does not change [its object], since change would be for the worse, and would already be a sort of movement.

First, then, if its substance is not active understanding but rather a capacity [to understand], it is reasonable to suppose that the continuity of its active understanding is laborious for it. Next, it is clear that something else would be more estimable than the understanding, namely, what is understood. And indeed [the capacity] to understand and active understanding will belong even to someone who actively understands the worst thing, so that if this is to be avoided (for there are in fact some things that it is better not to see than to see), the active understanding would not be the best thing. It is itself, therefore, that it understands, if indeed it is the most excellent thing, and the active understanding is active understanding of active understanding.

It appears, though, that scientific knowledge, perception, belief, and thinking are always of something else, and of themselves only as a byproduct. Further, if to understand and to be understood are distinct, in virtue of which of them does the good belong to it? For the being for an act of understanding is not the same as the being for a thing understood. Or is it that in some cases the scientific knowledge is the thing?

1075a1   In the case of the productive sciences isn't it the substance and the
essence without the matter? In the case of the theoretical sciences isn't
it the account, the thing, and its active understanding? In the cases,
then, where the thing understood and the active understanding of it
are not distinct, namely, in those where the thing understood has no
matter, they will be the same, and the active understanding will be one
with the thing understood.

   5   A further puzzle remains as to whether the thing understood is composite. For if it were, then the [divine] understanding would undergo
change in understanding the parts of the whole. Or is not everything
that has no matter indivisible? (Just as the human understanding [of
such things] is, or the understanding even of composite things in a
certain time—for it does not possess the good in [understanding] this
or that [part], rather, in [understanding] a certain whole it possesses
the best, being something else.) And is not this the condition of this
   10   understanding which, for all eternity, is an understanding of itself?

C. *Nicomachean Ethics* (All selections from Aristotle, *Nicomachean Ethics*, translated by C. D. C. Reeve, Hackett Publishing, 2014.)

1. 1094a1–19 [see 1.8.2, 3; 6.7.20; 6.8.7]

1094a1   Every craft and every method of inquiry and likewise every action
and deliberate choice seems to seek some good. That is why they correctly declare that the good is "that which all seek."

   A certain difference, however, appears to exist among ends. For
some are activities while others are works of some sort beyond the
   5   activities themselves. But wherever there are ends beyond the actions,
in those cases, the works are naturally better than the activities. But
since there are many sorts of actions and of crafts and sciences,
their ends are many as well. For health is the end of medicine, a ship
of shipbuilding, victory of generalship, and wealth of household
management.

   10   Some of these fall under some one capacity, however, as bridle making falls under horsemanship, along with all the others that produce
equipment for horsemanship, and as it and every action in warfare fall
under generalship, and, in the same way, others fall under different
ones. But in all such cases, the ends of the architectonic ones are more
   15   choiceworthy than the ends under them, since these are pursued for
the sake also of the former. It makes no difference, though, whether the
ends of the actions are the activities themselves or some other thing
beyond them, just as in the sciences we have mentioned.

2. 1097b22–1098a21 [see 1.4.1]

But to say that happiness is the best good is perhaps to say something that is apparently commonplace, and we still need a clearer statement of what it is. Maybe, then, this would come about if the function of a human being were grasped. For just as for a flute player, a sculptor, 25 every craftsman, and in general for whatever has some function and action, the good—the doing well—seems to lie in the function, the same also seems to hold of a human being, if indeed there is some function that is his.

So are there some functions and actions of a carpenter and of a shoemaker but none at all of a human being? And is he by nature inactive? Or, rather, just as of eye, hand, foot, and of each part generally there 30 seems to be some function, may we likewise also posit some function of a human being that is beyond all these?

What, then, could this be? For living is evidently shared with plants as well, but we are looking for what is special. Hence we must set aside the living that consists in nutrition and growth. Next in order is some 1098a1 sort of perceptual living. But this too is evidently shared with horse and ox and every animal.

There remains, then, some sort of practical living of the part that has reason. And of what has reason, one part has it by dint of obeying reason, the other by dint of actually having it and exercising thought. But "living" is said of things in two ways, and we must take the one in 5 accord with activity, since it seems to be called "living" in a fuller sense.

If, then, the function of a human being is activity of the soul in accord with reason or not without reason, and the function of a sort of thing, we say, is the same in kind as the function of an excellent thing of that sort (as in the case of a lyre player and an excellent lyre player), and this is unconditionally so in all cases when we add to the function 10 the superiority that is in accord with the virtue (for it is characteristic of a lyre player to play the lyre and of an excellent one to do it well)—if all this is so, and a human being's function is supposed to be a sort of living, and this living is supposed to be activity of the soul and actions that involve reason, and it is characteristic of an excellent man to do these well and nobly, and each is completed well when it is in accord with the virtue that properly belongs to it—if all this is so, the human 15 good turns out to be activity of the soul in accord with virtue and, if there are more virtues than one, then in accord with the best and most complete. Furthermore, in a complete life, for one swallow does not make a spring, nor does one day. Nor, similarly, does one day or a short time make someone blessed and happy.

3. 1177a12–1177b16 [see 1.4.1]

But if happiness is activity in accord with virtue, it is quite reasonable that it should be in accord with the one that is most excellent, and this will be the virtue of the best element. Whether, then, this element is understanding or something else that seems by nature to rule, lead, and understand what is noble and divine, whether by being
15   something divine itself or by being the most divine element in us— the activity of it, when in accord with the virtue that properly belongs to it, will be complete happiness. That it is contemplative activity we already said.

And this would seem to be in agreement both with what was said before and with the truth, since this activity is also most excellent. For not only is understanding the most excellent element in us, but also,
20   of knowable objects, the ones that understanding is concerned with are the most excellent ones. Further, it is the most continuous activity, since we can contemplate more continuously than we can do any action whatsoever.

Moreover, we think that pleasure must be mixed in with happiness, and the most pleasant of the activities in accord with virtue is agreed to be the one in accord with theoretical wisdom. At any rate, philos-
25   ophy seems to involve pleasures that are wondrous for their purity and stability, and it is quite reasonable that those who have attained knowledge should pass their time more pleasantly than those who are looking for it.

Moreover, the self-sufficiency that is meant will belong most of all to contemplative activity. For while a theoretically-wise person as well as a just one and people with the other virtues all need the things necessary for living, when these are adequately supplied, the just one
30   still needs people to do just actions for and with, and similarly for a temperate person, a courageous person, and each of the others. But a theoretically-wise person, even when by himself, is able to contemplate, and the more wise he is, the more he is able to do so. He will do it better, presumably, if he has co-workers, but all the same he is most self-sufficient.

Moreover, this activity, and only this, would seem to be liked
1177b1   because of itself [alone]. For nothing arises from it beyond having contemplated, whereas from the practical ones we try—to a greater or lesser extent—to get for ourselves something beyond the action.

Moreover, happiness seems to reside in leisure, since we do unleisured things in order to be at leisure, and wage war in order to live in
5   peace. Now the activity of the practical virtues occurs in politics or in

warfare, and the actions concerned with these seem to be unleisured
and those in warfare completely so (for no one chooses to wage war
for the sake of waging war, or to foment war either, since someone
would seem completely bloodthirsty, if he made enemies of his friends 10
in order to bring about battles and killings). But the activity of a pol-
itician too is unleisured and beyond political activity itself he tries to
get positions of power and honors or, at any rate, happiness for himself and his fellow citizens—this being different from the exercise of
politics and something we clearly seek on the supposition of its being
different. 15

4. 1178b8–33 [see 1.2.1; 1.4.2]

But that complete happiness is some contemplative activity will
also be evident from the following considerations. The gods, in fact,
we suppose to be the most blessed and happy of all. But what sorts
of actions should we assign to them? Just ones? Won't they appear 10
ridiculous if they engage in transactions, return deposits, and so
on? Courageous ones, then, enduring what is frightening and facing danger because it is a noble thing to do? Or generous ones?
To whom will they give? It will be a strange thing, if they actually
have money or anything like that. And their temperate actions, what
would they be? Or isn't the praise vulgar, since they do not have base 15
appetites? If we were to go through them all, it would be evident
that everything to do with actions is petty and unworthy of gods.
Nonetheless, everyone supposes them to be living, at least, and
hence in activity, since surely they are not sleeping like Endymion.
If, then, living has doing actions taken away from it and still more 20
so producing, what is left except contemplating? So the activity of a
god, superior as it is in blessedness, will be contemplative. And so
the activity of humans, then, that is most akin to this will most bear
the stamp of happiness.

A further indication of this is that other animals do not share in
happiness, being completely deprived of this sort of activity. Hence the 25
life of the gods is blessed throughout; that of human beings is so to the
extent that it has something similar to this sort of activity, whereas of
the other animals, none is happy, since they in no way share in contemplation. Happiness extends indeed just as far as contemplation
does, and those to whom it more belongs to contemplate, it also more
belongs to be happy, not coincidentally but, rather, in accord with con- 30
templation, since this is intrinsically estimable. And so happiness will
be some sort of contemplation.

IV. Stoics

(Selections from *Hellenistic Philosophy: Introductory Readings*, 2nd ed., edited by B. Inwood and Lloyd P. Gerson, Hackett Publishing, 1997.)

A. Stoic Theory of Knowledge: Sextus Empiricus, *M.*
(pp. 126–127, 7.227–236) [see 5.3.5; 5.5.1]

227. Since the Stoic doctrine remains, let us next speak of it. These men, then, say that the graspable presentation is a criterion of truth. We shall know this if we first learn what presentation is, according to them, and what its specific differentiae are. **228.** So, according to them, a presentation is an impression in the soul. And they differed immediately about this. For Cleanthes took "impression" in terms of depression and elevation—just like the impression on wax made by seal-rings. **229.** But Chrysippus thought that such a view was absurd. For first, he says, this will require that when our intellect has presentations at one time of a triangle and a tetragon, the same body will have to have in itself at the same time different shapes—triangular and tetragonal together, or even round; which is absurd. Next, since many presentations exist in us at the same time the soul will also have many configurations. This is worse than the first problem. **230.** [Chrysippus] himself speculated, therefore, that "impression" was used by Zeno to mean "alteration"; so that the definition becomes like this: 'presentation is an alteration of the soul'; for it is no longer absurd that the same body at one and the same time (when many presentations exist in us) should receive many alterations. **231.** For just as air, when many people speak at once, receiving at one time an indefinite number of different blows, also has many alterations, so too the leading part of the soul will experience something similar when it receives varied presentations.

232. But others say that even Chrysippus' corrected definition is not right. For if a presentation exists, then it is an impression and an alteration in the soul. But if an impression in the soul exists, it is not necessarily a presentation. For if a blow to the finger or a scratch to the hand occurs, an impression and alteration are produced in the soul, but not a presentation, since the latter occurs not in any chance part of the soul, but only in the intellect, that is, in the leading part of the soul. **233.** In response, the Stoics say that 'impression in the soul' implies 'insofar as it is in the soul'. . . . **234.** Others, starting from the same basic position, have defended their position more subtly. For they say that 'soul' is meant in two senses, one referring to that which holds together the entire, continuous composite, and the other referring particularly to the leading part. For whenever we say that man is composed of soul and body, or that death is the separation of soul from body, we are speaking particularly of the leading part. . . . **236.** Therefore, when Zeno says that presentation is an impression in the soul, he should be understood to mean not the whole soul but only a part of it, so that what is said is "presentation is an alteration in the leading part of the soul".

B. Stoic Physics: Diogenes Laertius, Book 7
(p. 156–157, §132; §133, ll. 9–17) [see 1.4.2; 1.8.1]

132. They divide the account of physics into topics on bodies and on principles and elements and gods and limits and place and void. And this is the detailed division; the general division is into three topics, concerning the cosmos, concerning the elements and the third on causal explanation. They say that the topic concerning the cosmos is divided into two parts; for the mathematicians share in one branch of its investigations, the one in which they investigate the fixed stars and the planets, for example, [to ascertain] whether the sun is as big as it appears to be, and similarly if the moon is; and concerning the revolution [of the cosmos] and similar enquiries.

133. The other branch of the investigation of the cosmos is the one which pertains *only* to natural scientists, the one in which the substance [of the cosmos] is investigated and whether it is generated or ungenerated and whether it is alive or lifeless and whether it is destructible or indestructible and whether it is administered by providence; and so forth. The topic concerning causal explanations is itself also bipartite. For medical investigation shares in one branch of its investigations, the one in which they investigate the leading part of the soul, what happens in the soul, the [generative] seeds, and questions like these. The mathematicians also lay claim on the other, for example, [investigation into] how we see, into the cause of how things appear in a mirror, how clouds are formed, and thunder and rainbows and the halo and comets and similar topics.

(p. 136, §147; p. 137, §150)

147. God is an animal, immortal, rational, perfect in happiness, immune to everything bad, providentially [looking after] the cosmos and the things in the cosmos; but he is not anthropomorphic. [God] is the craftsman of the universe and as it were a father of all things, both in general and also that part of him which extends through everything; he is called by many names in accordance with its powers. They say that *Dia* [a grammatical form of the name Zeus] is the one 'because of whom' all things are; they call [god] *Zena* [a grammatical form of the name Zeus] in so far as he is cause of life or because he penetrates life; and Athena by reference to the fact that his leading part extends into the aither; Hera because he extends into the air; Hephaestus because he extends into craftsmanlike fire; Poseidon because he extends into the fluid; and Demeter because he extends into the earth. Similarly they also assign the other titles [to god] by fastening onto one [of his] peculiarities.

150. They say that primary matter is the substance of all things which exist, as Chrysippus says in book one of his *Physics* and [so too does] Zeno. Matter is that from which anything at all can come into being. And it has two names, 'substance' and 'matter', both as the matter of all things [as a whole], and as the matter of individual things. The matter of all things [as a whole] does not become greater or smaller, but the matter of the individual things does. Substance is, according to the Stoics, body, and it is limited, according to Antipater in book two of *On Substance* and Apollodorus in his *Physics*. And it is capable of being affected, as the same man says; for if it were immune to change, the things generated from it would not be generated. From this it follows that [matter] can be divided to infinity. Chrysippus says that this division is infinite, ‹but not to infinity›; for there is no infinity for the division to reach; rather, the division is unceasing.

C. Stoic Ethics: Diogenes Laertius, Book 7 (pp. 190–191, §84–89) [see 1.4.2]

84. They divide the ethical part of philosophy into these topics: on impulse, on good and bad things, on passions, on virtue, on the goal, on primary value, on actions, on appropriate actions, and on encouragements and discouragements to actions. This is the subdivision given by the followers of Chrysippus, Archedemus, Zeno of Tarsus, Apollodorus, Diogenes, Antipater, and Posidonius. For Zeno of Citium and Cleanthes, as might be expected from earlier thinkers, made less elaborate distinctions in their subject matter. But they did divide both logic and physics.

85. They say that an animal's first [or primary] impulse is to preserve itself, because nature gave it an affinity to itself from the beginning, as Chrysippus says in book 1 of *On Goals*, stating that for every animal its first [sense of] affinity is to its own constitution and the reflective awareness of this. For it is not likely that nature would make an animal alienated from itself, nor having made the animal, to give it neither affinity to itself nor alienation from itself. Therefore, the remaining possibility is to say that having constituted the animal she gave it an affinity to itself. For in this way it repels injurious influences and pursues that to which it has an affinity.

The Stoics claim that what some people say is false, namely, that the primary [or first] impulse of animals is to pleasure. **86.** For they say that pleasure is, if anything, a byproduct which supervenes when nature itself, on its own, seeks out and acquires what is suitable to [the animal's] constitution. It is like the condition of thriving animals and plants in top condition. And nature, they say, did not operate differently in the cases of plants and of animals; for it directs the life of plants too, though without impulse and sense-perception, and even in us some processes are plantlike. When, in the case of animals, impulse is added (which they use in the pursuit of things to which they have an affinity), then for them what is natural is governed by what is according to impulse. When reason has been given to rational animals as a more perfect governor [of life], then for them the life according to reason properly becomes what is natural for them. For reason supervenes on impulse as a craftsman.

87. Thus Zeno first, in his book *On Human Nature*, said that the goal was to live in agreement with nature, which is to live according to virtue. For nature leads us to virtue. And similarly Cleanthes in *On Pleasure* and Posidonius and Hecaton in their books *On the Goal*.

Again, "to live according to virtue" is equivalent to living according to the experience of events which occur by nature, as Chrysippus says in book 1 of his *On Goals*. **88.** For our natures are parts of the nature of the universe. Therefore, the goal becomes "to live consistently with nature," i.e., according to one's own nature and that of the universe, doing nothing which is forbidden by the common law, which is right reason, penetrating all things, being the same as Zeus, who is the leader of the administration of things. And this itself is the virtue of the happy man and a smooth flow of life, whenever all things are done according to the harmony of the daimon in each of us with the will of the administrator of the universe. So, Diogenes says explicitly that the goal is reasonable behavior in the selection of things according to nature, and Archedemus [says it is] to live carrying out all the appropriate acts.

89. By nature, in consistency with which we must live, Chrysippus understands both the common and, specifically, the human nature. Cleanthes includes only the common nature, with which one must be consistent, and not the individual. And virtue is a disposition in agreement. And it is worth choosing for its own sake, not because of some fear or hope or some extrinsic consideration. And happiness lies in virtue, insofar as virtue is the soul [so] made [as to produce] the agreement of one's whole life.

And the rational animal is corrupted, sometimes because of the persuasiveness of external activities and sometimes because of the influence of companions. For the starting points provided by nature are uncorrupted.

V. Skeptics

(Translation by Lloyd P. Gerson.)

A. Sextus Empiricus, *M*. (7.310–312) [see 5.3.5]

Let us take it as established through these arguments that man is unable to grasp the senses by means of the body nor again the body by means of the senses, given that these cannot perceive themselves or the other. Next, we should show that discursive thinking is not cognizant of itself as the dogmatists among the philosophers claim. For if intellect grasps itself, either it will do so as a whole or not as a whole, using one part of itself. But it will not be able to grasp itself as a whole. For if a whole grasps itself, the whole will be both the grasp and [the activity of] grasping. But the subject grasping is the whole so that which is grasped will no longer be anything. But it is entirely irrational for there to exist the grasping but not that which is grasped. Neither, indeed, can the intellect use a part of itself for the grasping. For how does the part grasp itself? If it does so as a whole, that which is sought [to be grasped] is nothing; if it does so by some part, again, how will it cognize itself? And so on, indefinitely. So, grasping is without a beginning, since either no primary subject is found to do the grasping, or there is nothing to be grasped.

ENGLISH GLOSSARY OF IMPORTANT TERMS

The references after most of the technical and semi-technical terms are intended to illustrate Plotinus's usage, especially in texts of central doctrinal importance. These references should serve to supplement the cross-references in the translation. Common Greek philosophical and non-philosophical terms are not referenced.

accident (συμβεβηκός): The Peripatetic term for non-essential attributes of sensibles, including both *per se* and non-*per se* attributes. For Plotinus, there are no accidental attributes in the intelligible world.

accompaniment (παρακολούθημα): also, secondary attribute. That which is extrinsic to the nature of something but is necessarily found with it. This is Plotinus's version of the Peripatetic *per se* or καθ'αὑτό attribute. See 3.7.10.1–7; 6.3.3.6, 23.

act (ἐνέργημα): also, activation. Used to refer to the result of an **activity** or **actuality**.

act of apprehension (ἐπιβολή): also, direct apprehension. A term of Epicurean provenance. An unmediated cognition of an object whether sensible or intelligible. See 4.4.1.20; 6.2.4.23; 6.6.9.14; 6.7.35.21.

activity (ἐνέργεια): also, actuality. A Peripatetic term referring primarily to intellection and implying no imperfection. When translated as 'actuality' the term is used in discussing sensible composites which include a **potency** (δύναμις) related to the actuality. Occasionally, activation. See 1.1.9.21; 1.4.4.10; 2.3.16.48; 2.5.1.3–9; 3.2.16.19; 3.8.7.19; 4.3.23.16; 4.4.4.18; 5.1.3.9–18; 5.3.5.32–42; 5.9.10.14; 6.1.6.14, 10.13, 16.1; 6.2.7.20, 18.7–9, 22.25–29; 6.6.6.36–38; 6.7.3.32; 6.8.4.28, 7.49, 12.22–33, 20.11.

acts of intellection (νοήσεις): see **thinking**.

actuality (ἐνέργεια): see **activity**.

affections (πείσεις): see **state**.

alteration (ἀλλοίωσις): also, qualitative change. See **change**, **motion**. See 3.6.2.60; 4.4.32.45; 6.1.20.3–4; 6.3.21.47.

always (ἀεί): Having no temporal limitations. See **everlasting** (ἀΐδιον) and **eternity** (αἰών), **eternal** (αἰώνιον). See 3.7.1.1–6, 6.21–34.

appetite (ἐπιθυμία): A state of the lowest part of the embodied soul. Sometimes, Plotinus uses the more general term ὄρεξις (**desire**) as equivalent. The appetitive faculty (ἐπιθυμητικόν) is the psychical power owing to which appetites are produced. The verb τὸ επιθυμεῖν is often used synonymously with the general term 'desire' and is rendered 'desiring'. See 1.1.1.1; 1.8.8.3; 2.9.5.2; 3.1.5.14; 4.3.19.20; 4.4.20.26; 4.8.2.17; 6.1.21.13; 6.8.2.4–5; 6.9.11.16.

appetitive faculty (ἐπιθυμητικόν): see **appetite**.

apprehension (ἀντίληψις): A general term for cognition, whether by sense-perception or intellect. Plotinus sometimes uses the term κατάληψις synonymously, although the latter, owing to its Stoic provenance, tends to be used for cognition of sensibles. A term used more broadly than ἐπιβολή (**act of apprehension**). See 1.4.9.17; 2.9.5.22; 3.2.14.26; 4.3.23.8; 4.4.23.2–4; 5.1.12.12–13; 5.5.1.17; 6.4.1.26; 6.7.7.25–26.

appropriation (οἰκείωσις): also, affinity. A term of Peripatetic or Stoic origin, it refers to acts or practices that are conducive to the happiness of living beings of a certain nature. The appropriation or affinity is always owing to an innate **sameness** in the subject and object. See 3.5.13.8; 3.6.3.27, 17.3; 4.4.44.24; 6.7.27.18, 23.

archetype (ἀρχέτυπος): Something at a higher ontological level projected at a lower level. See 1.2.2.3; 2.4.15.22; 3.2.1.25; 3.5.1.33; 3.8.11.20; 4.3.13.3; 5.1.4.5; 5.3.6.17, 7.332, 13.31; 5.7.1.22; 5.8.3.1, 12.15, 19; 5.9.9.6; 6.2.22.35; 6.4.10.3–6; 6.7.15.9; 6.8.18.27; 6.9.11.45.

ascent (ἀναγωγή): Practices or acts that result in souls being closer to the One or the Good. See 1.3.1.5, 18; 3.1.4.18; 3.8.10.20; 4.9.4.2; 5.4.1.2; 5.5.4.1; 5.7.1.2; 6.8.6.27; 6.8.21.22.

assimilation (ὁμοίωσις): Following Plato, this is the process of making oneself the same (ὅμοιον) as god. See **sameness, likeness**. See 1.2.2.4–8, 3.5, 6.26, 7.28; 3.6.7.43; 4.3.10.45; 6.7.26.3.

audacity (τόλμα): The term used for the characteristic of souls that leads to their separation from the intelligible world and of Intellect that led to its separation from the One. The term is of neo-Pythagorean origin indicating the separation of the Indefinite Dyad from the One. See 1.2.5.27; 2.9.11.22; 5.1.1.4.

autonomous (αὐτεξούσιον): Used by Plotinus as a synonym for **up to us** (ἐφ' ἡμῖν) or that over which we are authoritative with respect to action. It has no implication that we legislate for ourselves. See 1.4.8.9; 3.2.10.19; 4.3.16.15; 4.8.5.26; 5.1.1.5; 6.8.3.10–21, 6.19, 7.17, 27, 42–44, 10.27, 20.34.

beauty, beautiful (κάλλον, καλόν): also, Beauty. The term refers generally to the attribute of attractiveness of being. Like all attributes of being, the term can be used in a sense of the One or Good. The moral connotation of the term is practically inseparable from the aesthetic. Hence, when the term is used, for example, for souls or virtues or practices, the temptation to translate it as 'noble' instead of 'beautiful' should be resisted. Plotinus uses one term for all. Plotinus's terms for 'nobility of birth' are εὐγένεια or γενναίοτης. See 1.3.1.22–31; 1.6 *passim*; 1.8.13.8; 2.3.9.25; 2.9.17.40; 3.5.1.21; 4.3.10.27; 5.5.1.40–42; 5.8 *passim*; 6.2.18.5; 6.3.11.21–28; 6.7.32.3; 6.8.6.18; 6.9.11.16.

Being, being (ὄν): Being and Beings (ὄντα) are the terms used generally for the entirety of the intelligible world apart from the One. But Being also refers to one of Plato's μέγιστα γένη (greatest genera). The term 'being' ('beings') is used most comprehensively for all that exists in the intelligible world and in the sensible world. When used for the latter, it refers to the result or product of generation or production or becoming.

belief (δόξα): also, opinion. A cognitive state derived generally from sense-perception and distinct from cognitive states that have only intelligibles as objects. Belief admits of falsity; higher forms of cognition do not. See 1.1.2.26, 9.5; 1.8.4.11; 3.6.2.54; 5.3.1.21, 9.29.

blending (κρᾶσις): see **mixture**. See 1.1.3.19; 1.6.1.52; 2.3.1.25, 5.6; 2.7.1.6, 11, 22; 2.9.5.19; 3.3.4.49; 4.7.8.31; 8^2.2, 3, 12, 8^4.8, 15; 6.2.2.22; 6.3.25.9.

body (σῶμα): A composite of form and matter. The forms of bodies are expressions of nature, the lowest part of the soul of the cosmos. See 1.1.1.3, 3.1–4; 2.1.2.4–24; 2.3.9.17–27; 2.4.12.14; 2.7 *passim*; 3.6.6–19; 4.3.2.12–20; 4.4.18, 20.4, 29.1–5; 4.7.1.8; 4.9.2.11–15; 5.1.2.26; 5.4.1.17–19; 5.9.5.46; 6.3 *passim*.

boundary (ὅρος): also, definition. A broad term regarding anything with spatial limits or having a specific, limited nature. See 2.4.15.7; 2.8.2.6; 6.3.11.14, 12.15; 6.7.17.18, 20.

breath (πνεῦμα): The Stoic term for the vehicle of divine reason, used in refutation of their position on the materiality of soul. See $4.7.4–8^3$.

calculative reasoning (λογισμός): also, calculation. The term is closely related to διάνοια (**discursive reasoning**) used generally for the application of intellect to embodied life. The faculty of calculative reasoning is τὸ λογιστικόν, τὸ λογιζόμενον. It is sometimes used synonymously with τὸ διανοητικόν ('the faculty of discursive thinking'). The verb λογίζεσθαι is rendered 'calculating'. See 1.2.1.19; 3.2.2.8; 4.3.18.1–13; 4.8.8.15; 5.1.3.113; 5.3.3.14; 5.8.4.36; 6.2.21.33–37; 6.4.6.17–18; 6.7.1.20–38, 20.21; 6.8.2.4–16; 6.9.5.9.

capacity (δύναμις): see **power**.

category (κατηγορία): also, **predicate**. The Peripatetic term for the fundamental divisions of sensible reality. Plotinus also uses it for the divisions of the intelligible world according to Platonic principles. Often, Plotinus speaks of a category generally when he is referring specifically to a predicate within that category. The verb κατηγορεῖσθαι is to predicate. See 6.1 *passim*; 6.3.14.20; 6.4.2.12; 6.6.13.30.

cause (αἰτία, αἴτιον): also, explanation. The term is used both for the four Peripatetic causes and for the Platonic paradigmatic cause. Generally, the translation 'cause' is used when referring to one of the three hypostases or agents and 'explanation' is used when Plotinus is referring to a discursive account. See 3.1.10.2; 4.4.32.1; 5.8.7.36–45; 6.2.6.18; 6.7.1.58, 2.27–43, 16.27; 6.8.14.21–28, 41; 6.9.6.54.

chance (τυχή): also, luck, fortune. Used broadly for that which occurs without the guidance of reason. Occasionally, **spontaneous** (αὐτόματον) is used synonymously. See 3.2.1.1; 5.9.4.6, 10.6; 6.8.7.34; 6.8.10.5–6, 14.10–16; 6.9.5.1.

change (μεταβολή): also, **transformation**. The Peripatetic generic term for either locomotion, alteration, quantitative, or qualitative occurrences, events, or processes. Plotinus uses it in his criticisms of Peripatetic accounts of nature. Plotinus holds that **alteration** (ἀλλοίωσις) is a species of motion, not of change and entertains the possibility that motion is the genus of which change is a species. See 2.1.1.5; 2.4.6.3; 3.2.15.28; 4.4.2.20; 4.7.9.15; 5.9.5.33; 6.1.16.35–36; 6.3.21.24–42; 6.5.3.10.

character (ἦθος): Generally, a settled moral (as opposed to intellectual) disposition resulting from habitual practices. See 1.3.6.23; 1.6.5.13; 2.3.7.9; 3.4.5.7, 11; 4.4.45.40; 6.4.15.19.

choice (προαίρεσις): The Peripatetic term used for deliberate desire or the culmination of a deliberative process. Plotinus uses it, roughly, in reference to the result of a deliberative process that is **up to us** (τὸ ἐφ' ἡμῖν). See 2.3.2.17; 3.4.5.3–4, 14; 4.3.12.23, 13.3; 4.4.3.5–7, 22–33, 37.18–25; 5.4.1.29; 6.8.17.3, 8.

circuit (περιφορά): The complete (circular) path of the body of the universe or the cosmos. See **revolution**. See 2.1.7.21, 8.16; 2.3.9.3; 3.2.3.30; 3.4.6.51; 3.7.8.10, 12.46–51; 4.3.7.20, 26.

cognizing (γιγνώσκειν): see **knowing**.

combination (σύστασις): also, structural integrity, constitution. See 1.8.8.4; 2.1.2.22, 6.55; 2.4.11.1, 12; 2.9.5.19, 7.25–27; 3.2.16.33, 51; 3.3.6.24; 4.7.3.33; 5.9.11.3; 6.2.2.10, 14.4; 6.3.25.10; 6.7.20.5.

complex (συναμφότερον): see **composite**. See 1.1.5.8, 7.2; 2.3.9.31; 2.5.2.11, 13; 3.6.9.36; 4.3.26.1; 4.7.3.10; 6.1.30.30; 6.3.7.14; 6.7.4.19, 5.2.

composite (σύνθετον, τὸ κοινόν): Often used to refer to form and matter together, but also used for the complex nature of anything other than the One, that is, anything whose existence and substantiality are distinct.

The term σύνθεσις refers to the act of producing a composite, here rendered 'compositing'. See 1.1.2.2; 12.10–11; 1.7.3.21; 2.3.9.21; 2.4.2.6; 2.4.8.13; 3.3.6.5, 7; 3.6.7.4; 4.7.2.2; 5.3.1.5; 5.6.3.19; 5.9.3.18; 6.1.13.11, 26.16; 6.2.4.26; 6.2.18.12; 6.3.4.4–7, 10.21–23; 6.9.2.31.

comprehension (σύνεσις): also, comprehensive grasp, understanding. Used generally for compositional cognition, that is, the mental seeing of parts as a whole. See 1.6.3.30; 3.2.5.19; 3.5.1.18; 4.3.26.46; 4.4.13.14–19; 5.3.2.25, 4.15; 5.8.11.23; 6.4.6.19; 6.7.31.33, 33.27; 6.9.4.2, 17.

conception (ἔννοια): Stoic term used by Plotinus for an intellectual state derived ultimately from sense-perception. Closely related to conceptualization, conceptual distinction (ἐπίνοια). See 1.8.3.12; 2.4.1.3, 11.39; 3.7.1.4, 5.19, 9.83; 5.8.1.4; 6.1.3.22; 6.5.1.2; 6.8.1.17; 6.9.5.3, 40.

concord (συμφωνία): also, harmony. See **sympathy**. Especially, the operational coordination of the parts of the embodied soul. More generally, the coordination of any cosmic parts. See 1.2.1.19; 3.4.5.24; 4.3.12.16, 19; 4.4.40.2; 5.1.9.25; 6.8.14.27.

confidence (πίστις): also, trust, conviction. A settled belief-state of an embodied soul. See 1.3.1.34; 2.1.1.18; 3.6.6.67; 3.8.6.14; 5.3.6.9; 5.5.1.11–12; 6.3.10.16; 6.5.8.2; 6.9.4.32.

conscious awareness (παρακολουθία, παρακολούθησις): Term used, usually in a form of the verb παραθκολουθεῖν, as a contrary to a state of non-consciousness or unconsciousness. More often, the term is used for self-awareness or self-consciousness. See **self-awareness**. See 1.4.5.2, 9.1, 10.23–29; 1.6.3.31; 2.9.1.43; 3.9.9.12–19; 4.3.26.45; 5.3.13.7.

contemplation (θεωρία): Primarily, the relation between the intellect and Forms or intelligible reality. See 1.1.7.14; 1.2.6.13; 1.8.13.15; 3.8 *passim*; 4.3.4.35; 4.4.41.1; 4.8.7.28; 5.3.5.18, 21; 5.5.3.22; 6.2.6.18; 6.7.39.26; 6.8.6.21.

contraries (ἀντικείμενα, ἐνάντια): also, opposites. The Peripatetic term for attributes in a category that cannot be simultaneously true of a subject. For ἀντικείμενα, see 4.5.8.34; 6.2.10.7–8, 12.25; 6.8.21.3, 6; for ἐνάντια, see 1.1.11.7; 1.8.6.35–58, 11.1; 2.3.4.3; 2.3.16.45; 3.2.16.45–58; 4.4.18.33; 5.1.1.7; 6.1.4.40; 6.3.12.3, 20.2–36, 23.30; 6.6.3.28; 6.6.14.26.

controlling principle (ἡγεμονικόν): Especially, a Stoic term for the authoritative or ruling principle or part of the soul. For Plotinus, roughly equivalent to the rational faculty of the soul (τὸ λογιστικόν). See 3.3.2.14; 6.1.28.5; 6.9.3.29.

corporeal (σωματικόν): Referring to attributes of a composite of form and matter. Indicating three-dimensionality and solidity. See 1.1.9.16; 2.2.1.17; 2.3.9.24; 2.9.17.4; 3.1.2.10; 3.6.5.36; 4.3.29.34; 4.4.21.8; 4.5.1.10; 4.7.3.17; 5.1.10.15; 6.1.19.8; 6.3.2.12; 6.9.5.2.

cosmos (κόσμος): The organized or structured portion of the universe. The term is sometimes used for the intelligible world (κόσμος νοητός) alone or for the 'microcosmic' intelligible world that is each individual rational soul. See **universe** (τὸ πᾶν) and **heaven** (οὐρανός). Also, order or arrangement. See 2.1.1, 7.2; 2.3.9.17; 2.4.4.8, 5.28; 2.9.4.16, 8.26, 12.5–38; 3.2.1.16; 3.2.2.2; 3.2.17.3; 3.4.3.22; 3.5.5.12; 3.7.2.3, 11.27; 4.3.2.59; 4.4.10.1; 4.8.1.42; 5.1.4.1; 5.3.16.12; 5.7.1.10; 5.8.9.1; 5.9.3.3; 6.1.27.35; 6.4.12.43; 6.5.9.17; 6.9.2.29.

craft (τέχνη): also, craftsmanship. The ability to apply **expressed principles** to practical affairs or to products. See 3.1.3.14; 3.2.11.10; 3.3.5.51; 3.8.5.7; 4.3.10.16; 4.4.331.3; 4.8.8.15; 5.8.1.8–23; 5.9.5.40, 11.1; 6.3.26.10.

create (δημιουργεῖν): A term used primarily for the Demiurge who imports order into the pre-cosmic disordered receptacle. See 2.4.7.25; 2.8.4.8; 2.9.18.16; 4.7.13.8; 5.8.7.31.

creator (ποιητής): see **production**. Used principally for the Demiurge in relation to the cosmos. See 1.1.12.31; 1.6.9.8; 2.3.18.13; 3.2.16.9; 3.2.17.19–45; 3.8.11.37; 5.8.3.8, 7.2; 5.9.3.26, 34, 5.20.

daemon (δαίμων): Semidivine living beings inferior to gods. See 2.3.9.46, 15.4; 3.4 *passim*; 3.5.1.1, 4.5, 25; 3.5.5.16, 6.15, 41, 56; 6.7.6.28.

deficiency (ἔλλειψις): also, lack. Indicating an attribute of anything in relation to its paradigmatic cause. See 1.8.4.9, 24, 5.1, 12, 22, 8.23; 3.2.5.26, 28; 3.5.9.46; 3.9.9.23.

Demiurge (δημιουργός): also, **creator** (ποιητής). Referring mainly to the principle of order in Plato's *Timaeus*. This is a divine intellect (νοῦς). Sometimes the term is used generically and is rendered 'craftsman'. See 2.3.18.15; 2.9.6.24, 8.2; 3.9.1.2; 4.4.9.9; 5.1.8.5.

desire (ἔφεσις, ὄρεξις): The cause generally of psychical motion. All desire is for the Good primarily, but secondarily for anything that appears to be an instance or image of it. For ἔφεσις, see 1.4.6.17; 1.5.2.7; 1.7.1.13; 2.3.11.8; 3.2.4.21; 3.5.1.12, 9.46; 3.6.7.13; 3.8.7.5; 3.9.9.4; 4.3.26.42; 4.4.18.36; 5.3.11.12; 5.5.12.11, 17; 5.6.5.9–10; 6.4.8.45; 6.7.21.3; 6.7.27.4, 26–27; 6.8.15.7; 6.9.11.24; for ὄρεξις, see 1.1.5.21–27; 1.8.1.10, 15.6–7, 21; 2.9.15.7; 3.5.1.17; 4.3.23.32; 4.4.28.72; 4.7.13.4; 5.3.6.39; 6.1.21.13; 6.2.19.9; 6.5.1.14; 6.8.2.12–33, 4.1.

destructible (φθαρτόν): A property of everything corporeal. See 2.1.2.23.

destruction (φθορά): also, perishing, passing away. The term usually paired with the contrary **generation** or 'coming to be' (γένεσις), describing everything corporeal or part of the sensible cosmos, excluding the cosmos itself. See 2.1.1.6; 2.3.16.37; 2.4.6.4, 9; 2.9.6.58; 3.2.4.4; 3.6.8.9; 4.3.8.51; 4.7.12.17; 5.9.5.34; 6.3.25.2; 6.7.20.5, 24.29.

Difference (ἑτερότης): also, difference. A fundamental principle in the intelligible world accounting for the distinctiveness of each nature cognized by Intellect. Difference is one of Plato's 'greatest genera'. The differences among things in the sensible world image intelligible differences. See **identity**. 2.4.5.28–32; 2.4.13.18; 3.6.15.7; 5.1.1.4, 4.35; 6.2.15.15, 21.21; 6.3.22.42–43; 6.4.11.17; 6.7.113.12; 6.9.6.42; 6.9.8.32.

discursive faculty (διανοητικόν): The faculty of discursive or non-intuitive thinking. This is the lowest part of intellect and the highest part of the embodied soul. Discursive reasoning (διάνοια) is the activity of the discursive faculty. See **calculative reasoning**, faculty of discursive reasoning (λογισμός, τὸ λογιστικόν). See 1.1.9.9; 5.3.2.23; 5.3.3.20; 5.3.4.14–15; 5.3.6.20.

disposition (διάθεσις): also, condition. An acquired attribute owing to which someone or something is inclined to perform actions of a particular type. See **habit**. See 1.2.3.19; 1.4.5.17; 1.8.12.4; 2.3.11.4; 3.1.9.7; 3.4.6.23; 3.7.11.2; 4.3.13.5; 4.3.33.6; 5.9.2.3; 6.1.4.41, 10.35; 6.6.6.38; 6.8.5.28, 17.9.

distinguishing property (ἰδιότης, ἴδιον): also, essential property, property. It is that which distinguishes a species within a genus or individuals within a species. The term has both Peripatetic and Stoic provenance. See 1.1.8.4–5; 2.4.4.4, 13.23–27; 2.6.1.24, 3.6, 12; 4.4.18.2; 5.1.4.42; 6.1.2.16; 6.3.5.24, 15.1, 6, 22; 6.7.33.7.

divisible (μεριστόν): also, divided. Generally applied to bodies that have parts outside of parts, but by extension applied to intelligible composites. Opposite **indivisible**, undivided (ἀμέριστον). See 2.4.4.12, 14; 4.2.1.37–43; 4.2.2.40; 4.3.19.1–32; 4.7.8.11; 4.9.3.11; 6.4.3.30, 4.27, 34, 8.14–19, 13.20; 6.9.2.21.

Dyad (δυάς): Usually referring to the Indefinite Dyad, the principle with the One from which Being is produced. The Indefinite Dyad is Intellect in the initial phase of its generation from the One. It is not two, but is the principle of duality. Also, a group of units with the cardinality of two. See 3.7.8.43; 5.1.5.7–14; 6.3.10.3, 13.20; 6.6.4.8, 5.4, 7, 14.19–22, 16.26.

element (στοιχεῖον): Peripatetic term for the first constituent in a sensible thing. Elements are what primarily undergo change. See 1.6.3.20; 2.1.1.5; 2.4.1.8, 11; 2.4.6.14; 2.6.1.3; 3.1.3.2; 3.6.8.8; 4.4.14.2, 31.14, 34, 47; 5.1.9.7; 5.9.3.20; 6.1.1.10; 6.2.3.22; 6.3.2.14; 6.3.3.11–20, 9.14; 6.6.5.43; 6.7.11.66.

equivocal (ὁμώνυμος): Characteristic of word with more than one referent having no more than a name in common. See **univocal**. See 1.2.3.26; 2.1.7.27; 3.6.12.19; 6.1.8.7, 19, 10.19, 12.48; 6.3.1.21, 3.26, 16.5, 22.18.

error (ἁμαρτία): also, **moral error**. Usually having a moral or normative connotation, indicating a failure to achieve a goal that one ought to achieve. See 1.1.12.24–25; 1.2.6.1–2; 2.3.16.40; 2.9.9.13; 3.2.10.7; 3.8.7.23; 4.3.16.4; 4.8.5.6, 16.

essence (τι ἔστιν, τὶ ἦν εἶναι): Peripatetic term. Used both for substances and, by extension, for things not in the category of substance. Occasionally used by Plotinus as equivalent to **Substantiality**. The essence of something is that without which it loses its identity. See 2.1.6.29; 2.5.1.4; 6.7.2.15, 3.21, 4.18, 26. Sometimes, τι ἔστιν is used more broadly for a generic identification. See 1.4.4.33; 4.2.1.4; 5.3.4.18; 6.1.2.5; 6.3.27.36; 6.5.2.24; 6.7.2.12; 6.8.1.27; 6.9.2.13.

eternity (αἰών): also, eternal (αἰώνιον). Characteristic of everything above **Soul**. What is eternal is outside of time. See **always** (ἀεί) and **everlasting** (ἀΐδιον). See 3.7.3.36–39.

everlasting (ἀΐδιον). Often used synonymously with **eternal** (αἰώνιον), but sometimes indicating no temporal beginning or end. See 3.7.3.1–5, 5.12–18.

evil (κακόν): Plotinus identifies matter with evil. By extension, evil is that which tends to matter via deformation or disintegration. Evil is the complete absence of Good. It possesses a nature only in a sense because it is completely unformed. The plural 'evils' (κακά) refers either to vices or to things that at least appear to be undesirable. See **vice**. See 1.6.6.22, 25; 1.7.3; 1.8 *passim*; 2.9.13.28; 3.2.5.26; 3.5.1.64; 4.8.7.16; 5.9.10.18; 6.6.3.4; 6.7.28.7–18; 6.8.4.21, 21.3; 6.9.11.37.

excellence (ἀρετή): Usually used with a moral connotation, referring generally to ideal human achievement. See 1.2 *passim*; 1.4.2.43; 1.5.2.5, 6.20, 10.21; 1.8.6.19; 2.3.9.17–19; 2.9.15.6–39; 3.4.2.28–29; 3.6.2; 6.2.18.16; 6.7.10.16; 6.8.5; 6.9.9.19, 11.48.

exist (ὑπάρχειν): Often, when appearing with the prefix ἐν-, with the sense of (permanently) belonging to or found in something, and always with the sense of being extra-mental or concretely real. The prefix προ- indicates logically or temporally prior existence. See 1.2.1.9–10; 1.4.3.24–33; 1.7.3.1; 2.1.2.28; 2.4.2.24; 3.1.4.25; 3.6.4.22; 3.7.4.20–21; 3.9.8.3; 4.3.6.29, 8.27–28; 4.4.25.3; 4.7.10.12; 5.1.4.30; 5.3.5.18; 5.5.2.13; 5.8.6.17; 6.1.3.18, 6.2, 25.22; 6.2.2.11, 11.15; 6.6.3.20, 11.9–11; 6.7.1.48, 3.16; 6.8.2.2.

exist, come to (ὑφίστημι): Often used in relation to ὑπόστασις (**existence, real**), the result of ὑφίστημι in the middle or passive. The term can indicate both temporal and atemporal existence. The verb is often used as a synonym for γίγνομαι (come to be or exist). See 3.7.13.36; 5.1.6.1; 5.5.5.13–14; 5.6.3.16; 5.9.5.13; 6.8.13.50; 6.6.2.14, 3.1–2, 6.18, 10.35, 13.27; 6.8.11.33, 13.40.

Existence, existence (τὸ εἶναι): also, existing. The reality of anything logically distinct from the nature that it has. Existence refers to the principle for existing things in the intelligible world; existence refers to things in the sensible world. **Existence** and **Substantiality** are the two components of the primary endowment of the Good or One. The term τὸ X εἶναι (**essence**) refers to the nature of that which exists. Nothing exists without having a nature. Being (τὸ ὄν) generally refers to the existing thing along with its nature. See 1.5.2.9; 1.6.7.11; 1.8.5.10; 2.1.5.21; 2.3.15.22; 2.4.15.27; 2.5.5.3; 2.9.16.32; 3.1.1.10–12; 3.2.3.36; 3.5.2.39; 3.7.3.35, 4.22–30; 4.3.2.27; 4.7.3.10, 5.27, 9.1; 5.1.4.28, 6.2; 5.3.7.17–18; 5.4.2.37; 5.5.5.13–14, 22–24, 11.10; 5.6.6.19; 5.8.9.38–41; 6.1.27.6; 6.2.5.20–21, 6.2, 7.36, 8.4–5; 6.3.6.11, 7.9–28; 6.4.1.10; 6.6.6.2, 8.15; 6.7.2.17, 41, 24.26; 6.8.4.28, 7.49, 11.6–7, 14.31–32, 15.27–29; 6.9.1.10.

existence, real (ὑπόστασις): also, hypostasis, real existent, extra-mental existence (existent), separate existent. The term is used of the three principles, **One**, **Intellect**, and **Soul** but it is also frequently used for items other than these. The term often connotes both τὸ εἶναι ('existence') and οὐσία ('substantiality') together, indicating a real existent or something that is extra-mental or separate and hence not a mere appearance. It also connotes the existence of something that is a ground or basis for the existence of something else. The term does not, however, necessarily connote something independent of a cause of its existence. See 1.4.9.19; 3.5.2.23–38; 3.5.7.9; 3.6.13.52; 4.5.6.5; 5.1.3.9, 15, 6.5, 33; 6.1.8.3; 5.3.16.36; 5.4.2.35; 5.5.1.15, 3.23; 5.6.3.11–17; 5.9.5.46; 6.1.6.3, 7.24–29, 8.3, 27.42; 6.2.4.17; 6.3.10.15; 6.4.9.25, 39; 6.6.5.17–24, 10.30, 12.1, 13.55; 6.7.2.37, 4.14, 40.19, 22; 6.8.7.26, 47, 10.12, 12.27, 14.18, 15.6, 28, 20.11.

experience affections (παθεῖν, πάσχειν): also, experiencing, undergoing. The term is used both in a general or neutral sense for the attributes or states of something and in a particular sense for emotional or appetitive states of a living being. See **state**.

expressed principle (λόγος): As a technical term, the product of a higher principle at a lower level. In non-technical contexts, λόγος is used for items within the full range of elements of rational communication. The technical sense provides the ontological foundation for the non-technical senses. See 2.3.17.1–7; 3.2.2.36–37; 3.3.4.9–13, 5.16–20; 3.8.2.20–23, 30–35, 3.1–3; 4.3.5.8–10, 9.48–51; 4.4.13.3–5; 5.1.3.8–10, 5.13–14, 6.45–46, 7.42; 6.4.11.16; 6.7.5.5–6, 12.41–42; 6.8.15.33. The term λόγος is also used in a quasi-technical sense for any intelligible structure or its representation. It is variously rendered as 'formula', 'ratio', 'account', etc.

faculty (δύναμις): see **power**.

fate (εἱμαρμένη): Term used mainly in criticism of Stoic doctrine which identifies the unified cause of all things with reason, god, or nature. The term μοῖρα is used synonymously with εἱμαρμενή, and is so translated. The Fates (Μοῖραι) are a trio of Homeric gods referred to in Platonic myth. Plotinus uses the literary term μοῖρα, which is derived from the Greek word for a portion or share, to indicate not the result of an external imposition, but the result of human action, foresight (προόρασις), **providence** (πρόνοια). See 1.9.1.15; 2.3.9.28; 3.1 *passim*; 3.3.5.15; 3.4.6.32, 60; 4.3.13.20, 22, 15.11.

form (εἶδος): also, Form, species, Species, kind. This term refers either to Platonic Forms or to their enmattered images or to Aristotle's principle of hylomorphic composites. When used with **genus**, the term is rendered 'species.' See 6.1.1–21; 6.3 *passim* on the form of hylomorphic composites. On Forms in the intelligible world, see 5.5.1–6; 5.9; 6.7 *passim*.

function (ἔργον): also, deed, task. A defining activity according to the essence of something. More broadly, the term refers to the result of the defining activity.

generation (γένεσις): Indicates the beginning of anything that exists in time, or the entire world of becoming. In the latter sense, it is contrasted with **Substance**. The term is also used by analogy to refer to production in the intelligible world.

genus, genera (γένος, γένη): According to Peripatetic usage, the 'logical' matter in combination with the differentia, the 'logical' form, comprises the species which is the 'logical' hylomorphic composite. Plotinus adopts and adapts this usage, while preserving its Platonic provenance when applied to the intelligible world, especially for the μέγιστα γένη (greatest genera). He maintains that the intelligible genus contains species, but not in the way that the Peripatetic genus contains species, i.e., only logically. On the greatest genera see 6.2 *passim*.

goal (τέλος): Both a Platonic and Peripatetic term for the intended outcome of any action. The real goal of everything other than the Good is to achieve the Good insofar as possible even if this does not appear to the agent.

god (θεός): The term used for principles in the intelligible world, often virtually as an honorific adjective equivalent to 'divine' (θεῖος). The term is seldom used as a proper noun, even for the One.

Good (τὸ ἀγαθόν): The first principle of all, alternatively designated as the Idea of the Good and the **One**. See 5.5.6–13; 5.6.3–6; 6.7; 6.9 *passim*.

Good-like (ἀγαθοειδές): The property that an intelligible entity has as an image of the Good. See 1.2.4.12; 1.7.1.16, 2.7; 3.8.11.16, 18; 5.3.3.10, 16.18–19; 5.6.4.5, 5.13; 6.2.17.28; 6.7.15.9–24, 16.5, 18.1, 7, 14, 25, 21.3–8, 22.33; 6.8.15.19.

grasp (λαμβάνειν, often with prefixes κατα, μετα, προς, ὑπο): Generally, cognition of something real, whether intelligible or sensible.

growth, faculty of (φυτικόν): Includes faculties of nourishment (θρεπτικόν), increase in size (αὐξητικόν), and reproduction (γεννητικόν). Applies to both plants and animals. Alternatively, we find φυτικὴ ψυχή, θρεπτικὴ ψυχή ('growth soul', 'nutritive soul'), etc. See 1.4.9.27; 3.4.2.23, 4.38; 4.3.19.19; 4.4.22.3, 27.12, 28.11, 16, 59, 65; 4.7.8^5.25; 4.9.3.21.

habit (ἕξις): also, condition, disposition, settled state. See **disposition**.

happiness (εὐδαιμονία): The ideal human condition, identification with the intellect, i.e., the true person. See 1.4 *passim*.

harmony (ἁρμονία): also, attunement. The mutual suitability and cooperation of the parts either of a body or, by extension, of an intelligible entity. See 1.3.1.332; 1.4.10.18; 1.6.3.28; 2.3.13.46; 2.9.16.40; 3.2.2.29–33, 16.37–44, 17.44, 69–72; 3.6.2.5; 4.2.3.1; 4.4.8.57; 4.7.8^4.2–28; 5.9.10–11; 6.6.16.43–44; 6.7.6.3–5.

heaven (οὐρανός): The 'vault' of the planetary orb, containing the stars and planets and their spheres. Sometimes used as roughly synonymous with **cosmos, universe**. See 1.8.6.4; 2.1.1.12, 2.2, 15, 18, 5.14–19, 7.46; 2.9.5.10, 18.38; 3.2.3.28–34, 8.6; 3.5.2.15; 3.7.13.27–30; 4.3.7.4–5, 15.1, 17.1–3; 4.4.5.12, 8.55–57, 22.40; 4.5.8.1; 4.7.12.6; 5.1.2.17–39; 5.8.3.32; 6.7.12.4–19, 16.3.

human being (ἄνθρωπος): also, person. The composite of body and soul, distinct from the true self which can exist apart from the body, identified either with soul generally or with the highest part of soul, namely, intellect.

Idea (= Form) (ἰδέα): The term alternatively used for intelligible paradigms of reality.

identical (ταὐτόν): Always indicating oneness or unity as distinct from **same** (ὅμοιον), which always indicates two or more entities. Only the One is unqualifiedly self-identical. Therefore, the qualified or relational identity of two or more things entails their non-identity or difference. In this sense, identity and sameness are extensionally equivalent. See 1.1.2.5; 1.2.2.5; 1.4.4.15; 4.2.1.53, 2.41–42; 4.3.5.13; 4.9.1.8, 2.7; 5.3.5.5; 6.1.7.11, 8.22; 6.2.7.33–45; 6.4.1.23–25; 6.7.13.5–6.

Identity (ταυτότης): One of Plato's five 'greatest genera' and the principle of oneness. See **Difference**. See 1.2.5.2; 2.4.13.20; 3.7.2.15; 4.4.15.8;

5.1.4.34–35; 5.3.10.25–27; 6.1.6.19; 6.2.8.37, 15.15, 21.20; 6.7.39.6; 6.9.8.28.

image (εἰκών, εἴδωλον): see **imitation**.

imagination (φαντασία): The activity of the **imaginative representation, faculty of**. The result of this activity is a **semblance** (φάντασμα). In the plural, φαντασίαι, are imaginative representations. For φαντασία, see 1.1.9.8; 1.2.5.20; 1.4.10.19–20; 1.8.15.18; 2.4.11.38; 2.9.11.22; 3.1.7.14; 3.6.4.19–21; 4.3.23.33, 29.27, 30.3, 31.5; 4.4.3.7, 4.6, 8.3, 13.14, 17.12, 20.17, 28.41, 48; 5.1.10.26; 5.3.3.6; 6.8.2.8, 3.8–16; for φάντασμα, see 2.4.10.9, 11.27–29; 3.5.7.8; 3.6.5.3, 7.13; 4.3.29.23, 31.11; 5.3.2.8, 11.7; 6.2.22.39; 6.6.17.10.

imaginative representation, faculty of (φανταστικόν): see **imagination**. See 4.3.23.32, 30.2, 7, 10.

imitation (μίμημα): One of a family of terms indicating the relation between the lower and the higher, usually sensible in relation to intelligible, but also Soul in relation to Intellect and Intellect in relation to the One. Other related terms are **image** (εἰκών) and **likeness** (ὁμοίωμα) and **reflection** (ἴνδαλμα, εἴδωλον). For μίμημα, see 1.2.2.3, 3.27–28; 2.4.4.8; 2.9.8.28, 16.46; 3.6.7.28, 11.3, 13.26, 17.3; 3.8.7.7; 4.3.10.18; 4.4.13.22; 5.3.16.40–41; 5.4.2.25; 6.8.12.16; 5.9.3.37; 6.2.15.35, 22.38, 41; 6.4.2.2; 6.7.6.11, 28; 6.9.11.27; for εἰκών, see 1.2.7.28; 1.5.7.15; 1.8.3.8; 2.3.18.17; 2.9.4.26; 3.5.1.35; 3.6.5.5; 3.8.11.30; 4.4.10.12; 5.1.3.7; 5.3.4.21; 5.8.12.19; 6.2.22.43; 6.3.1.21, 15.32; 6.4.10.3; 6.7.35.17; 6.9.11.44.

immaterial (ἄυλον): That which is separate from matter in contrast to that which is enmattered (ἔνυλον). For ἄυλον, see 2.5.3.18; 3.6.2.52, 56, 16.27; 4.7.4.19; 5.1.10.20; 6.4.8.2; 6.5.11.33, 35; 6.8.6.26; for ἔνυλον, see 2.3.17.8; 6.5.8.26, 11.32, 34.

impression (τύπος, ἀντίτυπος): The intelligible residue of a higher principle in a lower, or of a sensible composite in the embodied intellect. An archetype (ἀρχέτυπος) is the higher principle in relation to the lower expression or representation of it. Even the One is sometimes referred to as an archetype. See 1.2.4.19–24; 1.5.6.4; 2.3.17.5, 16; 2.4.10.23; 2.9.6.4; 3.6.3.29; 4.3.26–29; 4.5.1.24, 3.30; 4.6 *passim*; 4.7.6.43; 5.3.2.10–12; 5.3.5.19, 23; 5.5.1.24, 2.1; 5.8.4.5; 5.9.2.27; 6.6.12.12; 6.7.15.9, 16.5, 29.12; 6.8.7.16; 6.9.3.5–6, 7.9–13.

impulse (ὁρμή): Stoic term for the source of psychical motion. In the passive, rendered **impelled**. Roughly synonymous with **desire**, although impulses, unlike desires, can be found in non-living things. See 2.3.13.12; 3.1.1.28, 4.15, 7.16, 23, 9.10; 3.3.1.9; 3.4.6.55; 3.5.2.6; 4.3.12.2, 23.13, 32; 4.4.7.7, 28.63, 32.42, 44.5; 4.5.2.43; 5.3.12.38; 6.2.8.22; 6.5.2.6; 6.8.2.3.

in charge of (κύριος): also, to be authoritative over, in control of. Used in reference to both moral agency and political rule.

in fact (ἤ): Literally 'or'. Gloss: 'or is it not the case that?' Very frequently used by Plotinus to indicate the start of the expression of Plotinus's own position after a dialectical discussion.

indestructible (ἄφθαρτον): Can be used of bodies, souls, and intelligible principles to indicate a nature incapable of decomposition. See 2.1.2.21, 23; 3.6.1.29; 4.7.12.20; 6.4.10.23.

individual (καθέκαστον): also, particular. Used generally of members of a species but in particular for human beings or human souls. See 3.2.9.12; 3.9.2.2; 4.3.8.25, 13.23; 4.4.32.15; 4.8.2.28; 5.6.6.24; 5.7 *passim*; 5.9.12.4–5; 6.2.2.24, 20.11–13, 28; 6.3.9.20, 38; 6.4.16.34; 6.5.1.10–11; 6.8.1.40, 18.37.

indivisible (ἀμεριστόν): See **divisible**.

Intellect (νοῦς): also, intellect. (Pl. νόες, νοοῖ). Intellect is the second hypostasis; intellect is the true identity of rational living beings. Our intellects are undescended and engage in the same activity that Intellect does. The mode of cognition of Intellect and all intellects is non-discursive.

intellection (νόησις): see **thinking**.

intellectual (νοερός): Used of the activity of intellect and also of that which participates in Intellect insofar as it participates.

intelligible (νοητόν): see **thinking**.

intelligible world (ἐκεῖ): Literally 'there', used generally for the realm of Soul, Intellect, and the One, and for other components of intelligible reality. The phrase νοητὸς τόπος (literally 'intelligible place') is also rendered 'intelligible world'.

interval (διάστημα): The space between bodies. See 2.4.11.18; 2.7.2.12; 2.8.1.50; 3.6.19.39–40; 3.7.7.25, 8.17–68; 4.2.1.19; 4.3.20.24, 26; 4.4.7.12; 4.5.4.17–21; 5.1.2.31; 6.3.11.3; 6.4.1.9, 2.8, 16.20; 6.5.4.22; 6.5.5.7; 6.7.39.3.

intrinsic (σύμφυτον): Belonging to the nature of a thing. See 1.2.1.36, 38; 2.6.3.15; 2.9.15.16; 3.6.11.21; 3.7.4.23; 3.8.2.2; 4.7.2.8; 5.4.2.32; 5.5.12.11; 6.7.1.16.

involuntary (ἀκούσιον, ἀπροαίρετον): All desire is for the Good. Hence, what is involuntary is a choice or an action based on a desire for the apparent, not the real, Good. For ἀκούσιον, see 3.2.10.7; 4.3.23.15; 4.8.5.8; 6.8.1.41, 42, 4.15; for ἀπροαίρετον, see 1.2.5.14–19, 6.3; 1.4.15.17; 4.4.35.43.

judgment (κρίσις): also, discernment. Sometimes with prefix δια. The result of a process of **calculative reasoning**. See 1.1.1.10, 9.9, 18; 1.3.4.13;

1.6.3.4; 3.4.6.13; 3.6.1.5, 7; 4.3.3.22, 26.8; 4.4.22.31; 6.1.6.22; 6.4.6.14; 6.7.19.2.

knowing (γιγνώσκειν): also, **cognizing**. The widest term for cognition above the level of sense-perception and imagination. Knowing can indicate acquaintance, recognition, awareness, as well as propositional knowledge.

knowledge (γνῶσις): The generic term. Also, cognition, cognizance. See **knowing**.

licit (θέμις): Term drawn from Greek religion, usually indicating behavior that is within an acceptable range of moral norms. See 2.9.2.29, 9.66, 17.16; 3.6.13.33; 4.7.11.14; 5.5.11.13; 6.7.15.15; 6.9.9.56.

life (ζωή): also, Life. The principle of self-motion in any **living being** (ζῷον). Plotinus uses the latter term broadly to include plants but more often refers only to animals. The principle of Life in the intelligible world is coordinate with the principles of Being or Existence and Intellect. Intellect is both said to have a life and to be Life itself. The term βίος (way of life) usually indicates a range of activities or specifically human activities that characterize someone over a lifetime.

likeness (ὁμοίωμα, ὁμοίωσις): see **assimilation, sameness, imitation**. The sameness of two things when one is ontologically dependent on the other. See 1.2.2.4–10, 7.28; 6.9.11.43.

living being (ζῷον): also, animal, Living Being. Generally, anything with a soul, including plants; often used for animals exclusively. The Living Being is the entirety of intelligible reality plus the Intellect or Demiurge. The universal or complete **living being** is equivalent to the **cosmos**.

longing (πόθος): Generally an impulse for the Good. See 1.6.4.16; 3.5.2.40–41; 4.3.1.12, 21.21; 5.3.10.48; 5.5.4.7, 12.6; 6.7.34.1.

magnitude (μέγεθος): Geometrical term indicating the length, breadth, and depth of bodies (σώματα), usually contrasted with number (ἀριθμός) or multiplicity (πλῆθος) which pertains to that which is numerable.

mass (ὄγκος): A property of things with **magnitude**.

matter (ὕλη): A Peripatetic and Stoic term used by Plotinus both in his criticisms of these schools and to indicate total privation or non-being, that which is equivalent to evil.

memory (μνήμη): The presence in the soul of images or representations either of previous embodied experiences or of the life of the undescended intellect. See **recollection**. See 4.3.25–4.4.12 *passim*.

mixture (μίξις, μίγμα): Used mainly in criticism of Peripatetic and Stoic theories of the composition of sensibles. See **blending** (κρᾶσις). For μίξις, see 2.1.7.17; 2.3.9.43; 2.7.2.39; 3.5.1.28, 38, 56; 6.3.10.3, 25.9; for μίγμα, see 1.1.1.4–5; 1.6.5.35; 2.4.7.3–8; 2.7.1.40; 2.9.5.20; 3.2.7.6, 16; 3.5.7.21; 4.3.19–23; 4.4.17.19, 22; 6.3.1.22; 6.3.8.26; 6.7.30.33–34.

moral error (ἁμαρτία): see **error**.

motion (κίνησις): also, Motion, one of Plato's five 'greatest genera'. A broad term used both for bodies and for psychical and intellectual activities, an alternative to ἐνέργεια (= κίνησις νοῦ).

multiplicity (πλῆθος): The general term for the opposite of unity, therefore applying to everything except the One. The term refers to anything complex, not just quantitatively. Primarily, it refers to that which is numerable as opposed to magnitude (μέγεθος), which is measurable.

nature (φύσις): The lowest part of the soul of the cosmos. Also, synonymous with form, essence, or intelligible structure. Nature is variously present in plants, animals, and human beings. Nature is prior to the sensible composite and determinative of it.

necessity (ἀνάγκη): Used for both physical and logical necessity.

non-being (μὴ ὄν): That which is without being or Being, primarily matter but including also everything that has a principle of difference in it.

nutritive faculty (θρεπτικόν): see **growth, faculty of**. See 3.6.4.32; 4.9.3.23, 25.

One (τὸ ἕν): also, one, unity. The first principle of all and a property of everything that exists in any way. Generally, the contrast between ἕν and πολλά is translated as 'one-many' and the contrast between (τὸ) ἕν and ὄν is translated as unity-being. Plotinus distinguishes between the One, the first principle of all, and unity as a hierarchically gradable property of both intelligibles and sensibles, using the same term τὸ ἕν for both.

order (τάξις): also, ordered parts, system, arrangement, rank. Sometimes with prefixes δια, συν. Refers generally to the intelligible arrangements of parts of a paradigm or paradigms and all that exists in imitation or likeness of them. Disorder (ἀταξία) is intrinsically unintelligible. Sometimes, κόσμος (**cosmos**), which usually refers to the entire world order, is used for some portion of that and so synonymously with τάξις.

partake of (μετέχειν): Platonic term used to indicate the relation of an instance of an intelligible to the intelligible itself. Synonymous with participate in (μεταλαμβάνειν). See 1.7.2.3–5; 1.8.4.1; 2.1.6.46; 2.4.7.7, 13.8–9, 15.9; 2.9.17.21; 3.6.13.33, 14.22; 3.8.9.24; 4.4.32.9; 4.5.8.21; 4.9.2.26; 5.3.15.22, 19.9; 5.5.4.29–30; 6.1.26.33; 6.2.12.5; 6.7.23.20; 6.8.14.3; 6.9.1.38.

passible (παθητικόν): also, passive, subject to affection. See **state** and **experience**.

perceiving (αἰσθάνεσθαι): see **sense-perception**.

persist (μένειν): also, be stable. Refers to the state of a higher principle which, although having an activity outside of itself, remains unchanged.

place (τόπος): also, region. Narrowly, the innermost boundary of a containing body. More broadly, a largely undefined section of the universe.

potency (δύναμις): see **power**.

power (δύναμις): also, potency, capacity, potentiality, faculty, virtuality. The term has both Platonic and Peripatetic provenance. When used according to the former, it indicates a principle in relation to whatever it is a principle of; when used according to the latter, it indicates a contrast with ἐνέργεια (**actuality**). It is also used technically for any distinct part of the soul as the source of a particular function. 'Power' and 'capacity' are used to render what for Aristotle would be an active potency. Virtuality indicates the fact that the higher principle is, or has the lower expression of it, but at a higher level of unity. If A is virtually B, then B is or has an expressed principle (λόγος) of A.

predicate (κατηγορία): see **category**. The result of the act of predication within a category. The verb κατηγορεῖσθαι is rendered 'to predicate'.

principal (κύριος): also, authoritative, proper, in charge, dominant. Generally, refers to that which in a system determines its direction or structure.

principle (ἀρχή): also, starting point. Used mainly in metaphysical contexts for that which is the *explanans* of any phenomenon. By extension, used for the axioms or definitions deployed in an argument that provides an explanation.

privation (στέρησις): Peripatetic term, along with form (εἶδος) and the substrate (ὑποκείμενον) indicating the principles of change. Plotinus argues for the equivalence of privation and underlying principle understood as matter. See 1.8.1.17, 19, 4.23, 5.24, 11.1–15, 12.1–2; 2.4.13.10–23, 14.1–21, 16.4–6; 3.6.9.24; 6.1.10.42; 6.6.14.5; 6.7.27.37.

procession (πρόοδος): The derivation of an order from its principle. See 4.8.5.33, 6.5; 5.5.3.9; 6.3.22.7, 47.

produce (ποιεῖν): also, cause, make. To be the efficient cause of something.

production (ποίημα): also, creation. Used both for ordinary efficient causality and especially for the operation of the Demiurge, where creation is the imposition or form on the utterly formless. See 2.3.16.32; 3.2.7.43, 9.29, 12.9, 17.32, 43, 50; 4.4.15, 17, 35.6; 5.8.2.17.

proper (οἰκεῖον): That which belongs to something's nature or is appropriate for it. See **produce**.

providence (πρόνοια): also, foresight. The direction of the lower sensible world by the higher intelligible world. Especially, a Stoic term for the rational, causal order of nature. See 2.2.1.25–26; 2.9.15.8, 11, 16.15, 28, 31; 3.2, 3.3 *passim*; 4.4.26.19; 4.8.2.25; 6.1.22.23–24; 6.7.1.19, 28, 26.11, 39.27; 6.8.17.4, 7, 10.

rational (λογικόν): Used for the differentia of the human soul and also for the faculty of discursive reasoning.

reason (λόγος): also, statement, argumentative procedure, argument, theory, rational discourse, account, definition, etc. A general term for any unit of intelligible communication. See **expressed principle** for the technical meaning of λόγος.

recognition (γνῶσις): see **knowledge**.

recollection (ἀνάμνησις): Generally used as synonymous with **memory** (μνήμη), but always with the connotation of the originative experience being in the intelligible world. For this reason, time is not attached to recollection, as it normally is to memory. See 1.8.15.28; 2.9.12.7, 16.47; 3.5.1.34; 3.7.1.23; 4.3.25.32, 37; 5.5.12.13.

reflection (εἴδωλον, ἔμφασις, ἰνδάλμα): An imperfect representation of a higher principle on a lower level. For εἴδωλον, see 1.1.7.12, 12.24–32; 1.4.10–11; 1.8.3.37; 2.4.5.18–19, 15.22–26; 2.9.1.62, 10.26–27; 3.3.7.12; 3.6.7.13–28; 3.7.11.53; 3.9.3.11–15; 4.2.10.39; 4.3.29.3; 4.5.7.44; 4.9.4.18; 5.1.6.46, 7.40; 5.3.8.9; 5.5.2.7; 5.9.5.18; 6.1.10.58; 6.3.15.30; 6.4.16.40–44; 6.6.2.13, 9.35; 6.7.5.14; 6.8.18.35–36; for ἔμφασις, see 4.3.18.12; for ἰνδάλμα, see 1.4.3.35; 1.8.4.30; 2.1.5.7; 2.3.18.12; 2.5.4.17; 3.8.5.7; 4.4.13.3, 19.3–4, 29.53; 5.3.8.47; 5.9.5.42, 6.19; 6.2.22.33, 43; 6.4.9.37, 40, 10.12; 6.7.40.19; 6.7.18.27.

relation (σχέσις): also, spatial relation, status, position. Sometimes used synonymously with ὁ πρός τι. Used especially in criticism of Peripatetic and Stoic categories. See 2.4.14.24; 3.1.5.11, 34, 39, 44, 50, 58, 6.15, 7.5; 4.4.26.2, 29.23, 33.4, 34.22; 4.7.4.18; 6.1.6.3, 21, 7.2–31, 8.6–19, 9.2, 26, 14.10, 15.15, 17.5, 11, 18.16–17; 6.2.16.2; 6.3.21.16–17, 28.5–6; 6.6.14.24–31.

reversion (ἐπιστροφή): Literally 'turning toward'. The process or result of the reconnecting of the lower with the higher. See 1.2.4.18; 2.2.3.9; 4.3.4.25; 4.8.4.2, 7.26; 5.1.7.5; 5.3.6.40; 5.8.11.9.

revolution (φορά): Used generally for the motion of the heavenly bodies (heaven) and of the universe itself. See **circuit** (περιφορά). See 2.1.8.18; 2.3.1.1, 9.25; 2.9.4.30; 3.1.2.11, 3.3, 5.2, 15, 6.4.

same (ὅμοιον): see **identical** (ταὐτόν). See 1.1.2.6; 5.3.5.4; 5.6.3.8.

sameness (ὁμοιότης): also, Sameness. For Plotinus, the use of the term implies that there is something (self-) identical (ταὐτόν) 'over and above' the things that are the 'same'. See 1.1.9.23; 1.6.2.11–12; 3.1.5.3; 6.1.9.13; 6.3.15, 28.11. See **likeness** (ὁμοίωμα) referring to the sameness in something in relation to its model or paradigm. Sometimes, Plotinus speaks of the sameness or likeness of two things indifferently. See **assimilation**.

science (ἐπιστήμη): see **scientific understanding**.

scientific understanding (ἐπιστήμη): also, **science**. The non-intuitive cognition of necessary, eternal truths or the formal expression of these. In the latter case, the term is rendered 'science.' See 1.2.7.3; 1.3.4.8; 1.8.1.13; 3.9.2.1; 4.3.2.23, 50–54; 4.8.7.16; 4.9.5.7; 5.3.1.19; 5.4.1.9, 2.48; 5.5.13.14; 5.8.4.40, 51; 5.9.5.30, 8.5, 13.9; 6.1.1.9; 6.2.17.2, 18.8, 20.3–4, 16; 6.3.4.11; 6.4.11.23–24; 6.5.7.4; 6.6.6.20–29, 15.19–20; 6.7.1.25; 6.8.3.5; 6.9.4.1–9.

self-awareness (συναίσθησις): The activity of cognizing one's own cognitive or affective states. The prefix συν indicates a level of cognition over and above that found in αἴσθησις (sense-perception), which implies a certain passivity and an external object. See 1.1.9.20, 11.11; 3.4.4.10; 3.8.4.19–20; 4.3.26.45; 4.4.2.31, 8.20, 24.21, 45.8, 34; 4.5.5.29; 5.1.7.12; 5.3.2.4, 13.13, 21; 5.4.2.18; 5.6.5.3–4; 5.8.11.23; 6.4.9.36; 6.7.16.19, 41.27.

self-control (σωφροσύνη): One of the classical virtues, variously defined according to whether the soul is considered with or without the body. See 1.2.1.18, 7.4; 1.6.1.46, 4.11, 5.13, 6.1, 7, 9.14; 2.9.14.12; 5.9.113.8; 6.2.18.15; 6.7.31.14, 33.6.

self-evident (ἐναργής): What is cognized without inference.

self-transcendence (ἔκστασις): also, inclination toward, displacement. Indicates generally the ascent from a lower to a higher principle. See 1.1.5.23; 5.3.7.14; 6.3.2.20; 6.9.11.23.

semblance (φάντασμα): see **imagination**.

seminal principles (σπερματικοὶ λόγοι): Stoic term for the internal principles of growth and order in the cosmos.

Sensation(αἴσθησις): see **sense-perception**.

sense-datum (αἴσθημα): see **sense-perception**.

sense-perception (αἴσθησις): also, perception, sensation. The process or activity of using one or more of the five senses. Sometimes used of immediate cognition that is not of sensibles. When rendered 'sensation,' the term refers to the corporeal aspect of the cognitive process. **Sensibles** (αἰσθητά) are the actual or potential direct objects of sense-perception. A **sense-datum** (αἴσθημα) is the internal result of an act of sense-perception. **Perceiving** (αἰσθάνεσθαι) is the act of using one or more of the five senses. The faculty of sense-perception (αἰσθητικόν) is that power of which sense-perception is the actualization. When rendered 'perception', the term indicates some sort of awareness broader than that found in the five senses. For αἴσθημα, see 4.2.2.20; 4.3.25.44, 29.33; 4.7.6.11, 20, 31; for αἰσθητικόν, see 2.9.1.13; 3.4.4.13; 4.3.19.11, 22.17, 23, 31, 29.2–7, 26; 4.9.3.26; 5.3.2.3; 6.7.3.22–30, 6.1, 18, 28, 8.1.

sensibles (αἰσθητά): see **sense-perception**.

signification (σημασία): Used generally for the theory that the heavenly bodies and their positions and motions bear meaning or indications of terrestrial events. See 2.3.7.7, 10.1; 4.4.34.16, 23, 26, 39.17.

sort of (οἷον): also, in a way, as it were, in a manner of speaking. A quasi-technical term for the analogous application of a term, usually derived from the sensible world in application to the intelligible world.

Soul (ψυχή): also, soul. The third hypostasis. Also, soul is the principle of motion in any living being.

species (εἶδος): see **form**.

spiritedness, faculty of (θυμοειδές): The part of the soul that is the source of emotions or passions. See **spiritedness**. See 3.6.2.27, 55, 4.4; 4.4.28.64–65, 41.10.

spiritedness (θυμός): also, passion, anger. See 1.1.5.22; 1.9.1.10; 2.3.11.5; 4.3.19.21, 28.13; 4.4.17.15, 28.9, 32.29, 35.29; 6.9.11.10.

spontaneous (αὐτόματον): see **chance**.

stability (στάσις): also, Stability, positioning, standstill, rest. One of Plato's five 'greatest genera'. This term refers to the contrary of motion in the sensible world and also the eternal state of non-sensible Being without the implication of inactivity. The related verb ἵστημι is sometimes rendered 'to be stable' or 'come to a standstill' or 'be at rest', indicating a prior motion.

star (ἄστρον): Fixed planet, constellation.

state (πάθος): also, experience, affection, feeling, emotion. A broad term used sometimes as equivalent to property or attribute; more often, used for a non-intellectual property of a living being. Also, πάθημα. Sometimes, Plotinus uses these terms interchangeably and sometimes he follows Stoic usage and reserves πάθος for states of the soul and πάθημα for certain non-psychical, that is, bodily properties. For πάθος, see 1.1.5.18; 1.4.2.3–4; 2.4.10.21; 2.8.1.34; 2.9.2.10; 3.3.5.40; 3.5.1.1–8; 3.6.3.19, 4.35, 5.5, 10.2; 3.8.4.11; 4.3.9.10; 4.4.7.3, 42.21; 4.6.3.69; 4.7.11.14–15, 12.19; 5.8.11.34; 5.9.10.19; 6.2.15.12; 6.3.16.40, 44, 19.18–21; 6.4.1.20, 8.18; 6.7.26.17, 33.23; for πάθημα, see 1.1.3.4–7, 5.27; 2.3.9.10, 16.29; 3.1.3.24;

3.3.5.7; 3.5.1.65; 3.6.6.53, 12.13; 4.2.1.53, 76, 2.28; 4.3.26.56; 4.5.3.37; 4.7.3.12–13; 4.9.4.22; 5.3.2.6; 6.1.5.11, 27.41; 6.3.1.29; 6.6.12.2–18; 6.8.3.12, 6.11; 6.9.4.19.

stillness (ἡσυχία): The condition of Intellect and intellects in contemplation of intelligible reality. A term with a strong positive connotation. See 1.2.5.30; 1.3.4.16–17; 2.9.1.27, 6.19; 3.6.1.23; 3.7.11.6, 14, 12.11; 3.8.6.12; 3.9.1.17; 5.3.6.15, 7.13–16; 5.9.8.8; 6.3.2.27, 22.29; 6.3.23.4; 6.8.5.17–18.

structured ordering (σύνταξις): An order or arrangement implying purpose or intention. See **order**.

Substance (οὐσία): also, substance, Substantiality, substantiality. Term with both Platonic and Peripatetic provenance. When used Platonically, Substance refers to Intellect or to any distinct **Being** in the intelligible world; Substantiality refers to the essence of Intellect or of any distinct Being. **Intelligibles**, that is, Platonic Forms, are variously referred to as Substances or the Substantiality of Intellect. When used Peripatetically, the term 'substance' refers to an individual 'this something'; 'substantiality' refers to the essence of a substance, that is, its core reality or being. For Plotinus, true ontological primacy is found in Substance and Substantiality, not in substance and substantiality. Nevertheless, Plotinus follows Aristotle in making a distinction between Substance and Substantiality in the intelligible world which reflects Aristotle's distinction between substance and substantiality in the sensible world. The adjective **substantial**, **Substantial** usually indicates an implicit contrast. Thus, Substantial Numbers (οὐσιώδεις ἀριθμοί) are contrasted with quantitative (i.e., non-substantial) numbers.

substrate (ὑποκείμενον): also, underlying nature. A Peripatetic term indicating the putative subject of change or a principle of composition in relation to form. See 1.4.3.14; 1.8.10.9; 2.4.1.1, 4.7, 5.19–22; 6.2, 12.15, 13.1–6, 14.16; 2.5.1.30; 2.8.1.38; 3.3.4.31–323; 3.6.6.30; 9.13; 10.8, 12.8, 16.5; 3.7.3.9, 24; 5.17; 4.4.23.17; 4.7.4.19; 5.6.3.2; 5.8.4.18; 5.9.2.14; 6.1.3.13, 5.11, 25.23, 33, 27.7–37; 6.2.4.4; 6.3.4.26; 6.4.13.13; 6.6.13.59; 6.7.30.11, 40.7; 6.8.18.51.

susceptibility (ἀσθένεια): also, weakness, both physical and moral. See 1.4.8.13, 17, 15.10; 1.8.14.1–49; 2.1.8.25; 2.3.13.41; 3.8.4.33–41; 4.6.3.46; 4.9.5.26; 6.4.15.20.

sympathy (συμπάθεια): The capacity of the parts of an organic whole, including the cosmos, for mutual affectivity indicating an affinity owing to sameness of origin or structure. The capacity is based on the shared possession of one or more **expressed principles**. See **concord**. See 3.1.5.8; 4.3.8.2; 4.4.40.1; 4.5.1.35, 2.15, 17, 3.17.

thinking (νοεῖν): The general term for cognition apart from sense-perception. There are a number of other closely related terms. The term νόησις is sometimes used as equivalent to νοεῖν, but more often indicates the highest type of thinking, the activity of Intellect or of disembodied intellects. In these cases the term is rendered **intellection**. A thought (νόημα) is the result of the activity of thinking. An **intelligible** (νόητον) is the object of thinking.

transcendent (ἐπέκεινα): also, transcend. Literally 'beyond'. Refers to the One or Good in relation to intelligibles and Intellect. Occasionally the term refers to the intelligible world in relation to the sensible world. Also used as a verb to translate ὑπερέχειν.

transformation (μεταβολή): see **change**.

truth (ἀλήθεια): The property of Being in relation to Intellect and to intellects. By extension, the term is used as a semantic property of propositions. The One or Good is the source of truth for Being.

unaffected (ἀπαθής): also, impassive, impassible, without passions. Not subject to change or alteration; especially applied to the (higher part of the) soul. See 3.6 *passim*.

unit (μόνας): Any principle of a number or numerable quantity.

unity (τὸ ἕν, ἕν): see **One**.

universe (τὸ πᾶν): The cosmos plus the higher causes of the cosmos. Often used synonymously with **cosmos** (κόσμος).

univocal (συνώνυμος): Characteristic of word with identical meaning in all its referents. See **equivocal**. See 1.4.3.3; 6.1.1.18, 8.6; 6.3.1.21.

unlimited (τὸ ἄπειρον): also, absence of limit, infinite regress, unlimitedness. Generally, a property of something insofar as it is without Substantial Being or substantial being, for these provide limit, etc.

up to us (ἐφ' ἡμῖν): also, free. Alternative translations include 'dependent on us', 'in our power', 'authoritative over ourselves'. See **choice**.

variegated (ποικίλος): also, complex. Refers to anything non-uniform and, by extension, non-simple. Used especially for Intellect or Being which is one (simple)-many (variegated).

vice (κακία): Any state or action tending toward evil. Vice is generally owing to an association with a body and hence with matter. See **evil**. See 1.1.10.13; 1.5.6.14; 1.8.4.7, 10, 13, 6.6.13–17, 9.1–10, 11.6, 12.2, 13.4–20, 14.50; 2.3.1.9; 16.38; 2.9.8.35; 3.2.5.14–16; 3.5.7.45; 3.6.2.1–66; 4.4.45.22; 4.8.5.22; 6.3.18.24; 6.4.15.32–33; 6.7.20.15, 23.10, 28.13–15; 6.9.3.19.

virtuality (δύναμις): also, virtually (δυνάνει). See **power**.

virtuous (σπουδαῖος): Term used for a person of elevated character. See 1.2.7.13; 1.4 *passim*; 1.9.1.12; 2.9.1.46, 9.3, 7–8; 3.1.10.11; 3.2.15.52–54; 3.4.6.1–2; 3.8.6.37; 4.4.43.1.

void (κενόν): also, empty. Used in criticism of Stoic doctrine and in defense of Plato against Peripatetics.

volition (θέλησις): The principle of connation, always used of rational beings. See **wanting**.

voluntary (ἑκούσιον): Adjective used synonymously for the verb **wanting** and the noun **volition**. All and only desire for the Good is voluntary; desire for apparent goods is involuntary. See 3.1.9.6, 11; 4.3.15.18; 4.8.5.3, 4, 7; 6.8.1.33–43, 3.19.

wanting (θελεῖν): see **volition**. Also, **willingly** (ἕκων).

wickedness (πονηρία): The generic term whose species are defined by their location in the soul and the manner in which they incline the soul to evil. Roughly synonymous with **vice**. See 1.8.5.17; 2.3.14.13–14; 3.1.6.10; 3.2.5.19, 16.1.

will (βούλησις): The power in virtue of which something can be **up to us**. In practice what is 'up to us' is usually equivalent to **voluntary**, though they are not identical in definition. See 1.4.4.17, 6.14–20, 11.17; 2.1.1.2; 2.4.8.18; 3.3.5.37; 4.4.12.16; 5.2.2.10; 6.7.3.4; 6.8.3.3, 5.23, 6 *passim*; 6.9.6.40.

willingly (ἕκων): see **will**.

wisdom (φρόνησις): also, practical wisdom. Often used synonymously with σοφία. Sometimes, φρόνησις and σοφία are contrasted, where they are rendered 'practical wisdom' and 'theoretical wisdom'. In this case, the former is viewed as an application of the latter. See 1.2.1.8, 6.12; 1.3.5.7, 6.10; 1.6.6.2; 2.3.18.7; 2.9.5.6; 3.6.6.17; 4.2.2.48; 4.4.11.23–24, 28, 12.6–47; 4.7.10.16; 5.8.2.39; 6.6.1820–33; 6.8.16.36.

wishing (θέλησις): Used mainly for the One to indicate its perfectly unimpeded or unmediated activity. Often close in meaning to **will**, sometimes also used for the One. See 6.8.13.27, 30, 38, 45, 16.22, 23, 18.42.